What would it mean to live
in a city whose people were changing
each other's despair into hope?—
You yourself must change it.—
what would it feel like to know
your country was changing?—
You yourself must change it.—
Though your life felt arduous
new and unmapped and strange
what would it mean to stand on the first
page of the end of despair?

—Adrienne Rich

UNWINDING THE VIETNAM WAR
From War Into Peace

Edited for Washington Project for the Arts by
REESE WILLIAMS

The Real Comet Press
Seattle 1987

Unwinding the Vietnam War is an original publication of The Real Comet Press, a division of Such A Deal Corporation. For further information: 3131 Western Avenue #410, Seattle, WA 98121-1028; telephone 206 283-7827.

Library of Congress Catalogue Card Number: 87-12142
ISBN 0-941104-20-6 (cloth), ISBN 0-941104-21-4 (paper)

87 88 89 90 10 9 8 7 6 5 4 3 2 1

FIRST EDITION

Contents

With the admission of murder in the form of executions, self-defense, wars, there may be a semblance of morality, but no real morality. The recognition of the sacredness of every man's life is the first and only foundation of all morality.

—Tolstoy
from *The Kingdom of God is Within You*

Introduction

In 1973 an American president declared "peace with honor" to mark the end of a war that began without a declaration of war. Millions of people were dead or injured in Southeast Asia and Vietnam was a land in ruin. The United States was also in ruin—not on the physical level but on the spiritual level. The country was divided and confused, and underneath the surface of daily life was the collective pain of having lost so many pieces of ourselves and of having taken part in the killing of so many human beings.

The statement "peace with honor" was one of many lies that our national leaders told us about the war. During the time of our involvement in Vietnam, lying to the public became a standard practice. Despite a change in the people who run the government, the lying continues today. The dishonesty about our military intervention in Central America is related to the dishonesty about the Vietnam War; the lies of the Iran-Contra affair are related to the lies of Watergate.

Part of the work of this book is to support more people in the difficult awareness of the death and suffering created by these lies.

As a nation we have not yet taken responsibility for our role in the catastrophe of the Vietnam War, nor have we offered any apologies or significant gestures of good will to the people of Vietnam. In the years immediately following the war, Americans wanted to forget about the war. It was too painful. The people who knew the war first hand, the veterans, were often treated with hostility; their knowledge and experience was perhaps too threatening. The nation tried to be done with the war without acknowledging how terrible it was, without searching for any of the source dynamics.

After nearly a decade of avoidence, people slowly began to listen to the veterans. The dedication of the Vietnam Veterans Memorial in Washington in 1982, as well as the controversy surrounding the design, served as a catalyst to focus attention on veterans and what they had to teach about war. The memorial gave the country permission to reflect back upon the war. It also helped many Americans who had opposed the war to find a way to honor the sacrifice of the veterans and accept that a larger national healing depends first upon hearing the anger and pain of the veterans.

In the early stages of the aftermath, the nation let the veterans carry the burden of the war, but in the past few years that has begun to change. More and more people are looking back to that critical period in our history. People who spent years in silence—wives and children of vets, nurses who served in the war, war resisters who went to prison, served time as conscientious objectors, or left the country, and many others—are now openly communicating their pain, their anger, and their knowledge.

Unwinding the Vietnam War is grounded in the political, cultural, and aesthetic issues of the mid-1980s; it is not about the war, nor is it about the early stages of the aftermath. The book is a "bringing together" of many voices into one space—veterans, refugees, peace activists—people who work as teachers, as healers, as writers, as artists, as community organizers. The work of some of the most distinguished writers in the country appears next to the work of people who don't usually spend much time in front of a typewriter. Some people offer personal reminiscences, others critical analysis, others poetry. What connects these people together is the need to speak out against war.

My editorial process has been associative rather than systematic, personal rather than objective. This anthology is one orientation within a vast subject. During the time of my work on the book, I have picked up two things in almost all the people I have talked with: an anger with the policies of our government and a desire to explore a synthesis of the many voices in the aftermath of the war. Conversations that began as discussions of the consequences of the war often developed into more general reflections on the direction of our country. What I heard repeatedly was, "We are an America we never wanted to be."

The postwar baby boom generation came of age during the Vietnam era. For millions of young men and women the myth of America's goodness and invincibility was shattered. The war demonstrated irrefutably that the policies of the U.S. government often fail to uphold the basic philosophical tenets of democracy. Our policies (then and now) reflect a double standard, granting the human rights evoked in the Declaration of Independence to some people while denying them to others. The war forced some Americans to ask tough questions about their nation:

Do we need to kill people to sustain our society?
Do we need to dominate and exploit other countries to prosper?
Do we need to be a militarized society?
Do we need to use violence to resolve conflict?

These questions, and many others of similar nature, helped to create the largest antiwar movement this nation has ever known.

This antiwar movement helped to bring the war to an end, but the questions remain. U.S. foreign policy is still centered around physical violence and military intervention. Each year our government spends billions of dollars on military weapons and practically nothing toward the building of peace.

But policies of the U.S. government do not reflect the will of the majority of the American people. Public opinion polls consistently show that U.S. citizens do not want the U.S. to give financial support to the contras in Nicaragua. Yet, as of this writing, the president continues to vigorously champion his "freedom fighters." In many respects, the executive branch of the government is operating autonomously, with its own agenda, its own imagination. This government's vision of the future, as manifested in the combination of high technology and irrational fear underlying Star Wars, is not the future that individuals universally desire. A subtle death wish is advancing in the policies of our nation. As Martin Luther King said, "A nation that continues year after year to spend more money on military defense than on programs of social uplift is approaching spiritual death."

Our foreign policies are in conflict with the desires that exist at the community level in our country. While the "nation" pursues its policies of death, something quite different is going on in the "country." A strong new momentum is building in the peace movement. To quote from Jan Barry's essay:

The peace movement of the 1980s has grown far beyond the protests of the Vietnam War. It has grown from a few dozen peace groups thinly-scattered across the nation in 1967, the year the Vietnam peace movement mobilized its first massive march on Washington, to hundreds of peace groups able to turn out nearly a million marchers for a disarmament demonstration at the United Nations headquarters in New York in 1982, to some six thousand organizations estimated to be working for peace in 1986. It has grown from a focus of working for peace in one place to working for peace in the world.

Perhaps the most important, underreported news story of the 1980s is the geometric growth of a widespread, deep-rooted citizens' peace offensive. While the governments of the United States and the Soviet Union have been deadlocked in fruitless negotiations on nuclear arms control, millions of citizens in both nations have been seeking each other out in an extraordinary effort to prevent nuclear war and make peace in bloody clashes involving the superpowers in Central America, the Middle East, and wherever Cold War tensions overheat.

The ongoing injustice of U.S. foreign policy is part of a much larger social and cultural crisis, a crisis of perception that is affecting every aspect of our lives. Worldwide economic instability, the growing polarization of the rich and the poor, pollution and environmental disasters, the constant threat of war, high levels of violence and crime, etc., are all aspects of the same crisis which derives from clinging to the concepts of an outdated world view: the thinking of Cartesian-Newtonian science which sees the universe as a mechanical system; the view of life as a competitive struggle for existence; and the belief in unlimited material expansion through economic growth.

We live in a world in which biological, psychological, economic, environmental, and spiritual phenomena are all interconnected and interdependent. The new momentum in the peace movement is part of a larger cultural transformation—the shift from a mechanistic to a holistic conception of the world, one which acknowledges the cause-and-effect relations among all phenomena.*

Part of the work of this book is to support this cultural transformation that is already under way in our country and in many other places in the world.

What would happen if we let our memories of the war become instruments of peace?

I chose the word "unwinding" for the title because our national healing process appears to have much in common with the healing process of an individual. The word "unwinding" is often used to describe a phase in the healing process when an individual has stopped the expansion of a neurosis and is working back through the layers of armoring to the original trauma, to the source of the "dis-ease." Part of the work of this book is to continue tracing our way back to the source of the war. One essayist suggests that this path may lead all the way back to the founding fathers of our country. Until we, as a nation, recognize the source and accept responsibility for it, there is the danger that we will repeat it again in another war.

The book closes with the urgent voice of Martin Luther King, Jr. "A Time to Break Silence" is as timely today as it was twenty years ago. The name of the country has changed and the number of casualties is not as great, but once again our tax dollars are being used to kill people of a

---

*For a thorough presentation of these ideas, see *The Turning Point* by Fritjof Capra (Bantam Books, 1983).

different culture in a small foreign country. One thing stands clear in the violence and turbulence of the past twenty years. Peace will not be given to us. If we want it to exist in the world we will have to work hard to create and sustain it. We will have to allow the recognition of the sacredness of every life to be our first cause.

Southeast Asia

1,921,000 Vietnamese dead
200,000 Cambodians dead (1969-75)
100,000 Laotians dead (1964-73)
3,200,000 wounded (Vietnam, Laos, Cambodia)
14,305,000 refugees (Vietnam, Laos, Cambodia) by the end of the war

In South Vietnam:

300,000 orphans
800,000 children who lost one or both parents
131,000 war widows
200,000 prostitutes

Between 1965 and 1973 approximately one out of thirty Indochinese was killed; one in twelve wounded; and one in five made a refugee.

The United States

2,500,000 soldiers served in the war
58,135 soldiers were killed,
303,616 wounded,
33,000 paralyzed as a result of injuries
110,000 veterans have died from "war-related" problems
since returning to the U.S. (at least 60,000 are suicides)
35,000 U.S. civilians killed in Vietnam (noncombat
deaths)
2,500 missing in action

15,500,000 tons of bombs and munitions were used by
U.S. forces (6,000,000 were used by U.S. forces in all of
World War II).
18,000,000 gallons of poisonous chemical herbicides
such as Agent Orange were sprayed over forest and
croplands in South Vietnam.
$168.1 billion—direct financial cost of the U.S.
government to fight the war (including military and
economic aid to Vietnam, Laos, and Cambodia).
$350 to $900 billion—estimated final cost of the war
(including veteran benefits, interest, etc.).

Sources: *Indochina Newsletter* (November-December 1982), Disabled American
Veterans, Veterans Outreach Program for Vietnam Vets.

. . . *and a hard rain fell*

From Part I: The Draft, the Decisions, and the Nam

Exactly twenty-three days before I was supposed tó leave Vietnam, I stopped worrying about dying. We were called out with a wrecker to haul in some trucks from a convoy that had been ambushed on the road to Dak To. As we neared the firefight, dump trucks loaded with bodies, or over-loaded with bodies, swirled out of the dust, sailed past the windows, and retreated the way we had come. Perhaps it was the sight of the bodies in disarray. Obviously, no one had taken time to stack them like firewood, and limbs hung over the sides at crazy angles. No, that was fitting for the circumstances, understandable. Perhaps it was the very attitude of the limbs; broken, interrupted, torn, and bloodied. Or the mud, like thick brown paste, clinging to rumpled fenders and ravaged jungle uniforms, all-encompassing sticky goo that deformed and defiled all it touched. In an instant they were gone, four or five truckloads with kids going home. A couple of escort vehicles, with flat sheets of armor plate and twin fifty-caliber machine guns, and naked torsos in flak jackets, and the calm, grim, matter-of-fact stares that said these guys had just been to hell and didn't have enough energy left to show emotion. And we were heading into what they had just left!

I was riding shotgun. At twenty-three days you let somebody else fight the fuckin' war. We must have been doing sixty when the shooting started. I simply opened the door and jumped for the ditch. Somehow, I got turned around in midair and landed on a canteen of Kool-Aid that I had riding my right kidney. I knew, I just knew I had been shot in the back, and I was going to lie there in that stinking ditch and bleed to death and never see the world again.

Sorry! Over two million Americans went to The Nam. Nearly fifty-eight thousand died there. Everyone dreamed about The World, talked about The World, cried about The World. There was nothing more important. The World wasn't a planet. It was your hometown, your tree-lined street in the suburbs, your tenement in the ghetto. It was your wife, your girlfriend, or mom, or just a female with round eyes and swelling bosom. The World was a 427 Chevelle with cheater slicks and tripower carbs, parked way at the back of the drive-in, with footprints on the headliner and beer cans under the seat. It was fake proof so you could see the bands, and the gas station where you could buy condoms from a machine on the restroom wall. The World was where your kid brother lived, and if he ever thought of leaving to come over to this cesspool you'd chop his toes off with a hatchet, for his own good. The World was flush toilets and doorknobs and fishing streams. A mythical, magical place that had existed once, and would again, and had been interrupted by the Vietnam War as a TV show is interrupted by a commercial. Excuse me, I'll capitalize The World. If you were there, you'll know. If you weren't, you never will. And I don't plan to refer to the Vietnam "conflict." LBJ saw it as a "conflict." To a pfc, nineteen years old, that many dead guys earned it the title of "war."

The World existed. All too often the fantasy became clouded over by the day's events. It seemed far away, intangible, even alien; but you couldn't let go of the fact that it existed, or you might never make it back. You might be lying in the mud listening to some guy beg because his intestines are spilling out of a hole in his belly, and some fool down the line starts singing some old Smothers Brothers thing about falling into a vat of chocolate, and The World comes back to life, and everybody struggles just a little big harder, and you make it.

Every single thing I had ever taken for granted in my life was a fantasy. The kitchen. My car. The folks. Clean sheets. Toilet paper. My arms, my legs, my face, even my brain . . . might not exist ten seconds from now.

Survive. Make it to the next second, it could become a minute. Minutes became hours, and hours, days. A day was an accomplishment, a square on your calendar. One three-hundred-sixty-fifth of a year. You remembered every story of survival you'd ever read, ever seen on TV or at the movies. You became Ben Hur and Moses and anyone else Charlton Heston had ever played.

Someday medical science will discover how many brain cells a man can lose and continue to function. A strong man can learn to live without an arm or leg. A scared kid can learn, if he has to. But brain cells are different; microscopic particles in a group, sorting out life. A lot of brain cells are burned out in a war, overloaded and short-circuited and gone.

They don't regenerate. You know they're gone, but the folks back home only see that you've brought all your arms and legs, and the inside hurts stay inside, and there's a void you can feel.

That's if you make it home before you eclipse that magic, terrible number. I came close, twenty-three days before I was supposed to leave Vietnam.

I felt the pain. My eyes watered. I couldn't see, and my ears couldn't stand much more of the noise. I ignored the hurt, concentrated on the fear, and on surviving. I pushed every muscle, every tissue, into the brown slime. I wanted to be invisible, to sink up to my nostrils, to buy some time till my eyes cleared and I could at least see it coming. God, I didn't want to die without even being able to focus! There was gunfire everywhere. I had to sort it all out, put it into some recognizable form. The M-60 machine guns cracked a snare drum's beat. The M-16s and M-14s rattled the intricate, high-pitched, driving tinkle of thin-ride cymbals. A fifty-caliber thump-thumped a bass beat. I began to get it together. My eyes were clearing. Four or five tiny men in black were moving toward us across the field. They were crouched, firing from the hip. At least a hundred guns were roaring at them, the percussion section of a great symphony orchestra, and they were in plain sight, and they just kept coming closer. Grinning. You could see the white of their teeth. Off to the left one went down, then reappeared. The top of his head was completely blown away, but the crazy bastard got back on his feet, grinned, and just kept coming!

And then I realized it was over. It was quiet. And I was lying on my belly in the mud, tapping my foot to the abstract rhythm my head had found woven into the chaos of twentieth-century warfare. I had never even shouldered my rifle. I was lying in the dirt tapping my foot to a rhythm only I could hear, and a war happened, and I missed it. I got to my feet. It seemed no one had noticed that I hadn't been shooting. The field had been cleared, and the grass and rubble were only about knee-high. I could see the dead Cong a few yards away. A few of us wandered out to take a closer look. There could have been, should have been, booby traps hidden in the tangle at our knees; fascination made us oblivious. I had seen terrible auto crashes, broken bodies among fenders and chrome. I had never gawked. Twenty-three days before I was supposed to leave The Nam, I walked out into the stubble and looked down on torn men, desecrated flesh, and felt no emotion. It was like walking down the aisle of a supermarket. A couple of guys kicked the gooks. I knelt beside one and removed his belt, canteen, medical kit, and a few empty ammo belts. Another guy picked up his Chicom machine gun. "Go ahead," I said, "I've got one." A few moments before I had been tapping my foot to the rhythm of death as though I was at a rock concert; now I was handing out the spoils of a war I had ignored. I was aware that I was confused, that somehow this wasn't the way it should be. But I kept that canteen for many years, and I don't have it now, and I don't remember getting rid of it.

The Nam was like that. The strangest things happened, and everybody just sort of shuffled by and accepted it, and you can't explain it to someone who wasn't there. It just happened and you were a witness to something profound, momentous, but it didn't seem important at the time. You expected to die any minute or any second, and you wondered how you would do it. Tough, grittin' your teeth and pushing the hurt in with your hands; or small and damaged and vulnerable, crying and screaming for your mother, your panic sapping your strength, the very tension rolling out into a stain that darkened the mud. How would you do it? What would the guys say? What would they write to the folks back home? I mean, everybody hopes to die in bed, just go to sleep, but in The Nam guys were dying and it wasn't like that, and you wondered how you would do at it.

The dead gook was torn up bad. He had been hit twenty, maybe thirty times, and in places there were big holes with bone and tissue sticking out at crazy angles, and most of him was painted with a dark brown stuff that had to be blood, but it was muddy and soaked into the dark pajamas and really didn't resemble the stuff that came out of you. Somebody rolled him over, and I lost the critical brain cell. That dude had the biggest hard-on you ever saw; and it shouldn't have fit the situation, but it did. To my mind, his agony was over, and he felt the warm, comforting, electric surge of pleasure a woman brings, and he was happy! I wandered in a numb fog, gazed at gook after gook, torn, smashed, destroyed, but with the telltale bulge to say, "Fuck you, GI, I'm enjoying this!" and I've never looked at death the same since that day.

Don't get the wrong impression. I'm not John Wayne. I was nineteen when I arrived in The Nam, and scared to death. Six feet and a hundred and twenty-five pounds of skin and bones, glasses, silver fillings in my teeth. Scared to death; never a hero. I hadn't wanted to come to Vietnam. I was in the Central Highlands. If I'd been on the coast I might have tried to swim east till I drowned. The most heroic thing I'd ever done in my life was reassure my family before I left. I wasn't even sure they were real anymore. Nothing existed except right now; and right now was muddy and worn and torn and desolate and hopeless. Barren. The most wretched existence I had ever known; just stumbling through it; and if you survived the day it was an occasion. If you survived the year . . . well, there wasn't much chance of that, and you wondered how you would die when your turn came. You were so damned deep-inside-you glad you had made it through a day, you couldn't imagine the relief and joy of going home. It was so far away, so far beyond the imagination. You knew The World existed, but deep inside you knew it was spinning without you, and damned few people had even noticed you weren't there.

When I was about six my family moved to an eighteen-acre farm near one of the Finger Lakes. I was brought up with room to run, among fields of corn, alfalfa, and wheat. We had a large fruit orchard and about three acres of garden. My dad was a bus driver and rented the fields to area farmers. He left for work at 4:00 A.M. and returned about 6:00 P.M., so we never spent a lot of time together. Dad had been poor and forced to work at an early age, so he never knew the intricacies of football or basketball. The local school was athletic-oriented, and too far away to allow me to take part in afterschool activities. We played ball in the yard, but I was never an athlete. I have always read a lot, and somewhere I had discovered hot-rod magazines. I smuggled them inside my textbooks. I devoured them while I was supposed to be studying my homework. My marks were high until about eighth grade, when I began to know what I wanted to do with my life. Cars and drums, drums and cars. I bought a set of drumsticks and beat the paint off the windowsill. I built plastic model cars by the scores. I read the daring tales of the European racing drivers, scarves dancing merrily in the wind. I shoveled snow, mowed lawns, delivered newspapers, and spent my money on car magazines and rock 'n' roll records. I think my parents expected my interest in automobiles to wane, but it never did. I wanted to become an automotive engineer, but there was no money. I washed cars and pumped gas while other guys practiced football; I tortured my parents with a set of drums while other guys practiced lay-ups and fast breaks. My marks weren't bad, but I failed chemistry until the final exam. I was in a college-preparatory program, but my mind was on tune-ups and four-on-the-floor gearboxes. I fell in with some older guys who were building a '34 Ford into a dragster and felt more at home studying fuel injectors than algebra. I loved history and social studies, enjoyed literature but disliked grammar, and resented the demands homework made on my time. There were girls and pranks and camaraderie, but I felt school was keeping me from cars.

America had entered the space age, and it was taken for granted that a young man would go to college. I had earned a number of scholarships when I graduated with the class of '65, but my heart wasn't in the classroom. I was accepted by Syracuse, Cornell, and the Universities of Buffalo and Rochester, but I couldn't justify borrowing money to do something I didn't want to do. Two weeks after graduation my dad fell ill, and I got a job jockeying cars at a Chevy dealership. My scholarships were extended for a year. My classmates went off to college, and I found new friends among the mechanics at work. I bought a new set of drums, started playing regularly, and dreamed of being "discovered." The race car was running near national record times. I had money and girlfriends. My employer sent me to a GM school in auto body repair, signed me up as an apprentice, and got me a draft deferment. The news had begun to talk about a place called Vietnam, but I paid little attention. This was the freest, most exuberant period of my life.

The boss suggested a haircut. In 1966, no rock drummer got a haircut. I refused, he insisted, and I quit. I was working at another dealership when I was summoned for a preinduction physical. I laughed. I didn't want to be a soldier, and I couldn't conceive of being forced to do something against my will. I had little to offer the military, and I knew some way out would emerge.

The physical was in Buffalo. We gathered for the bus trip: fellow classmates, total strangers, a mixed lot. As the bus moved closer to Buffalo, we laughed. I was nervous, rehearsing the proper answers, but the idea of forced servitude was beyond my comprehension. Everyone had prepared himself, carefully wording answers to offer no more help than necessary. Many had medical records to bear witness to physical problems. The inspectors were contemptuous, herding us like animals, poking, probing, laughing about "cannon fodder for Vietnam," and announcing that "if you are walkin' and breathin', you're going." They asked for voluntary enlistments, and no one stepped forward. On the way home the bus was quiet, with occasional outbursts of rage and frustration. I still didn't believe they could take me if I didn't want to go. I felt no sense of duty. If anyone did, he didn't mention it. Most of the whispered conversations concerned atrocities and indignities. "Did you see what they did to the kid with polio?" "They told Jackson he's One-A, and he's got a heart murmur." "Can you imagine two years of being treated like that?" "Shit, they couldn't do anything to us. We're civilians. My brother told me about boot camp. That's where they really get rough." Somebody in the back hollered, "Hey, driver, do you do charters?"

"Sure."

"We would like to see Niagara Falls . . . from the Canadian side!"

It was a strange time in American history, a time when many seemingly unrelated events were combining to shake the very foundations of our most cherished institutions. It was a time of the Beatles and suborbital flights, of civil rights marches in the Deep South and black-and-white TV. After the simple satisfaction of the fifties and the patriotic frenzy of the New Frontier, and after the Bay of Pigs and the Cuban missile crisis and that day in Dallas, we all felt some kind of ominous tension. Even the high school teachers had seemed somewhat bewildered. You couldn't watch police dogs attacking Blacks on the evening news and believe the United States was the land of the free and the home of the brave. You used to think the commies were far away, then they showed up ninety miles from Florida. You used to think boys had short hair, but then the British invaded, and you looked at history books, and there really wasn't anything wrong with long hair. The grown-ups objected, then suggested you go to church, and Christ's hair was on his shoulders, and everything seemed suspect. They spoke of obligations to your country and whispered about tax breaks. They told you to defend freedom and used cattle prods on the Freedom Riders in Alabama. If you were young, it was an exciting world. You worked all week, and on the weekend you watched fuel dragsters or British rock bands or X-rated movies, and you believed you could change the world and make it a better place. Thirteen years of public school had created a generation of believers. "Do your own thing." "The Times They Are A-Changing." "We Shall Overcome." Born in the late forties, we were the first generation to grow up in the shadow of the mushroom cloud. Hate wasn't the answer. Material goods weren't the answer. The church wasn't the answer. Get yourself a surfboard and a girl, ride a wave, do your thing, and don't hurt anybody. There was plenty of world to go around; everyone had a right to his piece of it. They told us so in school. This was a democracy. It didn't always work just right, they said, but your generation will have to get it all together because now there's a bomb that can eliminate the whole population of the planet. So we grew up believing we could do it, and that the answer was peace, or love, or the golden rule, or whatever you wanted to call it.

After all those years of preparation in the schools, you walked out the door, and they told you it was your duty to kill the commies in South Vietnam. If you wouldn't volunteer, they could draft you, force you to do things against your will. Put you in jail. Cut your hair, take away your mod clothes, train you to kill. How could they do that? It was directly opposite to everything your parents had been saying, the teachers had been saying, the clergymen had been saying. You questioned it, and your parents said they didn't want you to go, but better that than jail. The teacher said it was your duty. The clergy said you wouldn't want your mother to live in a communist country, so you'd best go fight them in Asia before they landed in California. You asked about "Thou shalt not kill," and they mumbled. And you felt betrayed. You sat and drank beer and talked to all your classmates, and they agreed, but their folks were paying to keep them in college, and they had a student deferment. For thirteen years you had been through it all together, and now they were taking the easy way out, buying their way out, and you didn't have much in common anymore. You only knew it was all a bad dream, that the placid suburban street had become divided into us versus them, and they were copping out on everything they had ever told us. How could it have gotten so serious so quickly? It was all a bad dream. You tried to wait it out, hoping it would just blow over like the Cuban missile crisis. You saw more and more about Vietnam in the papers, a coup against Ngo Dinh Diem, Buddhist monks in flames, a "Dragon Lady." Maybe, if you just waited, it would all go away. Gee, California had all those cool cars, and surfers, and movie stars, and you had never met anyone who had ever been there. Too far away, too expensive. Vietnam? Yeah, you saw the thing in the papers, but right now you were trying to scrape up the bucks to see Sonny and Cher in concert.

16

Jimmy Rollins had been ahead of me in school. He had been on the basketball team, and was always friendly, but we weren't close. I assumed he had gone to college. I was at a Friday night football game. I had a date with one of the cheerleaders, and I watched her strut her stuff. I felt kind of special, a graduate. This year's students, teachers, parents stopped to say hello. In a small town everybody knows you. Belinda came over to the snow fence to talk about our plans for after the game. Suddenly her eyes darted to the crowd, and she called out.

"Jimmy! Jimmy!" Jimmy Rollins ambled over to the fence. Belinda leaned across the splintered wooden slats and threw her arms around him. He seemed to fall back under the impact. "Jimmy! It's so good to see you!" She said it over and over, and there were tears in her eyes. Rollins was hunched into a heavy mackinaw, his hands buried deep in the pockets. It was cold, and there was a detachment that had become fashionable with the Rolling Stones. He looked at his feet and said nothing. Belinda was rattling on. "I'm so glad to see you! Are you all right?" Rollins mumbled something and wrestled out of her embrace, coming face to face with me.

"Hi Jim. How ya been?" I held out my hand. He didn't. He looked at his feet. Belinda went back to her pom-pons. I nodded her way. "What was that all about? You been away?"

He looked up now, almost as if he were surprised at the question. His faced looked, well, tired, or strained. Different. Older. I couldn't put my finger on it. "Yeah, away." I sensed a tension.

"School?"

"No. How 'bout you?"

"Naw, I'm fixing dents in Chevy fenders." He shrugged himself deeper into the mackinaw and tilted his head a funny way, as if he was seeing me out of the corner of his eye. Cool. Mature. He kicked at the brown grass with a loafer toe.

"How do you stand with the draft?" He sounded sincere, concerned. It took me a little off guard.

"The army doesn't want me. I had a physical, I'm One-A, but I don't think they'll want me."

His face turned to mine, and it was twisted somehow. "Listen to me, asshole. The fuckin' army wants anybody that's walkin' and breathin'. There's a war on. Get in the fuckin' reserves, man, or the guard, or school, or get married. Do somethin'!" He was getting loud. "This ain't a fuckin' game! One day you'll find your ass in the fuckin' jungle, and you'll wish to God you'd listened!" It was an explosion now, a startling, loud explosion of profanity and emotion that shocked me. His eyes were wild, crazy, spooky. "Nobody told me! I didn't know! You ever see your best buddy die? Shit, no! And you better pray to fuckin' God you never do! You think that fuckin' football team is rough? Huh? That's a fuckin' game, and what we're talkin' about is no game! It's serious; deadly fuckin' serious! You gotta do something!" He was screaming now, crazy. People were looking. You didn't use language like that in small towns in 1966. Rollins took a deep breath, looked at me with those eyes, turned, and melted back into the crowd. I was bewildered, and I guess it showed. A teacher from my junior year had been a few paces away along the snow fence, and he came over to me.

"Jimmy's been through a lot." I liked Mr. Gott, had missed him.

"What's his problem?" I asked.

"You don't know?" Gott's eyebrows arched. "He was an ammo carrier in Vietnam. His arm was blown off at the shoulder."

The earth rocked under my feet. "No shit!" I looked toward the spot where Jimmy had disappeared. "No shit!" I dug for a cigarette. My hand was shaking as it raised the lighter.

Mr. Gott had a reputation for talking too much, but it was informed, insightful talk. The man read the papers, thought about what he had read, and challenged you to do the same. He always seemed to ask "Why do you think this happened?" as if all the world's news were interrelated.

I was still fumbling when he changed the subject. "You didn't go to college?" Before I could answer, he went on. "I hear you're working on cars. Should've had some auto shop. I didn't really think you wanted to go that way." He paused to light a cigarette.

"I just didn't want to spend any more time behind a desk. I always liked cars. I just couldn't get enthusiastic about going back to school."

"Uncle Sam after you yet?"

"I had a physical. I'm One-A."

Gott dragged at the cigarette, turned, and looked me straight in the eye. "Enlist."

"Mr. Gott?"

"Enlist! You can get some education. Training. How to fix cars, if that's what you want. Guaranteed. They send the draftees to Vietnam. You'll probably go to Germany. Even if you do go to Vietnam, you won't be infantry. Enlist. I did. It'll make you a man, do you a lot of good. Teach you some responsibility, get you out from under momma's apron. You can get out after three years, with benefits. You'll never regret it. Best years of my life were in the army."

I mumbled something, the team burst back onto the field, and Mr. Gott returned to his friends. It all seemed so far away. I looked to Belinda. I would think about it later. Tonight . . .

One night a few weeks later I was driving in a blinding snowstorm when I saw a dark figure with his back turned to the wind and his thumb extended. I stopped. He was half frozen and very appreciative. As he thawed, we talked. He was heading for Pennsylvania. Coming from Buffalo. He worked at the preinduction center giving draft physicals. I pulled over to the edge of the road and asked him to get out. He couldn't believe it. I insisted. I left him huddled against the snow and wind, in the night, a long way from home. My friends laughed at the story, but it was no laughing matter. Somewhere, deep inside, it felt deadly serious.

I-Feel-Like-I'm-Fixin'-to-Die Rag

C'mon all of you big strong men
Uncle Sam needs your help again
He's got himself in a terrible jam
'Way down yonder in Vietnam
So put down your books and pick up a gun
We're gonna have a whole lotta fun

And it's one-two-three what are we fightin' for
Don't ask me I don't give a damn
Next stop is Vietnam
And it's five-six-seven open up the Pearly Gates
Why, ain't no time to wonder why
Whoopee! We're all gonna die

Well, come on generals, let's move fast
Your big chance has come at last
Gotta go out and get those reds
The only good commie's the one that's dead
And you know that peace can only be won
When you blow them all to kingdom come

And it's one-two-three what are we fightin' for
Don't ask me I don't give a damn
Next stop is Vietnam
And it's five-six-seven open up the Pearly Gates
Why, ain't no time to wonder why
Whoopee! We're all gonna die

Come on Wall Street, don't move slow
Why, man, it's war a-go-go
There's plenty of good money to be made
By supplying the army with the tools of the trade
Just hope 'n' pray that if they drop The Bomb
They drop it on the Vietcong

And it's one-two-three what are we fightin' for
Don't ask me I don't give a damn
Next stop is Vietnam
And it's five-six-seven open up the Pearly Gates
Why, ain't no time to wonder why
Whoopee! We're all gonna die

Well, come on mothers throughout the land
Pack your boys off to Vietnam
C'mon fathers, don't hesitate

19

Send them off before it's too late
Be the first one on your block
To have your son come home in a box

And it's one-two-three what are we fightin' for
Don't ask me I don't give a damn
Next stop is Vietnam
And it's five-six-seven open up the Pearly Gates
Why, ain't no time to wonder why
Whoopee! We're all gonna die

Joe McDonald
(Country Joe and the Fish)

The next few weeks were agonizing. Thinking slows the movement of time, and I was going over and over the options in my mind. I spent too many nights in a little bar in the city, sipping wine by candlelight and listening to a folk group called Onja and the Loose Ends. No one called them hippies in those days. They were beatniks or bohemians, they did a lot of Bob Dylan songs, and every night's assembled audience made me feel comfortable. I could hide in the darkness, be soothed by the soft acoustic guitars. I was trying to bide my time, waiting for the miracle that would save me. Time was running out. In a scant sixteen months the optimism of high school had been replaced by hopelessness and confusion. I would probably be drafted within six months. If I escaped to Canada, my family would be social outcasts. They didn't know what to suggest either. We discussed Canada, and they weren't at all enthusiastic. They insisted they didn't want me to be drafted, but day after day expired, and there were no good alternatives. "Enlist. At least you won't be infantry." But I would have to go for an extra year. "Sure, but you're young." Yeah, and I wanted a chance to get old.

The waiting lists for the reserves and National Guard were too long, but I added my name. I thought about just running away, but to where? Again, it would dishonor my family, and I could never come home. Two years was a long time, but never was forever. I begged a doctor to write something about my damaged right knee. He encouraged me to do my duty. It was too late to register for school and get a student deferment, and I had a car payment to think about. At eighteen, school seemed as much a prison as the army. I only wanted to be free to do what I was doing. Advice came from everywhere. Try to get in the air force or navy, they live better than the army. They weren't accepting any more recruits. I didn't want to join anything or go anywhere. I only wanted to be free.

It was a bright and sunny Sunday in late November. I drove with my parents to Batavia, to a small storefront office. We were greeted by a portly, balding, kindly man who seemed to exude self-confidence and dignity. His clothes were crisply starched, and there were rows of multi-colored ribbons on his lapel. He laughed at Vietnam. We've got a few men there, sure, and it makes good news copy, but you'll probably go to Germany. We have bases all over the world. You'll live in modern barracks, like a college dorm. He held out a brochure. How long did I think a bunch of jungle savages would be able to stand up to the full might of the United States? I would be guaranteed months of schooling; chances are it would be over before I finished. Frankly, though, the best advice he could offer was not to let myself be drafted. They'll be the first to go to Vietnam. Second-class soldiers. Stand up to your obligation, go along with the army, and it would go along with you. Basic training is a kind of orientation. The hardest part is the physical conditioning, but you're young and healthy, and it won't bother you. After basic, it will be just like any other nine-to-five job.

In my eighteen years, I had never been far away from home more than a week in my life. I knew I wasn't cut out for the heroics I saw on *Combat*, but I could work on trucks and cars. I was scared and confused. Three years. Three years ago I had been a sophomore in high school. It seemed long ago. Three years from now I should be making good money. God, I was scared. I didn't want to shoot anybody, and I didn't want anybody to shoot me. I took a few days to decide. I had to make a decision soon, or not get my guaranteed army training. I met a girl who told me about her brother. He had been totally blind in one eye since birth, but they had drafted him, and he was in basic training. I called the recruiter. Could I at least stay home for the holidays? In order to make the class date, I would have to go in December 30. I signed the papers. The agony was over. I didn't like the outcome, but the terrible question was answered.

It was a strained Christmas. The family tried to make it jolly. Maybe they tried too hard; maybe it was the gifts. A shaving kit. A pocket radio. Traveling things. I was going away. I was dating a girl named Maggy. We went to a concert, the Who, the Blues Magoos, and Herman's Hermits. The teenybopper girls screamed and passed out. I hated that baloney. I had paid a good buck to hear the music. There was something different about that night, and I made some excuse to Maggy and went out into the corridor. Stretchers with unconscious girls were everywhere, while nurses in white uniforms rushed about. I stood and watched a long time. The papers said it was like a battle zone.

Knowing he would have to hire me back, the boss fired me "because my hair was too long." That, I assured him, was what I would be defending. American ingenuity. I sorted catalogue orders in a Sears warehouse till Christmas, then took a vacation. I tried to cram a lot into those few days, and they ticked away, one by one. On the morning of December 30, 1966, my parents drove me to that horrible building in Buffalo. Everyone was pleasant and respectful while the parents were there. We raised our hands and repeated some kind of oath. I thought I would throw up or feel my knees collapse. The parents left, and we were allowed to get something to eat and meet at the train station at midnight. I bought a bottle of Scotch.

I drank to the very limit of my endurance, threw up, and slept on the floor of the train. It was as if my life had ended, or I wanted it to. I was among total strangers, being carried away, and the drinking wasn't pleasurable. I wanted to get "dead drunk." It was self-destructive, the way I poured the booze down. I never wanted to see the morning, but I did. My eyes were bloodshot, and my headache was immense, and the train rolled on. In New York City we transferred to buses and arrived at Fort Dix, New Jersey, in the early afternoon. I was digging deep, looking for strength. As the bus stopped the DIs, or drill instructors, attacked. In uniforms with knife-edge creases and their stereotypical Smokey the Bear hats, they burst through the bus doors, screaming. We jumped, we hustled, we shuddered, but it really didn't upset me as I had expected. It was obviously an act. If a person really had that temperament, he would be committed. Rational adults don't behave like that. The secret was to act intimidated when confronted personally and blend into the background whenever possible.

From Part III: The Aftermath

Not long after my return, I was invited to a birthday party for one of my high school classmates. The party was in Buffalo, where she was doing graduate work. Another former classmate drove, and I was amazed by his Fiat roadster. For so long I had dreamed of returning to "muscle cars," the awesome 427 Chevies and Hemi-Dodges. I found it difficult to accept the high-backed bucket seats, federally mandated safety features that made it impossible to retrieve anything from the back of the car, or the asthmatic wheezing of the smog-controlled seventy-horsepower engine. But the car was nimble, agile, and fun. It was a cold and rainy autumn day, otherwise we could have put the top down. I was disoriented. The world (The World?) I had come home to had changed so significantly, and yet it had a great deal to offer. Surely this little buzz bomb was reminiscent of the tiny Japanese cars I had grown to accept in Thailand.

The party was also disquieting. Many of my classmates were there, and I was buoyed by their warm greetings. We reminisced, and for a few moments the carefree, optimistic joy we had shared comforted me. Then their conversations turned to college life, and I watched raindrops weaving psychedelic patterns down a steamy window pane. Since graduation, we had little in common. Once we had been seedlings on the same stalk. They had fallen upon the fertile soil, and I had been blown among the rocks and briars. They saw a rosebud and anticipated beauty. I recognized its teardrop shape and felt sadness that it would wither away so soon.

I had come to know despair and disgust. I had lived in a world characterized by the stink of death and the horror of disfigured, hopeless children. I had seen poverty, starvation, atrocity, corruption, incompetence, brutality, and suicide. Their world revolved around graded papers and a professor's outrageous neckties. I had lived among rodents and reptiles while they had been carrying laundry home on the weekends. They had never seen a religious penitent; I was unimpressed by athletic letters on cardigan sweaters. The girls pretended to be shy virgins. The guys snickered about sexual adventures at drive-in movies. A letter from exotic Malaysia had widowed me.

I had been cleaning a rifle while they were cramming for exams. They spoke with great conviction of the agony of studying without sleep, the enormous amounts of No-Doz and coffee it took to pass a trig final. I remembered Dak To, Ohio, Tet. They protested the war. They had diplomas to prove their wisdom, implying subtly that my views were not being sought because they lacked credentials. I had no diploma, no report card granting a 2.5 in horror or 3.8 in social studies for my research into the peasantry of Thailand's rice paddies. Almost apologetically, their eyes avoiding mine, they said they had taken part in marches opposing the war, then changed the subject.

I, too, protested the war. I had my reasons. I had known the thunder of a B-52 at work, the difference in sounds of an M-16 and an AK-47. I could sleep through an outgoing artillery bombardment but be awake and screaming a warning to my friends before a first incoming round struck. I had seen body bags and coffins stacked like cordwood, had seen American boys hanging lifeless on barbed wire, spilling over the sides of dump trucks, dragging behind an APC like tin cans behind a wedding party bumper. I had seen a legless man's blood drip off a stretcher to the hospital floor and a napalmed child's haunting eyes. I knew the spirit of the bayonet and the sizzle of a rocket tearing across the night sky. I slumped in a faded armchair sipping wine while the stereo played the score from the musical *Hair*. It sang of the joys of masturbation while I sat alone, remembering a place called The Warehouse. They opposed the war. They didn't ask my opinion. They had diplomas. I guess they thought I was stupid for having gone. If you weren't part of the solution, you were part of the problem. I, too, opposed the war. They were twenty-one, eager to try their wings. I was twenty-one, my life nearly over. We recalled the prom and the pizzas and went on with our lives.

I was on unemployment, reading the classifieds. I saw Arlo Guthrie in concert, then Country Joe & The Fish. I caught *Yellow Submarine* at the movies. The disk jockeys wondered if Paul McCartney had died. The Beatles' new album, *Abbey Road*, was everywhere on the airwaves. Onja had gotten pregnant, and the Loose Ends had broken up. Everyone told me to relax, take a few weeks to rest. I had rested in Thailand. I was eager to go on with my life, to build a future. I was eager to put the past behind me.

In a shiny silk suit hand-stitched by my Malaysian tailor, I arrived for an interview at an employment agency. Without a degree, I was referred to life insurance companies as a manager trainee. For days I bounced off the walls of a concrete canyon, filled in the squares of the aptitude tests, and endured rejections because I wasn't "aggressive enough."

My clothes had been custom tailored in the Orient, part of my preparation ritual. They were hopelessly out of style. My hair was unfashionably short, my army-issue glasses weren't "cool." Overweight middle-aged men in brightly colored dress shirts, their hair "styled" to transform receding hairlines into Beatle bangs, asked if I had any "management experience."

I had been a platoon sergeant in Thailand, in charge of forty-three Americans and numerous Thais. It counted for nothing. In fact, it counted against me. I might as well have arrived for the interviews dressed in jungle fatigues and carrying an M-16. No one knew what to say to a Vietnam veteran, and no one wanted to meet one at the water cooler.

I ate lunch at the greasy restaurant across the street from the Chevy dealership where I had worked. I sat with Harry, who had been one of my best friends. I had looked up to him. While I was away, he had dumped his wife and baby to live with a go-go dancer. He was into drugs and motorcycles, wearing an earring. "Fuck the world," he said, and I had just spent two years dreaming of returning to The World, and we didn't have very much in common anymore.

I found a job selling cars in a quiet, out-of-the-way foreign car dealership. Before the army, I had worked with Detroit iron. The World had changed, and so had I. Perhaps no aspect of my outward personality was more changed than my automotive tastes. I had always read the sports car magazines, but the foreign cars seemed exotic and unapproachable. I could understand Fords and Chevies, and the straightforward acceleration of drag racing. Now I surrounded myself with complex little Triumphs, MGs, Fiats, Jaguars, Lotuses, Volvos, and Saabs. Front-wheel drive. Rear engine, rear-wheel drive. Air-cooled engines. Exotica. I heard about, and began to try, apexing corners and four-wheel drifts. I sold my beloved T-Bird and bought an outrageous Triumph with roll bar, a multitude of high-power driving lights, and a rally odometer. Rallying was a passion at this dealership, and the bug hit me. My car was anything but basic, but I was learning. Alone on twisting country roads, I pushed the Triumph and myself to death-defying limits. Perhaps memories of the road to Dak To entered into it; I don't know. I had great confidence in my driving ability. This was freedom!

The responsibilities of job and car payments brought frustrations. Thousands of Vietnam veterans gathered in Washington to protest the war and throw their medals onto the steps of the Capitol. I knew I should have been there, but I also knew I wasn't ready to say anything in public. The job gave me a convenient excuse. I read the papers and felt a knot in my stomach, and sadness and disappointment in myself. Once again I had conveniently sidestepped the issue. Might my presence have kept someone alive? But I told myself the war hadn't happened, and I was usually able to fool myself.

There was a blind date, a disaster. I wasn't much for beer or crowds anymore. The psychedelic light show reminded me of the past, and I was concentrating on the future. The girl was ill at ease, alone with a Vietnam veteran. I was thinking with my glands. I said the wrong thing and offended her, and took her home. I tried a few taverns; I needed a drink now and then, but the taverns were full of college students laughing about their student deferments. I sat quietly in the shadows, feeling terribly out of place, even frightened, though I didn't know why.

For almost three years the word *home* had brought a mental picture of the big yellow house on the shaded suburban street. Dad's job was twenty-five miles away, and the family decided to move to the city. I had nowhere else to go, I didn't want to be alone, so I went along. It was disquieting, the loss of something dear. The city was intimidating, and I retreated to my small room. It began to snow in October. The fun lasted only a few moments. I was cold, and resented the time spent scraping a windshield or shoveling the driveway.

One night I sat cross-legged on the floor of my room, handling the feeble mementos I had brought home, thinking back to another time when I had been better able to cope. I had so little in common with the people here. My world was thirteen thousand miles away, as fleeting as the smoke from my cigarette. The idea came from nowhere. I attacked the phone book. I had a friend from The Nam, someone who had known me in that context and had never been ashamed of me. The number was local. I hadn't written Carolynn in a year. At the very least, I owed her a thank you for her wonderful letters. If things didn't work out, I could easily hang up. We talked for over four hours that first night. She seemed so glad to hear from me. One of the other guys to whom she had been writing hadn't made it home. She invited me to her house. Eager to have a friend, and ever mindful of parents who were about to see their daughter invite a Vietnam veteran into the living room, I shut the car off and coasted into the driveway. She was far prettier than her pictures, far kinder than even her letters had indicated. We dated. I took her to a bar where an all-woman band from Thailand was playing, a band I had seen in Korat just a few weeks before. She seemed to understand and had the courage to ask questions. I had written about Lin. Was I married? At a rock concert a joint was passed my way, and I took a hit. In a huff, Carolynn demanded I drive her home and warned that she wouldn't see me again if I used drugs.

We found a little coffeehouse where we sat on the floor in the dim light of flickering candles, drinking hot cider with cinnamon sticks. The place was owned by two young folksingers and named after their cat. It was always crowded, but it felt warm and intimate when Carolynn and I were together. The snow melting off hundreds of boots made the floor damp, but we didn't mind. She hooked her arm in mine, and we swayed as the soft voices and acoustic guitars led us down a path neither of us had traveled before. We talked her mother into allowing Carolynn to spend the night with me, not in passionate lovemaking, but strapped into a rally car, racing at unconscionable speeds across miles of snow and treacherous road conditions. Carolynn was the navigator, reading the complex route instructions as I wrestled against Mother Nature and fatigue. There was a heavy snowfall, about eighteen inches, and I managed to lay the car on its side in a ditch. We scrambled out Carolynn's door into a raging blizzard. I rushed to the trunk to get the shovel and winch, and when I returned she was gone. I found her under the front of the car on her belly, frantically pulling out snow with her arms. At that moment I knew I would never find another girl like this.

I spent long hours alone in my room. I had to resolve Lin before I could accept Carolynn's affections. My passionate letters to Malaysia had gone unanswered for months. I had been dumped, and it hurt. As soon as I had taken my wallet back to America, Lin's passions had cooled. She was an artist, able to make five-day dreams come true, but unable to break out of that time barrier and dream dreams of months or years. Outside of a bedroom Lin's imagination was limited. She had never taken a ferry to the mainland, a scant half-mile away. Like Penang, she would always be an exotic island. She talked about New York or California with ease, but her worldliness was a facade she slipped into as easily as her clothes. She always reserved the ability to slip back to the comfortable familiarity of Penang's peasantry. When there was no GI to be entertained she wore cotton nightgowns. Nudity was her business suit, and nostalgia about The World was the balm she used to soothe the wounds of war.

She had learned her craft well. Many tormented visitors had vacationed between her thighs. She had learned from each of them, compiled a repertoire of illusions designed to invite dreams. On a five-day holiday from hell, her man was supposed to dream of a better future, but only within limits she would set. She wasn't ready to leave her island or her family to face the future in an unknown land. She was a relief pitcher, talented for an inning or two but unable to start the game and face the challenge of going all the way. It wasn't that she was afraid, I decided; she had made the simple choice.

I remembered the inner agony when I had left Pleiku, left my friends behind. There had been a strong urge to stick it out to the end, to apply what I had learned that they might have a better chance of surviving. Perhaps Lin knew better than I the value of what she was doing for men in dire need. The nurses comforted the physically wounded. Lin nursed the emotionally wounded.

Yes, she was a prostitute. A whore. I had accepted that fact for eighteen months, dared to dream of a lifelong relationship. I had committed myself, "till death do us part." Had her simple handwritten note altered my values? Had my return to The World signaled some mysterious moral awakening? Had I shed immorality and lust when I had stripped off my army uniform? Certainly the protestors, with their "baby killer" accusations, had made morality a question of prime importance. To ascribe responsibility for the immorality to the uniform would be to condemn my friends. Every kid in uniform was somebody's next-door neighbor. My life had rested in their hands, and theirs in mine. They were not degenerate or immoral because they had slept with whores. They were lonely, afraid, and confused, caught up in a merciless web, shipped halfway around the world, and subjected to violence and death the next-door neighbors would never imagine. I felt no remorse, and I would make no excuses to the detriment of the guys I left behind.

I had seen friends in Vietnam react to Dear John letters. Lin had been a sensitive, caring person. She had waited until I was back in The World to shatter my fantasies. She knew there would be a kaleidoscope of diversions to ease the hurt, that I would have different perspectives. She would not be hurt. She had freed me to find another woman; fate had been kind, and I hadn't waited long. Carolynn offered more kindness and understanding than I was likely to find again. I would be a damn fool to live in the past.

It was fate! I had been thirteen thousand miles away. I could picture the mail shack. Carolynn had chosen three names with her eyes closed. Her finger had come to rest on my name, and she had accepted me in olive drab, now again in jeans and sweaters. She seemed to know far more than her words could say about the hurt I felt inside. I needed her, and I willingly accepted her kindness without regret. Lin became a pleasant memory in the midst of a nightmare, and Carolynn became my future.

The war continued, both in Southeast Asia and at home. Four antiwar protestors were gunned down at Kent State University. Thousands were arrested in Washington, D.C. There was an invasion of Cambodia, and a lot of Americans died when the South Vietnamese ran. It all seemed far, far away. Carolynn and I were planning a wedding, and the world stopped turning. Oh, I knew I should have been with the protestors, trying to save the helpless kids. Tired of the war, I had found something so beautiful, so wonderful, I very selfishly enjoyed it. I had given far too much to the war. Carolynn had rescued me from myself, and I committed myself to her. The economy was not good, and I needed to apply myself if we were to have a future. The war was the past. We concentrated on finding an apartment and furniture. I was so wrapped up in wedding plans I scarcely noticed that we had set the date for September 12, barely a year since I had returned.

Of course, there were reminders. One Saturday morning I woke with a terrible headache. My eyeballs had swelled until they literally grated against the sockets. I was rushed to the hospital, where I underwent a spinal tap. The doctors were rushing in and out, obviously concerned. Carolynn was frantic, but the swelling gradually went away. The doctors explained they didn't really know what it was, but there had been a dozen cases reported . . . all in Vietnam veterans.

Carolynn and I were married on September 12, 1970. We had hoped to have the folksingers from the coffeehouse sing, but we couldn't work it out. The church organist played our song, Simon and Garfunkel's *For Emily, Whenever I May Find Her*. Our apartment had been servant quarters, in the attic of a stately mansion in the finest section of the city. Our landlord and his family lived downstairs, and their kindness did a great deal toward starting our marriage on the right foot. It was a long climb to our third-floor hideaway, but worth it. Converted gaslights with crystalline globes arched out of the walls, the woodwork was polished oak, and the bathtub was a Victorian clawfoot antique. Learning to live with each other was a great adventure. Like kids in a tree house, we retreated from the dizzying world. We never seemed to have extra money; it was years before we had a couch, but Carolynn covered a foam mattress with corduroy, and we made ourselves very comfortable. At Christmas we built elaborate Victorian decorations. I fashioned a peace sign out of cardboard and lights, and let it shine down upon the richest neighborhood in the city.

We found some Thai friends, students and doctors, and rang in the New Year 1971 with a Thai feast and good fellowship. In February, Laos was officially invaded. Fully half of the South Vietnamese invaders were casualties, and President Nixon declared his policy of Vietnamization a success. The *Pentagon Papers* was released, a mind-numbing exposé of our government's long history of lies and distortions concerning Vietnam. I read it nights, while Carolynn was at work. We didn't talk much about The Nam, but I had a peace sign in the window of my car. Lieutenant Calley was found guilty of the My Lai massacre. Carolynn thought he should go to jail, and the public wondered how anything like that could have happened. They couldn't accept what the war had done to their sons, the realities of survival and betrayal. I couldn't give my reasons for seeing Calley as just a scapegoat. I might have been prosecuted for the incident with the fire truck, and I had a wife to think about. It was better to just leave the past behind.

There were hard times. Dock strikes and assembly-line strikes dried up our flow of cars, leaving me with a salary of $75, or $54.23 after taxes. I became a salesman and delivery man for a foreign auto parts store and took a few night courses at the community college. The VA benefits were meager, so I couldn't afford to consider full-time school. In 1972 Carolynn and I won a rally championship and put on a charity event to buy toys for kids confined to local hospitals. The papers said American troops were coming home from Vietnam, but I didn't believe it because I didn't see the amputees and paraplegics on the street. Richard Nixon campaigned for reelection, and Young Republicans in three-piece suits cried out for "four more years" while less fortunate Americans continued to bleed into Southeast Asian swamps. I was convinced Nixon was postponing the peace to aid his reelection hopes, and predicted peace would come November 1. The announcement came October 26, and "Tricky Dick" was reelected November 7. He didn't get my vote. I pulled George McGovern's lever, opened the curtain, and loudly announced, "That's for all the guys who have died in Vietnam while the president played politics with peace!" A lot of matronly ladies were shocked, and I was hurried to the door. On December 18 the president ordered the most concentrated bombing in history. Over a hundred thousand bombs fell on Hanoi in just twelve days. Thirty-three American planes were lost, twenty-six of our fliers killed, and another twenty-six captured. Damage to civilian areas of Hanoi was heavy. The war continued.

American combat troops left Vietnam in 1973, and (some of?) our POWs were released. I found a job opportunity in a South Carolina Toyota dealership, and in two weeks had moved Carolynn and the furniture a thousand miles from home. My new boss admitted he couldn't pay what he had promised, so Carolynn drove more than sixty miles a day to and from work. Richard Nixon was "tormented" by Watergate. Carolynn miscarried. I decided our best hopes depended upon my success in the new job, not for the boss, but in spite of him. We managed to buy a house. A "gas crisis" brought long lines at service stations. The endless supply of fuel that had been keeping our troops moving in Vietnam had mysteriously dried up when the troops came home. Richard Nixon left office in disgrace but was pardoned by his successor, Gerald Ford. The American people never seemed to connect the deceptions of Watergate to the deceptions of Vietnam, although they may simply have been too bone-weary to demand an accounting. The vets and protestors seemed to forget their differences, and amid the silence they raised families and gained car payments and mortgages. I was no different, at least outwardly, but started a beard. The boss ordered me to shave it. I refused. I quit, and we moved again. I gave Carolynn two paperback books for Christmas, and she gave me three pairs of underwear.

Nineteen seventy-five was a better year. I did well at my new job, earned a promotion, and we had a new house built. Carolynn got pregnant. She was working in labor and delivery, and wanted a baby of her own. I had been in no hurry to have children. Although I never attributed my feelings to Vietnam, I'm sure the memories of starving or napalmed children made me hesitant to bring an innocent child into the world. Once we were sure she was pregnant, it was full speed ahead. Carolynn was the authority on these matters, and we were careful to do everything just right. We attended Lamaze classes and prepared a nursery. Meanwhile, Saigon fell to the communists on April 30. Ironically, on the same day CBS-TV canceled *Gunsmoke* after twenty years. Our son was born December 31. Our joy was indescribable, and I smuggled a bottle of champagne into the hospital.

On the morning of January 14, 1976, I received an emergency call at work. Carolynn was hysterical; the baby was dead! I dropped the phone and started running toward home, a distance of sixteen miles, until one of the secretaries caught me and gave me a ride. I burst in the door to find Carolynn holding him, singing soft lullabies through great, choking sobs. In the distance the ambulance siren came and went, as they couldn't find our house. I was frantic, refusing to believe the unbelievable, and I drove madly to the hospital. Carolynn, of course, knew he was gone, and her face was horrifying. It became official, and a terrible numbness set in.

I had seen horrors before, but never anything like the sight of Carolynn cradling that baby. I had felt loss before, but never a loss like this. Here it was again. Within seconds, everything important to me had been snatched away. Carolynn, the most precious thing I had ever known, was a desolated shell of her former self. All our plans had been an illusion. Our parents were heartbroken. The nursery, once a joyous room, had become a chamber of horrors. They call it crib death or Sudden Infant Death Syndrome (SIDS). It takes ten thousand American babies a year. No one expects it to happen to them.

The autopsy showed certain anomalies. The baby had three spleens. That, in itself, was not life-threatening, but I went berserk. Long, long ago in a place far away, I had smoked some marijuana. I quit before I came home, had puffed a joint only twice in the past seven years. There was research suggesting marijuana might cause genetic defects, but research has indicated almost everything causes diseases. You ignore most of it. Now it was thrust into my face in the most terrible manner. Had I brought this heartbreak and suffering down upon the woman I loved? The pediatrician assured us it had been SIDS, that there was nothing we might have done to avoid it. The questions and the guilt remained.

I had forgotten lessons learned; forgotten that life is, in essence, only day-to-day survival. I had allowed my good fortune to become reality. A loving wife, a son, a comfortable house and two cars in the driveway . . . you can't take any of it for granted. I knew. Why hadn't I prepared Carolynn? For the first time in years, my thoughts returned to Southeast Asia. At times during the next few months, Carolynn thought I was insensitive. I was sad, confused, bitter. We had to go on. But had Vietnam scarred my emotions until I could scarcely shed a tear at my son's funeral? Our marriage was a commitment to life, which, I knew, included an unspoken pledge to love our children fully and without reservation. The war was far behind me. Or was it? Had it rendered me incapable of loving, at least of loving in the same sense of the word Carolynn expected? If, though using the same word, we were saying two different things, was that not a misrepresentation of the very foundations upon which our marriage had been built? Of course I loved her, and I had loved my son. But was it love in the conventional sense, or love with conditions? I hadn't cried at the funeral. Death, I told Carolynn, was an inevitable part of life. We just had to go on. Was I a monster? Was I truly insensitive, or simply realistic? Sadness overwhelmed me; I contemplated suicide, but I couldn't cause Carolynn any more pain, and we struggled on. I resented our Lamaze classmates, playing with their healthy children. Carolynn saw a baby at the supermarket, burst into tears, and fled the store, abandoning a cartful of groceries. She found work as an industrial nurse. I concentrated on rallying and my job, and earned honors in both.

On Saint Patrick's Day of 1977, Carolynn presented me with a beautiful, healthy, red-haired daughter. For all these years, the Simon & Garfunkel song had been special to our relationship. We named the baby Emily. At long last, we had found her. There was little relief, however. We flew to her crib at every burp or gurgle, sat watching her sleep by the hour, and prayed that she would survive each night's sleep.

The job began to go poorly. I tried to start my own business, but the financing fell through. We moved again, to the suburbs of Washington, D.C., and scratched to pay both rent and mortgage till the old house was sold.

A second daughter, Theresa, was born in June 1980. Another redhead, she is the clown to counter Emily's seriousness. There is no boy to carry on the family name, but girls are especially close to their daddies. We have chosen to do without a lot of material things so that Carolynn can be a full-time mommy. I've been fortunate. I have a successful career, and a beautiful and loving family.

I think the war started to creep back into my life in the spring of 1980. *The Deerhunter* had won a bouquet of Academy Awards. I thought Vietnam was far behind me, but the prisoner-of-war scenes started me shaking uncontrollably, and then I was crying, and I had to leave the theater and smoke a cigarette. The American military had botched the Iranian hostage rescue attempt and was pleading for funds. A new militarism was dawning in America, and the presidential election brought us Ronald Reagan as its chief spokesman. The rhetoric tightened my stomach. Had we learned nothing? I had been unable to shed a tear when my son died, but one December morning I pulled my car over to the edge of the road and cried great gasping sobs. John Lennon had been gunned down. For the first time in years, we fashioned a peace sign from cardboard and Christmas lights, and hung it in an upstairs window.

In late 1981 *Newsweek* did an article about a company of Vietnam veterans, what they remembered and what they felt today. The article lifted the lid of my secret box. I begged my parents to read it, the first time I had acknowledged my war memories in years. Nightmares woke me more often now.

Everything exploded one January night in 1982. There was snow on the lawn, but the fireplace was crackling a cheerful tune. The kids were tucked in, and I was twisting the TV dial, looking for mindless escapism. I found the famous documentary about phony enemy troop counts during the Vietnam War. My box fell off its shelf, and the contents scattered all across the living room floor. "It's coming out! My God, it's finally coming out!" Here was General Westmoreland, the commander of American forces in Vietnam, a genuine four-star lifer of lifers. Questionable troop strength reports had been relayed back to Washington for "political reasons," and the larger-than-expected enemy force shocked the world with the Tet offensive of 1968. I fell apart that night, and dawn was breaking before Carolynn was able to settle me down. I wrote for a transcript of the program and carried it for days, reading and rereading it. This was the war I had known. All of the deception, agony, treachery, and waste of Vietnam were wrapped up in those few sheets of paper. The lifers had felt so much contempt for us they had even lied to the president of the United States to earn their goddamn oak leaf clusters! We had been expendable. Now everyone would know.

But despite the enormous implications, the methods used to uncover the story have attracted as much attention as the story itself. Westmoreland has sued CBS for besmirching his professional reputation. I will never forget the Tet offensive. I only hope the truth will be exposed. I have written numerous letters to each of my congressmen and senators suggesting an investigation. I have never received a reply. I remember another letter to another congressman, long ago. "I've had dinner with . . ."

After the TV documentary, I got myself back together. Vietnam was eating away at me now. The warlike rhetoric flowed out of Washington in ominous torrents, and my stomach twisted into knots. My children were in danger. All of humanity was in danger. Why were we quietly accepting this terror? I wanted to speak out, but I couldn't even talk to Carolynn about the things I had seen in The Nam. I felt trapped and powerless.

I enjoy books and bookstores, but it was Carolynn who discovered our first book about Vietnam. I had never dreamed that someone might write about that awful place. How could they let it out? I was stunned. I rushed to a bookstore, filled a shopping bag with books about the war. There were strange, almost biblical titles: *A Rumor of War, The End of the Line, Fire in the Lake, Hell in a Very Small Place, Winners and Losers*. I devoured each one and attacked another. My collection has outgrown our assortment of bookcases. Each time I start another book about Vietnam I am on edge. Is it anticipation, fear, the pain of memories? I only know that I'm searching for something, I have to find it, and I don't even know what it is.

Hindsight can be confusing. Vietnam had fallen to the communists. So had Cambodia. Saigon was now called Ho Chi Minh City. Cambodia had become Kampuchea. Had the architects of America's policy been right? Would the communist horde sweep into my beloved Thailand, then Malaysia? Cambodia had died an ugly death; perhaps uglier than even the Nazi holocaust. Afghanistan. Nicaragua. El Salvador. I watched my children learning to walk and talk, heard the news reports about "windows of vulnerability" and "covert" forays into foreign politics. This would be the world my children would inherit, if it lasted long enough. I attempted to make sense of "contras" and "Sandinistas," mined harbors and death squads. I wanted to leave my children a better world. I wanted to settle whatever was gnawing at my guts. I started swallowing ulcer medicine before each meal. Once before I had been unknowing, and I carried the scars. The newspaper articles seemed ominously familiar. I had to take sides. I had to resolve Vietnam, but I didn't know where to begin.

It had been fourteen years. I didn't want to be cross-examined or interrupted until I had reached a conclusion I could defend. Until I was satisfied and at peace with my memories. There was no cataclysmic decision to blurt it out. One Saturday afternoon I jotted down a list of the most important incidents I had seen. That evening I began to type. I would describe my experiences. Perhaps Carolynn would read and understand. Perhaps I would save the papers until the girls were older, and they might learn from Daddy's mistakes. Carolynn encouraged me, then left me alone. After about two weeks of typing, I added to my list. I had expected this project to use about twenty sheets of paper. Incidents long buried were surfacing at an alarming rate. I got up in the dead of night to jot a note, or pulled over to the edge of the road to record another memory that had just exploded out of my subconscious. I typed late at night, every night. The old records that had been background music of many of my adventures helped bring those adventures back to life. It was a painful journey. I relived all the horror and fear in the living room. Sometimes Carolynn had to come downstairs to help me through the ordeal. I was obsessed; there was no stopping. The pages accumulated.

Carolynn was concerned. Where would this explosion lead? She sought out the author of that first book about Vietnam, a nurse who had worked with civilian casualties. I worked up enough courage to meet the lady, and she was as honest as her book. She knew; I could see it in her eyes. She said her nightmares didn't take her back to The Nam but brought Vietnam into the present.

Sometimes, in the night, I dream I'm looking out toward the backyard. The kids are in the sandbox, Carolynn is puttering with her flowers, and the neighboring yards are swarming with Vietcong sappers in black pajamas. I scream, but my girls cannot hear me. I am frozen, and the approaching gooks are all grinning that maniacal grin I once saw on the road to Dak To, twenty-three days before I was supposed to leave The Nam. I am prickly with terror. Insane. Frantic. I can feel each hair leaping out of my skin. Sweat lies cold upon my rib cage, burns my eyes. Then I wake with a start and prowl the house. The children are sleeping peacefully, looking like angels; and I sit and smoke or read magazines until I am ready to sleep again.

I dream I am leaning over the bed to kiss a forehead goodnight, and there is a stir, and a beautiful, trusting face has been transformed into the bubbled, flaking, disfigured black horror of the kid I once saw in the hospital.

I dream we are crouched behind the sandbags, watching the horde of Charleys approaching. There is no escape. There are only four bullets left. I remember the fire truck in the midst of a clearing, and know what I have to do to save my girls from being violated. But the girls look at me with eyes full of love and trust, and I can't do it, and I am deeply sorry I brought them into the world. There is a frantic explosion of action, and I wake to find the blankets wrapped tight around me, the sheets soaked with sweat, and my fists twisted frantically into the pillow. The dream never reaches its unspeakable conclusion, and I lie awake and quake at the awesome responsibilities of parenthood.

I'm not the only one with nightmares. Talking with other Vietnam vets has taught me that. I wonder if I'm crazy, but I know the psycho wards could never hold all of us. The experts say we are normal, just more aware than other people, and better for it.

I was typing every night now, the story bubbling out of me like pus from an infection. I couldn't stop the flow. And as my writing progressed, so did my nerve. I began to talk with other Vietnam vets, to check details, compare feelings. I became aware of the Agent Orange controversy. I have no idea if I was ever exposed to this state-of-the-art military miracle. Outside our barbed-wire perimeter there was a free-fire zone of six-inch grass for about fifty yards, then a wall of ten-foot elephant grass. The free-fire zone was booby-trapped with mines and flares. No one mowed that grass, but it never grew. Why? One night I took an ominous inventory of the Vietnam veterans I knew personally. At that time there were nine, plus myself. (One has since committed suicide.) Two have never fathered children since the war. Of the remaining eight, one was a woman. She had suffered numerous miscarriages and many severe health problems. Another vet's first child was stillborn. Four of us had known the agony of Sudden Infant Death. Seventy-five percent of all Vietnam vets I knew had buried their children! A macabre coincidence? Perhaps, but I began to ask questions of acquaintances, my students, total strangers. The percentage has never dropped below 65! Did we lose our son in The Nam? Are our beautiful daughters carrying a time bomb in their bodies? Will our grandchildren be Vietnam casualties? Had we been aware of the Agent Orange connection to infant death, we would not have risked having other children. Our daughters are beautiful and healthy. We wonder what their future holds.

I didn't ask to go to Vietnam. The authorities said it was my "duty," and they had a relentless force of agents ready to invade any neighborhood to force compliance. No such show of force exists today to answer the questions about Agent Orange. The VA often suggests psychiatric help. The air force's "Ranch Hand" study has reported three times the normal mortality rate in children under twenty-eight days of age, children of Vietnam vets exposed to Agent Orange. But, in announcing the findings, the air force was quick to add "we see no reason not to use it again." All we ask are some honest answers, but the government fears the cost, and there is heavy vegetation in Nicaragua and El Salvador.

"Be all that you can be," the TV commercials say, invading my living room to shine their rainbow-colored message over the innocent bodies of my children. Is *that* all they can be? I see those commercials on Saturday mornings, interspersed with cartoons for preschoolers. But cigarette commercials are banned from television because smoking is "hazardous to your health." Have we learned nothing? Or is this propaganda, as insidious as the brainwashing we hear about behind the Iron Curtain?

I was deep into my story when I found the key. I was searching for a word, and *expendable* came into my head. My *Webster's Dictionary* defines *expendable* as: "in military usage, designating equipment (and hence, men) expected to be used up (or sacrificed) in service." I cannot be expected to experience the war and its aftereffects, to relive it in hundreds of hours of self-analysis, punching out hundreds of typewritten pages with only one finger, without reaching conclusions. The Vietnam War is too deeply significant for me to have learned nothing. I am not comfortable with my conclusions, but I am satisfied that they are realistic.

I'm afraid that our leaders, civilian or military, are so obsessed with power that they have come to view us all as expendable. What mother cradles a child to her breast and considers him "cannon fodder," or wants to think that he is "expected to be sacrificed"? By law, we are allowed to nurture and teach children until they reach the tender age of eighteen. After that, the state can seize them for military service. The authorities speak of a child's "duty," of his "obligation to his country." These same officials have ignored the majority public opinion, demonstrated in referenda, polls, and surveys, that the American people favor a halt to the arms race, a nuclear freeze.

In the wake of the Tet offensive, an American military officer described the action around the village of Ben Tre with the words, "We had to destroy it to save it." Did America's military leaders lie to Congress and the president about enemy troop strengths and expose half a million Americans, mostly teenagers, to unnecessary suffering and death? On December 27, 1983, in Washington, President Reagan publicly accepted "full blame and responsibility" for the deaths of 241 marines in Beirut, despite a Pentagon report outlining critical errors by marine lifers on the scene that had contributed to the slaughter, perhaps caused it. Ironically, just across town that day, General Westmoreland told a press conference, "If I were guilty as charged by the CBS broadcast, I could be court-martialed." Clearly, there is no precedent to cause the general any alarm.

Under the guise of "security," the press was not allowed to accompany our marines to the invasion of Grenada. Approximately five thousand of our boys took part. More died as a result of accidents and "friendly fire" than by hostile action. There has been no disciplinary action, but 8,666 medals have been awarded to this date.

The tragedy of Agent Orange continues. The only assurances we have seen from the government or the military are statements that they would not hesitate to use it again—birth defects, premature deaths, and suffering of the American people notwithstanding.

The sacrifices made by American veterans in all wars have been terrifying and heroic, but once their usefulness has been "used up," the VA hospitals to which they are committed are a disgrace. Ron Kovic had volunteered for his second tour in Vietnam when a Vietcong bullet smashed his spine and left him paralyzed. In his book, *Born on the Fourth of July*, Kovic writes of life in a VA hospital. The patients tossed bread crumbs onto the floor at night so that the marauding rats would not gnaw at their lifeless toes.* Conditions in VA hospitals today are little im-

---

*Ron Kovic, *Born on the Fourth of July* (New York: McGraw-Hill, 1976).

proved, and the Reagan administration's budget cuts have not helped. America's arsenal, and budget deficits, have mushroomed.

Government officials have assured us that we can survive, even win a nuclear war, if we will just dig a hole in the backyard, place a door over the hole, and cover it with dirt. I refuse to spend any more time in a muddy hole at my government's pleasure. If they have a nuclear war, the survivors will just have to bury me or live with the stink. I'll be damned if I will quietly and conveniently dig my own grave to make it easier for them!

I am not anti-American. The wholesale murder of civilians is horrible regardless of whether it is done by American or communist forces. The bloodbaths in Vietnam, Cambodia, Afghanistan, and Nicaragua are equally repugnant. The threat of more bloodshed in the Middle East or Central America dominates today's news. Are we helping the peasants repel communism or simply allowing our military to play with their terrible space-age toys and forcing the battered peasants to embrace communism as a means of self-preservation? Our military leaders have shown contempt for the poor from our own country, as well as the poor in Lebanon, Grenada, El Salvador, Nicaragua, South Africa, and the Philippines. They hold all of humanity hostage with their nuclear arsenals. Might they decide to destroy the entire planet "in order to save it"?

Long ago, the army pointed to my IQ scores and suggested I volunteer for Officer Candidate School. I never attended OCS, but I think I have learned a great deal from my military experience.

November of 1982 brought a tidal wave of emotions and long-suppressed memories into my life, all centered around the shaded corner of the mall in Washington, D.C., where a Vietnam Memorial was being constructed. A television camera scanned the vast wall of names, my eyes recognized a ghost from the past, and I burst into tears. I didn't know he hadn't made it. The children were upset at the sight of their daddy crying. We hustled them into the car and drove to Washington. The memorial was surrounded by snow fence and security guards, waiting quietly to be dedicated the following weekend. Television hadn't prepared me for the power of those huge, black walls; it takes a lot of space to print 57,939 names. We stood on a small knoll beneath the naked branches of hickories in winter dress. Perhaps a hundred strangers were scattered around us, many sobbing, none ashamed. My eyes were watering uncontrollably when the children spotted a squirrel and rescued me with their delighted chatter.

"Haec Olim Meminisse Juvabit": The Sixties

The Latin words appear in thin Imperial script on a dark placard in the State College Hotel, downtown from Penn State University where, twenty years before, I debated Vergil's phrase with two friends from the advanced Latin class—Andrew Stapp and Timothy Reussing—who, like myself and many other young Americans, would soon be swept off into political waters of which six months earlier we had no sense at all. "Perhaps someday it will help to remember these things." Now, long after my friends' burning of a draft card and after their flight from the FBI, after my cover-up of their disappearance, and still later, after Stapp's court-martial at Fort Sill, and after the three years I spent in Vietnam, Vergil's words have an ironic ring. *How*, I've sometimes wondered as my youth passed and our lives changed irrevocably, how will remembering the tumultuous events of the sixties and the war in Vietnam be a help to me or to anyone else?

Nonetheless, helpfully or not, my thoughts have often returned to events which engulfed my friends and shoved their lives in strange directions. The other day, the shores of memory were given an oceanic wallop as I passed Reussing's old place—long dubbed the Pugh Street Zoo—and saw a ball-and-crane swinging into the blistered, dry-rotted, and surely termite-eaten, clapboard, fleabag rooming house. The roof of that warren was already collapsed and I pictured the rungless chairs, three-legged desks, and squeaky bunk bed frames washed in sunlight and I remembered the room where Reussing lived twenty years before after he had dropped out of the fraternity which had become for him "irrelevant." I remembered letting myself into his room day after day after he and Stapp

38

had fled to Cuba (or so I thought, though I had told the FBI I was pretty sure they were heading to Canada). Then, for about a week—in order to delay knowledge that Reussing and Stapp were *both* gone (because at first the FBI was only looking for Stapp, who had burned his draft card at one of the first antiwar demonstrations in our sleepy football town)—I got into Reussing's room each evening when no one was looking and pulled his shade down, turned on his ceiling light, and rumpled his bedcovers; in the morning, on the way to my classes, I'd sneak back in, make his bed, turn off the light, and let up the shade. Getting in was easy: the large cast iron key from my room just up the street turned as nicely in Reussing's lock as it did in mine . . . and now this memory recalls Mrs. Mary Homan Ross, the large, bespectacled elderly widow with a bun of white hair and heavy doughy arms that shook when she rolled a pie crust as she often did for the "boys" in her rooming house, myself among them. She would be dead by the end of that school year. Old as she was, I think her heart attack was advanced by the following events and by a particular visit from the FBI.

And so, twenty years later, standing across the street in the bright sunlight while the wrecking ball splintered the white siding of the Zoo, I remembered standing in Reussing's room and listening to his abandoned radio playing the Beatles' new song, *Yesterday*. I think I was crying or on the verge of tears. After all, I was nineteen years old; my closest friends had taken off on a motorcycle after learning that the FBI wanted to "talk" to them just when other draft card burners were being arrested in other college towns as the attorney general's office was sorting its cases to decide the most prosecutable. (Wasn't the final conviction based on destroying government property, i.e., the draft card itself?) Anyway, Andy and Tim had been gone for about two weeks. I had been lying to FBI agents regarding their whereabouts. Someone had told me that this itself was a crime punishable by law, as also was flight to avoid prosecution. I had been telephoned by a Mr. Storch, the Dean of Men, about the false report I had given our Latin teacher about Andy and Tim's absences. ("You said they were sick, Mr. Balaban. Why did you say that?"—"Well, last time I saw them they didn't look too good to me.") And, most upsetting, the FBI had questioned me on three occasions about my two friends and other student "activists," a term which hadn't reached popular use.

In order to throw the FBI off the trail, I had led them to believe I was a stooge. Sure, I'd tell them what I knew about Andy: he was upright, honest, a good student; no, I didn't think he believed in violent overthrow of the government. Yes, he had burned his draft card; no, I did not see him do it. No, I did not know about the May 2nd Movement or the Progressive Labor Party (pro-Castro and pro-Mao groups which Andy had joined). For a while, at least judging by the questions put to me, our Happy Valley was the home of the Rabid Maoists as well as the Nittany Lions. After the first three visits to my rooming house, the FBI seemed bored by my replies. Two weeks had passed since my friends had disappeared.

I was able to escape too much guilt about lying because in fact I did not know where Stapp and Reussing were. The last I had seen them was when they had rounded a corner on Tim's motorcycle and stopped when I waved them down. They were both giddy and wild-eyed with a look that one saw later on the faces of American soldiers rolling out of Hue on operations, armed and standing up in truckbeds and armored personnel carriers as their dust-billowing convoys roared on to battle. Exhilarated. Scared. My friends were going to Cuba, or so they said, but for weeks I didn't really know where they were so I wasn't really *lying* to the FBI. Even after Andy called me from New Orleans and asked me to wire them fifty dollars I figured I still wasn't actually lying unless the FBI asked me again. Unfortunately, they did. One day as I was crossing the parking lot of the newly-built Sheraton, I ran into Mr. Jones, as we'll call him, the State College agent, along with several other agents that had been sent in to cover the case (at one point eight agents!). Jones asked me if I knew yet where my friends were. I hesitated and said no. "Okay," he said, and turned away with his colleagues and I knew I was in trouble. I must have gone around wearing a worried look because I remember Gordon Smith, my seventeenth-century English poetry professor, stopping me after class and asking me if anything was wrong. I told him only that the FBI had questioned me repeatedly about my friends and then I remember his saying, "Look, you're a first-rate student who should be thinking about a graduate school, not the FBI. You tell me if they bother you again." Whatever he intended to do, it was nice to have someone on my side.

What developed, as my thoughts were diverted from my studies of Donne and Marvell, was a political consciousness—nothing grand or systematic, mind you, but an attitude, a clearer viewpoint on the state and the individual, for things became clearer almost immediately when my mail started to arrive opened. I stormed down to the FBI office over the Penn-Whelan drugstore and shook my fist of opened mail at the roomful of agents having morning coffee. Jones, bluff, square-jawed, and soft-spoken, told me that the FBI didn't open mail without a court order and that he would tell me when they had one for me.

Then things became clearer still some days later when, taking a shower in the metal stall of our rooming house bath, I heard my name called dimly through the soap in my ears and the hiss of the shower spray. I looked out to see a trenchcoated Jones standing in the doorway.

"I want to talk with you," he said, and he sounded angry.

"Now?"

"Yeah, now."

"Go in my room," I said, gesturing from behind the plastic shower curtain with a sudsy hand. When I got to the room myself, covered by a wet towel and feeling that Christ this was a pretty humiliating way to get arrested, Jones was still in his trenchcoat, something I found slightly comic, even then.

"We know you're lying to us," he began.

"How," I said, giving up further pretense, "would you know that unless you read my mail or tapped my phone?"

"Never mind how," he said. "You lied and I trusted you."

Even at nineteen I thought this a weak argument for an FBI agent. Jones, I later decided, had gotten in trouble with higher-ups because what he said was, although lame, also true: I had . . . well . . . *misled* him and maybe he had trusted me.

"I want to say," he continued, "that the next time I come I'll have a warrant for your friends and one for you unless you want to tell me where Stapp is."

So they *didn't* know. They only knew I knew. With some pride, I now remember what I said just then, two years before I was old enough to drink or vote.

"Mr. Jones, what would you arrest me for?"

"Harboring a fugitive and withholding information."

Holding my towel with one hand, I opened the door to my closet and said, "You can see that no one's here so I'm not harboring a fugitive and as far as 'withholding information' I don't know about that. You FBI agents, I do know, usually have some background in law . . ."

Jones shook his head.

". . . so maybe you know better, but I think it's my right to withhold any information I want."

"Okay," he said with a bit of a snarl. "I warned you." (He talked like that.)

"Do you like what you are doing?" I asked as he turned to leave. To my surprise Jones stopped and considered my question. "I mean, the Mafia runs prostitution and heroin up the road in Altoona. They kill and hurt people. Wouldn't you rather be chasing real criminals?"

"Maybe I would," Jones said.

In retrospect I think of him as a pretty decent guy. Ten years later, I was kind of proud of him when he rescued a kidnapped woman and maybe saved her life.

After Jones left I was so scared I actually considered calling my parents (during World War II my father had given the FBI information that had helped the Allies target the cleverly camouflaged Ploesti oilfields of his boyhood Romania). But if what I was doing was confusing to me, it certainly would have made no sense to my parents. Instead, I had sense enough to call the American Civil Liberties Union in Philadelphia. I told them that I was going to be arrested by the FBI. It was a Friday. The ACLU guy asked me some questions, said "Uh huh," and then said he would try to get a lawyer to come into their office to meet me the next morning.

That evening I drove my '53 Chevy two-door the ten miles to Bellefonte to use the Western Union. (Would the State College clerk be told to look out for me?) I wired the fifty dollars and also sent Stapp and Reuss-

41

ing a telegram telling them to flee because I didn't want to know any longer where they were in case the ACLU lawyer told me that I had to tell the FBI. When I had last spoken to my friends they had cooled on going to Cuba and were working at a construction site in New Orleans, which sounded like fun. I wasn't going to go to jail for *that*, so I devised a telegram that would alert them, defy easy reading, and get me off the hook: "FUGITE FUGITE FABIUS BITHYNIUS INSPECTUS INVENIT." (Five years later, when I next saw Stapp, he still carried the telegram folded in his wallet.) "Flee. Flee. F.B.I. is coming."

Leaving my message with the clerk at the Bush House Tavern, I drove the thirty miles across the mountains to Lewistown to catch the 11:00 P.M. "Spirit of St. Louis." I was early; the train, as always in those pre-Amtrak days, was late, so I had a couple of hours of waiting outside the locked and deserted station where I watched the foundry smoke drifting across the constellations and wondered what the hell was going on. Maybe, I thought, I'd join Andy and Tim rather than tell anybody anything. I pictured the cops finding my dusty Chevy in the station lot a couple of weeks later . . . Mr. Jones kicking the license plate and saying ruefully, in his TV-script way, "Yep, Balaban's. You can bet he's with them now."

Nothing so drastic, nothing so dramatic happened. In Philadelphia the next morning, the ACLU lawyer told me that Jones was bluffing, that I hadn't done anything illegal and that the FBI was just trying to scare information out of me. A week later I heard from Andy again. The FBI *had* found them. They had been questioned. They hadn't been arrested. But the FBI had indeed tapped my phone because they had overheard one of his calls to me or so, Andy said, an FBI friend of the Stapp family had told his worried parents.

Tapped my phone. Opened my mail.

And then I learned that they had searched my room. When I returned to school after that Christmas break (Stapp and Reussing never returned to finish degrees) I learned that my landlady, Mrs. Ross, had died of a heart attack. The chemistry student from across the hall, whom Mrs. Ross had set store by, told me that she had reluctantly let the FBI into my room on two occasions and that they had asked her not to tell me or anyone else because I was "involved with criminals," and she, who lived most of her life on a dairy farm until her husband died, had agreed but got so upset that she had to tell somebody so she told my fellow roomer just to get it off her chest, and he was now getting it off his.

She had died just before Christmas. By New Year's her children already had the place up for sale. No more baking in that oven for her "boys." I remember Tom (was that his name? Tom what?) as a dried-out sort who looked like Mister Rogers and who studied all the time. He went to church which I think was pretty unusual among college students then and so, to make this brief, in the choosing-up-sides atmosphere of the sixties, I figured he was definitely on *theirs* . . . so I was surprised when he blurted out his conclusion. "I think they killed her," he said. "How could they ask an old lady like that to lie?"

In the 1960s thousands of Americans, many now nearing middle age, were forced to make their own political judgments—often against the activities of their government. One wonders what this will mean for the country, especially since they were the baby boom generation and the American electorate now has a bigger percentage of them than of anybody else. If some of them were nudged into political consciousness, others, who may have been pushed harder, were propelled into political action.

When I first met Andy Stapp he was more interested in the factual errors of our recent lecture on Trajan's column than in the moral errors of Johnson's escalation. Stapp was largish, gat-toothed, sloppy, talked and ate a lot, told very funny jokes, liked to be right, and was generally a good-natured wise-guy. His more mainstream friend, Tim Reussing, was—except for his interest in his Greek classics—a typical frat rat: preppy and more concerned with sorority mixers than with the Gulf of Tonkin. In the normal course of things, Andy would have gone on to finish a Ph.D. in classics and Tim would now be a business executive with literary interests. These possibilities were eliminated one weekend in 1965, when Andy, who was increasingly aroused by the war, boarded a bus chartered to join a march in Washington. (His parents, searching for some clue to his agitation over Vietnam, could recall only that when Andy was fourteen or fifteen he had gotten so upset over the Soviet crushing of the Hungarian revolution that they had made him see a counselor.)

In Washington, where police with nightsticks charged the demonstrators, Stapp was clubbed, arrested, stripped, and handcuffed naked to a pole that ran from the floor to the ceiling in the detention room. He said he saw a girl dragged by her long, red hair down a corridor in the station. Whole hanks had been pulled from her scalp. Earlier, in the first mayhem when the police charged the demonstrators who had linked arms and sat down on some government lawn, Andy recalled seeing a kid, who had been the only one to wear a helmet and so had been the butt of some wisecracks on the bus, standing helmetless, dazed, and his nose dribbling blood as he looked down into his open palm where one of his eyes lay. Andy was never the same after that. His political talk became remorseless and by degrees the less radical Reussing, who had never marched or demonstrated, was pulled into the wake of Andy's rage.

So Stapp's radical career should have come as no surprise. Pushed harder than most of his contemporaries, he pushed back with the cleverness that characterized the activists of the sixties. When he fled Penn State, he lost the 2-S Selective Service deferment that kept him and thousands of other (mostly white) American males out of Vietnam. Andy was nonplused. As far as he was concerned, all the rules had been broken and he was now free to play according to his own. School, first of all, was plainly a waste of time. He wanted to learn about guns and guerrilla combat. He volunteered for the marines.

The marines wouldn't have him, but his local draft board put him in the army, where, at Fort Bennington, he volunteered for special training in assault weapons. He was learning about machine guns before the army realized that something wasn't quite right about the eager recruit, so even before completing his training, he was transferred to Fort Sill, Oklahoma, where he was kept under surveillance.

It would have been hard *not* to notice him. Stapp was always talking— in the barracks, in the chow line, on duty, and on breaks—about the military-industrial complex, about the power elite's manipulation of the war for economic ends, about the oppression of the poor, about racism in the United States, about the aspirations of the Vietnamese people. I pictured him tanned, leaner, and really enjoying his missionary work. I don't imagine that he was ever a wind-up radical reiterating a fixed tirade. Like Mac in Steinbeck's *In Dubious Battle,* Andy knew how to listen, to joke, to insinuate: he talked from your side of things. And while he was to some just another grunt with a gripe, he was also beginning his American Servicemen's Union which, in the late sixties in Vietnam, and especially through its Black membership, caused the army another worry in the management of its huge and increasingly disaffected forces.

Thinking back on it now, I can see that the army was wise to take special measures with Andy, but the lengths to which the Fort Sill command went still seem amazing. He was placed in a kind of quarantine, his duty as isolated as possible but not *too* isolated because, left entirely on his own, Andy tended to wreck equipment, once backing a truck into a wall and destroying both. Who could prove that he had done it deliberately? He wrote me in my first year at Harvard (in a letter stamped "opened by the military censor" or something like that) that "it was an accident. Ha. Ha. Ha."

To remove him even further from contact with other troops, Andy was obliged to sleep in a different barracks each week. Of course this only aroused sympathy for him, especially since he was ordered to carry his bed from barracks to barracks, on his back, like some biblical figure. When punishment and isolation failed to break him, the army looked for some means of getting rid of Stapp which would also be an example, I suppose, to the soldiers who knew him. His inevitable court-martial came when he refused to open his footlocker to an officer conducting a surprise inspection. Andy had "refused to obey a legitimate order." They had him.

When his trial came up he turned it into an attack on U.S. policies in Vietnam. Later, he sent me a copy of the court-martial proceedings. Among the various "subversive publications" listed by the prosecution as being concealed in the footlocker for illegal dissemination was a *Harvard*

Crimson that I had sent him.

Certainly what happened to my friend affected me as it had earlier affected Tim Reussing (who, after the New Orleans adventure, had gone to work in a tool-and-die shop near Atlanta). Shortly after, I too dropped out: leaving graduate school to go to Vietnam as a conscientious objector. When Andy and I met again, he was running his union with his radical wife and I had spent two years in South Vietnam, first as an instructor of linguistics at the University of Can Tho and then, after the university was bombed during the Tet offensive in 1968, as a field representative of the Committee of Responsibility, a private group that arranged hospital care for war-injured Vietnamese children. My job had been to send to the United States children—children with no noses, with obliterated jaws, with exploded eardrums and blinded eyes, with missing hands and arms and legs, with shattered spines, with severed sciatic nerves, with scalped heads, and with chins glued to their chests by napalm and white phosphorus. When these children were more or less patched up, my job then was to return them to their families, if their families still existed and if I could find them. In this context, Andy's attempt to undermine the military seemed to me no idle radical exercise.

That was in 1970. I haven't heard of Andy since. Is this significant? It surprises me. Why didn't he join a really radical group like the Weathermen or the Symbionese Liberation Army? Indeed, it now strikes me as amazing that in the United States where true atrocities were perpetrated by the government, no serious terrorist groups sprang up as there did abroad. Here we had the Kent State murders, the shotgun woundings of demonstrators in San Francisco, the murders of Black students at Southern University in Baton Rouge, and beatings administered routinely all across the country by local police and National Guards. How interesting it should be to us that American protestors, with far more grievance, remained largely peaceful, in comparison to foreign radicals like the German Baader-Meinhof group, the Japanese Red Army Faction, and the Italian Red Brigades. Indeed, our few bomb throwers now seem far less dangerous to the public weal than the governmental agencies that pursued them with lawlessness or only a charade of legality. Our near lack of violent protest remains to me a mystery; maybe it says something good about America.

But setting aside the radical fringe, what about all the people who witnessed the political events of the time, including the countercultural events so often political in nature? What permanent effect did the sixties have on the general population, the workaday breadwinners and their families, and through them, on present American society? They are no small number. Do you know how many American armed forces were sent to Vietnam? 8,744,000. Nearly 9 million. After all, we were there for ten years with 500,000 on regular rotation. Nine million is more than twice the number of American troops in World War I (4,734,991) and compares with the number involved in World War II (16,112,566).* But

Americans at home during those earlier wars did not watch the battles on their televisions. They were not forced to witness. Vietnam was a different war and 9 million is only a portion of those Americans directly affected by the slaughter. What are all these people thinking about now? Can they have forgotten Vietnam and its impact on the sixties? Can we possibly dare to ignore so vast an amount of conscious and unconscious thought when something so large must surely have changed, is changing, the national character? Presidents since Johnson have wanted to forget Vietnam and the divisive sixties and get on with business as usual. Is this possible? To do so obliges America to continue to wander into the twenty-first century with the vulnerabilities of an amnesiac. Jimmy Carter, in his Sunday school way, sensed this when he lectured us on our lack of moral fiber. He read the symptom but couldn't identify the disease. Moral fiber grows from recognition of problems, from decisions, from action, and from responsibility for actions. As a nation, we cannot afford to forget Vietnam.

The deceits of U.S. involvement in Vietnam led to the deceits of Watergate and perhaps even more disastrously—because Watergate, God bless Sam Ervin and John Sirica, at least forced a partial coming to terms—to the politics of Ronald Reagan who, when recently questioned, could not accurately describe the Geneva Accords, the natures of the two Vietnams, or events which led to U.S. involvement, *but who nonetheless* had told an American Legion convention during his 1980 campaign that Americans should be proud of what we did in Vietnam. This, despite the millions of civilians killed there and in Cambodia and Laos by our troops and bombs, despite the thousands of our own dead and wounded and maimed, despite our irretrievable loss of national treasure and the corresponding ruination of Johnson's Great Society, and despite the damage done to American prestige throughout the world and the resulting increase in Soviet sway.

Remembering the sixties—and hoping to see it reflected in films, novels, plays, poems, and essays—isn't so dreadful a task. During the sixties, one could argue, the young people of this country helped save it from total moral disgrace by protests which still provide lessons in traditional American resourcefulness, team work, and rugged individualism. With the failure in the received wisdom of the establishment, many learned to make their own judgments about political and personal affairs. I remember an event that took place in Philadelphia where the local SDS had announced that it was going to burn a dog publicly, with a homemade napalm concoction in order to protest the use of napalm on people. The

---

Information Please Almanac, 1982, p. 400.

46

local papers seethed with outraged editorials and letters and, heeding the large public outcry, a contingent of police and firemen and SPCA officials showed up to stop the demonstration. The SDS appeared on the appointed day with some gas cans and a waggly dog. Before an angry crowd and a ready cordon of cops, one of the radicals stepped up to a microphone and said, *"Of course* we aren't going to burn a dog. That would be horrible. Can you imagine how horrible it is to burn a human being?" And with that, they left.

Did the knowledge gained on mental perimeters, in Vietnam and in the United States, disappear like a drug trip? Was the popular wisdom just so much pot smoke? For those young in the sixties, the music made America inhabitable. But the heroes and heroines of rock were risky models. Joplin and Hendrix and Morrison died miserable deaths. Woodstock quickly became Altamont with attendant Hell's Angels. The spiritual seekers of the sixties degenerated into the Moonies and the Campus Crusades for Christ. Etc. Etc. Does this discredit the counterculture? I don't think so and I am reminded of an episode in Tennessee Williams's *Camino Real* where Casanova and Marguerite are trapped in the deadly city surrounded by a howling Terra Incognito. Lord Byron will soon go off alone into that unknown wasteland and Casanova says to his beloved: "You must learn how to carry the banner of Bohemia into the enemy camp." And Marguerite replies: "Bohemia is no banner. It survives by discretion." Well, our heroes and heroines in the sixties had little discretion, yet they sometimes ventured into *terra incognito* and while it cost some of them their lives and their sanities, the paths they made are still there and *terra incognito* is less threatening. In retrospect, one admires their bravery, sees in it something very American and strong, and wishes more of it were alive in the eighties.

Despite all the tomfoolery, mayhem, flash, and rhetoric of the sixties we learned things. We relearned, like those Philadelphia SDSers, like Stapp, like Reussing, the power of the individual who has the courage to assess his condition honestly and then act with resource and imagination. In this respect, our elected officials are still far behind us as they insult the ordinary person's intelligence every year at election time and then, when they have won office, continue to fail at the tasks at hand. Why do we let them do this? My notion is that one cause lies in the sixties and in the resultant disaffection of millions of people with a corrupt and unresponsive government. We are stalled. Americans can't move forward until we see where we have been. Recognizing and understanding the complex causes of our defeat in Vietnam are crucial to our national progress. *Forsan et haec olim meminisse juvabit.* Aeneas says this to his men after their ten-year war at Troy, after their defeat, and after their difficult flight across an unknown sea. "O comrades," he says,

. . . we knew—we suffered—evils before.
Together we have been through worse:
the loud chambers of Scylla's rocks;
the thundering cliffs of the Cyclops' shore.
Our god will grant an end to this as well.
So pluck back courage; banish anxious fears.
Some day, perhaps, remembering these will help.

RECOMMENDED READING

John Balaban, ed., *Ca Dao Vietnam: A Bilingual Anthology of Vietnamese Folk Poetry*. Greensboro, N.C.: Unicorn Press, 1980.

Maurice Durand and Nguyan Tran Huan, *An Introduction to Vietnamese Literature*. New York: Columbia University Press, 1985. A survey.

Timothy J. Lomperis, *Reading the Wind: Literature of the Vietnam War*. Durham, N.C.: Duke University Press, 1987. American survey.

David G. Marr, *Vietnamese AntiColonialism*. Berkeley: University of California Press, 1971. Intellectual history.

Tran Van Dinh, *Blue Dragon, White Tiger: A Tet Story*. Philadelphia: TriAm Press, Inc. 1983. A novel.

My Home in the Country

I

I'd climb into the wicker baby carriage in the barn—I must've been five or so—and it was my pleasure to picture the cavalry riding up to rescue me. The commander, a sergeant, would pull up to an abrupt halt and dismount. He was very quick and sure of himself. Gold buttons cascaded down his trim torso. He'd come over to the carriage and look in. He'd say, "It's her," and nod to all the other men and then he'd lift me up in his arms. I'd be a "baby in swaddling clothes" which to me meant something like a little bundle of bound and trembling flesh. I'd replay this over and over. There they'd be in the middle distance, then closer, closer, dismount, step, click, nod, and whoosh, up I'd go. I don't know whose baby carriage it was. And now I don't know who's left around to ask, but I'd be interested in the facts.

I am ten years old, nearly eleven. I'm standing in galoshes smack in the middle of the stream that cuts across the yard out front of the house and heads down past the barn through the fields and on into the creek about a quarter of a mile away. It's late winter. Rain pounds the snow into ice and water, and all of it steams up out of the hillsides like a sigh rising in my throat. I'm a kid in my birthday month about to trudge that sweet, treacherous slip of mud bank down the stream to the creek and back.

A mother and a father move about somewhere behind me in that "dog of a house," as an aunt will say of it, much later. It's a two-storied white-shingled corpus with a single stone wing jutting out of it that chills the parental bedroom. The whole affair is dug into a hill that I can get to by crawling out my bedroom window. At a run I can burst in through the front door, tear upstairs through my bedroom out the window onto the hill down the slope and back into the stream just in time for my mother to walk out on the front porch and yell at me. The house breathes out trails. The children have marked its floors and walls with family life, drenched it with the urge to go from inside out.

My mother seems to hate it. I don't think she cares so much what the house looks like but she hates living on a dirt road in the farthest reaches of the school district with no neighbors to talk to during weekdays when she is home by herself. She has neighbors but they are the wives of truck drivers and factory workers. My mother never walks up the road to visit them, though I am all the time riding the range with their kids. They are godfearing and their houses are even doggier. Mrs. Williams once banished me from her house for making up a drama about the Devil and casting her kids in supporting roles.

My parents lack fundamental religious feeling. My father was never baptized and only goes to church so he can sing in the choir, which he loves to do. He sent me to Sunday school once with a chicken bone fastened into the pony tail sprouting on top of my head. The teacher said it was barbaric, but my father really loves practical jokes.

I can tell my mother is bored by church, though she would never say so to me. I think her lack of faith disturbs her. She'd like not to pass it along just in case, you know, there is redemption. I worry about that too. So sometimes we make resolutions to go to church. I get dressed up like Alice in Wonderland in petticoats that make me nervous and cranky. We go to hear about God from Reverend Allen and adopt a submissive reverence that we'd rather not feel, especially because we don't really know why we're doing it. After awhile, we give it up.

I know things about my mother by what she says and by what she does. She is the daughter of a draftsman with an eighth-grade education who worked on the first nuclear-powered submarine in Groton, Connecticut. Her mother is a charming and complete alcoholic about whom she expresses no warmth.

My mother stays up late reading Jane Austen and historical novels about places like China. Sometimes she shows me her scrapbook from high school. She was a star basketball player and a good scholar back then and should have gone to college. But her father didn't have enough money to send all three children, so only the son could go. When she was seventeen her parents divorced. A strange woman took her to lunch and told her she was about to acquire her as a stepmother.

This crushed my mother. She was ashamed of her parents. She left home, found my wonderful father and his wonderful family and married into them, like a girl desperate to get home. She explains these things to me with a ferocious seriousness but no details. I repeat them to my friends during contests over whose parents are the most mysterious and infirm, but I don't understand how to dramatize them. I don't quite get what an alcoholic is, though the word carries weight. Katy's dad has a war wound. That's real evidence.

I know my giddy father by what he does. He's Good Time Charlie to me and my friends. He teaches a bunch of us how to ski, and calls us "messy fellas," or names he makes up. Kablookerhonkies. Mizzible houndies. Zounds Daddy! Yikes! We go for midnight hikes during the full moon. He fixes everything that breaks and makes hot dinners for the dogs. He licks his own plate after meals so that nothing gets wasted. Once I saw him crying during a very sad movie about the Civil War. Just after that he fell asleep in his chair.

He used to be Canadian but now he's not. All that family came down to New England from Nova Scotia by way of Saskatchewan some time in the twenties. He did go to college and because he's so good with mechanics he became an aeronautical engineer. I think he wasn't in the war at all because he worked for Electric Boat. Part of the defense industry. I can't imagine him killing anything. I think he and my mother met at Electric Boat and fell in love. I think they were both handsome and shy and yearning for each other and his mother treated my mother like her own daughter and he was very good about it when her mother fell asleep drunk and set fire to the bed. I don't know in what house. My mother has always been excessively grateful to him and his family.

They married and went to the World's Fair in New York City. There's a picture of them walking along in a crowd wearing saddle shoes and holding hands. There's another of them kissing each other on the mouth. I stare at this picture for a long time, whenever I come across it. The first few months of their marriage they lived on a sailboat my father had raised off the coast of Groton and restored. This was hard on my mother but I don't know if she complained. They had my sister and probably lived happily in a house within hearing distance of foghorns on Long Island Sound. Afterward my father got a job offer and they moved to Pennsylvania. Then they had my brother and me.

My father works on small planes for AVCO. He doesn't ever seem to be concerned about promotions and I don't think he ever gets any. I never know too much about this. To me his place of work is down cellar, out in the garage, out shoveling paths or mowing the fields in the summer. I like it when he pulls the car onto the bridge over the stream, moves the planks and stands in the furry moss and water tinkering with the underside of the car. He runs a line out from the garage for light and turns on the radio, singing along up to the point where concentration overtakes him and he starts chewing his tongue. I can't really talk to him when he's working. His confident hands manipulate the interior of the machine. I pad about in the stream bed and create the role of the little fellow who helps the big fellow who needs no help.

He has two suits and some workclothes. T-shirts. Chinos. In the summer he wears short shorts that double as bathing suits all over town. This profoundly embarrasses my sister. Mom has three or four navy blue and black skirts, some white blouses that button up the back, maybe a summer dress or two, two vinyl purses, and a winter coat and a summer coat. I don't remember seeing her in anything else, though there is a picture of her looking rugged in chinos before I was born.

My parents sleep in one big bed in one small room next to the garage. I've been through their closet and drawers, fingering his wool socks and rifling through her bargain nylon underwear to get to the box that holds my mother's jewelry, her high school charm bracelet and her jade ring. I've sniffed the daytime smell of my father's two suits and stared, without thinking anything much, at her brown loafers, her navy blue pumps, his dirty sneakers and his wingtips, all lined up in a row. My parents have broad, big feet and broad, big bodies. I've stood at the closet gazing into the evidence of their flesh, the grime embedded inside her shoes, his boxer shorts hanging used and limp on the hook next to my head.

It's February 1963. I carry certain truths in my body. The parents are behind me in the house. I know that we are a very, very happy family. My mother has depth and my father knows what to do about things. My sister is off at college and my brother is getting ready to go. I am the remaining child with my own room, poised to be the darling hope of my mother's eye.

I am ten years old and out in the world. Christmas is over and the landscape takes back its own from a frenzy of straw-haired angels trumpeting that swamp of gifts on the living room floor. No one but me goes out in sleet, not the kids up the road, not my mother and not my father, not for the sheer thrill of the thing. I feel my own muscle. That cool, athletic girl cuts a swathe through the thick hide of snow, rocks, and mud just before spring, in her own country, drenched to her thrilling skin with the disintegration of winter's clarity.

II

Williamsport used to have only two-lane roads. Route 15 went south to north with no passing lanes all the way and a lot of trucks. You could hear them while you were sitting in the woods on the hill. They roared down the highway that slid like a snake past the new Robert Hall, over the creek and into cornfields and past the place where Billy Reigle rode in that horse show. I would sit in the woods on the hill looking out over all this and squint at that dot that was the stables. I'd get a picture of Billy Reigle in my head and match that up to the dot so I could pinpoint a little shiver of anticipation and stay with it for hours, stopping now and then to dig my hands through sun-warmed pine needles into the dirt which felt sweet and cool. Letting all that tension drain out of me into the fixed border of my father's property, a safe place, our land, my spot on the hill, the impress of my own body on the pine needles swept into anonymity later by a little bit of wind and rain.

52

When Billy got close I was less interested. I was a wild woman. I liked
the idea of horses and I liked the idea of him fitting on the back of one and
I liked thinking about Doug Klopp up the road, too. His daddy drove
trucks. His brother looked mean. Doug was good-natured and more
interested in my friend Katy. I think he kissed her in the barn once while I
sat on another hill in melting snow believing my friendship with her had
come to an end. Just about, but it wasn't because of Doug. He treated me
like a kid frothing at the mouth until one late wet afternoon he tried to
kiss me underneath the Meyers' summer cottage down by the creek and I
got real cold and went home. I didn't like the way the day was getting
dark or the way it felt like I was being circumscribed by some boy's meaty
embrace from up the road.

I bet my mother saw that and didn't like it either.

Katy and I used to play at sex by making Ken and Barbie mate. Then
I'd put on dark clothes and a hat and she'd strip down to her underwear
and I'd be the man, a gangster. I'd crawl on top of her and press down
hard. We were both as rigid as planks. I kissed her with my mouth shut
and collapsed giggling into her neck. We were both excited.

A curtain went down on Katy's and my friendship the next year when
she landed in 7-5 and I landed in 7-1. I was entering my accelerated peri-
od and probably took biology that year along with Latin. No, it was earth
science. I don't know. The whole seventh grade was in the auditorium.
Billy Reigle was in 7-6 in the back of the auditorium next to 7-5, and I
think that's when he and Katy went steady. Mr. Shifflet was the wrestl-
ing coach and also my homeroom teacher. He liked to pull several of us
girls up on the stage for some infraction and bellow out things like,
"Whatsa matter, Rinella, ya got diarrhea of the mouth?" and then smack
the offending girl on the hand with the wooden hall pass in front of three
hundred budding adolescents. We didn't know whether to laugh or to
cry. Mr. Probst taught history and was more serious. He commanded 7-6
like a drill sergeant we thought, but he was probably just a straight out
sadist constrained by the puffery of societal limits. He liked to beat his
kids up.

I see numbers. 1961 and 1962 have an inky look. They nest in green Penn-
sylvania hills. 1963 and 1964 go amberish. 1965 goes red, mid-decade. In
this image I can see my girlish ankles flickering about the perimeters of a
landscape inhabited by the demise of girl scout training and the arrival of
my period. I'm thirteen years old and growing distant from my father's
gregarious activities. I have moods and acquire a Princess phone on
which my mother urges me to take the initiative and call recalcitrant boys
myself. We enter a conspiracy. She reports on their movements as she
sees them about town. We start going to baseball games together because
my heart throb is the bat boy and because she loves the game. When I
lose interest she continues to go alone. On the first day of May my father
goes to bed early and dies in his sleep. I am at a high school production of

1984 and my mother is at a game. When we get home he is already gone.

I learn something about the world by who grieves for him. Several of his friends are heartbroken. They are men who cannot stop crying. Mattie Givens sends us fried chicken. She is an older black woman who is his civic choirmate. I come to understand that they were very good friends. We children go to visit her in shared grief because his death has made us want to cross boundaries and because she makes us feel so at home, but my mother never comes. My father is buried in a cemetery that disallows the burial of blacks. We overlook this because we're all so miserable. There is so much personal pain. Some of it makes me special among my peers. I walk down school halls with a solemn authority. Some of it gnaws, incomprehensible, at the gut.

1966-67 go inky again, a descent into a deep pool, my father's mother dies and an aunt commits suicide in Connecticut. My mother adopts her widow's weeds and slips from the society of familied couples without a whisper. She has to get a job. She works for one day as a plainclothes detective at a bargain-rate mall. I go where she is on Saturday afternoon and hang out at the cosmetics counter watching her shuffle up and down the aisles in her coat. We love to shop. But this is different. We pretend not to know each other. My mother is undercover. She is playing the role of a dowdy, middle-aged housewife who cannot stop to rest even though her legs hurt her. It takes exactly eight hours to get to check out.

She has friends on the school board who take pity on her and give her a job as a secretary in their offices next to the bowling alley. This they are glad to do because she's a good worker. Very organized. We sell the house and land because without my father we have become incompetent to take care of it. My mother and I move into a pretty little red house in the suburbs near my school. Now when my brother and sister come home they are visitors and must sleep in the basement.

1967-68, sixteen, a pale yellow dress, a beloved olive-green sweater skirt outfit that makes me feel adultish, and at least one of my friends is doing adultish things. Sexual liberation has pretty much not arrived en masse in Williamsport, but Chris manages somehow to combine espousal of sex with loyalty and devotion, a winning over of men friends through vibrant talk and avoidance of the term "putting out." Partly she can do this because she is afflicted with seizures of mysterious origin that occur in moments of stress around friends and lovers. Though I am suspicious of this aspect of Chris it doesn't really matter because I admire and love her. Her seizures project a seriousness that deflects the more traditional categories like slut and pig.

We learn U.S. history from The Boot, so known because his head is shaped like Italy. We memorize dates and treaties up to World War I and have a debate on how the building of Interstate 80 direct from New York is going to allow a lot of city criminals free access to our front yards. I know this is ridiculous. My brother and sister now live in New York City. And even if it is true, anyone as boring as The Boot probably deserves to have his porch lights knocked out by criminals. We do not discuss civil rights or the Vietnam War. Psychedelics. Hippies. These subjects come in over the hills from older siblings and their record collections. Phil Ochs. Joan Baez. Bob Dylan. Jimi Hendrix. Some of us begin to adopt phrases— *What a trip!* and *feelin' groovy*—without fully knowing whereof we speak. We sway like flowers to the lyrics of the times.

After awhile my mother starts working as one of two librarian's assistants, both widows, at my high school. She teases me about keeping a close eye on me but really we are engaged in sharing my friends and romances. I run hot and cold and stop telling her everything. Sometimes she's my mother and sometimes she's my closest friend. She's my closest friend over beef burgundy or fried clams on all-you-can-eat night at Howard Johnson's. We gossip about real and possible boyfriends. She's a good conversationalist and spends more time talking with some of them than I do.

She's my mother when I come home tipsy and she runs to her room crying and slams the door. She slams the door to let me know how she's feeling, it's a kind of discipline. We scream and rage sometimes about politics which is hard because neither of us knows very much. I know for certain that war is wrong and that this war, the Vietnam War—which is all so confused in both our minds with the subversion of my brother and sister living in Greenwich Village and me growing up and her eventually being left alone—is a maniac's creation. I know this because my brother talks to me about it like I'm a thinking person which is far more than anyone who seems to support the war has. She knows it too because she lost a lot of sleep studying the medical deferment forms to get my brother out. She has worked and worked for her children.

I don't know who she is when she asks me to promise that after she dies and I am on my own, I will move her and my father back to Groton, within sight of the water.

1968-69 burn white hot. They glare out of that swamp of years like the way God wrote the Ten Commandments on Charlton Heston's tablet in the movie of the same name. Chris is rapidly tracking down Mike for baby and eventual free love marriage. I am working at getting my ears pierced while my mother gets kidney stones taken out. This provokes a crisis on my cheerleading squad because pierced ears will destroy the symmetry of the squad. Since I am slated to be captain in my senior year, this makes for confusing signals in the ranks. I've been to Greenwich Village with my brother and bought a peace symbol button. We've attended an antiwar demonstration and I've been excited and unnerved by big city police on the largest horses I have ever been close to. I wear the button on my coat back in Williamsport and Charlie Hayes says, "What's that?" and I get frightened, mumble something about "it's a peace symbol," and take it off. I drop off cheerleading because there's a war going on.

I apply to colleges out of state. My mother, who has been studiously tracking my test scores throughout high school, reluctantly assents to this, signs my financial aid forms, and speaks vaguely about moving back to Connecticut. My mother and I act like Siamese twins under the scalpel. We are joined at the breast, with one heart. There is a crescendo of noise, like an airplane taking off, 1969. She dies of a stroke on March 6, just days after I've received acceptances from colleges in New York and Boston.

I learn a lot about the world by who grieves for her. My sister comes home to fold up the house. We live out the summer packing. We dispense with the excesses of family life—furniture, hardware, my mother's clothing. My sister divides the family photographs into three neatly labeled albums, one for each of the children. Sometimes we play soul music loud and drink wine in the evenings, spraying each other with the lawn hose until I'm too drunk to hold myself up. We retreat into denuded rooms, hating each other because no one else is in sight.

Six months later I stand in a cruddy apartment near Fenway Park. I have gained twenty pounds and will never again wear the plaid skirts and knee socks my mother and I shopped for together. I wear instead big flowered pants and a sweater vest one of my slut girlfriends stole for me back in Williamsport. A B.U. sophomore with thin lips has invited me back here after a dreary mixer. I think we are trying to talk. I think that maybe I will even try sleeping with him because I need a window to open up inside me, I feel so fat and slow, and maybe he's not as mean as he looks, Mother. He fingers a copy of *The Tibetan Book of the Dead*, and says something along the lines of "this is heavy." He tells me about some really hip chick he knows who loves to masturbate with Coke bottles. He grabs my hand as if it were not, in fact, attached to my body and slaps it on the bulge in his crotch. His jeans are correct, quite faded and dirty enough to walk on their own. "Are you a virgin?" he asks. I lie and say no and I leave.

"Did you ever, I mean you yourself, kill anyone?" I ask my veteran boyfriend a year later. He lies and says no and he leaves.

III

I thought I saw my father in 1977 in the body of a Kalash villager high up in the Hindu Kush, just ten miles east of the Afghan border. The Kalash worship their ancestors. When I was there they were being advertised by the Pakistan government as a tourist's jewel, an exotic fruit, a quaint remnant of pre-Muslim times. I saw a mannequin of one in a dishevelled museum of national treasures in Peshawar. Translated to literal ground, this seemed to mean they were infidels, they couldn't own land, and their unveiled women were ripe for rape, forced marriage, and prostitution.

This man had the same blue eyes, the same barrel chest. He had a look on his face as sweet as the peaches my father used to try to grow. He was grinning and walking down the road away from me and away from a group of vacationing Muslim men who spat in his direction.

I was androgynous, American, traveling in jeeps and buses halfway around the world to prove myself capable of outdistancing the eclipse of family and home. I was a woman capable of crossing continents, unlike my mother. I stood sobbing after a strange man despised in his own country. He was as much my father and as much himself as I could ask for. Distinct from me. Vulnerable to power. Alive.

November 7, 1985

I approach by the east panels. The pathway descends into the V. The names begin at ankle height and reach a depth of about ten feet at the center. The single chain link fence cordoning the path suggests to visitors that they not distance themselves more than ten feet from the black granite surface. You can see yourself. You can get a sense of how you look, and as you look the names of the dead superimpose themselves over the image of yourself as you wander through clusters of families, school groups, or the isolated individuals who are undergoing the same transfiguration. There are over fifty-eight thousand names but I am not looking for anyone in particular. Others are. People locate names, touch them, and lay wreaths, or leave notes, letters to the dead. Some are weeping. When I walk I must be careful that I don't cross into the camera range of someone photographing a name.

No one can back up enough for the long view. We are all held to the text, a formal succession of names that are made particular by the shapes of the bodies leaning into someone engraved, a face.

If you stop, if you just stand at any point and stare at the wall, the names begin to move. *Jimmy Rollings. Alfredo Ostolazo-Maldonado. Daniel L. Garrison. Alphonzo Holoman, Jr. King D. Washington.* The bodies of the living roll through them like a stream passing over rocks, lending them a metallic, nearly animate lustre. It is an illusion of the monument that the quick make communion with the dead. It is also, probably, a fact.

Ascending the path along the west panels the visitor arrives at the secondary monument commissioned in the aftermath of protest over what was termed to be the abstract and depressing nature of the black V lodged in the ground. The statue sits sheltered in a grove of trees. It depicts three GIs who, the sculptor has said, are "consistent with history. They wear the uniform and carry the equipment of war; they are young. The contrast between the innocence of their youth and the weapons of war underscores the poignancy of their sacrifice. There is about them the physical contact and sense of unity that bespeaks the bonds of love and sacrifice that are the nature of men at war."

I used to play here some summers when we'd come to visit relatives. This whole tip of Constitution Mall is known to me through the measure of a child's legs. Mostly I remember spilling out of the car into this grass paradise and springing up Lincoln's steps to gaze rapturously at his marble flesh. I loved the giant lifelike foot and the kindly expression in his face. I loved the columns and the way I could race around the Lincoln Memorial as if it were my own godlike house.

I was fascinated by the Iwo Jima statue set like a storm into position somewhere across the Potomac. I can just about sense where. I imagined I could smell the jungle mud. I heard the grunts and gasps exiting the throats of those men as they hauled themselves hand over fist to raise the flag. I perhaps imagined an interesting future of modest and heroic men striking more casual poses in my grown-up house while they told stories about liberating concentration camps somewhere in the world. The act of saving ravaged and degraded survivors—whose experiences I recall knowing from spending hours riveted to picture magazine coverage of the Eichmann trial—belonged to the principled stance of a nation realizing itself in the bodies of its men.

Men like these three who gaze into a middle distance. Their magnificent youth is intact, their vulnerability poignant but masterful, irreducible, sexual.

Men haven't been like that, neither as literal, nor as vigorous, nor as fixed in history or in my life. My desires haven't been so simple. A VFW contingent lays a wreath at the feet of the three GIs who have no name on my first day at the Vietnam Veterans Memorial. Somewhere buried in the trees Vietnam veterans drink beer. They're singing *We Gotta Get Outa This Place.* I wish to join them but don't. I am a woman from the antiwar movement. I haven't fought overseas. Flesh is porous, capable of being in fever. We're not young, nor are we entirely innocent, but we're consistent with history. Behind me the wall bristles with its names.

November 10, 1985

Today I am aware of wearing soft black cotton clinging pants, a pink sweatshirt, black sneakers, green earrings, and a beautiful aging maroon wool jacket with antique Tibetan cloth sewn into it. The persons I most resemble in style at the Vietnam Veterans Memorial are a class of ten-year-old girls who are ferociously unto themselves and glittery in the bright sunlight. We stand near each other at the statue of the three GIs. At least a third of the girls have cameras they whip out of shoulder bags. Canon instamatics, it looks like, and one quaint Brownie.

They shoot efficiently. Some of them freeze, the way I am frozen looking at them, and gawk at sinews, sculpted veins, and the idealized solemnity of the statue. Little girls. Big bronze men. I'm a sentimentalist myself, I'm telling you. Their skin is fresh, their manner girlish, suburbanly snotty. They cast glances my way and I sense I'm not dressing my age.

I have the sense I'm not dressing my age. What does it matter? They surrender their spot and round the chain descending the V's west wall, and I follow, the sun behind us. It all looks like a picture to me. I'm distracted, annoyed by the seriousness of the granite. I'm noting perspective, angle of the shadows, keeping in mind the highlights of the memorial's placement—aiming its wings at the Washington Monument and Lincoln Memorial. I'm a serious child on tour. I follow the girls, who are in a hurry. They stop abruptly midway through the west wall. Shoosh, click. They spin a neat reverse and flood past me on their way out. I slide through the subtropic humidity of their youth.

The scene where John Wayne plays Davy Crockett getting nailed to a door by a Mexican's sword in *The Alamo* inserts itself as my first introspective moment regarding the look and feel of violent, glorious death. He breaks the sword in half when he twists himself off the door, staggers, and falls. He dies—the way my mind puts it together—to these lyrics: "It was good to be young then/to be close to the earth/and to stand by your wife at/the moment of birth." I learned that song with my classmates in fifth grade along with *Sink the Bismarck* and *High Hopes*.

Paul J. Lively. Donald W. Keep. Perhaps a sucking chest wound, or death by friendly fire. Maybe crispy critters burned up in a rocket attack. Was it good to be young then? They were close to the earth. I'm no longer as young as that. How do these girls see it? Are they frightened? Do they sleep over at each other's houses and try to picture sex?

Ho Chi Minh could have been president of Vietnam before the reason for this memorial ever existed. No Vietnamese are listed here. Another generation of kids grows up. They are stroking their hair in this sunlight.

November 11, 1985

It's Veteran's Day. I get here at 10:00 A.M. People come and spend a lot of time. Vets have held garage sales and carwashes to get their companies here. It is ten years after the fall of Saigon. The only thing certain among them is that they are in a lot of pain. How do I know? Men are standing around crying. Women are crying and holding men. Men are holding each other.

This week marks the sixteenth anniversary of my first march on Washington against the Vietnam War. Today Vietnam vets are trampling flowers to put their arms around the three bronze GIs and demand that their pictures be taken.

They say: This is for us. We've earned it. This is our statue.

A T-shirt reads: I RISKED MY ASS FOR THIS—LEGALLY BLIND, FORMER MECHANIC, FORMER TEACHER, UNEMPLOYED, DISABLED.

The memorial is a neat, black, shiny gash in the ground. A man is on his knees toward the end of the east panel searching for a name, his shoulders all hunched over. His two young daughters stand behind him and one finds the name—Here it is Dad! He lurches at it. His body convulses in a panic of grief. His fingers play over and over it, the name, Ronald Ferry I think, and he is inconsolable. His daughters (maybe eight and fourteen) are hushed. He is wearing a plaid shirt and forest green polyester pants. The seams are mended in places with an awkward color of thread. I hear sobbing, snuffling, an intake of breath. His eldest gets behind him and holds on.

This one and that one crumple and cry. A chorus of fingers trace the Rafael, the Jesse, Daniel, Oscar. People tell stories. They talk about the POW/MIAs. A meticulous hand-carved wooden plaque is placed before a panel, commemorating a man who died in 1983 from Agent Orange.

Overheard:

—Ralph. I'll be back next year. I miss you so much. I shoulda died with you.

—They lied about Tet. They cut the numbers of VC on the offensive. If they did that they're sure lying about how many are dead up on that rock.

—Now I go around protecting nuclear plants from people.

—I feel okay at this distance. When I get close to those names they jump out at me. It's terror down there. There's vibrations on that wall.

—I asked him if he had post-traumatic shock disorder. He said no, but he sure did feel *words lost.*

A shoulder patch reads: Vietcong Hunting Club.

I know my boyfriend Fred lied when he said he didn't kill anyone because I sneaked a look at his citation the day he was handed the Distinguished Service Cross in a formal ceremony. We had just gotten involved and were spending the summer in Northern California pretending to be earthy and family-oriented. We ate awful macrobiotic food and spoke of babies. He painted a yin-yang symbol on the bedroom ceiling using orange and yellow paint. I did temp work at the phone company and talked about not returning to college. When the moon was full he'd get real quiet and disappear. I'd get horrible cramps. We never talked details. The cycle went—stone-cold silence, regret, romance renewal, heightened sense of maternal and paternal proclivity, then we'd drop off the cliff again. It was like doing calisthenics.

I attended the ceremony in a last-ditch effort to exhibit my loyalty and perseverance. I wore the one dress that still fit me from high school, some bell-sleeved hideous polyester that used to float around my waist, and sat next to his extremely proper, extraordinarily severe parents around whom I felt like a bowl of pudding. He looked handsome and stiff as a board. He was dressed in a suit but had declined to cut his hair and it hung to his shoulders. Fred had been a medic. His citation said he shot a sniper out of a tree under heavy fire. He never argued it. I thought that was supposed to mean something big about his psychological state but I could never pinpoint what.

The summer the Vietnam War spread into Laos I could have gotten pregnant, married Fred and gone for the quick divorce, but I deferred. As did he. "I love you to death," he once whispered in my ear and I moaned and I said I love you too. It was all the language that we had so we thought we meant it.

The politicians at the Vietnam Veterans Memorial on November 11, 1985, speak of defense of family, homeland, place. They exhort the assembled to be conscious of the need for family. This is a time for reflection, they say, and the memorial reflects us, the distinct image of people who lost sense of family and purpose in pursuit of this nation's duty.

Typed note, west wall: TO THE GRUNTS: You get the feeling that the lucky Nam vets are the ones that didn't come back. DEDICATED (for the Grunt) -YOU- Whenever you start loosing grip remember them guys. Remember those promises. Even if that's the only thing you stay alive for. You promised . . . You might be the only thing they died for.

What is it I wanted to remember and can't remember? Late night at the memorial scattered vets are cursing the park guards for keeping them from sleeping here.

Ten years later there is peace with honor. Home is a little spot of ground administered by the National Park Service. On Veteran's Day, President Reagan speaks to a crowd of six thousand at the Tomb of the Unknown Soldier. He says war is the result of a peace process that failed. Thousands more flock a J.C. Penney outlet where Prince Charles and Princess Diana review a display of British-style clothing. A few hundred people stand here applying their hands to the granite, trying to find a way into the wall as if punching through it would release them into the grit of the other side. I have heard that four hundred thousand vets have died since the war from the following causes: war wounds, police killings, in defense by abused spouses, car accidents, suicides.

The Vietnam Veterans Memorial has to do with some of the consequences of a criminal U.S. policy in Southeast Asia. A number of veterans are just beginning to find their voices at the wall. The problem has to do with the language of criticism.

I meet an official from a Vietnam veterans organization. He turns into someone else, Dennis, a one-legged veteran with no rank. He has blonde hair, longish. Burning eyes (blue). An articulated sense of the dilemma about reintegration into the society. He seems to vibrate, sitting still. He is a little frightening to me. I become a naive woman with long brown hair. Someone else. Her.

He courts her.

She passes a number of his tests regarding her desirability. His skin is always hot. Two men friends form a circle with him, a bonding. They are all vets.

Everything happens in rambling, three-story houses.

He finds her staying in a feminist stronghold, her safe place. They fall in love, a sweaty, desperate embrace.

He is getting it together. He walks faster than she on his artificial leg. Without it, he can swing very fast on his arms. He swings very fast on his arms because sometimes he is a double amputee.

In the houses, everything can be seen on all floors from the stairway.

She worries for him. She is afraid he will fall off the stairway. She becomes increasingly feminine and earnest, like a preacher's daughter from the Midwest.

They marry. At the wedding reception two cars line up facing each other. One is a Corvette and one is a red pickup called "Merit." At the signal they peel out and crash headlong at high speed. The celebrants applaud.

He has to change clothes during the wedding in front of all the guests. They can scarcely believe the extent of his wounds. A guy in a baseball cap shouts to the people next to him, "I didn't know his scars were that bad!" Dennis hears this and turns to his buddy, a "ragged vet." Dennis falls into his arms sobbing and they kiss, long, deep, and hard.

After awhile their lives develop normalcy, as she sees it. She is loyal, but she cannot fathom the rapid succession of Dennis's moods. She becomes long-suffering. Her suffering grows large enough to include me. I move back into her body and gaze dumbstruck out of her eyes.

A social pattern develops with the three war buddies and their wives. Richie begins to ferociously batter his wife. Richie gets crossed off the friends list. Dennis says, "You don't do that to women."

The women start to talk. A support group forms downstairs in the house where I live with Dennis. Elise is bloody and bruised. We test the boundaries between each other and these husbands. I say we support her leaving Richie, he has become too brutal. Even Dennis supports her. I don't say that he mocks me, or that I think he loves me with a passion I don't fully understand. Elise is preparing to heal herself by leaving town.

The other woman, Holly, tells us she has a lover and is leaving her stable vet husband for him. I can't believe my ears. I think there is something vaguely wicked about Holly for doing this but I am drawn to support her.

Dennis comes home and slowly goes up the all-seeing stairs. Elise leaves, or becomes somebody else not hip to the palpable tension. This woman reads aloud a card Holly has just received from her lover. The lover is a high school teacher from Miami. Sweet. Goofy.

Dennis has already descended the stairs swinging on his arms to hear this. I am on a couch. Holly is standing near me. He is now in a wheelchair coming at us. Though he is fully clothed, I see him coming naked from all sides. I notice, as if I have never seen it before, a brown birthmark across his ass.

Holly vainly tries to cover up this information. She gives up. She and Dennis get into tough, know-it-all banter which I am not sophisticated enough to follow. I am fully myself as that other, the feminine preacher's daughter. I am lying on the couch strung like a bow.

Dennis turns to me shrieking and demands to know if I've been thinking of leaving him. I sob like some dream of a fifties innocent. "No! I love you! I would never leave you!" He laughs and it sounds like a car backfiring. He looks scathingly at Holly. Now he is a double amputee and he's everywhere at once. He pulls me off the couch. I feel like a bird, poultry, his palms pressing fully around my ribcage. He throws Holly on the couch and begins to rape her. She is screaming. Her screams become rhythmical but the pitch and the terror never change.

I am not thinking about the distinctions between love and hate as I start to run. I've become a powerless slip of a girl trying to get out because whether he is raping her or killing her it seems to be all the same and I can feel him ready to come crushing through my body and I have nothing to stop him.

He rapes her. That birthmark glows in an enveloping darkness. She screams.

IV

I have been working as a defense committee organizer on the deportation case of a woman whose present circumstances, like those of many others, are linked with the interpretation of history. Margaret Randall has returned to the U.S. after spending over two decades working and writing in support of women and revolutions in Latin America. The Immigration and Naturalization Service is trying to deport her partly because she once wore a ring made from a U.S. plane shot down over North Vietnam. It was given to her by a Vietnamese woman.

Part of the problem Margaret has with Immigration has to do with how she interprets the bombing of North Vietnam and the bombing of Cambodia.

Part of the problem has to do with low-intensity warfare and the policy of destabilization applied by the United States government in the past and currently to countries like Chile, Cuba, Nicaragua, El Salvador, Honduras, and Guatemala but it's not as simple as that, is it?

Part of the problem has to do with the popular overthrow of a U.S.-backed dictatorship in Nicaragua, and the subsequent efforts by myriad people like Margaret to represent the diverse, indigenous faces of a revolution.

Part of the problem the U.S. government has with Margaret is the language of criticism. The consequences of dissent.

Black granite from Bangalore. A deep cut into Constitution Mall made by mineral resources from the Indian subcontinent, Asia, a place where other people live. What would it sound like if all the names started talking at once, if a collective roar rose up out of the wall? I mean, the collective voices of all those serving in the U.S. armed forces from 1959 to 1975 who lost their lives in Vietnam? Let's just say we're standing here, right now, peering from a clump of trees where you can see the whole slice of pie from tip to tip, the ragged edge of the columns of names feathering the panels let's say, the sound from each throat at the moment of expiration, all of it at once?

Veterans Day. A 15-by-25-foot American flag made of roses, carnations, and bachelor buttons sits atop the wall in a driving rain. The flag was the inspiration of a housewife in Virginia who wanted a flower in place for each of the names on the wall. She is there along with Chuck Norris, hero of martial arts war movies, who supported her efforts. People speak respectfully about him: "He has a brother on the wall."

The rain influences the small talk. Voices spit forth: This is just like the Nam. Shit, we're back here in the mud and trees like always while the big shots sit up front. The fucken press corps, Je-Sus! Someone will be quoted later as saying, "It looks like the wall is crying."

The POW/MIA activists have become their own army. I recognize some of their faces from last year. POW daughter Lynn Standerwick and veteran Gino Casanova are fasting in a cage. They are on this year's Last Patrol to call attention to the plight of men left among the communists in Southeast Asia.

Since the rules say the area of the Vietnam Veterans Memorial must not be politicized, the activists dig in on the perimeter. At the Last Firebase you can buy buttons, receive free literature, sign petitions, and donate funds to the Live POW committee. A larger-than-life prop of Jane Fonda in her leotard urges a boycott of her Workout Tapes. Hanoi Jane Sucks. Stop Communism. A plastic knife is pitched through her head and someone has cut out her heart.

A Vegas-circuit all-male band performs on the steps of the Lincoln Memorial. They are billed as would-be top of the line except for their devotion to the POW/MIA issue, which has caused them to be blacklisted. Maybe so. The lead singer is a big bearded guy wearing a two-piece white polyester suit with fringes. The backup singers wear red polyester one-piece—jumpsuits, I guess, that fit tight over white shirts and bulky bodies. I'm looking into the Reflecting Pool when they start up with a song called *Missing*, which makes me think about the disappeared in Chile.

They are followed by speakers who invoke Martin Luther King, Jr. to underline the plight of men held captive. "Freedom Now!" they chant. Almost everyone is white. The same group of people have been here for days. Maybe fifty, maybe a hundred, they wrestle an outpost and a cause out of the river of individuals who come to pay their private respects to the names on the wall. This group has sung *We Shall Overcome* behind the White House. Some of the more outspoken have been arrested trying to occupy territory on the lawn of an indifferent government official.

A guy stands in front of me at the wall amidst what now seems to me to be a sea of brand new fatigues, bought for a career of remembering Vietnam as opposed to being pulled from the back of the closet in honor of intimate remembrance. Someone has carefully embroidered in gold thread a column of words that shiver down the back of his camouflage shirt:

TO THOSE
WHO HAVE FOUGHT FOR IT
LIFE HAS A FLAVOR
THE PROTECTED
NEVER KNOW

Part of the problem has to do with the language of criticism. Wreckage from a U.S. plane shot down over North Vietnam. I'm standing in muck, cold but never as cold or as fucked up and under assault as most of these men who surround me. I want to tear that shirt to pieces, throw that man down and beat his face until we know where we are, on national ground pulling ourselves apart. Until his mouth and nose are bloody and he is pleading with me to stop, just to let him know I can, if I have to, protect myself. *I'm sorry, I had no idea.* So much of what we are is blood and guts. Individuals going after dignity with grappling hooks. *Did you ever, I mean you yourself, kill anyone?*

"A battle is something that's in a war. A war has many battles," the mother explains.

"Did all these people die in one battle?" the daughter asks.

"No, they died in one war. They died in many different battles at different times, which all happened in the one war," answers the mother.

The daughter takes it in, along with that business about "the wall is crying." The war is a concept she's putting together from what she's seen on TV. Wars flatten into a nebulous expanse. They have plots that are lifted from anecdotes and are edited down into a kind of sitcom in perpetual motion. From which we are to gather that wars mostly just happen, though some of us might wish they wouldn't. If they're going to happen then the battles ought to be interesting. Which they might be, depending on where you're standing.

Some girls think they know some things and others think they know less. That's true for boys as well. We judge accordingly. Today I am wearing an old army raincoat borrowed from friends, my tweed jacket, and jeans. I have had one conversation with a sweet-speaking veteran who I liked very much and who told me he reckoned that pretty soon it wouldn't just be Texas, but all of Mexico we'd be defending against communists along that slim stretch of southern border with Central America. I have been interviewed by Taiwanese television journalists while trying to lose myself in a crowd whose ebb and flow depended on how many crying persons drew video crews. It was late in the day and I must have looked mournful. They wanted to know if I had anyone on the wall. I don't have anyone on the wall so I started talking about fighting against another war in Central America and that's true and all our eyes glazed over.

My problem is I don't know the names of those I tried to help only to have them die in my arms. In my sleep I hear their cries and see their faces. As a young kid I was raised around the lakes of Indiana. I used to live for nothing more than spending time boating, swimming, or being around the cool shoreline of a lake. In Vietnam at age 20 I was put in charge of the riverboat. Now every time I get on a boat I only see the red blood running over the deck and into the water. I try to take my two sons fishing but we never stay out long. The fish don't seem to bite when I take them out, like they do when they go with someone else's father. They are too young to understand that their father does not like the reflections he sees in the water. For these reasons I write to say I'm sorry. I am the third son in three years to serve in Vietnam from my family. Like my brothers before me, I did the best I could. To all you mothers fathers brothers sisters wives and lovers of those men, I am sorry, I could do no more. I can count the numbers. 113 missions to extract. My boat was always first, I made sure of that. You know, never send anyone somewhere you wouldn't go yourself. I wish I knew your names, so I could touch your names in the black stone. But I don't and I'm sorry. "So Sorry."

—Excerpt from a note left at the wall

November 13, 1986

Here's what will be lost after awhile. People peering into the wall who can actually see what happened, hear choppers, shouts of "Incoming!," pwhoosh of mortars delineating the sound of an arc fulfilling itself by dropping back to earth to, in short, blow the heads off those boys, our boys. Somebody who saw Bobby Ray Jones go down, some friend or other who can pull Bobby W. Jobe out of the wall by adopting a pose of irreducible anguish when confronted by his name. Like somehow Bobby and Bobby leapt out of the wall into the last possible flesh still alive to tell it, the war, this particular war not as some universal human condition, but as the thing it was. That'll be gone.

Here's what will continue. People trying to "get it." Its texture. The smell. Applicable terms. For instance:

Triage—a system of assigning priorities of medical treatment to battlefield casualties on the basis of urgency, chance of survival, etc.

Cadaverine—a colorless, bad-smelling, liquid ptomaine, $NH_2(CH_2)5NH_2$, produced by the hydrolysis of proteins, as in putrefying flesh.

I lost four members of my family between 1965 and 1969. I didn't see any of them go. There are days when that's all I care to know.

Millions of Vietnamese, Cambodians, and Laotians dead in my lifetime. But it's not as simple as that, is it?

Bright light, pristine morning at the wall. A few folks roam about amidst the echoes of others, as befits a site said to represent the national preoccupation with the healing process in the aftermath of the Vietnam War. Few landscapes remain as intact in my memory as the rectangle stretching from Capitol Hill to the Lincoln Memorial. My old hometown is so transformed by modern highways and malls that I can barely find the spot where my parents are buried. Here everything is more like it was, more like what I remember, a static arrangement of national heroes, consistent with history.

A chubby kid and his father walk by me. They are both wearing fresh army camouflage and ribbons signifying their identification with the Live POW committee. The kid sports a button that says, "Never Again." That guy will never send his kid to war until all the POWs are brought back home. Maybe then he'll send him.

These are my fellow citizens. I am as responsible as they for what has been allowed to occur, for what will happen. We're alive. Still here.

RECOMMENDED READING

Etel Adnan, *Sitt Marie-Rose*. Post-Apollo Press, 1982.

W. D. Ehrhart, *Carrying the Darkness: American Indochina: The Poetry of the Vietnam War*. New York: Avon Books, 1986.

Gabriel Kolko, *Main Currents in Modern American History*. New York: Pantheon, 1984.

Anthony Smith, *Nationalism in the 20th Century*. New York: New York University Press, 1979

HARRY A. WILMER

The Healing Nightmare: A Study of the War Dreams of Vietnam Combat Veterans

It seems to most of us that Vietnam was a long time ago, that it is past history. It is not. It still lives in the nightmares of combat veterans and the collective unconscious of us all. It is an illusion to declare that the Vietnam Syndrome is over. Denial never killed anything.

In a dream seminar I directed for schizophrenic patients at the Audie Murphy Veterans Hospital in San Antonio, a Vietnam veteran I shall call Jim told his recurring nightmare. I had been listening to veterans' dreams for four years before that day, but Jim's nightmare was somehow different, and the group of twenty-five fellow patients who heard it were unusually affected. Jim had had his nightmare several times a week for twelve years, and his terror and grief were vivid.

When the session was over it struck me that while I had been listening to Vietnam nightmares for years, I had not yet really *heard* them. So I began to work analytically with Jim. We met two to three hours a week for the next three months in the hospital and less frequently for the following two years in the outpatient clinic, and I followed him off and on for the next four years.

In the first two months Jim's dream was about a tragic ambush, viewed first from this angle, then from that, now about this part, then about that part, but always the precisely identical event. The dream never varied from the images of the real event—never, that is, until after we began working. It had previously recurred hundreds and hundreds of times, and yet it was the same dream coming back again and again. I reasoned that there must be some biological or psychological purpose, some meaning in its repetition.

But what could that meaning be? What interpretation could one make of a dream about the same event happening again and again in an unchanging manner? Unless—and this was the idea that intrigued me—the reality dream could be translated into conscious metaphor by the dreamer in order to decipher his meaning of the sacrifice of war.

Could it be that the war nightmare, which is the exact replication of a catastrophic trauma, is the archetypal dream of war?

Jim described his dream as if it were a film replayed in his mind, like *cinema verité*. The story of the dream is the narrative of the time when he, acting as point man, and another sergeant led a platoon of seventeen newly arrived men to their deaths in an ambush on their first firefight. Jim had been in Vietnam for almost a year when the ambush happened.

The dream tells of sudden panic when the platoon was passing through a ravine and the Vietcong opened fire. The men fell screaming and crying, wounded and dying. The other sergeant escaped, running back to the camp, while Jim, standing in the foxhole of a VC he had killed, looked down on the slaughter and the carnage. He held a grenade in his hand and froze. Try to imagine this: he sees a VC officer picking up the heads of each of the wounded men by the hair and shooting them, one by one. If Jim throws his grenade he will kill his own men. He waits until they are all dead, then he throws the grenade and runs until he finds his way back to the base camp.

In the dream, as in real life, he returned to the ravine the next day with other soldiers to bring back the bodies. They had been decapitated and the heads put on punji sticks and smeared with shit. Some of the bodies had been mutilated in other ways. After this, Jim broke down and was medivaced back to the United States. He felt guilty, banished, rejected.

For twelve years Jim had been in and out of Veterans Administration hospitals and maintained on large doses of medications. He also drank excessively, became addicted to heroin, and smoked pot as often as he could. In a vain attempt to blot out his insomnia and nightmare, he began to take six to eight downers a night—barbituates he bought on the street which made his consciousness hazy and even more at the mercy of the dark forces of the collective shadow which haunted him in the night with terrifying specters.

When I reviewed Jim's large VA treatment records I found not a single mention of his nightmare. Even more astonishing, there was no record of his Vietnam combat experiences. Neither nightmares nor combat experience were recorded in the VA hospital records of any of the Vietnam veterans with whom I worked. Why do you suppose their records were silent on this score?

I asked Jim. His reply was characteristic of the Vietnam veteran. He said, "Nobody asked me."

After two months of analytical psychotherapy, Jim's nightmares began to change. At last the loop of precise dream repetition was broken, as I had hoped. He became in turn each of the people in the high drama: the executor, the executed, the soldier he killed to take his foxhole above the ravine, the other sergeant. When he was decapitated his head rolled down the hill towards the sea, and he, headless, ran to retrieve it. He explained that he could see with his soul, which came out of his neck: psyche means soul.

In another month, Jim finally dreamed of me. I was a doctor in his platoon; I was in the ravine and badly wounded in the head. With the help of a woman nurse Jim rescued me and bandaged me. His feminine side was personified by the actual nurse on the VA ward who, incidentally, was pregnant and had been assigned especially to his care. They were working together to save the *wounded healer*. He carried me back to the base, where I told the soldiers that Jim was not guilty. He was exonerated and there was a parade for him.

In a moment of naive relief, I thought that at last the story had been fulfilled and the nightmare resolved. But that was not the case, and in retrospect, I should have known better. Namely, his salvation was not in saving me in order that I might resolve his guilt and his shame, for then I would have usurped his own heroic role. No, the turning point was to be different.

Dreams in which he rescued me recurred for a while. Suddenly there was a change. He decapitated me, and in another dream I decapitated him—we both lost our heads. Finally the transformation and resolution occurred when after rescuing me he woke from his nightmare not drenched in sweat, trembling and panicky, as always before, but crying. At long last he would mourn his irretrievable losses and the sacrifices in his Vietnam experience. In his grief he could at last cry and begin that search for meaning which I characterize as The Healing Nightmare.

The nightly dreams no longer tormented him at infrequent intervals. Now he shrugged off his dream as "Oh, that damn thing again," and lost interest in discussing it with me. The unconscious transference of the twin heroes and the healing of both the wounded and the wounded healer was played out.

Jim's recovery had its ups and downs. One day about six months into his therapy, after reading newspaper stories of the nine hundred Americans who had committed suicide in Guyana and the three thousand Vietnamese boat people arriving in America, he burst into my office demanding a gun. He had just been swimming in the pool at the VA hospital and suddenly became convinced that the Vietnamese were invading America, having tunneled all the way to San Antonio, and were coming up out of the drain in the pool. He said that they were going to do to our country what we had done to theirs. He was now delusional, and everyone in the hospital seemed to be Vietnamese. He took my wrist as if taking my pulse. I told him that he knew I was not going to give him a gun and he would have to sit down in my office and talk to me. We spoke about Guyana and the boat people, about how far-distant things come into our minds wherever we are, and that we would have to try to sort out his fear and rage after he calmed down. I put my arm around him and led him back to the ward, where I told him he would be restricted for a while. I told him I was going to increase his medication.

A few days later he told me why he had held my wrist. He was checking to see if I was a Vietnamese invader wearing a plastic Dr. Wilmer disguise or the real thing. Convinced I was Dr. Wilmer, he did as I asked.

If, as I propose, war trauma nightmares are clues to healing, then what were all the other Vietnam veterans dreaming? The literature was no help. This was in 1978 and no one had published material on the Vietnam combat nightmares. Convinced of the practical therapeutic and theoretical importance of such a study, I persuaded the chief of staff of the VA hospital to give me a sabbatical leave to devote my full time to this project. I worked with 109 veterans from 1978 to 1981.

The combat nightmare has been clearly identified as the hallmark of the psychological trauma of war. In World War I, it ws called shell shock or war neurosis; in World War II, battle fatigue; and since 1979, Post-Traumatic Stress Disorder, or PTSD.

My study included 103 men, and 91 of them told me 359 dreams of Vietnam. Twelve veterans recalled no war nightmares. (Since nightmares begin as long as ten years or more after the war, these twelve men are at risk all of their lives to have them. It is quite likely that these twelve veterans had dreams about Vietnam after returning home; it would be most remarkable if they had not. But this much is certain: they were not troubled by any recurring war nightmares.) I counted each repetitive dream only once, and since these nightmares recurred week after week, month after month, year after year, the total is tens of thousands of dreams. But even 359 dreams present an overwhelming number of images, memories, and feelings to try to organize and understand.

This is how I went about my study: I explained to each veteran that I had not been in Vietnam but had been working for years with Vietnam veterans. I had been a captain in the navy during the Korean War. As each man came to see me I explained that I would meet him for two or three hours at least two or three different times, and I would tape-record our interviews, but I had to have their signed, informed consent. I explained I was going to write a book and give lectures and write papers based on these interviews. Three men refused to sign the consent form, each one floridly delusional. I did not use these cases.

The diagnosis of PTSD had not yet been officially accepted by the VA. The usual psychiatric diagnoses created a mind set that made it easy for the general public to slip into calling these men "VA psychos," losers," "dope fiends," "walking time bombs," "crazy vets," "baby killers," or whatever stereotype came to mind. Anyway psychiatric labeling side-steps the real issue, that war trauma is an existential experience, and maladaptation to it is not necessarily a psychiatric disorder. Even the formal diagnosis of PTSD, which is now a legitimate way into the mental health system, often brings into play drugs and therapies that are irrelevant to those suffering from war neuroses. Automatic treatment with sedatives, tranquilizers, and sleeping pills by personnel psychologically trained to seek childhood conflicts as the cause of later distress may be useless or counterproductive. (Moreover, compensation for disability has its problems. Monthly checks, rather than a lump-sum settlement, tend to pay the veteran to be sick; and as has happened to many veterans and their families, continuing but reducing payments makes it easy to forget that these men are not aberrations but ordinary people.) While the developmental history is important, ultimately we face an archetypal war experience. It is here that the Jungian approach offers help, insight, and meaning beyond traditional psychiatry.

Talking with these veterans would sometimes open their wounds, awakening disturbing effects. For those whose interviews raised more dust then they settled, I offered psychotherapy. To my surprise, I found that even a few sessions of listening, I mean really listening with a non-judgmental motivation to help, was adequate. It was not necessary to say much.

On the rare occasions when I felt that I was hearing "war" stories with embellishments or distortions or even fabrications, I ignored them. With few exceptions I accepted what each veteran told me as *his truth*—his authentic individual perspective. I had no intention of trying to corroborate his history, which would have been impossible anyway. I knew that if there were more than one observer to a battle, there would be a Rashomon effect and as many perspectives as there were observers.

Let me give you one veteran's war nightmare:

> We came in by helicopter. My buddy and I are about two feet apart in a foxhole on top of Hill 101. We got to know each other pretty good over three or four days. We had to stay in the same foxhole. We couldn't even get out to stretch our legs because of sniper fire. I am talking with my buddy. It is real dark. He lit a cigarette and all of a sudden his head blows off. His brains come out all over me. I wake up screaming.

War nightmares are a unique form of dreams. There are no other dreams like them. Freud despaired of working with or considering them because they were exceptions to his theory of dreams. They were not wish fulfillment, and they were not explainable in terms of libido theory. He did not treat any war neuroses. Jung, too, was pessimistic about treating them, saying that one had to wait and let the dreams more or less play out and stop of their own accord. However, in 1983 at Davos, Switzerland, I asked Marie-Louise von Franz, Jung's collaborator and one of the most illustrious Jungian authorities, why Jung didn't work with these combat nightmares. She told me that, in fact, he did and related this (unpublished) case:

> A British officer came to Jung because of a war nightmare that had

tormented him for several years after World War II. In the dream, the man is in his home and suddenly becomes terrified. It is night. He goes to the front door and locks it. Then the back door. He locks all the windows on the first floor. But the sense of terror and panic continues to build, and he goes upstairs and locks all the windows, but just as he begins to close the last window a grenade explodes outside the window. This dream recurs again and again during three months of analysis, until suddenly one night, when he goes to close the last window, a roaring lion appears and the dreamer wakes in terror.

Jung thought, "Ah, that's good. The instrument of danger has become an instinctual animal." And so it continues until finally one night, as the dreamer closes the last window, he sees the face of a man. Jung said to himself, "Now he will not have the dreams any-more." And that was the case. The danger had been faced and was his own reflection, and that could be analyzed.

So frightening were the Vietnam combat nightmares that the veterans were usually reluctant to talk about them at all. And who wanted to listen? The American people wanted to forget Vietnam, and veterans with their grim dreams were a hideous reminder of what happened to countless veterans.

The war nightmares are symbolic of our national nightmare, which is just beginning to go away. But it will not fully go away, and so we run a high risk of repeating it in another way, in another international police action, unless we face that nightmare horror—hear it, see it, know it. Then having remembered it, perhaps we can begin to forget it when we realize that what we are facing is the personal and collective shadow, and that these are part of each one of us. Then there can be a healing, a reconciliation with the wholeness that is also holy, the centering Self, the central archetype, which is our own inner religious experience.

Probably 400,000 to 500,000 combat Vietnam veterans are suffering psychologically from the aftermath of war and need help. Until now we have let the Vietnam veteran carry our odious shadow. That way we don't have to see that it is our own reflection in the window that would heal us if we faced it.

This phenomenon is also described by William Broyles, a Vietnam veteran, in an article about visiting the Vietnam Memorial in Washington, D.C.[1]

> I cried too. It was as if a common emotion held back in so many private corners was all at once coming out into the sunlight. I cried for the men who had been there, for their families, for the country, for myself. I cried because I couldn't help it. It was beyond knowing. As I stood in front of the polished granite I saw the names, but I also saw my own reflection. It fell across the names like a ghost. "Why me, Lord?" we asked ourselves in Vietnam. It was a question

that came back as I stood there: "Why them?" It was a terrible sadness that brought the tears. But also, beneath it, there was a deep relief tinged with guilt: my name isn't on the wall.

I had an unusual opportunity as a Jungian psychoanalyst to study the psychological trauma of war. I talked to combat veterans from the psychiatric wards in the hospital, from the outpatient clinic, and from the Vet Center Outreach in downtown San Antonio. I also saw veterans who were not patients but were referred by veterans I had seen.

I came to the conclusion that what I was hearing—no, what I was experiencing—was an absolutely unique, unconscious history of the impact of combat violence on the human psyche. This was the unconscious history of the Vietnam War as reflected in the minds and souls of the men who were its psychological casualties. Thus a unique story of war emerges from the veterans' nightmares.

The war was still alive and real in the minds of these veterans. These dream images are perhaps our only living, uncontaminated record of the war trauma—that is, not altered by consciousness.

Franz Kafka wrote:[2]

You can hold back from the suffering of the world, you have free permission to do so, and it is in accordance with your nature, but perhaps this very holding back is the one suffering you could have avoided.

In the inner world of spirit and the collective unconscious dwell the shadow of human beings, the dark side of the psyche, the rejected, unwanted, repressed unconscious, and ultimately evil, even absolute evil. This is not an atavistic throwback but the emergence of the primitive, archaic psyche that lives in civilized man.

Archetypes have positive and negative sides. When we face our shadow, accept it as our own, and don't project it onto others, the shadow may become positive, our so-called best energy. The negative shadow is a menace so long as it remains unconscious, unrecognized, and we fail to own it as our own. We tend to forget that the shadow is unconscious and therefore seen only in its projection as evil onto other people, things, races, ideas, and nations.

For the American people, the Vietnam War revealed the American shadow in almost inescapable ways. It was pumped into our psyche's bloodstream by nightly television reports of the war in living and dying color. Horrors and atrocities are never committed only by the enemy, and not since the Civil War—when it was brother against brother, a quarter million Americans died, a million men were wounded, and the slaves were freed—has the American shadow been so agonizingly conspicuous.

No one who has not known war at first hand can exactly imagine what it is like. I submit that the next most available way is to experience the war dream world, not as a clinical phenomenon to be reduced to psychoanalytic interpretation, but as human experience.

It is no wonder people shy away from systematic, subjective study of war nightmares. They reveal information that no traditional, clinical, statistical work can reach. Statistical analyses give us impersonal facts, averages, and generalizations, in which the individual is nothing but a unit like all the other units. Such studies do not explore exceptional and unusual cases. Jim may be number 28 on my computer analysis, but no other Vietnam vet was beheaded by me in a ravine in Vietnam, and this is an interesting psychological fact.

I am not particularly drawn to the horrors of war, but neither do I turn away from them. Acceptance of these horrors in another person may impart hope. Listening without contempt, depreciation, or condescension means accepting the dreamer and his dreadful images and memories. That, I regret to say, is a rare healing experience.

However, caution is the watchword. Inexperienced people who are not trained in dream analysis should not dive into these troubled, dangerous waters, but should know that listening itself, without *any* interpretation, allows the dreamer to retell his story, and in the process, possibly change his attitudes and dreams.

It is imperative that Americans learn about the psychological impact of catastrophe in order to comprehend today's world of terror and wars. The acceptance of the Vietnam soldier is the first new order of old business.

The shameful way in which our country welcomed our veterans back from Vietnam compounded the Vietnam failure in which we all shared. It played a significant part in the veterans' subsequent sufferings and alienation.

A case in point: When Mike arrived at San Francisco airport, wounded, frightened, feeling both guilty and proud, he told me, this is what happened:

> I went to a bar at the airport and someone at the bar said, "Well, what are you doing here? You're crazy. Why don't you get out of here?" It seemed to me that the media had depicted us as being crazy. When I left the service, I considered myself normal. I just wanted out. I did my thing and now leave me alone.

Tom, who prided himself on being a grunt, had spent twenty-six months in Vietnam and survived the Tet offensive at Hue, which was captured by the Vietcong and the North Vietnamese. He told me how it was when he landed in Washington, D.C.:

> A lady came up to me and called me a "murderer," and she hit me in the face with her purse. I said, "Shit." This is what I came home to. I went out and got a drink. I didn't want to come home if this was how it was gonna be.

Cervando, a tough ex-marine with a drawer full of medals, said to me:

Look around you. There are still people who are ashamed to say, "I'm a Vietnam veteran," because they are scared that people won't talk to them. I've been insulted. "Sir, were you one of them butchers over there? Did you really enjoy killing babies and people?"

Another veteran remembered one event that haunted him when he was awake and in his dreams:

I see this kid, twelve or thirteen years old, with his leg blown off, telling us in Vietnamese to go home and let the Vietnamese do their own fighting. At the same time, he was yelling to kill us. I turned away and somebody killed him.

Bill, who lost his leg in a mine explosion, told me this nightmare, which recurred several times a week for four years:

We were on a search-and-destroy mission and were going through a friendly village. A baby was crying in a hooch, and no one else was anywhere around. My buddy went into the hooch and the captain shouted, "DON'T PICK IT UP!" But my buddy didn't hear the warning and reached for the infant. The baby was booby-trapped with a grenade. It exploded. There was nothing recognizable left of the baby and only parts of my buddy. I'll never get that cry and explosion out of my head. Never.

Mike, a paraplegic, had been accidentally shot in the back by what was called "friendly fire." A buddy's M-16 went off and severed Mike's spinal cord. Now confined to a wheelchair, with excruciating, intermittent pains in his thighs, Mike was referred to me by the Vet Center because of his severe depression and nightmares. He said:

Vietnam was a high for me. I was seventeen years old, and that shit was better than any combat movie I had ever seen. It was for real. Sometimes I would think it would be nice to stay there, and at the end of a year I extended my time in Vietnam. Six weeks later I was shot in the back.

Mike's dream:

The Americans have turned on me. It is as if I am the enemy. They tied me to a tree and threw axes at me. Sometimes I dream I am a POW being captured by the Americans.

I worked with Mike once a week for eleven months. Only once did he complain about having been shot by an American and wonder what his life would have been if he hadn't been shot. Mike dreams:

We called one of the guys Coke Bottle because of his thick glasses. They blew the top of his head off. "PICK HIM UP, MAN!" There were pieces of his brain and shit on my boots. We took his body to the LZ [loading zone] and the AK-45s [enemy machine guns] were cracking. Pass the word—"They got Coke Bottle!" We dropped napalm. I dug in, scared, crying my ass off. "Maybe he's not dead." There was artillery fire all night. I fell asleep and had a frightening kind of dream of the sounds of elephants coming at me. I woke up screaming. We moved out in the morning. They lifted Coke Bottle sitting up in a hoist, blood and all.

After I had been working with Mike for three months, his nightmare stopped completely and his depression lifted, but then he began to bleed from his bowels. He was admitted to Ward 13 at Fort Sam Houston. He remarked that the first time he had been admitted to that ward was thirteen years before on the thirteenth day of the month, and he had weighed eighty pounds. He said, "There was something about that ward from the first day I saw it. It seemed to me that it was going to be a part of me for the rest of my life."

Although Mike was afraid that his depression would return, it never did. He didn't know why his war dreams had changed and then stopped. He said:

Maybe it had something to do with seeing you. In the past, if I had one of those dreams or flashbacks, I'd start trembling and sweating. It would worry the hell out of me. Now I sit back and accept the fact that talking about Vietnam is not going to change anything. I don't think of Vietnam. But how the hell can I live like this?

The surgeons removed a cancer of the colon and performed a colostomy. Mike was convinced that his cancer was caused by Agent Orange.

The last time I saw Mike on that ward, he was semicomatose and weighed eighty pounds again. I wanted to say something to him, but I didn't know what, and the silence was painful to me. His loving wife was at his side. Seeing him there, I thought back to Christmas time eight months previously, when he had told me how he had envied the simple Vietnamese lifestyle and the beautiful countryside, and that he had never hated the Vietnamese. Mike said to me last December, "What would I say if a doctor told me I had so many months to live? I'd probably go apeshit!" But of course, he didn't. He died rather peacefully.

He and I had been relieved that his depression, nightmares, and flashbacks had gone away, but at the same time he had developed symptoms of cancer. That was both bewildering and disheartening. For one brief moment I wondered if he would have been better off with his depression, as if that had warded off the cancer, rather than heralding it. He and I had done the best we could. Fate had its own hand to play. His healing nightmares had done their work.

I reviewed all the audiotapes of our meetings: I found no clue that his unconscious was reacting to his impending death. Not even in his dreams. Perhaps, as Jung noted, the unconscious does not take much notice of our death but rather reacts to our attitude towards dying. Still I wondered why this had happened just as his spirits were lifted, his life was joyful, and his marriage more happy than ever before? Was it possible that the depression had been the alarm signal of impending peril, and unconsciously he had sought me out to help him die? I thought perhaps that was the case.

What I could do for most of the veterans I saw was to give them a handle on their dreams and terror, to convey an attitude that there was meaning to their suffering and sacrifice. Even if the situation was not *so* hopeful after all these years, there was hope.

It goes almost without saying that my work with these men was often painful to me. Many times I asked myself why I had taken it on, or more correctly, why it had taken me on. At times I experienced war nightmares and dreams of combat. Then I knew that the suffering of the men was getting to me, and I would take a few days off from working with them.

This is one of my dreams:

I see the silhouette of a large aircraft carrier off the shore of Vietnam. It was a dark night, and I could just make out the outline of things. Then I am on the deck. Suddenly all over the deck I see muzzle fire of revolvers and rifles. I am running to avoid being shot, but the firing seems haphazard and I am not really in any danger.

I am astonished that while men were shooting every which way, no one was getting hit. At that point it dawned on me that these were all security officers, naval intelligence, CIA, and FBI, and that they were trying to kill an enemy somewhere on the ship. Then the shooting stops, and a naval intelligence officer tells me that the man has escaped off the ship, which was now tied up at a Vietnam pier.

What does that dream mean? How was it trying to help me? What was all this shooting about? Surely it was a dream of the shadow, the whole image of the dream was shadow. And the dark forces that were holding out escaped, as is always the case with the shadow. You cannot kill the shadow. It always survives or is recreated. I knew that. Here on the ocean of the unconscious, close by Vietnam, all of the intelligence powers of America were trying in vain to kill the shadow. And so it became obvious to me that even the most intense concentration of intelligence of all the thinking powers could not cope with the enemy I was trying to find. In short, I had to reach my subject from a feeling more than a factual approach to the American shadow. Perhaps this is best explained in the final lines from *King Lear:*[3]

> The weight of this sad time we must obey,
> Speak what we feel, not what we ought to say.
> The oldest hath borne most; we that are young
> Shall never see so much, nor live so long.

And so it is important to point out that the most stressful dreams the veterans had were not of their own danger—of being shot, maimed, or killed—but of seeing others, particularly their buddies, and next the children, and then women, being killed and slaughtered.

George's dream:

> We get into this village about six miles north of Da Nang. A bunch of little children are running towards us. Our captain yells, "FIRE!" When we fire, they explode. They were loaded with grenades. They were booby-trapped. We really blew them away. They just blew to pieces.

Children were often killed because they were armed or booby-trapped. George said, "That's what's shattering my nerves." We all know about My Lai and atrocities involving shooting children in cold blood, but do we know about grenades killing booby-trapped babies and the shooting of armed or booby-trapped children and civilians? These occurred often enough so that the men involved, as well as those who heard stories from buddies, and who became psychological casualties, carried a heavy burden of guilt and a great sadness.

Wilson, a marine sergeant who spent two years in Nam, told me this nightmare, which recurred once or twice every week:

> There is a big flash and everybody is hurting and crying, "MEDIC! MEDIC!" Then everyone is kinda lying there, hearing the helicopters come in. I see an army lieutenant walking across the field with no foot. It was blown off. I hear him getting on board the damn helicopter, dragging the bone across the steel deck. I'm being medivaced in that helicopter. DAMN. It hurts to look at it. He doesn't even know what is happening. I wake up sweating and say, "Oh shit! That happened all over again." I get a real bad headache then. I just lie there. I feel like something is coming apart at the seams. I lie there, trying to relax. Waiting for the sun to come up. I can't sleep.

Now a story that demonstrates the soldier's identification with his dead buddy and his survivor's guilt. And that touches the heart of my paper—death and compassion.

Mario, a tall, brooding marine sergeant, was sent home to escort the body of a buddy who had been his close friend since childhood. Mario said to me:

> I came back to stand in the funeral with two other marines as honor guard. My buddy's wife came up to me and said, "Why did you let him die?" I just flipped out there. I took off out of the funeral home, and for a long time I held that guilt within me. I wasn't sure if it was my fault or not. Maybe she just needed someone to blame it on. When I went back to Vietnam, I went back to be killed. I really didn't want to go back home at all. Now I have a nightmare about how it actually happened.

Mario's dream:

79

My buddy gets hit. I am close enough to reach him but I can't do anything. He is dying. The right side of his head is totally gone. It looks like hamburger, and the other side is a mess. I don't know what hit my buddy, but for some ungodly reason he is still alive. I hold him between my legs and he bleeds to death.

That is the psychological, social, and physical reality of death.

That is the story of bravery and selflessness of the hero who became the American anti-hero.

That is what the conflagration of war does to men and women.

That is the primitive basis of the pain that comes when people are slaughtered and maimed and butchered, when there are *no words* to articulate what happened . . . and no one wants to hear them anyway. And it comes relentlessly in the dream, in the black of night.

> To sleep: perchance to dream: ay, there's the rub;
> For in that sleep of death what dreams may come. . . .[4]

Until only a few years ago Americans had turned their backs on the Vietnam veteran. Since symbolically our shadow is at our back, the metaphor is apt. But it is changing, and at long last understanding of the Vietnam veteran becomes possible. Yet we Americans have not yet faced our shadow, and we project our evil. We are still caught in the American myth of the hero and the hubris that always attends the hero motif. The hero myth is also the myth of invulnerability expressed in the good-bad guy westerns and the shoot-out between the sheriff and the lawbreaker. As in Dr. Jekyll and Mr. Hyde, unleashing the powers of good and evil to go their separate ways is a fatal mistake. The integration of both good and evil is the way to heal the nightmare. That is what the transpersonal psyche is trying to do in dreams of war. And without mourning and grief worked through, the inner shadows continue to torment us all.

> He that lacks a time to mourn, lacks a time to mend.
> Eternity mourns that. 'Tis an ill cure
> For life's worst ills, to have not time to feel them.
> Where sorrow's held intrusive and turned out,
> There wisdom will not enter, nor true power,
> Nor ought that dignifies humanity.[5]

The characteristic war nightmare, as I have said, is recalled as precisely as the real event. It is perceived as the reality. At first the reality of the trauma images in these dreams led me to think that they were something like the substance of what nightmares are made, rather than ordinary dreams. And in the end, it might be that these are indeed the archetypal dreams of war. As expressions of circumstances to which human beings are subject and in which the reality image itself is the most powerful expression of the feeling involved, they have no basis for metaphorical transformation. And there is no antecedent human resource or experience that can mollify the intensity of the images. Such archetypal dreams are both symbol and metaphor inherent in the original image, which is frozen in time and place.

I have classified the war dreams into three categories. The first is the characteristic war (trauma) dream, in which the dream is reported to be a replication of the actual trauma *exactly* as it happened. This represents 53 percent of the dreams told to me. The second group of dreams are the *variable* dreams, which portray the exact trauma but elaborated with sequences that did not happen but which might conceivably have happened. Such dreams might include images of the here-and-now and life experiences from the past. They constitute 21 percent of the dreams. The third group of dreams are like ordinary hallucinatory nightmares and constitute 26 percent of the total dream sample of 359 war dreams.[6]

All these men suffered because they were caught in a tragic situation. Each one is innocent, in the sense that what happened to him was far greater than anything he had done to provoke it. They are like the mountaineer (in Northrup Frye's image) whose shout brings down an avalanche.[7] He is guilty in the sense that he lives in a world where injustices are an inescapable part of existence. I am referring to the collective guilt as personified in the shadow of the hero—the anti-hero.

It is well known that most veterans came back home and made successful re-entries into society. For vast numbers of Vietnam veterans, the experience in Vietnam was a positive one. While most of the men I saw felt positive about the closeness, tightness, even brotherhood among the combat veterans, the war still raged. Some of the dreams of the veterans are allegorically prophetic. A Texas veteran dreams he is on a street in Dallas:

> I am trying to warn people that another war is coming. People are laughing at me. I yell, "Hey, there's a war going to happen! You'd better take cover and get off the street!" But the people laugh at me. They wouldn't listen to me. I am going to secure a position by chopper, but the helicopters fly off and leave me there. I wake up angry and afraid. When the choppers leave, I have lost my last link. Without it, I am not part of the unit anymore.

In our world today, too much evil is done and too little is said about it. There is no shortcut to facing the depth of the impact of war on the human psyche, and denial wears off. "There is no pill called salvation," says the Mayo Clinic psychiatrist Howard Rome. No pill will cure the wounded psyche of the warrior.

Novalis said, "Whatever the spirit that calls, a kindred spirit will answer." This is the way to help the wounded warrior. We who try to help these men must realize that we ourselves are wounded healers.

Once, long ago, when I was sitting in the Stanford University Chapel during other troubling times, these words came into my mind: *Things are better than they are.* Many times since, these words have come when I needed them most. I hope they are the words of the human psyche speaking through me, not by me, to you.

NOTES

1. William Broyles, "Peace Be With You," *Reader's Digest* (March 1982).

2. W. H. Auden and Louis Kronenberger, eds., *The Viking Book of Aphorisms* (New York: Viking Press, 1962), p. 90.

3. Shakespeare, *King Lear*, V.iii.

4. Shakespeare, *Hamlet*, III.i.

5. Sir Henry Taylor, *Philip van Artvelde* (1839), part I, act I, scene V.

6. The format and motif of war dreams and their classification are reported in a paper: Harry A. Wilmer, "Combat Nightmares: Towards a Therapy of Violence," *Spring* (1987) [in press].

7. Northrup Frye, *Anatomy of Criticism: Four Essays* (Princeton: Princeton University Press, 1973), p. 41.

TRAN VAN DINH

The Tale of Kieu: Joy and Sadness in the Life of Vietnamese in the United States

Canh nao canh chang deo sau
Nguoi buon canh co vui dau bao gio
  (But her own gloom would tinge each sight or scene:
  when you feel grief, can what you see give joy?)

Cung chung mot tieng to dong
nguoi ngoai cuoi nu ghuoi trong khoc tham
  (Both heard the selfsame voice of silk and wood—
  she smiled and gloated while he wept within)

The first quote was used by a friend of mine, a 1975 refugee now settled in California, to express his feelings when we attended the Cherry Blossom Festival in Washington, D.C.

The nation's capital was at its most beautiful—politics aside—and happiest in April, yet my friend was lost in his thoughts. He was sad. The blooming forsythia reminded him of the *mai vang* (yellow apricot) flowers which Vietnamese use to decorate their ancestors' altar during Tet (lunar New Year).

The second quote served as a comment for a relative of mine, one of the "boat people" (1982), now living in Florida. We had just come out of a concert at the Kennedy Center. He remained unusually silent for the rest of the evening.

Both quotes come from the *Tale of Kieu* (or *Kim Van Kieu*), the early nineteenth-century, 3,254-line "literary Bible" by Nguyen Du (1765-1820), the greatest Vietnamese poet of all times.

The Tale of Kieu is the life story of Thuy Kieu, a talented, beautiful woman and a gifted musician. On a spring promenade with her brother and sister during Thanh Minh (the festival of the washing of the tombs in the third month of the lunar calendar) she stops by a secluded tomb, left in a dreary condition. She is told that the abandoned grave is that of Dam Tien, a famous songstress, "who in her life was a wife to everyone and at her death a ghost without a husband." Thuy Kieu, deeply moved by the "pale fate" of the songstress, bursts into tears and composes a quartet, which she engraves with her hairpin into the bark of a nearby tree. It is called "Bac Menh" or "Pale Fate." Then Kim Trong appears, a handsome student and a friend of her brother. Kim Trong is struck by her beauty and she by his.

That evening, alone in her room, Thuy Kieu is haunted by the encounters of the day: the fate of a dead songstress and the unexpected handsome young man. In her sleep, she dreams of Dam Tien, the songstress, who tells Thuy Kieu that her name, too, is in the *So Doan Truong* (Registrar of the Severed Entrails) of the "women with rosy cheeks and pale fate."

Kim Trong, on his part, thinks of Thuy Kieu constantly. He succeeds in finding a lodging next to Thuy Kieu's house, manages to approach her, and vows to marry her as soon as they have received the approval of their parents.

But shortly afterwards, Kim Trong has to leave to attend his uncle's funeral, and misfortune befalls Thuy Kieu's family. Her father and her brother, victims of a slanderous accusation of a silk merchant, are arrested and thrown into jail, and their house is looted. In the desperate situation she finds herself and her family in, Thuy Kieu has only one solution: she sells herself to a certain Ma Giam Sinh, who agrees to take her as his wife for three hundred gold taels, which Thuy Kieu uses to bribe the officials and set free her father and brother. She asks her sister to take her place and marry Kim Trong when he returns. Thuy Kieu leaves her home for her future husband's tavern. But Ma Giam Sinh, a self-proclaimed scholar, is actually a pimp, and he sells her as a prostitute to a "blue castle." Cruelly betrayed, Thuy Kieu tries to commit suicide. Again she sees Dam Tien, the songstress, who promised to meet her later in the Tien Duong River. She is saved in time and the "blue castle" madam, Tu Ba, does her best to console her, giving her a private apartment and promising to arrange for another marriage. Tu Ba then plots with So Khanh, a notorious playboy. He seduces Thuy Kieu, wins her confidence, and then leads her to run away with him. Credulous and impatient to get away from the "blue castle," Thuy Kieu falls into the trap. So Khanh deserts her at the rendezvous and she is taken back to Tu Ba, resigned now to receive guests. She meets Thuc Sinh, a scholar who falls in love with her, redeems her, and makes her his second wife. Thuc Sinh's first wife, Hoan Thu, out of jealousy, has Thuy Kieu kidnapped and submitted to all sorts of subtle, cruel punishments. Kieu runs away again, this time to a Buddhist pagoda where she becomes a nun. But soon afterwards, thinking that she is going to be adopted into a good family, Kieu becomes a prostitute a second time. At this new "blue castle," she meets Tu Hai, a rebel warrior and a generous heart who buys her out of her shame and marries her. He leaves her to pursue his conquests, but comes back triumphantly a year later as "the conqueror of half an empire." Soon, Thuy Kieu persuades her husband to return to the grace of the imperial court. Tu Hai accepts the peace offer but is attacked and killed during the surrender ceremony by government troops.

Bitterly disappointed with life, Thuy Kieu throws herself into a nearby river, which happens to be the Tien Duong—the same river the song-stress Dam Tien had mentioned in her second appearance. However, she is rescued by the same superior nun who had given her asylum fifteen years before. Meanwhile, Kim Trong, her first love, after looking in vain for her, marries her sister. When the two are finally reunited, they decide to remain friends and not become husband and wife.

The Tale of Kieu, which the Vietnamese unanimously consider a unique narrative in verses of six and eight syllables, was composed in the purest tradition of folk songs and popular sayings, and the highest literary style. It was so popular that for nearly two centuries even illiterates could recite by heart scores of couplets from it. The best translation in English is by Huynh Sanh Thong of Yale University (1973). Ten years later, a new bilingual revised edition was published and appropriately dedicated by the translator to "Vietnamese refugees and their friends throughout the world." Professor Alexander B. Woodside, a leading scholar on the history and civilization of Southeast Asia, in his "Historical Background" for this edition, wrote:

> To the Vietnamese people themselves, *The Tale of Kieu* is much more than just a glorious heirloom from their literary past. It has become a kind of continuing emotional laboratory in which all the great and timeless issues of personal morality and political obligation are tested and resolved (or left unresolved) for each new generation.

For the generation of Vietnamese refugees in the United States, *The Tale of Kieu* is the mirror of the society they have left behind: bad guys and good guys, beauty and ugliness, loyalty and treason, noble acts and vile tricks, secret dealings, open propositions, and unnecessary intrigues—all entangled in a seemingly hopeless tragicomedy. Kieu is Vietnam itself: beautiful, talented, often condemned to a "pale fate" by external forces beyond its control and comprehension.

When they landed in the United States, the refugees at first experienced a bursting joy, an ethereal relief. They found the American people usually friendly and generous, the country diverse and immense, the landscape inspiring.

But soon they realized that Americans are strangers who do not speak their highly musical (six-toned) language. And, no matter how majestic American mountains are, no matter how gorgeous American rivers can be, they are not the Trang Son ("long mountain range," also known as the Annamitic Cordillera, which separates Vietnam from Laos), the unpredictable Song Hong ("red river," in northern Vietnam), the meditative Song Huong ("perfume river," in Hue, the former imperial capital in central Vietnam), and the fertile Cuu Long ("nine dragons," or Mekong, in southern Vietnam). They began to miss their country, which is also known in Vietnamese as *non song* (mountains, rivers). They felt nostalgic for their *que huong* (native village), their *que me* (mother's native land) of the *noi chon dau cat ron* (place where the placenta is buried and the umbilical cord is cut). They thought of other members of their extended family still living in desperate poverty and anxiety back in Vietnam, now "desecrated by communist rulers," of their unattended or displaced ancestors' graves. They remembered the intimate details of the *huong vi* (flavor and taste) of the Tets (Vietnam traditional lunar new years) of yesteryears. Because the Vietnamese culture stresses the yin-yang relationship between *ngoai canh* (external scenery) and *noi tam* (inner heart), the natural unity between matter and spirit, body and soul, and because Vietnamese are romantic people extremely sensitive to poetic communication, the realization of the difference between the U.S. and Vietnam, between comfort and security "over here" and privations and uncertainty "over there," becomes the major source of a deepening sadness. Many refugees experience a sense of loss of history and values, of loneliness, of discontinuity with traditional patterns of life, of being betrayed. But the new existence in the new land must be built and must go on.

To do so, they "have learned how to construct a creaky armor in which to joust with the world outside . . . They have learned how 'to act American on the outside' while remaining Vietnamese on the inside."[1]

"To act American on the outside" is not so difficult. Vietnamese refugees adapt quickly and are relatively successful in business, in academic pursuits, in schools, and in offices. "To remain Vietnamese on the inside" proves to be difficult, complicated, painful, and to some, self-destructive. For these, especially men of old age, their acute sadness might lead to slow, quiet death in the middle of the night. As we say in Vietnamese, "they are so sad that their entrails rot" *(buon thoi ruot)*. As a matter of fact, the original title of *The Tale of Kieu* was *Doan Truong Tan Thanh* (New Cry of the Severed Entrails).

In sadness and in joy, to remain Vietnamese on the inside, the Vietnamese can find in *The Tale of Kieu* "some common denominator about their world that touches a chord in their collective psyche," according to Mr. Huynh Sanh Thong. He explains:

A clue perhaps, is a word that recurs throughout the poem: OAN. The nearest equivalent in English is a past participle: WRONGED. A story purporting to recount events that occurred in Ming China manages to project one stark, readily recognizable image about Vietnam—the picture of victims, of people punished for crimes or sins they are not aware they have committed.[2]

But also in *The Tale of Kieu*, Vietnamese can find a message of hope, Mr. Thong believes:

> Despite its grim details and sordid aspects, Kieu's story conveys a message of hope for both the individual and the country: if, like Kieu, the Vietnamese accept and endure with fortitude whatever happens to them, someday they will have paid the cost of their evil karma and will achieve both personal and national salvation.[3]

As a Buddhist, I share Mr. Thong's belief. As a Vietnamese, I understand the essence and the meaning of sadness in our individual life and national history as well as the romantic optimism that sustains the Vietnamese nation through its long path of survival and renewal.

During the war of independence against colonial France, my home town, Hue, the former imperial capital, famous for its Nui Ngu ("imperial hill") and Song Huong ("perfume river") was occupied in 1947 by the French troops after a hard battle and a stiff resistance by the Vietnam Liberation Army. The resulting desolation moved a poet to sigh:

> There is not even one tree left on the Imperial Hill,
> The lonely bird sleeps on the bare cold earth,
> There is not one passenger in the pleasure sampan on the River of Perfume,
> The songstress cries at the empty sky.

This note of pessimism and despair was quickly answered by a *ca dao* (folk song), a creation of the common people:

> Here is the River, there is the Mountain,
> they are still the same.
> Our land is as beautiful as brocade,
> why then worry, my love?
> Right now, we are going to rebuild our future
> to provide a tree for the bird and a sampan
> for you to cross the River.

NOTES

1. Lynn Darling, "Vietnamese: 'American on the Outside': Trauma Still Re-

mains for Refugees in Fairfax County," *Washington Post,* July 10, 1977, Section A, p. 1.

2. Huynh Sanh Thong, trans., *The Heritage of Vietnamese Poetry: An Anthology* (New Haven: Yale University Press, 1979), p. xxxii.

3. Ibid., p. xl.

RECOMMENDED READING

Huynh Sanh Thong, trans., *The Heritage of Vietnamese Poetry: An Anthology.* New Haven: Yale University Press, 1979.

David G. Marr, *Vietnamese Tradition on Trial, 1920-1945.* Berkeley: University of California Press, 1981.

Nguyen Du, *The Tale of Kieu,* a bilingual edition translated by Huynh Sanh Thong. New Haven: Yale University Press, 1983.

Paul J. Strand and Woodrow Jones, Jr., *Indochinese Refugees in America: Problems of Adaptation and Assimilation.* Durham, N.C.: Duke University Press, 1985.

Tran Van Dinh, *Blue Dragon, White Tiger: A Tet Story.* Philadelphia: TriAm Press, Inc., 1983.

For You

It was dusk that made me a felon. Not principle, not revolutionary fervor, not even the remorse of a wealthy kid who had sailed through childhood as if he owned the very sea of his own unexplored future.

The war wouldn't give way. It wouldn't stop because I was a poet, wouldn't stop because I had my first job, wouldn't stop because I was in love. It would always be there. Nineteen sixty-seven was, for me, the beginning of the end. Suddenly there was a new fact in the world, a patient and dramatic devastation that seemed to exist outside time. And because I took a walk at dusk one fine fall evening in Moline, Illinois, the next day I gave Whitman to my draft board ("Dismiss whatever insults your own soul") in a short but quotation-filled letter and returned my draft card to them.

By 1968 I had spent two years moving back and forth along the edges of the antiwar movement. I was grateful for the ragged, but necessary passion of those students who opposed the war. They taught me one of the first rules about how to be a citizen: you've got to be willing to be a pain in the neck. But crowds made me uncomfortable, mass chanting was an embarrassment no matter how right the cause, and breaking the law with deliberate pleasure seemed worse than reckless: its bad taste offended every bone in my Anglican body. It assumed that one was right beyond a shadow of a doubt and how could a movement—a crowd, a mass of laughing, chanting college students—make such an assumption? An Anglican with a love of the splendidly solitary view from his parents' bedroom to Reising Hill could never feel at home in a room full of people chanting, "Hell, no, we won't go!"

But the war was no respecter of good taste. It had become so wrong—so obscenely and ploddingly wrong—that any opposition to it had to be welcomed and joined, no matter how out of place some of its tactics made me feel.

Like everyone else I knew, I was in search of a position to uphold. I was more than a poet, it turned out. I was a citizen. But I wasn't sure what that meant and I hadn't devoted years to becoming a good citizen as I had trying to become a good poet.

Suddenly I was spending hours in my boarding house drinking instant coffee with a fellow who wore the same blue velvet shirt day after day. We took turns arguing one way, then another, about "what to do." We sat in the basement kitchen of the boarding house in Iowa City. Dried up catsup bottles, each one the deposit of a previous tenant, lined the open shelf above the refrigerator. Sometimes we yelled at each other, sometimes we sat silently, our hands around our mugs of coffee, our hearts confused. We were the men—because of teacher and student deferments from the draft—who could afford to choose a future. We were the ones who had to learn what it meant to decide rather than to drift or be pushed.

I had spent so many years learning just the opposite! How to drift, how to float on the dusk's shifting current, how to let go of choice and give the poem a chance to rise waveringly up into its own shape, its own existence.

I didn't want to chant slogans. I didn't want to be "right." I didn't want to judge. And yet, there I was, night after night, sitting at the table, trying to make a choice: deferment? Canada? (the army was out of the question), draft resistance and/or prison?

These weren't choices. They were entire lives, futures that could never be redeemed—or so it seemed then in the midst of it all—if the wrong choices were made.

Back and forth we went, the young man from the boarding house in the blue velour shirt and I, all of us on the edges of the antiwar movement, those of us given to reading Emerson and Thoreau, eating frozen dinners and drinking 3.2 beer, playing pinball or pool for hours at a time—helpless devotees of any game that would shut down our minds for a few hours. We were the ones who underlined CIVIL DISOBEDIENCE with yellow marker pens and wrote excited comments in the margins late at night, but who would have hated to follow through with disobedience of our own.

Though most of my friends were in Iowa City, I lived alone in Moline, Illinois, one dusty and dimly lit flight above a greeting card shop run by a red-faced, rather likeable John Bircher. I was one block from the Mississippi and frequently took walks with a view that gave onto the world's largest stockpile of conventional weapons: the Rock Island Arsenal. Or maybe it was the largest arsenal in the world located on an island. Whatever its actual statistical existence, it was my landscape. Lush foliage hid the real work of the place. From the windy distance of the nearest bridge it looking inviting, even serene.

There was an otherness about that island—something I couldn't name. It was unapproachable and an MP was always on duty on the other side of the bridge where the arsenal began. That was the year I lived next to an arsenal, the year I began—painfully, slowly, but with growing rage—to take responsibility for what my country was doing in my name.

It was also the year I didn't write any good poems. All I can remember now are some lines about a dusty window, a parking lot, two pine trees, and the bitterness of Ernest Hemingway. And it was the first year I got paid for teaching writing and literature. It seemed miraculous that someone would actually give me money to talk about what I loved, to have opinions about James Joyce and Thoreau that formerly I couldn't give away to the man in the blue velour shirt or any of my other friends.

It was a working-class college with the English department housed in the basement of an old Pentecostal church: a dreary place. The mixture of Sunday morning classrooms and poverty could be deadly on Monday mornings when the students sat sleepy-eyed on the waxed floors outside the classrooms like refugees waiting for their morning bowl of soup rather than students waiting for classes to begin. I was the razzle dazzle guy with the curly hair and hiking boots from the Big U in Iowa City. I didn't own a tie, I lived in a VW bus all fall, I had opinions that gave off the ferocious glitter of newly minted funny money. To the students I was a classy eccentric, and I had them with me from the first, those future postal clerks and nurses, those earnest would-be writers with their mixed bag of Sartre and letter jackets, pimples and acid, and—finally—of life and death.

Then two of my students quit school and within months were dead in Vietnam. The second student who died had sat in the back of the room, chair tilted against the wall, his long hair spread behind him against the blackboard like a scraggly fan. He often brought his guitar to class in a black case. He wrote his poems on cheap yellow paper and he wanted to know about mileage from my bus. These were the details I remembered when his girlfriend told me he had been killed.

It was winter by then and I was living alone above the greeting card shop. After that second student's death, I spent the weekend by myself. I was reading Suzuki at the time and wanted to believe in something, even if it was only the pull and release of my own breath as I sat cross-legged, meditating best I knew how. I liked Zen. For someone raised in Anglican it seemed, somehow, the closest thing to those rituals I loved growing up with, but could no longer accept as my own. While I sat meditating, I felt lonely: all my voluble and spontaneous love of poetry that fit itself so nicely into the fifty-minute school hour, my á là mode hiking boots. I thought of that dead boy with his guitar and his questions, and the careful but wasted economy of the cheap yellow paper he used for writing first drafts and I felt sick to my soul, for all my talk of Thoreau and Whitman. I wanted to be a citizen again, to Pledge Allegiance to something with the faith I'd felt in fourth grade, facing the flag behind Miss Rodger's desk. It was my country, too, not just the John Bircher's downstairs with his saccharine greeting cards and his private gun collection.

That weekend I drank green tea, believing it more Japanese than Lipton's Orange. I sat. I stared at the gray clouds of dust under the bed. I followed the flow of my breath in and out of my stomach—like a golden river, Suzuki said. I remember how hard I tried to shut out the sound of the radiator pipes, a peculiar crackle followed by a death-rattle gurgle, then a short mechanical silence before the next spit of heat. For two days I did nothing but alternately sit and then hobble on legs grown permanently sore from being crossed so much.

I quit thinking about everything: the draft, my dead students, the future, the past. I felt as if I'd grown three inches overnight: everything I saw looked slightly different, smaller and further away, the way a dream does as you wake up and it begins to leave you. Towards evening of the second day I'd had enough of the hush, pause, hush, pause, hush of my own breath and the shooting pains at ankles and knees. I wanted out and away from those motionless dust balls. It felt wonderful to walk into evening, alone in Moline, Illinois, in the middle of America, the weightless center of a centerless country.

I walked and I looked. I saw some men sitting at a bar. I stood outside, staring through the small pane of glass at the top of the door. Everything moved so slowly: my breath still deep and even, holding me rooted in the evening air like an anchor when men fish from a boat and seem to drift, but are only rocking back and forth between one known place and another. I saw the men, heads bent toward the neon light of a beer sign behind the bar: a man with a lasso in one hand and a beer in another. The lasso was red, the beer golden. The bartender stood beside the sign, white-aproned, holding a pencil. I watched as he gestured towards the bent heads of the men sitting before him. One of them nodded up and down and that simple, barely noticeable sign of agreement brought an assent of my own where I stood anchored by my own steady breath. And it brought tears to my eyes as well: if, in a moment of peace, the world could yield up such signs, then I wanted an equivalent inner peace, both permanent and casual. But I could not begin until I settled with the war. It was that dusk, that walk, that bartender that convinced me I could be sustained by the ordinary world if only I could abandon my soul searching and endless arguments over what to do, like a character in a Chekhov story so busy talking outside on a cold winter's night he almost dies of frostbite while trying to prove the existence of God. I had never felt more deeply the strangely calming power that comes from seeing clearly into the heart of everyday life.

I walked on, went up the hill that rose steeply away from the river where I lived. A sled had been left out for the night on a front yard's thin crust of snow. I saw this ordinary sight framed in a deepening gray like a

93

letter in a phrase, still undeciphered, but so important that once I understood it, it would change the meaning of all other words.

As I walked slowly up the hill, other objects I saw seemed part of the same phrase: a porch swing drawn up on its two chains waiting near the roof for spring; a car with a broken windshield glittering under a streetlight like the traces of a phosphorescent map; the corner of an old newspaper frozen into an iced-over sidewalk.

"For you," I found myself saying over and over as I neared the top of the steep hill. My breath came in short gasps, "For you, for you." It became a kind of greed. I couldn't get enough of the men with their bent heads in the bar, the sled, the swing. They gave and I took. I wanted it to go on forever, this greed for the world. I knew that it was for the sake of a sled left behind in the moment of impatience for dinner that I would go to prison. Not just for political reasons, not even for moral ones: not for reasons at all, or not the kind I could explain to a draft board. For you, sled. For you, bent heads. For you.

BRUCE WEIGL

Sailing to Bien Hoa

In my dream of the hydroplane
I'm sailing to Bien Hoa
the shrapnel in my thighs
like tiny glaciers.
I remember a flower,
a kite, a mannikin playing the guitar,
a yellow fish eating a bird, a truck
floating in urine, a rat carrying a banjo,
a fool counting the cards, a monkey praying,
a procession of whales, and far off
two children eating rice,
speaking French—
I'm sure of the children,
their damp flutes,
the long line of their vowels.

Monkey

Out of the horror there rises a musical ache that is beautiful . . .

—James Wright

1
I am you are he she it is
they are you are we are.
I am you are he she it is
they are you are we are.
When they ask for your number
pretend to be breathing.
Forget the stinking jungle,
force your fingers between the lines.
Learn to get out of the dew.
The snakes are thirsty.
Bladders, water, boil it, drink it.
Get out of your clothes:
you can't move in your green clothes.
Your O.D. in color issue.
Get out the plates and those who ate,
those who spent the night.
Those small Vietnamese soldiers.
They love to hold your hand.
Back away from their dark cheeks.
Small Vietnamese soldiers.

They love to love you.
I have no idea how it happened,
I remember nothing but light.

2
I don't remember the hard
swallow of the lover.
I don't remember the burial of ears.
I don't remember
the time of the explosion.
This is the place curses are manufactured:
delivered like white tablets.
The survivor is spilling his bedpan.
He slips a curse into your pocket,
you're finally satisfied.
I don't remember the heat
in the hand,
the heat around the neck.

Good times bad times sleep
get up work. Sleep get up
good times bad times.
Work eat sleep good bad work times.
I like a certain cartoon of wounds.
The water which refused to dry.
I like a little unaccustomed mercy.
Pulling the trigger is all we have.
I hear a child.

3
I dropped to the bottom of a well.
I have a knife.
I cut someone with it.
Oh, I have the petrified eyebrows
of my Vietnam monkey.
My monkey from Vietnam.
My monkey.
Put your hand here.
It makes no sense.
I beat the monkey.
I didn't know him.
He was bloody.
He lowered his intestines
to my shoes. My shoes
spit-shined the moment
I learned to tie the bow.
I'm not on speaking terms
with anyone. In the wrong climate

a person can spoil,
the way a pair of boots slows you down. . . .

I don't know when I'm sleeping.
I don't know if what I'm saying
is anything at all.
I'll lie on my monkey bones.

4
I'm tired of the rice
falling in slow motion
like eggs from the smallest animal.
I'm twenty-five years old,
quiet, tired of the same mistakes,
the same greed, The same past.
the same past with its bleat
and pound of the dead,
with its hand grenade
tossed into a hootch on a dull Sunday
because when a man dies like that
his eyes sparkle,
his nose fills with witness nuance
because a farmer in Bong Son
has dead cows lolling
in a field of claymores
because the VC tie hooks to their comrades
because a spot of blood
is a number
because a woman is lifting
her dress across the big pond.

If we're soldiers we should smoke them
if we have them. Someone's bound
to point us in the right direction
sooner or later.

* * *

I'm tired and glad you asked.

5
There is a hill.
Men run top hill.
Men take hill.
Give hill to man.

*

Me and my monkey
and me and my monkey
my Vietnamese monkey
my little brown monkey
came with me
to Guam and Hawaii
in Ohio he saw
my people he
jumped on my daddy
he slipped into mother
he baptized my sister
he's my little brown monkey
he came here from heaven
to give me his spirit imagine
my monkey my beautiful
monkey he saved me lifted
me above the punji
sticks above the mines
above the ground burning
above the dead above
the living above the
wounded dying the wounded
dying.

* *

Men take hill away from smaller men.
Men take hill and give to fatter man.
Men take hill. Hill has number.
Men run up hill. Run down.

Song of Napalm

For my wife

After the storm, after the rain stopped pounding,
We stood in the doorway watching horses
Walk off lazily across the pasture's hill.
We stared through the black screen,
Our vision altered by the distance
So I thought I saw a mist
Kicked up around their hooves when they faded
Like cut-out horses
Away from us.
The grass was never more blue in that light, more
Scarlet; beyond the pasture
Trees scraped their voices into the wind, branches
Crisscrossed the sky like barbed wire
But you said they were only branches.

Okay. The storm stopped pounding.
I am trying to say this straight: for once
I was sane enough to pause and breathe
Outside my wild plans and after the hard rain
I turned my back on the old curses. I believed
They swung finally away from me . . .

100

But still the branches are wire
And thunder is the pounding mortar,
Still I close my eyes and see the girl
Running from her village, napalm
Stuck to her dress like jelly,
Her hands reaching for the no one
Who waits in waves of heat before her.

So I keep on living,
So I can stay here beside you,
I try to imagine she runs down the road and wings
Beat inside her until she rises
Above the stinking jungle and her pain
Eases, and your pain, and mine.

But the lie swings back again.
The lie works only as long as it takes to speak
And the girl runs only as far
As the napalm allows
Until her burning tendons and crackling
Muscles draw her up
Into that final position
Burning bodies so perfectly assume. Nothing
Can change that; she is burned behind my eyes
And not your good love and not the rain-swept air
And not the jungle green
Pasture unfolding before us can deny it.

Amnesia

If there was a world more disturbing than this
Where black clouds bowed down and swallowed you whole
And overgrown tropical plants
Rotted, effervescent in the muggy twilight, and monkeys
Screamed something
That came to sound like words to each other
Across the triple-canopy jungle you shared,
You don't remember it.

You tell yourself no and cry a thousand days.
You imagine that the crows calling autumn into place
Are your brothers and you could
If only the strength and will were there
Fly up to them and be black
And useful to the wind.

They Name Heaven

Managua, December 1984

I see the moon over Plaza España
but it's not my moon
because of what this pale one has seen
pass in dark cells
at the hands of crazy rich men,
murder on their lips like salt.
Not the moon my little boy must see tonight
safe in his bed in another country,
in the place of the great Republic,
near enough his mother
so he may find her even in his sleep.
Not the clean and round moon he calls to,

this moon rises over Cuesta del Plomo
where the bones have already
grown back into the earth
until there is nothing
to mark the graves of the disappeared.
The moon who will no longer
let us understand each other:

how in darkness they come for you,
how in moonlight you pass through the city
your hands bound,
your shirt ripped over your face.
How you must know you will die

only wonder how long it will take,
what parts of the body they will relish
with their sticks and their long knives . . .
those who make pacts under the moon,
who wash the blood away with rum,
who return to their sleeping families
and lift the acquiescent
nightgowns of their wives,
their drunken lips
fumbling upwards, always
upwards to the moons of flesh they name heaven.

Amigo del Corazón

In a café in barrio Las Américas
a lovely dark man has become my friend
drinking so much beer
we fall into each other's arms
in the shadows of palms
while his daughter,
the flower named Ana Ester,
sips her juice through a straw
and can't help not sway to a salsa
coming in from someone's lonely radio.
Flower of the night garden,
her eyes are on her father as he speaks,
her face open to him
because a radiance is still possible.

He pulls his pants-legs up
for me to see the scar of the wound
where shrapnel burnt a white
crescent moon into his brown skin.
We live mostly in silence, he says,
in houses smaller than the shape
he draws with his finger
in the air around the room.

We have not done well enough, he says,
not even love can pull you from certain

memories, the beer spilling at his lips
until he's quiet, and the music gone
and the heart quiet too in its time
so we can hear the night bird
sing what sounds like loss
into the dark barrio, and sing again
but no song returns and I feel myself
lift away from the ghosts he recalls,
who crowd around us to sing
their own grind of troop trucks
to sing the rattle of weapons
in the houses of those
who will not let the terror return.
He reaches for my hand to pull me back.
He touches his heart
and then he touches my heart too.

DANIEL M. SWAIN

Brothers in Arms: The Death of an Antiwar Veteran

Another movie, called *Platoon*, is out about Vietnam. Another book, a new novel by Larry Heineman called *Paco's Story*, shows how the war still lives in some obscure part of a veteran's brain. Other attempts are being made every day to define the horror that was Vietnam, and as a Vietnam vet myself I suppose that I should somehow feel gratified to know that the era is not being forgotten, that the lessons we learned from that terrible mistake are being remembered, that those who served are being given the only tribute any war calls for, that its horror is portrayed for all to see so that we may never forget.

I should feel good about all of this, but I don't. As a matter of fact, I feel outraged that anyone finds it satisfying, that anyone who went through the sixties can so misinterpret what the war in Vietnam was all about and who its real victims were. They were not the soldiers and airmen who fought a dirty little war, but those who fought a much greater war at home, who not only never got a parade but who continue to be victims of the war because they continue to lose battles every day of the year, continue to see all that they believed in and fought for destroyed and ridiculed, ridiculed in one of many ways by this sudden glorification of the men who fought in Vietnam. And make no mistake about it, no matter how much you show the inequity of war, no matter how terrible you make the events, no matter how completely you show the Vietnam soldier as the victim of politicians, you still glorify him by making him the tragic figure in your dramas.

I should explain that my brother Philip died today, the twenty-first of December, 1986, in Maricopa County Hospital in Phoenix, Arizona. He died of liver failure, officially, but what he really died of was a life lived too fully in the mentality of the sixties. He wasn't a vet, so neither his name, nor the name of my brother John, who died of a drug overdose in San Francisco in the early seventies, will appear on that wonderfully artistic monument the country has erected in Washington, D.C. to honor those who died honorably for their country in Vietnam. But they were as much victims of the sixties and that war as anybody. The only problem is that they both were on the other side, among those who couldn't or wouldn't serve in Vietnam, and so the price they paid with their lives doesn't count. What I find ironic about current attitudes is that, if there was a right side to the war, they were the ones who were on it.

I know, I know, I'm being insensitive to those poor Vietnam vets who have to live with the terrible guilt of what they did. I've read the stories about the poor SOB who can't look at his darling children without wanting to break into tears because he blew away a little Vietnamese child about the same age so many years ago. Perhaps part of the reason I don't sympathize is that I am one of those vets. But the fact is, isn't that what we *should* feel, mind-torturing guilt for the rest of our lives? Can't anyone see that we *deserve* to feel guilty? Doesn't anyone see that the entire ball of rationalization that we built for ourselves—we were only nineteen, we thought we were fighting a war of liberation, we believed in our country—is just so much bullshit? Nineteen or not, we made a choice that revealed to us our basic inhumanity, and even if we never willingly killed little kids, in the final analysis we participated in an enormously immoral act, and the guilt we feel is a reasonable response to our acts. We should be forgiven, but we shouldn't expect to hear "that's okay," because the fact is it wasn't and never should be "okay."

If you need a tragic figure let me suggest my mother, Helene Swain. Her sin was raising five healthy boys who all reached the age of nineteen during the sixties. Of those, two served in Vietnam (myself and my brother Steve), one was classified a deserter because he refused to go to Vietnam (my brother John, who died of a drug overdose in 1974, still considered a deserter), one got lost in the counterculture (my brother Philip, who died today), and one got into the National Guard early enough not to get drafted (my brother Bill, now working as an oxygen therapist in San Francisco). Her second great sin was teaching her children that they should act on their beliefs, that bravery consisted of accepting the cost of following those beliefs. Perhaps she never understood, as she raised her sons in the placid fifties, how badly this prepared them to face the world of the sixties, where no choice was really satisfying and the cost for believing anything at all could be one's soul.

Philip died at the age of thirty-five, and it's tempting to ask "Where did he go wrong?" as if it were a great sin in our nation of prosperity and power to die at so young an age. But the fact is that Philip didn't choose to die so young, it was simply the result of a choice he made in the sixties, of a personality he accepted and stuck doggedly to long after it had gone out of fashion.

By the time he approached adulthood the world he entered was divided into two diametrically opposed camps. On the one hand, the college students were marching daily against the war and the draft, and on the other, the middle class was stubbornly holding on to what they saw as American values (many people forget that as late as 1971, a hundred thousand hard hats marched in New York City at lunchtime to show their support for "our boys in Vietnam"). Bob Dylan had sung of answers in the wind, and Timothy Leary had long before encouraged everyone to "Turn on, tune in, and drop out." The drug culture was less a political ideology than an alternative view of reality, but it did in theory support certain virtues that Philip's life in fact displayed: gentleness and a lack of concern for material things. Philip never went to college but he could have joined in on the easy sex and light drugs, as so many did, and still maintained his own self-interest, played it cool and been a part of it without losing himself in it. But he chose not to. He chose instead to believe in a world that probably never really existed, where a young man with a guitar could strum away his life and people would listen.

Years later Philip would call me long distance from Phoenix and ask me if I wanted to hear his latest song. If I did I had to call him back because he couldn't afford the phone call. He would then sit back and sing, sometimes a song, but more often than not a wandering group of melodies that never seemed to end. Sometimes he was high when he called and often very sentimental. He'd play and every so often he'd ask, "What do you think of that?" But with the phone set on the floor in front of him, I was never sure he heard my answer.

He got into drugs in a big way in the sixties. He didn't dabble, he invested his life in what was there, not only because it was a kick or a thrill, which it was, but because he could see how patently stupid the other side was. When the FBI raided my mother's home in Tucson looking for my brother John, and John fled up to the sanctuary of the Catalina Mountains, my brother Philip made a trip up the canyon with supplies. Philip told me later how John, who never fit in anywhere, found for a while a peace that he never knew before or after. When John died, Philip wanted to spread the ashes over that spot because John had loved being there so much. Years afterward Philip would speak of John as no one outside of my mother ever did, with love and tenderness.

Philip's life never left the sixties. Dylan always remained his hero, and even if that may seem trite and out of fashion now, I respect the way he clung to the belief that there was something there that he could add to, not only a way of life but a philosophy that he believed in. He went through several drug rehabilitation programs, suffered with hepatitis, and finally came out of it tired and beaten perhaps, but with his sentimental streak intact. His family, though it was spread throughout the country, was always important to him, and he would call me at all hours of the night whenever the spirit moved him, and he always ended those conversations with "I love you Danny." Two summers ago I went to visit

109

him and he met my two sons for the first time. I remember that he didn't have a thing to eat in the house, but he played the guitar for us and gave my youngest boy his clay bongo drum.

Perhaps there are Philips in every generation, and perhaps the sixties were no more responsible for what he became than anything else. Perhaps we never really make choices in life and it was simply coincidence that I ended up in Nam and Philip in Maricopa County Hospital, but I don't for a moment believe that. In a world where people can blindly march to a war that is as stupid and ridiculous as Vietnam, let's hope that there will always be another side that screams out in disgust and anger and simply opts out of even the margins we've created. If not, then we are doomed to repeat our lemmings' march to another war.

Helene Swain has to bury another one of her children. No one from the VFW will be there to help her. No one will see the death as the tragic loss of an American boy in a silly war. I remember that during the time when my brother John was being hunted by the FBI my mother wrote a letter to Stewart Udall, her senator. In it she said that two of her sons had already served in Vietnam. Wasn't that enough? she asked. How much did one family have to give? He never answered.

We often hear that we lost close to fifty thousand lives in Vietnam and that the suffering goes on for many thousands more who have to relive the anguish of having served. In the final analysis I guess that's true, but it certainly is only half the story and half the cost. If there is any solace in having served in Vietnam it's in the fact that people are beginning to see what the cost was. But there were other costs as well, in the lives of so many who chose not to be a part of the system that created the conditions for war. They suffer as well and the death count keeps mounting. God bless you Philip. I love you too.

The words and images on the following pages have been compiled by artist Kim Jones. They relate to performances which he has done over the past ten years in galleries and museums and on the street.

vietnam dong ha marines it's summer time 125 degrees heat sweat like pigs work like dogs live like rats red dust covered everything

celts druids or priests great festival once every five years colossal images of wicker work or of wood and grass were constructed these were filled with live men cattle and animals of other kinds fire was then applied to the images and they were burned with their living contents

running with friends killing birds and putting the feathers in our hair

macarther park on a bench near the lake shot a pigeon with a sling shot crippled was staggering around picked up panicked what to do had to finish off held under water looked around no one was watching the bird struggled could feel muscles eyes bulged wide one last time a powerful straining beak wide open relaxed pulled out of water feeling guilty looking around quickly hide in near garbage can

sunset on the oceanfront walk a black man standing near a burning garbage can said your rats are in there and laughed

north viets would hit us with rocket artillery and mortars we would jump in our rat holes we lived in a constant state of tension anger there were no hamburgers or ice cream only occasional warm beer or coke

vegetation wars picking special leaves and flowers laying them on the dirt and concrete attacking them with rocks and dirt clods some were killed some wounded a strong leaf could survive many attacks until its stem was crushed

the smell of burning leaves

east indian island of bali the mice which ravage the rice fields are caught in great numbers and burned in the same way that corpses are burned but two of the captured mice are allowed to live and receive a little packet of white linen when the people bow down before them as before gods and let them go

rats live on no evil star a palindrome on the side of a barn in ireland

vietnam dong ha marine corps our camp covered with rats they crawled over us at night they got in our food we catch them in cages and burn them to death i remember the smell

some enjoyed watching the terrified ball of flame run

vietnam dong ha marine corps feel sorry for one and let it go my comrades attack me verbally

vietnam dong ha marine corps guard duty it was my turn to sleep a duck was quacking bothered me threw a rock at the duck hit its head next morning it was staggering around crippled I couldn't kill it a friend crushed its head with his boot

crying very much afraid when my father accidentally kills a squirrel with a 22 rifle

shooting lizards for sport with a friend on his ranch

he told her on their first date how he used to throw cats out of a speeding auto on the freeway she said she loved cats later they were married

boardwalk venice california a woman is concerned about a crippled pigeon it should be put out of its misery she said i crushed the pigeon's head with a hammer on the concrete a spectator laughed with delight

making faces in the wet sand crushing them with rocks and fists

going out to the swamp near my house catching frogs and snakes laying in the tall green grass watching the sky

* * * * *

When they were burning and screaming, I bent down and screamed with them. I don't know whether it helped them or not. Probably, it didn't mean anything to them, but it meant something to me. It was my way of connecting with them somehow, although they were feeling the pain, not I. They were like scapegoats.[1]

* * * * *

I asked the audience to come into a very small room so that we were packed tightly into this small space. Then I tacked to the wall a piece of white paper. I took off all my clothes so that my whole body was exposed. I wore sticks on my head and pencils tied to the sticks. Then I cut myself with a razor blade twenty-seven times, three times for each segment on my arms and legs and across my chest. And I began to draw a self-portrait on the paper, first drawing with the pencils on my head, which was mostly scribbling, and then with my hands, making flowing lines. When I was bleeding enough, I pressed by body against the paper and there was a blood smear. I laid down on a small ledge off the floor, asked someone to turn off the lights, and then slowly started whispering: "Get out of my room get out, get out." I said this louder and louder until I was screaming. Most everybody left, and that was the end of the performance.[2]

*　*　*　*　*

The "Brotherhood" performance was about sharing with another man. It became a very quiet thing between us. We were sharing this cigar. We smoked it and then we laid it between our arms and let it burn our skin for a while. When it hurt too much, we took another puff. When it became too painful, we agreed between each other, that this was enough, we were through. It was a shared thing, like a tattoo, a little sacrifice.[3]

*　*　*　*　*

I walked Wilshire Boulevard from Wilshire One to Ocean Avenue on January 28 sunrise to sunset and on February 4 sunset to sunrise. The photographer drove a car and would meet me at various points along the route.

When I decided to do the piece, I wasn't sure I could walk the length of Wilshire Boulevard with the mud and the structure. I was concerned about the cold, the rain, the police, people in general, and the distance. After I started, most of these fears were more under control. I was concentrating on walking, balancing the structure, feeling the shoulder straps, crouching and turning sideways for obstacles like trees, buildings, lamp posts, and people.

We marked down an approximate schedule on a road map estimating how far along the boulevard I would be at certain times. I was able to walk very fast for about the first half of the distance, well ahead of schedule. After that, I began to progressively slow down, resting more and more until the end. My legs and feet felt all right, but my back and shoulders hurt from the straps digging into my skin.

Mailers were sent out. Some people were able to locate me while others couldn't. Some I talked with, some I sat in restaurants and had coffee with, and some I walked with for a few blocks. One woman met me at the Harbor Freeway overpass and walked a block or so behind me most of the way.

The piece was also observed by the Wilshire Boulevard public, an unannounced event, walking in and out of their lives. A laughing gas station attendant refused to let me use his restroom. I stopped to rest in front of a Wells Fargo Bank. The police were called. They checked me out and finally let me go after telling me to watch my step. A man in Westwood asked if it was a fraternity initiation. A little old lady said, "Oh, you must be one of those back packers from back East."[4]

NOTES

1. "Rat Piece," February 17, 1976, Cal State, Los Angeles. I burned three rats to death.

2. "Cut Piece," performance at University of California, Irvine, 1981, class in performance art taught by Barbara Smith. Substitute teaching: Kim Jones and Paul McCarthy. The last section of this performance was inspired by Bruce Nauman.

3. Exile Gallery, Los Angeles, 1982, series of performances with Paul McCarthy, Harry Kipper, Kim Jones. "Brotherhood" done with Gary Worrell, volunteer from the audience.

4. Sponsored by CARP, Barbara Burden, and Marilyn Nix, Los Angeles.

Big Bertha Stories

Donald is home again, laughing and singing. He comes home from Central City, Kentucky, near the strip mines, only when he feels like it, like an absentee landlord checking on his property. He is always in such a good humor when he returns that Jeannette forgives him. She cooks for him—ugly, pasty things she gets with food stamps. Sometimes he brings steaks and ice cream, occasionally money. Rodney, their child, hides in the closet when he arrives, and Donald goes around the house talking loudly about the little boy named Rodney who used to live here—the one who fell into a septic tank, or the one stolen by Gypsies. The stories change. Rodney usually stays in the closet until he has to pee, and then he hugs his father's knees, forgiving him, just as Jeannette does. The way Donald saunters through the door, swinging a six-pack of beer, with a big grin on his face, takes her breath away. He leans against the door facing, looking sexy in his baseball cap and his shaggy red beard and his sunglasses. He wears sunglasses to be like the Blues Brothers, but he in no way resembles either of the Blues Brothers. I should have my head examined, Jeannette thinks.

The last time Donald was home, they went to the shopping center to buy Rodney some shoes advertised on sale. They stayed at the shopping center half the afternoon, just looking around. Donald and Rodney played video games. Jeannette felt they were a normal family. Then, in the parking lot, they stopped to watch a man on a platform demonstrating snakes. Children were petting a twelve-foot python coiled around the man's shoulders. Jeannette felt faint.

"Snakes won't hurt you unless you hurt them," said Donald as Rod-

121

ney stroked the snake.

"It feels like chocolate," he said.

The snake man took a tarantula from a plastic box and held it lovingly in his palm. He said, "If you drop a tarantula, it will shatter like a Christmas ornament."

"I hate this," said Jeannette.

"Let's get out of here," said Donald.

Jeannette felt her family disintegrating like a spider shattering as Donald hurried them away from the shopping center. Rodney squalled and Donald dragged him along. Jeannette wanted to stop for ice cream. She wanted them all to sit quietly together in a booth, but Donald rushed them to the car, and he drove them home in silence, his face growing grim.

"Did you have bad dreams about the snakes?" Jeannette asked Rodney the next morning at breakfast. They were eating pancakes made with generic pancake mix. Rodney slapped his fork in the pond of syrup on his pancakes. "The black racer is the farmer's friend," he said soberly, repeating a fact learned from the snake man.

"Big Bertha kept black racers," said Donald. "She trained them for the 500." Donald doesn't tell Rodney ordinary children's stories. He tells him a series of strange stories he makes up about Big Bertha. Big Bertha is what he calls the huge strip-mining machine in Muhlenberg County, but he has Rodney believing that Big Bertha is a female version of Paul Bunyan.

"Snakes don't run in the 500," said Rodney.

"This wasn't the Indy 500, or the Daytona 500, none of your well-known 500s," said Donald. "This was the Possum Trot 500, and it was a long time ago. Big Bertha started the original 500, with snakes. Black racers and blue racers mainly. Also some red-and-white-striped racers, but those are rare."

"We always ran for the hoe if we saw a black racer," Jeannette said, remembering her childhood in the country.

In a way, Donald's absences are a fine arrangement, even considerate. He is sparing them his darkest moods, when he can't cope with his memories of Vietnam. Vietnam had never seemed such a meaningful fact until a couple of years ago, when he grew depressed and moody, and then he started going away to Central City. He frightened Jeannette, and she always said the wrong thing in her efforts to soothe him. If the welfare people find out he is spending occasional weekends at home, and even bringing some money, they will cut off her assistance. She applied for welfare because she can't depend on him to send money, but she knows he blames her for losing faith in him. He isn't really working regularly at the strip mines. He is mostly just hanging around there, watching the land being scraped away, trees coming down, bushes flung in the air. Sometimes he operates a steam shovel, and when he comes home his clothes are filled with the clay and it is caked on his shoes. The clay is the color of butterscotch pudding.

At first, he tried to explain to Jeannette. He said, "If we could have had tanks over there as big as Big Bertha, we wouldn't have lost the war. Strip mining is just like what we were doing over there. We were stripping off the top. The topsoil is like the culture and the people, the best part of the land and the country. America was just stripping off the top, the best. We ruined it. Here, at least, the coal companies have to plant vetch and loblolly pines and all kinds of trees and bushes. If we'd done that in Vietnam, maybe we'd have left that country in better shape."

"Wasn't Vietnam a long time ago?" Jeannette asked.

She didn't want to hear about Vietnam. She thought it was unhealthy to dwell on it so much. He should live in the present. Her mother is afraid Donald will do something violent, because she once read in the newspaper that a veteran in Louisville held his little girl hostage in their apartment until he had a shootout with the police and was killed. But Jeannette can't imagine Donald doing anything so extreme. When she first met him, several years ago, at her parents' pit-barbecue luncheonette, where she was working then, he had a good job at a lumberyard and he dressed nicely. He took her out to eat at a fancy restaurant. They got plastered and ended up in a motel in Tupelo, Mississippi, on Elvis Presley Boulevard. Back then, he talked nostalgically about his year in Vietnam, about how beautiful it was, how different the people were. He could never seem to explain what he meant. "They're just different," he said.

They went riding around in a yellow 1957 Chevy convertible. He drives too fast now, but he didn't then, maybe because he was so protective of the car. It was a classic. He sold it three years ago and made a good profit. About the time he sold the Chevy, his moods began changing, his even-tempered nature shifting, like driving on a smooth interstate and then switching to a secondary road. He had headaches and bad dreams. But his nightmares seemed trivial. He dreamed of riding a train through the Rocky Mountains, of hijacking a plane to Cuba, of stringing up barbed wire around the house. He dreamed he lost a doll. He got drunk and rammed the car, the Chevy's successor, into a Civil War statue in front of the courthouse. When he got depressed over the meaninglessness of his job, Jeannette felt guilty about spending money on something nice for the house, and she tried to make him feel his job had meaning by reminding him that, after all, they had a child to think of. "I don't like his name," Donald said once. "What a stupid name, Rodney. I never did like it."

Rodney has dreams about Big Bertha, echoes of his father's nightmare, like TV cartoon versions of Donald's memories of the war. But Rodney loves the stories, even though they are confusing, with lots of loose ends. The latest in the Big Bertha series is "Big Bertha and the Neutron Bomb." Last week it was "Big Bertha and the MX Missile." In the new story, Big

Bertha takes a trip to California to go surfing with Big Mo, her male counterpart. On the beach, corn dogs and snow cones are free and the surfboards turn into dolphins. Everyone is having fun until the neutron bomb comes. Rodney loves the part where everyone keels over dead. Donald acts it out, collapsing on the rug. All the dolphins and the surfers keel over, everyone except Big Bertha. Big Bertha is so big she is immune to the neutron bomb.

"Those stories aren't true," Jeannette tells Rodney.

Rodney staggers and falls down on the rug, with his arms and legs akimbo. He gets the giggles and can't stop. When his spasms finally subside, he says, "I told Scottie Bidwell about Big Bertha and he didn't believe me."

Donald picks Rodney up under the armpits and sets him upright. "You tell Scottie Bidwell if he saw Big Bertha he would pee in his pants on the spot, he would be so impressed."

"Are you scared of Big Bertha?"

"No, I'm not. Big Bertha is just like a wonderful woman, a big fat woman who can sing the blues. Have you ever heard Big Mama Thornton?"

"No."

"Well, Big Bertha's like her, only she's the size of a tall building. She's slow as a turtle when she crosses the road, they have to reroute traffic. She's big enough to straddle a four-lane highway. She's so tall she can see all the way to Tennessee, and when she belches, there's a tornado. She's really something. She can even fly."

"She's too big to fly," Rodney says doubtfully. He makes a face like a wadded-up washrag and Donald wrestles him to the floor again.

Donald has been drinking all evening, but he isn't drunk. The ice cubes melt and he pours the drink out and refills it. He keeps on talking. Jeannette cannot remember him talking so much about the war. He is telling her about an ammunitions dump. Jeannette had the vague idea that an ammo dump is a mound of shotgun shells, heaps of cartridge casings and bomb shells, or whatever is left over, a vast waste pile from the war, but Donald says that is wrong. He has spent an hour describing it in detail, so that she will understand.

He refills the glass with ice, some 7-Up, and a shot of Jim Beam. He slams doors and drawers, looking for a compass. Jeannette can't keep track of the conversation. It doesn't matter that her hair is uncombed and her lipstick eaten away. He isn't seeing her.

"I want to draw the compound for you," he says, sitting down at the table with a sheet of Rodney's tablet paper.

Donald draws the map in red-and-blue ballpoint, with asterisks and technical labels that mean nothing to her. He draws some circles with the compass and measures some angles. He makes a red dot on an oblique line, a path that leads to the ammo dump.

"That's where I was. Right there," he says. "There was a water buffalo that tripped a land mine and its horn just flew off and stuck in the wall of the barracks like a machete thrown backhanded." He puts a dot where the land mine was, and he doodles awhile with the red ballpoint pen, scribbling something on the edge of the map that looks like feathers. "The dump was here and I was there and over there was where we piled the sandbags. And here were the tanks." He draws tanks, a row of squares with handles—guns sticking out.

"Why are you going to so much trouble to tell me about a buffalo horn that got stuck in a wall?" she wants to know.

But Donald just looks at her as though she has asked something obvious.

"Maybe I *could* understand if you'd let me," she says cautiously.

"You could never understand." He draws another tank.

In bed, it is the same it has been since he started going away to Central City—the way he claims his side of the bed, turning away from her. Tonight, she reaches for him and he lets her be close to him. She cries for awhile and he lies there, waiting for her to finish, as though she were merely putting on make-up.

"Do you want me to tell you a Big Bertha story?" he asks playfully.

"You act like you're in love with Big Bertha."

He laughs, breathing on her. But he won't come closer.

"You don't care what I look like anymore," she says. "What am I supposed to think?"

"There's nobody else. There's not anybody but you."

Loving a giant machine is incomprehensible to Jeannette. There must be another woman, someone that large in his mind. Jeannette has seen the strip-mining machine. The top of the crane is visible beyond a rise along the Western Kentucky Parkway. The strip mining is kept just out of sight of travelers because it would give them a poor image of Kentucky.

For three weeks, Jeannette has been seeing a psychologist at the free mental health clinic. He's a small man from out of state. His name is Dr. Robinson, but she calls him The Rapist, because the word *therapist* can be divided into two words, *the rapist*. He doesn't think her joke is clever, and he acts as though he has heard it a thousand times before. He has a habit of saying, "Go with that feeling," the same way Bob Newhart did on his old TV show. It's probably the first lesson in the textbook, Jeannette thinks.

She told him about Donald's last days on his job at the lumberyard— how he let the stack of lumber fall deliberately and didn't know why, and about how he went away soon after that, and how the Big Bertha stories started. Dr. Robinson seems to be waiting for her to make something out of it all, but it's maddening that he won't tell her what to do. After three visits, Jeannette has grown angry with him, and now she's holding back things. She won't tell him whether Donald slept with her or not when he came home last. Let him guess, she thinks.

"Talk about yourself," he says.

"What about me?"

"You speak so vaguely about Donald that I get the feeling that you see him as somebody larger than life. I can't quite picture him. That makes me wonder what that says about you." He touches the end of his tie to his nose and sniffs it.

When Jeannette suggests that she bring Donald in, the therapist looks bored and says nothing.

"He had another nightmare when he was home last," Jeannette says. "He dreamed he was crawling through tall grass and people were after him."

"How do *you* feel about that?" The Rapist asks eagerly.

"I didn't have the nightmare," she says coldly. "Donald did. I came to you to get advice about Donald, and you're acting like I'm the one who's crazy. I'm not crazy. But I'm lonely."

Jeannette's mother, behind the counter of the luncheonette, looks lovingly at Rodney pushing buttons on the jukebox in the corner. "It's a shame about that youngun," she says tearfully. "That boy needs a daddy."

"What are you trying to tell me? That I should file for divorce and get Rodney a new daddy?"

Her mother looks hurt. "No, honey," she says. "You need to get Donald to seek the Lord. And you need to pray more. You haven't been going to church lately."

"Have some barbecue," Jeannette's father booms, as he comes in from the back kitchen. "And I want you to take a pound home with you. You've got a growing boy to feed."

"I want to take Rodney to church," Mama says. "I want to show him off, and it might do some good."

"People will think he's an orphan," Dad says.

"I don't care," Mama says. "I just love him to pieces and I want to take him to church. Do you care if I take him to church, Jeannette?"

"No. I don't care if you take him to church." She takes the pound of barbecue from her father. Grease splotches the brown wrapping paper. Dad has given them so much barbecue that Rodney is burned out on it and won't eat it anymore.

Jeannette wonders if she would file for divorce if she could get a job. It is a thought—for the child's sake, she thinks. But there aren't many jobs around. With the cost of a babysitter, it doesn't pay her to work. When Donald first went away, her mother kept Rodney and she had a good job, waitressing at a steak house, but the steak house burned down one night—a grease fire in the kitchen. After that, she couldn't find a steady job, and she was reluctant to ask her mother to keep Rodney again because of her bad hip. At the steak house, men gave her tips and left their telephone numbers on the bill when they paid. They tucked dollar bills and notes in the pockets of her apron. One note said, "I want to hold your muffins." They were real-estate developers and businessmen on important missions for the Tennessee Valley Authority. They were boisterous and they drank too much. They said they'd take her for a cruise on the Delta Queen, but she didn't believe them. She knew how expensive that was. They talked about their speedboats and invited her for rides on Lake Barkley, or for spins in their private planes. They always used the word *spin*. The idea made her dizzy. Once, Jeannette let an electronics salesman take her for a ride in his Cadillac, and they breezed down The Trace, the wilderness road that winds down the Land Between the Lakes. His car had automatic windows and a stereo system and lighted computer-screen numbers on the dash that told him how many miles to the gallon he was getting and other statistics. He said the numbers distracted him and he had almost had several wrecks. At the restaurant, he had been flamboyant, admired by his companions. Alone with Jeannette in the Cadillac, on The Trace, he was shy and awkward, and really not very interesting. The most interesting thing about him, Jeannette thought, was all the lighted numbers on his dashboard. The Cadillac had everything but video games. But she'd rather be riding around with Donald, no matter where they ended up.

While the social worker is there, filling out her report, Jeannette listens for Donald's car. When the social worker drove up, the flutter and wheeze of her car sounded like Donald's old Chevy, and for a moment Jeannette's mind lapsed back in time. Now she listens, hoping he won't drive up. The social worker is younger than Jeannette and has been to college. Her name is Miss Bailey, and she's excessively cheerful, as though in her line of work she has seen hardships that make Jeannette's troubles seem like a trip to Hawaii.

"Is your little boy still having those bad dreams?" Miss Bailey asks, looking up from her clipboard.

Jeannette nods and looks at Rodney, who has his finger in his mouth and won't speak.

"Has the cat got your tongue?" Miss Bailey asks.

"Show her your pictures, Rodney." Jeanette explains, "He won't talk about the dreams, but he draws pictures of them."

Rodney brings his tablet of pictures and flips through them silently. Miss Bailey says, "Hmm." They are stark line drawings, remarkably steady lines for his age. "What is this one?" she asks. "Let me guess. Two scoops of ice cream?"

The picture is two huge circles, filling the page, with three tiny stick people in the corner.

"These are Big Bertha's titties," says Rodney.

Miss Bailey chuckles and winks at Jeannette. "What do you like to read, hon?" she asks Rodney.

"Nothing."

"He can read," says Jeannette. "He's smart."

"Do you like to read?" Miss Bailey asks Jeannette. She glances at the pile of paperbacks on the coffee table. She is probably going to ask where Jeannette got the money for them.

"I don't read," says Jeannette. "If I read, I just go crazy."

When she told The Rapist she couldn't concentrate on anything serious, he said she read romance novels in order to escape from reality. "Reality, hell!" she had said. "Reality's my whole problem."

"It's too bad Rodney's not here," Donald is saying. Rodney is in the closet again. "Santa Claus has to take back all these toys. Rodney would love this bicycle! And this Pac-Man game. Santa has to take back so many things he'll have to have a pickup truck!"

"You didn't bring him anything. You never bring him anything," says Jeannette.

He has brought doughnuts and dirty laundry. The clothes he is wearing are caked with clay. His beard is lighter from working out in the sun, and he looks his usual joyful self, the way he always is before his moods take over, like migraine headaches, which some people describe as storms.

Donald coaxes Rodney out of the closet with the doughnuts.

"Were you a good boy this week?"

"I don't know."

"I hear you went to the shopping center and showed out." It is not true that Rodney made a big scene. Jeannette has already explained that Rodney was upset because she wouldn't buy him an Atari. But she didn't blame him for crying. She was tired of being unable to buy him anything.

Rodney eats two doughnuts and Donald tells him a long, confusing story about Big Bertha and a rock-and-roll band. Rodney interrupts him with dozens of questions. In the story, the rock-and-roll band gives a concert in a place that turns out to be a toxic-waste dump and the contamination is spread all over the country. Big Bertha's solution to this problem is not at all clear. Jeannette stays in the kitchen, trying to think of something original to do with instant potatoes and leftover barbecue.

"We can't go on like this," she says that evening in bed. "We're just hurting each other. Something has to change."

He grins like a kid. "Coming home from Muhlenberg County is like R and R—rest and recreation. I explain that in case you think R and R means rock-and-roll. Or maybe rumps and rears. Or rust and rot." He laughs and draws a circle in the air with his cigarette.

"I'm not that dumb."

"When I leave, I go back to the mines." He sighs, as though the mines were some eternal burden.

Her mind skips ahead to the future: Donald locked away somewhere, coloring in a coloring book and making clay pots, her and Rodney in some other town, with another man—someone dull and not at all sexy. Summoning up her courage, she says, "I haven't been through what you've been through and maybe I don't have a right to say this, but sometimes I think you act superior because you went to Vietnam, like nobody can ever know what you know. Well, maybe not. But you've still got your legs, even if you don't know what to do with what's between them anymore." Bursting into tears of apology, she can't help adding, "You can't go on telling Rodney those awful stories. He has nightmares when you're gone."

Donald rises from bed and grabs Rodney's picture from the dresser, holding it as he might have held a hand grenade. "Kids betray you," he says, turning the picture in his hand.

"If you cared about him, you'd stay here." As he sets the picture down, she asks, "What can I do? How can I understand what's going on in your mind? Why do you go there? Strip mining's bad for the ecology and you don't have any business strip mining."

"My job is serious, Jeannette. I run that steam shovel and put the topsoil back on. I'm reclaiming the land." He keeps talking, in a gentler voice, about strip mining, the same old things she has heard before, comparing Big Bertha to a supertank. If only they had had Big Bertha in Vietnam. He says, "When they strip off the top, I keep looking for those tunnels where the Vietcong hid. They had so many tunnels it was unbelievable. Imagine Mammoth Cave going all the way across Kentucky."

"Mammoth Cave's one of the natural wonders of the world," says Jeannette brightly. She is saying the wrong thing again.

At the kitchen table at 2:00 A.M., he's telling about C-5As. A C-5A is so big it can carry troops and tanks and helicopters, but it's not big enough to hold Big Bertha. Nothing could hold Big Bertha. He rambles on, and when Jeannette shows him Rodney's drawing of the circles, Donald smiles. Dreamily, he begins talking about women's breasts and thighs—the large, round thighs and big round breasts of American women, contrasted with the frail, delicate beauty of the Orientals. It is like comparing oven broilers and banties, he says. Jeannette relaxes. A confession about another lover from long ago is not so hard to take. He seems stuck on the breasts and thighs of American women—insisting that she understand how small and delicate the Orientals are, but then he abruptly returns to tanks and helicopters.

"A Bell Huey Cobra—my God, what a beautiful machine. So efficient!" Donald takes the food processor blade from the drawer where Jeannette keeps it. He says, "A rotor blade from a chopper could just slice anything to bits."

"Don't do that," Jeannette says.

He is trying to spin the blade on the counter, like a top. "Here's what would happen when a chopper blade hits a power line—not many of those over there!—or a tree. Not many trees, either, come to think of it, after all the Agent Orange." He drops the blade and it glances off the open drawer and falls to the floor, spiking the vinyl.

At first, Jeannette thinks the screams are hers, but they are his. She watches him cry. She has never seen anyone cry so hard, like an intense summer thundershower. All she knows to do is shove Kleenex at him. Finally, he is able to say, "You thought I was going to hurt you. That's why I'm crying."

"Go ahead and cry," Jeannette says, holding him close.

"Don't go away."

"I'm right here. I'm not going anywhere."

In the night, she still listens, knowing his monologue is being burned like a tattoo into her brain. She will never forget it. His voice grows soft and he plays with a ballpoint pen, jabbing holes in a paper towel. Bullet holes, she thinks. His beard is like a bird's nest, woven with dark corn silks.

"This is just a story," he says. "Don't mean nothing. Just relax." She is sitting on the hard edge of the kitchen chair, her toes cold on the floor, waiting. His tears have dried up and left a slight catch in his voice.

"We were in a big camp near a village. It was pretty routine and kind of soft there for awhile. Now and then we'd go into Da Nang and whoop it up. We had been in the jungle for several months, so the two months at this village was sort of a rest—an R and R almost. Don't shiver. This is just a little story. Don't mean nothing! This is nothing, compared to what I could tell you. Just listen. We lost our fear. At night there would be some incoming and we'd see these tracers in the sky, like shooting stars up close, but it was all pretty minor and we didn't take it seriously, after what we'd been through. In the village I knew this Vietnamese family—a woman and her two daughters. They sold Cokes and beer to GIs. The oldest daughter was named Phan. She could speak a little English. She was really smart. I used to go see them in their hooch in the afternoons— in the siesta time of day. It was so hot there. Phan was beautiful, like the country. The village was ratty, but the country was pretty. And she was beautiful, just like she had grown up out of the jungle, like one of those flowers that bloomed high up in the trees and freaked us out sometimes, thinking it was a sniper. She was so gentle, with these eyes shaped like peach pits, and she was no bigger than a child of maybe thirteen or four-teen. I felt funny about her size at first, but later it didn't matter. It was just some wonderful feature about her, like a woman's hair, or her breasts."

He stops and listens, the way they used to listen for crying sounds when Rodney was a baby. He says, "She'd take those big banana leaves and fan me while I lay there in the heat."

"I didn't know they had bananas over there."

"There's a lot you don't know! Listen! Phan was twenty-three, and her brothers were off fighting. I never even asked which side they were fight-ing on." He laughs. "She got a kick out of the word *fan*. I told her *fan* was the same word as her name. She thought I meant her name was banana. In Vietnamese the same word can have a dozen different meanings, depending on your tone of voice. I bet you didn't know that, did you?"

"No. What happened to her?"

"I don't know."

"Is that the end of the story?"

"I don't know." Donald pauses, then goes on talking about the village, the girl, the banana leaves, talking in a monotone that is making Jeannette's flesh crawl. He could be the news radio from the next room.

"You must have really liked that place. Do you wish you could go back there to find out what happened to her?"

"It's not there anymore," he says. "It blew up."

Donald abruptly goes to the bathroom. She hears the water running, the pipes in the basement shaking.

"It was so pretty," he says when he returns. He rubs his elbow absentmindedly. "That jungle was the most beautiful place in the world. You'd have thought you were in paradise. But we blew it sky-high."

In her arms, he is shaking, like the pipes in the basement, which are still vibrating. Then the pipes let go, after a long shudder, but he continues to tremble.

They were driving to the Veterans Hospital. It was Donald's idea. She didn't have to persuade him. When she made up the bed that morning— with a finality that shocked her, as though she knew they wouldn't be in it again together—he told her it would be like R and R. Rest was what he needed. Neither of them had slept at all during the night. Jeannette felt she had to stay awake, to listen for more.

"Talk about strip mining," she says now. "That's what they'll do to your head. They'll dig out all those ugly memories, I hope. We don't need them around here." She pats his knee.

It is a cloudless day, not the setting for this sober journey. She drives and Donald goes along obediently, with the resignation of an old man being taken to a rest home. They are driving through southern Illinois, known as Little Egypt, for some obscure reason Jeannette has never understood. Donald still talks, but very quietly, without urgency. When he points out the scenery, Jeannette thinks of the early days of their marriage, when they would take a drive like this and laugh hysterically. Now Jeannette points out funny things they see. The Little Egypt Hot Dog World, Pharaoh Cleaners, Pyramid Body Shop. She is scarcely aware that she is driving, and when she sees a sign, Little Egypt Starlite Club, she is confused for a moment, wondering where she has been transported.

As they part, he asks, "What will you tell Rodney if I don't come back? What if they keep me here indefinitely."

"You're coming back. I'm telling him you're coming back soon."

"Tell him I went off with Big Bertha. Tell him she's taking me on a sea cruise, to the South Seas."

"No. You can tell him that yourself."

He starts singing a jumpy tune. He grins at her and pokes her in the ribs.

"You're coming back," she says.

Donald writes from the VA hospital, saying that he is making progress. They are running tests, and he meets in a therapy group in which all the veterans trade memories. Jeannette is no longer on welfare because she now has a job waitressing at Fred's Family Restaurant. She waits on families, waits for Donald to come home so they can come here and eat together like a family. The fathers look at her with downcast eyes, and the children throw food. While Donald is gone, she rearranges the furniture. She reads some books from the library. She does a lot of thinking. It occurs to her that even though she loved him, she has thought of Donald primarily as a husband, a provider, someone whose name she shared, the father of her child, someone like the fathers who come to the Wednesday night all-you-can-eat fish fry. She hasn't thought of him as himself. She wasn't brought up that way, to examine someone's soul. When it comes to something deep inside, nobody will take it out and examine it, the way they will look at clothing in a store for flaws in the manufacturing. She tries to explain all this to The Rapist, and he says she's looking better, got sparkle in her eyes. "Big deal," says Jeannette. "Is that all you can say?"

She takes Rodney to the shopping center, their favorite thing to do together, even though Rodney always begs to buy something. They go to Penney's perfume counter. There, she usually hits a sample bottle of cologne—Chantilly or Charlie or something strong. Today she hits two or three and comes out of Penney's smelling like a flower garden.

"You stink!" Rodney cries, wrinkling his nose like a rabbit.

"Big Bertha smells like this, only a thousand times worse, she's so big," says Jeannette impulsively. "Didn't Daddy tell you that?"

"Daddy's a messenger from the devil."

This is an idea he must have gotten from church. Her parents have been taking him every Sunday. When Jeannette tries to reassure him about his father, Rodney is skeptical. "He gets that funny look on his face like he can see through me," the child says.

"Something's missing," Jeannette says, with a rush of optimism, a feeling of recognition. "Something happened to him once and took out the part that shows how much he cares about us."

"The way we had the cat fixed?"

"I guess. Something like that." The appropriateness of his remark stuns her, as though, in a way, the child has understood Donald all along. Rodney's pictures have been more peaceful lately, pictures of skinny trees and airplanes flying low. This morning he drew pictures of tall grass, with creatures hiding in it. The grass is tilted at an angle, as though a light breeze is blowing through it.

With her paycheck, Jeannette buys Rodney a present, a miniature trampoline they have seen advertised on television. It is called Mr. Bouncer. Rodney is thrilled about the trampoline, and he jumps on it until his face is red. Jeannette discovers that she enjoys it too. She puts it out on the grass, and they take turns jumping. She has an image of herself on the trampoline, her sailor collar flapping at the moment when Donald returns and sees her flying. One day a neighbor driving by slows down and calls out to Jeannette as she is bouncing on the trampoline, "You'll tear your insides loose!" Jeannette starts thinking about that, and the idea is so horrifying she stops jumping so much. That night, she has a nightmare about the trampoline. In her dream, she is jumping on soft moss, and then it turns into a springy pile of dead bodies.

I've always felt like I should apologize for my father being a "lifer" in the army. I believe it was the way the media portrayed the military in Vietnam during the years I became aware of the war in larger terms than just my father as a soldier fighting for his country. Sometimes I was even embarrassed that my father was an officer. It seems everything I've read and all the movies I've seen have dealt with the loss and suffering from the young enlisted draftee's point of view. Officers are given in stereotypical costumes, as either the bloodthirsty Patton type or the young inexperienced buffoon that gets you killed. I can't count how many times I've talked or worked with Vietnam vets and didn't mention that my father was an officer, because of the fear that it would place me in the position of defending my father as an officer. Until lately I didn't know how or even why I should speak up.

The profile of the "average" Vietnam vet is widely known now. He was young, often with little education, and poor. These were the guys who didn't have the privilege and means to refuse or evade service. In recent years, I've come to realize my father began his military career the same way.

My father was one of nine children born of illiterate Italian immigrants. He grew up in a poor neighborhood in Akron, Ohio. He won a football scholarship to Akron University but lost it and finished college only by joining the ROTC. Of his nine brothers and sisters, he was the only one to go to college. It was because of ROTC that he became involved with the military. He served his required time to pay back his education and then remained in the service due to his fear that he could not support his new family as a school teacher. In the military he was not only able to take care of us better but he was an officer, not just another poor Italian. I've come to believe these were the biggest reasons for his becoming a "lifer."

I lived in Okinawa for two years while my father went back and forth to Vietnam on his "missions." The Fifth Special Forces group used Okinawa, or "the rock," as their main base of operations. My father would come and go to Vietnam (and other places) for periods as short as two weeks. All of my friends' fathers were soldiers too. The SF took great care of the dependents; other soldiers on leave were always available (even assigned) to the wives and children of the men who were away. They organized picnics and events to keep us busy, but they couldn't keep us busy enough not to notice when our friends left because their fathers were killed or wounded.

We planned for our father's death, always wanting to know from my mother where we were going to live when he was killed, who she was going to marry when he died (another soldier?), and why he had to keep going back to eventually die.

For me the typical scenario of him leaving was: my parents arguing the last couple of days before he left, then at the time of his departure he would be in uniform, kissing my sister and mother goodbye and then me. I always got the traditional, "Take care of your mother and sisters, you're the man of the family now until I come back." There was always that feeling that I would be a soldier when he didn't return, like in Barry Sadler's *Ballad of the Green Beret*. The dying soldier's last words are, "Put silver wings on my son's chest, *make him* one of America's best." Sometimes he left at night and he would speak to me while he sat on my bed. It was very moving to me and I still feel it. I never remember going to the airport to see him off; we usually met him there on his return. The returns were quite wonderful. We were all excited with the relief of actually seeing him and touching him, as proof of his return. We always celebrated his return by having a meal of the foods he missed most while away.

In 1966, after two years of "missions," my father volunteered for a year's duty in Vietnam. My mother talked him into doing it, to get it over with because of the strain the combat duty was putting on the family. We lived during that year with my mother's parents in Kentucky. I remember that year for three reasons: it was the first time I lived in a real civilian town, my grandparents were incredible people, and my father was gone.

It was 1970 when once again my father left for a year's tour overseas, this time to Korea, to command a battalion on the DMZ. We had lived in Korea between 1967 and 1969 where my father at the time had been attaché to KMAG, with special operations, where I presume his SF skills were needed. It was also around 1970 that I started to become more politically aware. We moved to Washington, D.C. and for only the second time I went to a civilian school, a school where the military kids were outnumbered. For the first time I started to watch reports about the war on the evening news, and, more importantly, the antiwar coverage. Never before had my family been truly exposed to this type of news. Being in the Washington, D.C. area, not only did we get the news, but we actually saw some of the demonstrations take place.

I started having problems with the idea that my father had spent a great deal of time in Vietnam. On his return from Korea, I was radically altered in my respect toward him and what he stood for. It was the beginning of a very rough period in our relationship. Not only did I have the war/soldier thing to deal with, but I was also a teenager going through a rebellious time with a vengeance mostly directed at somehow hurting my father and showing him he had no control over me like he had over his "men." From 1971-1976 it was hell at our house. My older sister was going through a similar change—going out with a "long-haired" draft resister, participating in demonstrations, and eventually leaving home.

After all the years of calm obedience, my father lost control of his family. It became a small model of the country, there was a feeling of civil war. We could not talk about politics, much less the length of my hair or manner of dress, and eventually it came to a physical confrontation. I moved into an apartment soon after and finished high school away from home.

My father and I watched the fall of Saigon on TV together, and he said something that stayed with me: he was happy it was over and that, now that I was old enough, I wouldn't have to go. It was sad actually, the relief of the end. We had talked before about why we were involved, how to win, etc., but it was never easy. Usually I was too belligerent, placing him on the defensive, exactly where he didn't need to be. All the military men were on the defensive, placing the blame on each other and on the politicians.

Our military did not get us involved in Vietnam, our elected representatives did. The military was an easy target for all sides—it was easier for the press to show the defeat of soldiers than of men in office. Easier to single out a GI on leave to harass than to identify the guy in the suit who helped keep it going.

I feel bitter about the politicians, local and national, who clung to the nationalistic rhetoric that kept men dying. I'm also bitter about a less visible group that felt it was their duty to abuse soldiers. I have always wanted to meet one of the latter group (no desire the first), someone who spat on or cursed "baby killer" type lines at returning soldiers who were confused and wanted out of the war as badly as anyone.

I was never involved in the antiwar movement. On only two occasions did I take part in any type of visible reaction to the war. The first was in 1966 on Okinawa; we had a parade, an "anti-antiwar" parade in support of our fathers and all the soldiers in Vietnam. We were upset by the news of antiwar demonstrations, thinking that the people were actually criticizing our fathers. A photo and a long article ran in the *Stars and Stripes*. The second time was an antiwar event. I was in the eighth grade in 1971, and about twenty-five of us planned a school walk-out and sit-in. On the day of the walk-out, we wore our best "freak" clothes and someone carried an upside-down American flag. We yelled things walking in the halls of the school as we left. By the time we got outside there were only about fifteen of us left. We sat on the school's front lawn waving the flag and chanting antiwar slogans. I remember wearing my "Fly the Friendly Skies of Vietnam" T-shirt (a gift from my father). After about ten or twenty minutes the principal came out and talked us into coming back to class. He reasoned with us, told us it was good to see we cared, but that we had to come back in. We went back in with relief. I have no idea what we would have done next. It was actually kind of embarrassing.

I know from conversations with my mother that my father disagreed with government policies on Vietnam. He felt, like many other career military men, that we should not have become involved at all in Vietnam, especially militarily. He was not a political man. Officers are not allowed to voice their opinions on civilian matters—those who do ruin their careers or are fired.

My father killed himself the summer before last. The gun he used, a Browning 9mm, has a story that goes with it. One of the only war stories I ever heard him tell was that he was out at a base camp and a man in a suit landed by helicopter. It was his CIA liaison, who asked if he needed anything. My father requested the gun. When I asked him questions about what he did or saw over there the usual reply was, "I'm not allowed to say anything for ten years." I know now that some of it was true, the secrecy part. From my mother I've learned that he was involved in project "Phoenix," something that the government has tried to keep quiet. I've seen very little written about it, except one article in *Mother Jones*. Project "Phoenix," along with project "Delta" (my father was second commander of Delta project), were American counter-guerrilla organizations. Both groups operated in South Vietnam, Cambodia, Laos, and North Vietnam. Project "Phoenix" was not only a counter-guerrilla outfit, but also an assassination organization. Project "Phoenix" would pinpoint a high-ranking officer, military or civilian, and send in a team to assassinate him. Even a mayor of a small village who "supported" the north could be killed.

After his ten years of required silence, he still didn't talk about what he had done in Vietnam. I really learned nothing at all about Vietnam from my father. Everything I know comes from other sources: books, movies, newspapers, and other Vietnam vets. Just the word Vietnam will attract my attention and draw me into an article or even a bad movie, as if in hope of finding an answer to his death.

My mother maintains he was never the same man after his Vietnam service. I don't know, I guess I was too young to notice the changes. I do know he became very religious and gave large sums of money to relief efforts and sponsored an entire Ethiopian family. But he still never talked about his experiences. Now that I know something about the Special Forces programs he was involved with, I feel that he was in some way trying to make up for what he had done in Vietnam.

I knew something was very wrong, but we were never close enough for me to be able to ask him if he was having problems and if I could help. After he retired from the military, he cut himself off from all of his old army friends. He let himself go physically and had little to do with our family. I never thought it had anything to do with Vietnam. I always thought it was between my mother and him or with his business. After my father retired, he became involved with a company that sold military equipment to Third World countries. Sometime after the war between Argentina and England, my father's company was investigated by a grand jury, but he was not indicted for any wrongdoing. This trouble, along with waiting for commissions from Third World countries for sales, put a great strain on him. He was not a great businessman.

During the past two years, I've gone through all the phases of a suicide survivor and I've come back to guilt, the sense of not having been able to talk to him, to help him in some way. I know there was really not much I could have done for we had never reconciled our differences and remained, until his death, in a strictly "get along mode" without any real contact.

After his death I discovered that he had seen a psychiatrist for a time but then quit because he said it didn't help him. He was also involved with numerous different church organizations and was friends with many ministers, and as one, a friend for more than twenty-five years, said at his funeral: he was let down by everyone, the military, the church, and his friends. No one saw or helped him through his problems. Through the psychiatrist it came out that the things he did in Vietnam were a major conflict that he could not resolve. His suicide was classified a Vietnam-related death.

They have started (very quietly) adding the roughly three hundred and eighty names of the men who committed suicide in Vietnam to the memorial in Washington, D.C. If we were to honor and remember the vets who have died "at home" after the war, we would need a memorial that could carry many more names than the present one.

RECOMMENDED READING

J. M. Coetzee, *Waiting for the Barbarians.* Harmondsworth: Penguin Books, 1982.

Gwynne Dyer, *WAR*. New York: Crown Publishers, 1985.

Arthur Egendorf, *Healing from the War: Trauma and Transformation After Vietnam*. Boston: Shambhala Publications, 1986.

Gloria Emerson, *Winners and Losers: Battles, Retreats, Gains, Losses and Ruins from a Long War*. New York: Random House, 1976.

John H. Hewett, *After Suicide*. Philadelphia: Westminster Press, 1980.

The Soldier

The Soldier, particularly since the Vietnam War, is frequently maligned. The veterans of that war were not welcomed home as heroes. Sometimes they were not even welcomed home at all. The Soldier now is often seen as a mere custodian of weapons systems, and both friends and foe of military spending openly criticize the intelligence and the morale of the men in the armed services.

Before we can understand the Soldier as a heroic image of masculinity, we must recall his original function. He was the protector, the man who made the difference between survival and annihilation. He was the man who defended his loved ones and the entire community. He symbolized security. He was the man who did not hide from danger, who did not give in to fear. The Soldier was willing to risk his own life in order to protect those he loved.

The Soldier was not only male, he was a certain kind of male. He symbolized strength, courage, responsibility. He was the man who inspired other men to act bravely, who rallied a community and enabled its members to defend their sovereignty. In virtually every cultural system, the Soldier was a hero because without him, that system could not endure.

Great sacrifices were required of the Soldier. Hardship and deprivation, fear and anxiety, were unavoidable. Injury, captivity, or death were constant possibilities. But the Soldier endured because, in exchange for his services, his culture conferred upon him a priceless gift. It considered him a man. If he performed his duty well, he was a hero. As James Fallows wrote, war is "life's most abhorrent activity," and yet it "has been, in many eyes, the ultimate manifestation of masculinity."

Although this image of heroic masculinity often led men to brutality, it nevertheless seemed vital to civilization. To embody courage under the most gruesome circumstances, the Soldier had to repress his fear. To embody strength, he had to repress his feelings of vulnerability. To embody toughness, he had to repress his sensitivity. To kill, he had to repress compassion. No alternative existed. So men through the ages have measured themselves against what seemed to be male destiny. Rather than deny it, we have embraced it. Those who have not, we have called cowards. What war required was, by definition, manliness. The men who were the best soldiers were, in effect, the best men.

Under such circumstances, to call upon men to be more sensitive or compassionate, or to criticize them for being out of touch with their feelings or their bodies, would seem absurd to them. Facing Rommel in North Africa, an Allied tank commander was not concerned about anything except victory. Who would dare suggest that compassion or sensitivity could have disarmed the Third Reich? Clearly only brave soldiers could have defeated Hitler.

The postwar generation of American men grew up revering its heroes. Many of us believed that we, like our fathers, could prove our manhood through war. We wanted to become the ultimate man, the hero vanquishing the enemy. When Vietnam veterans recall what led them to Vietnam, what made them *want* and *need* to go, they do not speak of communism or domino theories or patriotism. They speak of John Wayne.

Ron Kovic, who grew up in the shadow of Yankee Stadium, remembers being reduced to tears by the Marine Corps hymn. "I loved the song so much, and every time I heard it I would think of John Wayne. I would think of him and cry," he said. "Like Mickey Mantle, John Wayne in *The Sands of Iwo Jima* became one of my heroes."

As a boy, Ron played in the woods near his home. "We turned the woods into a battlefield. We set ambushes, then led gallant attacks, storming over the top, bayoneting and shooting anyone who got in our way. Then we'd walk out of the woods like the heroes we knew we would become when we were men."

When the Marine Corps recruiters came to his high school, Kovic's response was preordained. It had been imprinted in his mind, and in the collective masculine unconscious, for centuries. "As I shook their hands and stared up into their eyes, I couldn't help but feel I was shaking hands with John Wayne and Audie Murphy," he recalled. "They told us that day that the Marine Corps built men—body, mind, and spirit." Since he wanted to be a man, he decided to become a marine. His introduction to manhood was a drill instructor shouting: "Awright, Ladies! . . . When are you people gonna learn? You came here to be marines!" And Ron became one.

Phil Caputo also imagined himself becoming the Soldier. He grew up outside Chicago in a safe, clean suburb. In the "virgin woodland" near his home, he would walk and "dream of that savage, heroic time . . . before America became a land of salesmen and shopping centers." Like so many white American males, he wanted "to find in a commonplace world the chance to live heroically." Although college bound, he yearned to enlist. "I saw myself charging up some distant beachhead, like John Wayne in *Sands of Iwo Jima*, and then coming home a suntanned warrior with medals on my chest." When a marine recruiting station was set up on his college campus, Caputo's response was the same as Kovic's, as he wrote:

> They were on a talent hunt for officer material and displayed a pos-
> ter of a trim lieutenant who had one of those athletic, slightly cruel-
> looking faces considered handsome in the military. He looked like a
> cross between an All-American halfback and a Nazi tank com-
> mander. Clear and resolute, his blue eyes seemed to stare at me in
> challenge. JOIN THE MARINES, read the slogan above his white cap.
> BE A LEADER OF MEN.

That's when Caputo realized that "the heroic experience I sought was war; war, the ultimate adventure; war, the ordinary man's most convenient means of escaping from the ordinary . . . I was excited by the idea that I would be sailing off to dangerous and exotic places after college instead of riding the 7:45 to some office."

But it was not mere escape from the white-collar world that he sought. It was entry into manhood. He admits that the motive that pushed him to enlist was the one "that has pushed young men into armies ever since armies were invented: I needed to prove something—my courage, my toughness, my manhood, call it whatever you like." His parents considered him still a boy; he wanted to prove them wrong. He wanted to do "something that would demonstrate to them, and to myself as well, that I was a man after all."

Caputo's and Kovic's articulateness should not mislead us, since both have written books about their experiences: for most men, the self-questioning was inchoate. Perhaps typical is this army sergeant, struggling to explain in Robert Jay Lifton's *Home from the War* why he decided that becoming a soldier "was the way you proved your manhood":

> I remember questioning myself . . . saying this can all be a pile of
> crap . . . this stuff about patriotism, and yet because of this indeci-
> sion . . . this confusion within myself, I said . . . I don't think I'll
> ever be able to live with myself unless I confront this, unless I find
> out, because if I do not I'll always wonder whether I was afraid to
> do it . . . and the whole question of whether I was a man or not . . .
> whether I was a coward.

Strictly speaking, the Soldier was not unemotional. He had feelings, but they conformed to pattern. Harold Lyon, a graduate of West Point and an army officer, says that soldiers were trained "to guide their emotions into acceptable channels . . . I excelled in this red, white, and blue school of callousness and went on to do graduate work in toughness by becoming a paratrooper, ranger, and counter-guerrilla-warfare instructor . . . I cannot remember during those years ever considering or suspecting or wishing that there might be a tender aspect to me. My toughness was my strength, or so I thought, and tenderness was a weakness."

The John Wayne syndrome meant keeping emotions buried. "You can't display emotion around here!" West Point upperclassmen would shout at plebes (freshmen) whose faces betrayed anger, fear, joy, sadness.

One plebe had a tendency to break down in tears when he was harassed beyond endurance. "I recall with shame and chagrin," said one of his tormentors, contrite in retrospect, "how we systematically ran him out of the Corps of Cadets [by] writing reports on his unsuitability as a potential officer with over- and undertones concerning masculinity and possible homosexuality of a cadet who cried or could not control his emotions."

Like the military tradition it represents, West Point's self-defense for hazing is unapologetically chauvinistic. It is, after all, preparing its cadets to lead men into combat, that ritual of organized aggression "where display of emotions could cause one to falter and fail." The abuse the soldier receives in training is justified, explained an army sergeant, on the ground that "they're doing it for a reason . . . They want to discipline us [to] function in the context of war."

This is the Soldier's credo. The John Wayne syndrome is an explicit, if unwritten, code of conduct, a set of masculine traits we have been taught to revere since childhood. It means to be hard, tough, unemotional, ruthless, and competitive; to be, in Lifton's words, "a no-nonsense sexual conqueror for whom women were either inferior, inscrutable or at best weaker creatures."

The military fostered a certain kind of manhood for the same reason that parents did: masculinity's bottom line was written in blood. Parents turned little boys into soldiers because they wanted them to survive. "Supermasculinity prepares one for war," concluded Lifton bluntly, and every generation of Americans has had one, or expected and prepared for one. We have sacrificed other traits—gentleness, openness, softness—because they were liabilities, not assets, in war. We have left them to women.

Even if the old masculine archetype is unfulfilling, many men refuse to let it go. As critics of male chauvinism argue, it conditions us to be aggressive, unable to express our feelings, power-oriented rather than person-oriented, robotistic male machines. But what men's liberation advocates often fail to mention is that we were raised that way by our parents and our culture for a reason. We were raised that way in order to survive.

At least until the nuclear age, wars were considered virtually inevitable, so parents raised their sons to fight in wars. Just as they reinforced in their sons the virtues of war—aggressiveness, competitiveness, toughness, lack of emotion—they reinforced in their daughters counterbalancing traits—passivity, gentleness, expressiveness, nurturance. As long as men fight wars, or are prepared to do so, liberation will remain elusive.

The military promoted the supermasculinity that the women's and men's liberation movements of the seventies found so offensive. It promoted it on purpose. The epithets of drill instructors or fellow soldiers—"maggot," "faggot," "snuffy," "pussy," or simply "woman"—left no doubt that not becoming a soldier meant not being a man.

No wonder the men's and women's liberation exhortations still fall on deaf ears. The character structure they want us to abandon—toughness, aggressiveness, insensitivity—has been bred in us for generations. It is not some vague force called socialization, but the vicious imperative of war. From a military perspective, it is ideal that men are expected by most Americans to be "very aggressive," "not at all emotional," "very dominant," "competitive," "rough," "unaware of others' feelings." These traits are essential for survival.

The critics of male chauvinism are well versed in itemizing the sacrifices required by this kind of manhood. Perhaps it does make sex unfulfilling, marriage barren, friendships superficial, work stressful, and politics a ritualized cult of toughness. But before we can understand why men do not readily leave this hell of machismo for the heaven of liberation, we must understand why a woman whose son has just left for Vietnam could say, "Every man must have his war." We must ask the questions that too many manifestoes of liberation have overlooked. How does masculinity depend on war, and war depend on masculinity?

To answer this, we must remember that the Soldier is an ancient figure. His image as epitomized by John Wayne—whether against Indians (in innumerable films), Mexicans (in *The Alamo*), Vietcong (in *The Green Berets*), or other more contemporary villains—is but the last in a long line of military heroes that have excited men's imaginations. The Soldier was defined long before America was even born.

More than two thousand years ago, Julius Caesar wrote in *The Conquest of Gaul* that the men who inhabited what is now France, Switzerland, and the Benelux nations "do not even pretend to compete with the Germans in bravery." After respectfully describing Gallic culture and customs, Caesar stressed that the less civilized Germans were completely different in that they spent their lives "in hunting and warlike pursuits." To this end, they prized chastity in men because they believed it made them better soldiers. They did not cultivate their own land but instead moved each year from place to place. The reason for this custom, Caesar believed, was that if men were permitted to settle they would "lose their warlike enthusiasms and take up agriculture instead." To raid and plunder other tribes was not forbidden by the Germans because they believed that such raids kept the men in shape and prevented them from "getting lazy."

For centuries Caesar's view prevailed. Man's inherent aggressiveness has been cited as proof that war is inevitable. "War is a biological necessity," wrote the German general Friedrich von Bernhardi. "It gives a biologically just decision, since its decisions rest on the very nature of things." In 1911, General von Bernhardi called on his countrymen to abandon hopes for peace, which he felt would "poison the soul of the nation." This was not a uniquely German viewpoint, but one common throughout European intellectual circles on the eve of the twentieth century. From Spain: "When a nation shows a civilized horror of war, it receives directly the punishment for its mistake. God changes its sex, despoils it of its common mark of virility, changes it into a feminine nation, and sends conquerors to ravish it of its honor." From Ireland: "Bloodshed is a cleansing and sanctifying rite and the nation which regards it as a final horror has *lost its manhood.*"

According to this masculine-militarist interpretation, violence is the principal catalyst of human evolution. The capacity to communicate or to cooperate—which, as the feminist biologist Ruth Hubbard points out, is also part of our evolutionary achievement—is considered secondary, if not irrelevant. Masculine aggressiveness is not considered a trait that should be redirected into nondestructive competition or even constructive achievement; it is a trait to be extolled and developed to the fullest. It is to be nurtured by training for war and brought to maturity by war itself.

The equation of masculinity with soldiering was readily adopted in America. We brought with us to the New World a military tradition that had changed relatively little since Caesar's time. When America was born, battle was still considered the most basic and universal rite of passage into manhood. Americans were trying to become manly by at last leaving, in John Adams's words, "mother Britain's lap" to make our fortune in the world as a mature and independent nation. We achieved maturity through violence, through a ritual called war. The self-made American man did not call himself a son of England, but a "son of a gun."

The Revolutionary War triggered a reverence for the man in uniform; he was the midwife of the new republic. "Oh, that I were a soldier," exclaimed John Adams in 1775, embroiled in the complexities of the Continental Congress. "Everybody must, will and shall be a soldier."

Adams's wish came true. America had been, and would continue to be, almost constantly at war. We were never a peaceful nation. There was King William's War (1689-1697), followed five years later by Queen Anne's War, then the war against the Spanish (1739-1743), against the French (1744-1748), and against the French again (1754-1763). Then, in the Revolutionary War, virtually every major town experienced attack or occupation by the British. The Revolution was soon followed by the War of 1812, the Mexican War, and the Civil War. To all this must be added the never-ending campaigns against the Indians. No generation came of age in America without war, or the threat of war, confronting it.

Before the Civil War, eleven of the men nominated or elected president were military figures. George Washington was the "Father of Our Country" because he gave birth to it through battle. Later presidents, even those with strong civilian identities, like Zachary ("Old Rough and Ready") Taylor, portrayed themselves in full uniform in campaign posters. Heroism in warfare constituted, said one military historian, "an important claim to America's chief office."

Noting in his diary "the pernicious influence of military glory," Alexis de Tocqueville asked himself, "What determines the people's choice in favor of General Jackson, who . . . is a very mediocre man? What still guarantees him the votes of the people?" If given a choice, we wanted a man of heroic stature in the White House. It was by his uniform that we identified him. We assumed that the hero of war would be the hero in peace.

Unfortunately, heroism is more complex. Even in our own century, men have sometimes fought for the fuzziest reasons. On the battlefields of France in 1917, the American writer John Dos Passos experienced a "curious hankering after danger that takes hold of me." In the "drunken excitement of a good bombardment," Dos Passos admitted that he felt "more alive than ever before." Scores of other articulate men of letters jumped pell-mell into the fray. None could explain what attracted them.

"What an odd thing—to be in the Italian army," says a woman to the eager American lieutenant in Ernest Hemingway's A Farewell to Arms.

"It's not really the army," he replies. "It's only the ambulance."

"It's very odd though," she insists. "Why did you do it?"

"I don't know. There isn't always an explanation for everything."

This inarticulateness is typical. Frantically searching for the action, these American volunteers would speak of their desire to experience danger, their feeling that all else was insignificant, their fascination with courage and injury—and with heroism. "These," observed an expert on American writing after the Great War, "were for the most part the prevailing motives. In scarcely any case was there a clear, pure reason." Thoughtful, well-educated, middle-class American men rushed into the war because they "envisioned the battlefield as a proving ground where they could enact and repossess the manliness that modern American society had baffled."

A half-century later, young Americans would rush off to Vietnam with the same phrases rolling off their tongues. Many Vietnam vets were just as confused as Hemingway's lieutenant. "It is easy to look at the war in Vietnam and know why one should hate it," reflected a veteran in one of the many oral histories of the Vietnam War that began appearing in the early 1980s. "What is infinitely more difficult to articulate is why I loved it."

When John Bell, the hero of one of James Jones's war novels, The Thin Red Line, asks himself if all war is basically sexual, he is struggling with this puzzling connection between virility and violence. One of the obvious links between the two is the emotion of fear.

Behind the gleaming medals and starched uniforms is the terror of injury and death. This fact is at the heart of strategies of military leadership. The most critical element in military leadership, wrote Lord Moran in *The Anatomy of Courage*, is the "care and management of fear." Thoughtful military analysts, beginning with the nineteenth-century military historian du Picq, have all recognized that men fight out of fear— fear of punishment (as a consequence of not fighting) and fear of death (as a consequence of not fighting well).

But what the American soldier fears above all, according to S. L. A. Marshall in *Men Against Fire*, is "losing the one thing he is likely to value more highly than life—his reputation *as a man among other men*." After interviewing two groups of infantrymen just returned from combat (against the Japanese in the Pacific and the Germans in Normandy), General Marshall concluded: "Whenever one surveys the forces on the battlefield, it is to see that fear is general among men, but to observe further that *men are loath that their fear will be expressed* in specific acts which their comrades will recognize as cowardice." His interviews also revealed that, even in infantry units with high morale and intense fighting, only one out of every four fighting soldiers ever used his weapons against the enemy. Marshall observed that

> [modern Western man] comes from a civilization in which aggression, connected with the taking of life, is prohibited and unacceptable. The teaching and ideals of that civilization are against killing, against taking advantage. The fear of aggression has been expressed to him so strongly and absorbed by him so deeply and pervadingly—practically with his mother's milk—that it is part of the normal man's emotional make-up. This is his greatest handicap when he enters combat.

To overcome this powerful, almost unconscious prohibition against violence, a civilized handicap that General Marshall correctly identified as a feminine influence, the military enterprise must create an equally powerful and unconscious prohibition against *avoiding* violence.

To lose one's "reputation as a man among men" means to be identified as a coward or, more explicitly, as a woman. In *The American Soldier*, his exhaustive and definitive study of the American soldier in World War II, Samuel Stouffer found that the fear of showing cowardice in battle stemmed from "the more central and strongly established fears of sex-typing." To lack the Soldier's qualities means to risk "not being a man. ('Whatsa matter, bud—got lace on your drawers?' 'Christ, he's acting like an old maid.')" According to Stouffer, in such cases "there was a strong likelihood of being branded a 'woman.'"

The fear of being considered a woman—or, as marine drill instructors still call their recruits, "faggots"—is the sexual underbelly of combat. The Soldier's ultimate epithet and his ultimate (professed) love are identical: woman. But this contradiction appears perfectly logical when set against the inherently contradictory military landscape. The first woman the Soldier loved—the one from whose womb he emerged, on whose breast he sucked, by whose hands he was bathed and clothed—is the same woman who bred in him commandments against violence, which he is now trained and paid to violate. To become the Soldier, the real leader for whom the armed services are so desperately advertising, the boy must reject his mother's voice ("Don't hit, Johnny!"), reject his (woman) teacher's voice ("Stop that fighting, boys!"), reject his (effeminate) minister's voice ("Thou shalt not kill!"), and identify with that all-male voice of the drill sergeant ("Kill! Kill! Kill!").

Only something as repugnant as being considered a woman or a faggot—which Stouffer, in the prose of the social scientist, calls "a dangerous threat to the contemporary male personality"—is sufficiently terrifying that men are willing to die to avoid it.

But what exactly does the epithet "woman" signify? When the Soldier blurts it out venomously, it means that he is without fear, while women are fear-ridden; that he is strong, while women are weak; that he has courage, while women are cowards.

This fear of our feminine side, the "anima" in Jungian terms, seems inextricably involved in triggering our capacity for destructiveness. It is as if war provides men with a periodic exorcism of the anima—a ritual cleansing and purification of masculinity. The anima is banished from the Soldier's consciousness because it disturbs, in Emma Jung's words, "a man's established ideal image of himself."

We encase ourselves in muscles, which symbolize manhood. When attacking, our body is a weapon; when defending, it is a shield. Some psychologists actually call this process "armoring," a primitive defensive reaction designed to protect the organism against external threats. We sacrifice sensuous pleasure on behalf of the only instinct that is stronger—survival.

Always on duty, the soldier pays a price for his bodily armament. As we have seen, despite all our protection, men in America die much sooner than women. Women may openly suffer more emotionally. For example, six times as many women as men suffer from depression. But while they are feeling low, we are dying. Inside our armor, we degenerate. Like good soldiers, we keep on marching. We tell ourselves that we are well, and we numb ourselves to our deterioration. Ironically, it is often our heart that reveals our lies.

This paradox is reflected in the weekend TV football games that punctuate the fall and winter months. Covered with padding, crowned with helmets, bulging with muscles, and weighing over two hundred pounds, the armored men will die sooner than the scantily clad cheerleaders dancing on the sidelines. Put the two figures side by side and they are diametric opposites: the woman exposed, her erogenous zones accentuated and (to the degree the law allows) revealed; the man encased, vulnerable parts of his body insulated against injury. Yet a few decades later, the ranks of the protected will have lost more members than the ranks of the exposed.

If our bodies are so strong and women's so weak, it is paradoxical again that it is women who dare to be shown naked. Whether in film, on the stage, or in glossy, full-color photographs, our culture exhibits the naked female form far more often than the naked male's. Despite such latecomers as *Playgirl* (with a mere fraction of *Playboy*'s circulation), the fact remains that the male-controlled media have been far more zealous in their portrayal of the soft and tender reaches of women's bodies than men's.

One of the most sexually explicit films to receive critical acclaim in the seventies was Bertolucci's *Last Tango in Paris*. A man, played by Marlon Brando, has anal intercourse with a young woman. Bertolucci languorously displays the woman's entire body, from every detail of her breasts to the finest strands of pubic hair, before the camera's unflinching eye. Although he is portrayed as the aggressive and dynamic lover, the Soldier on the battlefield of Eros, the man remains unexposed; his genitalia are invisible throughout. It is the woman who is expected to take her armor off. It is the woman who is exposed, not to enemy fire, but to the uncaring eyes of tens of millions of strangers. Asked why he left the shots of Brando's genitals on the cutting room floor, Bertolucci first claimed that he "cut it out for structural reasons, to shorten the film." Then he admitted, "It is also possible that I had so identified myself with Brando that I cut it out of shame for myself. To show him naked would have been like showing myself naked."

Our bravery, it seems, is as contradictory as our bodies. We have the courage to fight, but not to be naked. We have the kind of courage required to put on armor, but not the kind required to take it off.*

What happens to the Soldier's bravery when he is in bed, naked, with a woman? "I'm sorry they never found out they could have orgasms too,"

---

*In 1969, a writer in *Cosmopolitan* argued that men suffer from a "John Wayne neurosis," an inability to express deep emotions with women. Such men want to be in control at all times. The man who models himself on the Duke is prepared at any moment to rush away on his horse (or drive away in his Mustang) to his more important business back in Marlboro country.

This traditional frontier image is being replaced by a more sophisticated, but equally repressed, modern urban image. As John Wayne symbolized the Cowboy, James Bond epitomizes the Playboy—"the old cowboy in modern dress." As sociologists Jack Balswick and Charles Peck described him, the Playboy wears a different kind of armor. He is a "skilled manipulator . . . knowing when to turn the lights down, what music to play on the stereo, which drinks to serve, and what topics of conversation to pursue." He specializes in love affairs. He shares his bed with women, but little more. The Playboy prides himself on his ability to move on—to have sex with different women without the complications of human emotions.

laments the protagonist of Joseph Heller's *Something Happened*. As long as men were the only ones with sexual passions, our satisfaction was enough. But when women, too, are sexual beings, men are no longer the center of the sexual universe. Before sexual liberation, men fretted about women's lack of sexual appetite. Now, as Christopher Lasch points out, we fret about our capacity to satisfy it.

As Soldiers, our bodies have been devoted to combat. We have cultivated its toughness. The penis—called a tool, rod, prick, or pistol when our language turns coarse—becomes the sole repository of our sexuality. Through it we shall give pleasure; through it we shall receive. Trapped within these self-imposed limitations, the Soldier is virtually incapacitated when he meets women. We reduce our sexuality to an organ requiring periodic discharge. If women wish to be quickly overpowered, a shot of semen will suffice. But few if any women find such sexuality fulfilling. Women do not want to be targets in some sexual shooting range. They want to be lovers, held in a mutual embrace.

The Soldier assumes that whatever pleases him pleases women. If it doesn't, he assumes something is wrong with *them*. If women are not satisfied by our lovemaking, then they are frigid or oversexed. If they do not love the Soldier, then they are not real women. We want women to act like "women," even if they have to pretend, because we have forced ourselves to act like "men."

In Burke Davis's *Marine!*, one of an endless stream of books on military heroes, the legendary Colonel "Chesty" Puller is glorified. In one scene, Puller is talking with a shell-shocked marine. The young man is lying on a hospital bed, staring forlornly at a picture of his girlfriend. After tasting battle, he is so frightened that he feels he cannot face it again.

"Too bad you'll never see her again," the Colonel said.

"What do you mean?"

"Why, she'll never look at you again after this. She wouldn't spit on you."

"She'll never know. How could she hear?"

"Oh, she'll find out . . . She'll find out all right."

The colonel's strategy works. The marine returns to duty and is later decorated for bravery.

A man who is raised in body, mind, and soul to embody the conquering Soldier, always dominant and in control, cannot go to bed and take off his armor. We cannot extol victory over others in public and then make love with our wives in sensuous surrender in private. We cannot devote our bodies to erecting invulnerable defenses and then become tenderly vulnerable in bed.

Harold Lyon explains that even at the moment of orgasm, he kept his emotions under iron control. He would try "to emit bass-sounding groans—instead of the tender, uncontrolled cries which would naturally come from me." With considerable pain he recognized that for years he had been camouflaging his real self, which wanted to be vulnerable, behind a more "masculine" exterior. "I realized," he wrote, "that I had been afraid that my partner would think of me as a boy and not a man if my love cries sounded childlike. How incredible! Even at the moment of release, to be so controlled."

But our language is misleading. The Soldier is not in control. On the contrary, he is controlled by his conditioning. That is why he is so dangerous.

Every age, even (suicidal as it may be) the nuclear age, has its soldiers. It is not the uniform that identifies us but our masculine attraction to violence. We experience what Rollo May called a "joy in violence," an ecstasy that "takes the individual out of himself and pushes him toward something deeper and more powerful than anything he has previously experienced." As May described it, the experience is a form of transcendence: "The ego is dissolved . . . 'I' passes insensibly into 'we': 'my' becomes 'our' . . . *Through violence we overcome our self-centeredness.*" General George Patton called it "the cataclysmic ecstasy of violence."

But many men now repudiate the Soldier. Some men consider him not a hero but a fool. Most Western nations have not fought a war for nearly forty years; some, like Sweden, have not had a war for more than a century and a half. The wars since 1945 have not bred heroism. Neither Korea nor Vietnam was a "real" war; neither was won and neither had heroes. All conflict now takes place under the shadow of a computerized network of strategic nuclear weapons that dwarf the actions of any individual pilot or infantryman. Consequently, the Soldier seems almost obsolete. In nuclear war, aggressiveness is no longer considered a virtue. It no longer implies survival but, rather, annihilation.

Young men who seek heroism through soldiering often return home today disillusioned. For Ron Kovic, the shock came with sudden brutality: a bullet ripped through his spinal cord. When he asked himself why, he had no answer. When he returned home from Vietnam, paralyzed for life, he began to question more. His questions took him to the 1972 Republican Convention, where, seated in his wheelchair, he shouted, "Stop the bombing! Stop the war!" until the police threw him out into the street.

Others returned from Vietnam with their bodies intact but their minds shattered. "I had thought there would be a parade with banners when I returned," said Eddie Graham, the son of a Boston factory worker. Eddie had served two tours of duty in the marines. "I thought confetti would be thrown . . . that's what I had dreamed about." Instead, venomous shouts of "murderer" and "fascist" greeted him as he stepped off the plane and onto the soil of the land he had been defending. He had been the Soldier, but he was no longer the hero.

When Vietnam veterans reminisce, they often mock themselves. They realize that they were emulating an age-old masculine archetype that has become obsolete. "Always," reported Robert Jay Lifton, who interviewed scores of Vietnam veterans for his book *Home from the War*, "the men came back to the John Wayne thing." They came back to it again and again because they knew that they—and we who never fought—must free ourselves from our identification with the Soldier. Eddie Graham, Phil Caputo, Ron Kovic, are men raised in a nuclear age yet still infatuated with pre-nuclear heroes. Our consciousness lags behind history, our self-awareness behind our weaponry.

Ultimately, this is what makes the nuclear age so dangerous. It has shifted the meaning of heroism. If we annihilate ourselves, it will not be because we are cowards. It will be because we are still trying to be yesterday's heroes.

RECOMMENDED READING

Helen Caldecott, *Missile Envy*. New York: William Morrow, 1984.

Franco Fornari, *The Psychoanalysis of War*. New York: Anchor Press, 1974.

David Halberstam, *The Best & The Brightest*. New York: Random House, 1972.

John Keegan, *The Face of Battle*. New York: Viking Press, 1976.

Richard Slotkin, *Regeneration Through Violence*. Middletown, Conn.: Wesleyan University Press, 1973.

Poem

At first it's cold
A wish for long underwear
Then something pulled close up
All night in a blur, a fire
And you say you understand
Enough black coffee to choke morning
A lot of words strung up to move your heart
A childish fear where things come true
The year you needed more baseball
Days you squeeze out near the finish
Something in the holy somehow
In the DO DAH distance, bases loaded
A chopper to third
The sacrifice to lawn gods

L'éclatante victoire de Khe Sanh

The main thing
you must remember
is the jungle
has retaken the trenches—

think it forgiven,
look on it healed
as a scar.

Willie

Sometime someone will renovate this block,
they'll dig the ruins out
and the time you spent

Your pain and the bottles
it took to hold the war,
your memory is where?

Some bunker near the suburbs,
ready to break in shooting
pull some kind of rescue

Some of the glass will survive.

Pool

You've got everything you ever asked for
and one shot. Plenty of cushion, the hole
wide open and

You've tested this a thousand times—
you can't look at the page—newspaper,
novel, poem and miss the words
Viet Nam. It might as well be neon.

If they are there
it's this huge warehouse
and you want to get to the place
you can walk through in the dark
and be glad it is cold for Christmas.

For Ed Hodson

Reunion

They don't mind if we do this,
stop here and mention
each other's family, some
buddy, the "how longs"
and "why for"
it ends like this
and name the places and
who's not here.
We keep talking the war,
sure it happened, sure
something wore out in that light.

For Raz

For the Duration

The first things to go have gone.
Bodies enter the dirt, color
shifts transparent, changing
the system from within.

What is lost has to be
remembered to be at all.

Fleshed out,
sculpted,
dust of the story,
flowering.

ROBERT BLY

The Vietnam War and the Erosion of Male Confidence

The following essay was given as a talk at the symposium "Understanding Vietnam," held in Salado, Texas, in 1982.

My subject is the erosion of male confidence in general during the last thirty years, and, specifically, the part the Vietnam War had in that erosion. Everywhere I go in the country I meet men roughly twenty to forty years old who live in considerable self-doubt. Many of them have few or no close male friends. I meet young fathers who do not know what male values they should attempt to teach their sons. These men, often separated from their own remote fathers, and out of touch with their grandfathers, do not feel they belong to a community of men. When they reach out toward truly masculine values, they find nothing in their hand when it closes.

The old anger against the father, so characteristic of the nineteenth century and earlier centuries, has been replaced in many men by a kind of passivity and remoteness, which springs from a feeling that the father has abandoned or rejected them. In some cases, the father lost his sons in divorce proceedings, and many sons interpret that event to mean that men are untrustworthy. Still other sons have lived with remote, overworked, impassive, silent, controlling, or condemnatory fathers; and one feels in these men a longing for male values mingled with a kind of helpless bitterness. Some men in recent years admire only certain values which they associate with women—tenderness, concern for the environment, nurturing, the sense of cooperation, ability to feel deeply. These men characteristically confide during a crisis only in women. That is fine; what is missing is the confiding in men. We could conclude by saying that women came out of the sixties and seventies with considerable confidence in their values, but men lack this clarity and belief. We all know many exceptions to this statement, and yet we sense a significant alteration in male confidence since, say, 1950 to 1960.

Because men of all social classes have lost confidence, it's clear that many forces affect this change. The Industrial Revolution has sent the father to work many miles from the home, and given him a work that he cannot teach his son. Male societies have disappeared, along with opportunities for older and younger men to meet each other and to do ordinary physical work together. The mythological layer, with all its models of adult male energy—Apollo, Dionysius, Hermes, Zeus—collapsed long ago, as have models of adult female energy for women. More recently, the relatively humane, or humanized, male battle disappeared, destroyed by machine-gun slaughter and bombing from the air. In old Irish and Greek stories we meet men who obey the rules of combat and honor their male enemy.

We all notice that suburban life gets along without male community. My parents brought me up on a Minnesota farm during years in which men lived in a community. My father ran a threshing rig, and all through the threshing season the men—young, old, and middle-aged—worked together, doggedly and humorously, in a kind of high-spirited cooperation at its best. I felt a confidence in the male community and I felt the goodness of it. But for men living in the suburbs all that is gone. We can all suggest many other forces and events that have contributed to erosion of male confidence. I would say that the two major causes for erosion are the attacks launched against men by the separatist part of the women's movement and the Vietnam War.

The women's movement has brought considerable psychic health to women, but we need to distinguish the women's movement from its separatist component: the attacks that heap together virtually all male values and condemn them as evil, and that locate the source of women's pain entirely in men. At a seminar three days ago a woman said to me, "Since all good poetry comes from our reaction to oppression, and since white males are not oppressed in any way, then how could they possibly write poetry?" So I asked, "Does your mother oppress you?" "Oh, not at all," she said. "Women don't oppress, men oppress." So I said, "How do you feel about the matriarchies?" She said, "Oh, there was no oppression in the matriarchies." I said, "Read Margaret Mead sometime." Some feminists are determined to save men even if they have to destroy them to do it.

An ancient story from north England about the ugly dragon man called the Lindworm says that the transformation of the Lindworm to a man takes place in four stages. The Lindworm's "bride," rather than fighting the Lindworm, asks him to take off one of his seven ugly skins, and she agrees to take off some of her seven blouses if he does that. After he has removed all seven skins, he lies helpless and white on the floor. She then whips him with whips dipped in lye, then washes him in milk, and finally lies down in the bed and holds him a few minutes before falling asleep. Connie Martin, the storyteller, has suggested that women in the seventies got the whipping part down well, but did not wash the man or hold him. They were too tired after the whipping to do the last two steps.

Let's turn now to the Vietnam War and its influence on men's confidence. That subject is what concerns us here. To introduce the subject, I'll tell two stories that I heard. A friend in Boston told me the first story. He stems from an old and wealthy family that carries a lot of military tradition and so much emphasis on male values that even civilians in his family receive a sort of military burial, with only the men present. My friend, whom I will call John, entered, as one would expect, the military service during the Vietnam War willingly, trustingly—became an officer and served in the field. After some duty in the field, he returned to Saigon on leave. One day he found himself by the river talking to an old captain, both of them speaking French. The Vietnamese river captain told him, in the course of many anecdotes, that the American soldiers were not welcome here, any more than the French. John had experienced inconsistencies in the field, but at that instant he felt a terrific shock. He understood that he had been lied to. The men who had lied to him were the very men that his family had respected for generations—military men and men in responsible government positions. Last night we saw a section of the new PBS documentary of the war. In that section one can watch McNamara and McGeorge Bundy lying about the Tonkin Gulf incident. I said to John, "What did you do then when you realized that you had been lied to about the major issues of the war?" "Well," he said, "a strange thing happened. A female anger rose up in me." I said, "Why do you use the word 'female'?" He said, "All at once I understood how a single betrayal could bring a woman to furious anger. The Greeks talked about that. I understood that female anger, and I felt it." I said, "What happened next?" He said, "Well the anger continued and turned into rage and I had to live with that the rest of the time I was in Vietnam, and I'm still living with it." He is a friend of John Kerry, who organized the Vietnam Veterans Against the War. He remarked that John Kerry has entered politics in Massachusetts—holds a high office—and Kerry still has a nightmare every night. Not one night goes by that he does not have it.

I know anecdotes don't prove anything; they only suggest. To me they suggest that a new situation evolved during the Vietnam War which amounts to older men lying to younger men. This is the grief I want to discuss.

I enlisted in the Second World War when I was seventeen and I, like most of the men I knew, did not feel that older men lied to me during the war. The older men, I felt, were aware of the younger ones, and though many younger men died, the older men died as well. There was a certain feeling of camaraderie and trust all up and down the line. My friend John emphasized that the military and civilian leaders this time did not labor to awaken the sense of patriotism that gives battle labor some meaning. That sense of meaning bound old and young together in the Second World War. Johnson didn't declare war because to do so would have necessitated a full congressional debate. Did you see Dean Rusk lie about that point last night in the documentary? He said, "Well, we didn't try to declare war because, you see, we were afraid that it would be, you know, you mustn't make people angry." Dean Rusk was lying. As the Vietnam War went on, Walt Whitman Rostow, McGeorge Bundy, Dean Rusk, all lied. And I felt lied to by them. But at the time, I didn't fully realize how the soldiers and officers in the battlefield would feel when, their lives at stake, they recognized the same lies.

I will tell a second story. I met recently in San Francisco a veteran who had been an ordinary draftee. When I told him I would be attending a conference in Texas about the war, he looked interested, and I asked him how he felt now about the war. He said, "Well, I must tell you that I still feel tremendous anger." I said, "What about?" "Well," he said, "I've been thinking about it, and it has to do with my background. At the time I was a young Catholic boy from Pennsylvania. I had taken in certain moral values, simply through being in that background. One was that killing was wrong. A second was respect for women. We even believed some of the moral declarations that racism was bad. All at once we were out in the jungle, and told to shoot at anything that moves. We couldn't tell if the people we were killing were men or women, let alone communists or peasants. Moreover, everyone, officers included, called them 'slopes' and 'gooks.' The older men never mentioned this nor told us what we were to do with the ideas we had taken in during Catholic grade school. After a month or so in the field suddenly I was shipped for R and R to a whorehouse in Thailand. Something was wrong with that. A lot of us still had feelings toward women. We had feelings about respect for women and what a woman means this way. Something got broken in me, and I'm still angry about that."

So the question we have to ask ourselves is, Who made that decision? I remember that during the Second World War the army supported the USO, where one went and danced a little with a woman, who was equally shy. It was very square, but nevertheless, the whole thing helped to preserve some continuity between civilian life and war life. Older men like Eisenhower supported such arrangements. The older men in the Vietnam War led the way to the whorehouses and made no attempt to preserve the continuity between civilian life and war life for these young males. It was a violation of trust. To repeat: when I came out of the Second World War there was a bond between younger and older men and it helped all of us who served to move through our lives.

Let's turn now to body counts. The army didn't announce body counts of Germans during the Second World War. As a speaker mentioned yesterday, we measured our progress in Vietnam not by land taken but by lives taken. "Attrition" is the sugar-coated way of putting it. But the fact is that counting dead bodies is not a way for civilized human beings to behave, especially when your culture emphasizes the dignity of life. How can the same culture that prides itself on respecting the dignity of human life be in favor of body counts? The counting of bodies and the release of that information daily was approved by the Joint Chiefs of Staff, and agreed on by the generals. You can't tell me that they didn't know the implications of this. Even worse, the generals and the Pentagon began to lie about the number of bodies. As we now know, the staff often doubled the count from the field. General Shoemaker, who led the incursion into Cambodia, is present, and several speakers have addressed polite questions to him during their talks here. I'd like to ask him a question also. General Shoemaker, I would like to ask you now: "Were you aware of the false body counts being passed through you?"

"Yes, I was aware that some of them were inflated."

"Have you apologized to the young men in the country for this lie?"

"Well, I would prefer to listen to you."

"All right. Thank you."

You heard the answer General Shoemaker just gave us, "No, I have not apologized to the young men in the country." And we can add that he doesn't intend to.

Our subject here is the bad judgment of older men that resulted in damage to younger men or death of younger men. John mentioned one more decision. The generals decided to have a 365-day field term rotation. Such a plan broke with the traditional situation in which a company lives and dies together as a unit. The company learns to act as a unit; and each man learns to trust, or whom to trust. But the 365-day rotation breaks all that. Everyone is thinking, as John mentioned, about his own survival, and then suddenly the others can't depend on him, or he on them. I think the average age of the soldiers in Vietnam was around eighteen years old; in the Second World War it was around twenty-six. The average age of the company commanders in Vietnam was twenty-two years old; in the Second World War, thirty-six. The decision for rotation was a bad one, and I think General Westmoreland made it; others here would know. General Westmoreland throughout did many stupid things, and his advisors showed a specialist mentality, and a massive insensitivity to the needs of the younger men. The use of Agent Orange is a perfect example. Our first step in recovering from the war, I think, is simply to say this.

So the eighteen-year-olds were out in the jungle with men only two or three years older, and these eighteen-year-olds felt completely isolated and separated. Who made the decisions that led to this isolation? Did anyone approve of the public body counts? I will recite to you a poem I wrote in the spring of 1966 about those body counts. It's called "Counting Small-Boned Bodies."

> Let's count the bodies over again.
>
> If we could only make the bodies smaller,
> The size of skulls, maybe we could get
> A whole plain white with skulls in the moonlight!
>
> If we could only make the bodies smaller,
> Maybe we could get a whole year's kill
> In front of us on a desk!
>
> If we could only make the bodies smaller,
> Maybe we could fit a body
> Into a finger ring, for a keepsake forever.

I always thought that we never made good enough use of the Vietnamese heads. Maybe the Pentagon should have encased them in plastic and put them up on motel walls around the United States. Couldn't American men and women make love well below those heads?

Walt Rostow made a remark this morning which you all heard. I don't want to single him out above the others of his sort—it happens he is the only one here representing that group of advisors, and it is brave of him to come. But I could hardly believe my ears this morning when he declared that the true brutality in this war was the brutality of Congress when it refused to vote more money toward the end. Did you hear that one? It was marvelous. Our feelings get damaged when we misuse our own language. All through the war, men like Rostow refused to use language in a clear and honest way. "Brutality" comes from the root, "brute"; and "not voting funds" comes from a decision based on rationality and debate. Words and phrases like "friendlies," "incursion," "communist infrastructure," and "strategic hamlets" testify to a time in American history when language failed. And it was the older men who brought in that language, and led the movement toward failure of language. They had the responsibility to keep the language clear. The young men can't do that. They are helpless. They believe the older men when they call a dictatorship "democratic," or when they call a certain liquid "Agent Orange" rather than "Poison number 465." Doesn't "Orange" imply nourishing?

We can say then that when the Vietnam veteran arrived home he found a large hole in himself where his values once were. What is the veteran going to do about that? Many veterans I meet say they still cannot find any values to put in there. The earlier values were blown out, the way acid blows out the brain. Harry Wilmer moved me tremendously when he talked about the dreams of Vietnam veterans yesterday. The dreams of certain veterans, he said, repeat events in exact detail, endlessly, meaninglessly. Only when the veteran is able to find a possibility of meaning—what a wonderful word that is—meaning, meaning, meaning—can his dreams begin to change. Then a veteran can begin to put something into this hole. But most veterans are not receiving help in moving toward meaning; they have not succeeded in finding a man like Harry Wilmer. They live in rage and in a sense of betrayal.

It is clear that this issue is a very serious issue, and the implications go far beyond the mistakes of the Vietnam War. When men lose their confidence in older men, what happens then? When older men betray younger men, and lie to them, in government and in the field, what happens then to male values? What happens to a society in which the males do not trust each other? What kind of a society is that? Do you feel it coming now? That mood in the country? Do you feel how the distrust erodes the confidence that males have in themselves? Did you know that the practice of "fragging," that is the killing by enlisted men of their own sergeants and lieutenants, was statistically not a factor until the Vietnam War? And I feel the poison of that distrust moving through the whole society now. The older men associated with the Vietnam War continue to lie to Vietnam veterans about chemical poisoning, and birth defects. Every man in the country knows that. It is no wonder that in Comtrex advertisements on television men are always presented as weak. What does the army's constant lying about Agent Orange do to our respect for men and for male values?

Our general subject is the Vietnam War and its effect on the erosion of male confidence. How can this nightmare end? Harry Wilmer suggests, and I utterly agree, that no healing can take place until we decide to take in the concept of the dark side, or the shadow. Each of us has a dark side. If I shout at my small sons, I can say that I have a fatherly duty to discipline them, but we know that this shouting has a dark side. When so many whites moved to the suburbs during the fifties, wasn't that a simple longing for open space? But it had a dark side. The dark side was that we let the centers of our cities disintegrate, in the same way that we let the center of our psyche disintegrate. When entertainment, in the form of television, floods our house every night, we are only sitting and listening—this is a simple thing surely, isn't it? But it has a dark side. It has a very strong dark side, in that we don't have to entertain others, or enter any larger sort of community to be entertained. Why don't we ever talk about that one? Well, when Johnson decided to raise troop levels sneakily, without public debate, that looked like a simple act, perfectly reasonable under the circumstances, as Dean Rusk says. But we know that it had a dark side. The decision to send eighteen-year-olds to whorehouses, whether they wanted to go or not, has a dark side, and the cool dryness with which Robert McNamara and McGeorge Bundy and Dean Rusk discussed hideous realities has a dark side. Have you ever noticed that? How calm the older men are? Some rationalists don't want to get into feeling at all. Did you notice how boyish McNamara looked in the documentary last night? I was shocked. Probably he looked that way because he was a boy. What is a boy? A boy is a person who takes an act and does not think about the dark side of it. An adult is a person who takes an act and remains aware of its dark side. What happens in the psyche when Reagan repeats over and over that we fight our wars with noble purpose while the other side fights its wars with evil purpose? What happens when we say that Russia is an "evil empire"?

Some Europeans studied the dark side of colonial wars, and Joseph Conrad studies it marvelously in his story, *The Heart of Darkness*. We have to think of the possibility that we are adopting European diplomatic phrases and adopting European global responsibilities, but adopting them not as adults but as boys. When we decisively entered Vietnam culture around 1966, we had virtually no one in the State Department who spoke Vietnamese, and very few in the academic community who had close knowledge of Vietnamese culture. Do you think that deterred our people? Not a bit. We invaded a nation and made decisions for it when we had only two or three scholars who could speak the language. That is not adult behavior. Our behavior in Central America is not adult behavior either. Reagan is another boy, an aged boy. How to embalm a boy so he always smiles forever? How could we be so lucky as to find a president who never sees the dark side of anything he does? These boyish men—so cheerful—are among the most dangerous men on earth. One group of Americans carries the knowledge of their danger: the Vietnam veterans. They carry that knowledge for us.

I am going to read now some sections of a poem I wrote during the Vietnam War called "The Teeth Mother Naked at Last." I don't want to read this poem. During the last ten years or so various people have asked me to read the poem in public and I have said no, I'm not going to read it. I don't like to read it any more. I don't want to read it. But since one purpose of this conference is to dip down into that old water, I will read some of the poem here. It tries to say how the war felt—not to a poet, just to a human being. I will start with the first section.

Massive engines lift beautifully from the deck.
Wings appear over the trees, wings with eight hundred rivets.

Engines burning a thousand gallons of gasoline a minute sweep
over the huts with dirt floors.

The chickens feel the new fear deep in the pits of their beaks.
Buddah with Padma Sambhava.

Meanwhile, out on the China Sea,
immense gray bodies are floating,
born in Roanoke,
the ocean on both sides expanding, "buoyed on the dense
marine."

Helicopters flutter overhead. The death-
bee is coming. Super Sabres
like knots of neurotic energy sweep
around and return.
This is Hamilton's triumph.
This is the advantage of a centralized bank.
B-52s come from Guam. All the teachers
die in flames. The hopes of Tolstoy fall asleep in the ant heap.
Do not ask for mercy.

Now the time comes to look into the past-tunnels,
the hours given and taken in school,
the scuffles in coatrooms,
foam leaps from his nostrils,
now we come to the scum you take from the mouths of the dead,
now we sit beside the dying, and hold their hands, there is
    hardly time for good-bye,
the staff sergeant from North Carolina is dying—you hold his
    hand,
he knows the mansions of the dead are empty, he has an empty
    place
inside him, created one night when his parents came home
    drunk,
he uses half his skin to cover it,
as you try to protect a balloon from sharp objects. . . .

Artillery shells explode. Napalm canisters roll end over end.
800 steel pellets fly through the vegetable walls.
The six-hour infant puts his fists instinctively to his eyes to keep
    out the light.
But the room explodes,
the children explode.
Blood leaps on the vegetable walls.

Yes, I know, blood leaps on the walls—
Don't cry at that—
Do you cry at the wind pouring out of Canada?
Do you cry at the reeds shaken at the edge of the sloughs?
The marine battalion enters.
This happens when the seasons change,
This happens when the leaves begin to drop from the trees too
    early
"Kill them: I don't want to see anything moving."
This happens when the ice begins to show its teeth in the ponds
This happens when the heavy layers of lake water
    press down on the
    fish's head, and send him deeper, where his tail swirls slowly,

and his brain passes him pictures of heavy reeds, of
vegetation fallen on vegetation. . . .
Hamilton saw all this in detail:
*"Every banana tree slashed, every cooking utensil smashed, every
mattress cut."*

Now the marine knives sweep around like sharp-edged jets; how
    beautifully
    they slash open the rice bags,
the mattresses. . . .
ducks are killed with $150 shotguns.

Old women watch the soldiers as they move.

II

Excellent Roman knives slip along the ribs.

A Stronger man starts to jerk up the strips of flesh.

*"Let's hear it again, you believe in the Father, the Son, and the Holy
Ghost?"*

A long scream unrolls.

More.

*"From the political point of view, democratic institutions are being built
in Vietnam, wouldn't you agree?"*

A green parrot shudders under the fingernails.
Blood jumps in the pocket.
The scream lashes like a tail.

"Let us not be deterred from our task by the voices of dissent. . . ."

The whines of the jets
pierce like a long needle.

As soon as the President finishes his press conference, black
    wings carry off the words,
    bits of flesh still clinging to them.

*   *   *

The ministers lie, the professors lie, the television lies, the priests
    lie. . . .
These lies mean that the country wants to die.
Lie after lie starts out into the prairie grass,
like enormous caravans of Conestoga wagons. . . .

And a long desire for death flows out, guiding the enormous
    caravans from beneath,

170

stringing together the vague and foolish words.
It is a desire to eat death,
to gobble it down,
to rush on it like a cobra with mouth open

It's a desire to take death inside,
to feel it burning inside, pushing out velvety hairs,
like a clothes brush in the intestines—

This is the thrill that leads the President on to lie

* * *

Now the Chief Executive enters; the press conference begins:
First the President lies about the date the Appalachian
  Mountains rose.
Then he lies about the population of Chicago, then he lies about
  the weight of the adult eagle, then about the acreage of the
  Everglades

He lies about the number of fish taken every year in the Arctic,
  he has private information about which city *is* the capital of
  Wyoming, he lies about the birthplace of Attila the Hun.

He lies about the composition of the amniotic fluid, and he
  insists that Luther was never a German, and that only the
  Protestants sold indulgences,

That Pope Leo X *wanted* to reform the church, but the "liberal
  elements" prevented him,
that the Peasants' War was fomented by Italians from the North.

And the Attorney General lies about the time the sun sets.

Do you want me to stop this? Do you feel depressed? Good. I want you to
listen to these next lines. I believe that the way the older men lie implies
self-destruction. Older men do not betray younger men with the con-
sistent betrayal that happened in the Vietnam War unless there is some-
thing deeply disturbed way down inside.

These lies mean that we have a longing to die that we do not
  recognize.
It is the longing for someone to come and take you by the hand to
  where they all are sleeping:
where the Egyptian pharaohs are asleep, and your own mother,
and all those disappeared children, who used to go around with
  you in the rings at grade school. . . .

171

Do not be angry at the President—he is longing to take in his
    hand
the locks of death hair—
to meet his own children dead, or unborn. . . .
He is drifting sideways toward the dusty places

III

This is what it's like for a rich country to make war
this is what it's like to bomb huts (afterwards described as
    "structures")
this is what it's like to kill marginal farmers (afterwards described
    as "communists")

this is what it's like to watch the altimeter needle going mad

*Baron 25, this is 81. Are there any friendlies in the area? 81 from 25,
negative on the friendlies. I'd like you to take out as many structures as
possible located in those trees within 200 meters east and west of my
smoke mark.*

diving, the green earth swinging, cheeks hanging back, red pins
    blossoming ahead of us, 20-millimeter cannon fire, leveling
    off, rice fields shooting by like telephone poles, smoke rising,
    hut roofs loop up huge as landing fields, slugs going in, half
    the huts on fire, small figures running, palm trees burning,
    shooting past, up again; . . . blue sky . . . cloud mountains

This is what it's like to have a gross national product.

I think I'll skip a little here.

This is what it's like to send firebombs down from
    air-conditioned cockpits.

This is what it's like to be told to fire into a reed hut with an
    automatic weapon.

It's because we have new packaging for smoked oysters that
    bomb holes appear in the rice paddies.
It is because we have so few women sobbing in back rooms,
because we have so few children's heads torn apart by
    high-velocity bullets,
because we have so few tears falling on our own hands
that the Super Sabre turns and screams down toward the earth.

It's because taxpayers move to the suburbs that we transfer
    populations.

The marines use cigarette lighters to light the thatched roofs of
    huts
because so many Americans own their own homes.

IV

* * *

I know that books are tired of us.
I *know* they are chaining the Bible to chairs.
Books don't want to remain in the same room with us anymore.

New Testaments are escaping . . . dressed as women . . . they
    go off after dark.
And Plato! Plato . . . Plato wants to go backwards. . . .
He wants to hurry back up the river of time, so he can end as
    some blob of sea flesh rotting on an Australian beach.

V

Why are they dying? I have written this so many times.
They are dying because the President has opened a Bible again.
They are dying because gold deposits have been found among
    the Shoshoni Indians.

They are dying because money follows intellect!
And intellect is like a fan opening in the wind—

The marines think that unless they die the rivers will not move.

They are dying so that the mountain shadows will continue to
    fall east in the afternoon,
so that the beetle can move along the ground near the fallen
    twigs.

One more small piece. I hate this section.

VI

But if one of those children came near that we have set on fire,
came toward you like a gray barn, waking,
you would howl like a wind tunnel in a hurricane,
you would tear at your shirt with blue hands,
you would drive over your own child's wagon trying to back up,
the pupils of your eyes would go wild—

If a child came by burning, you would dance on a lawn,
trying to leap into the air, digging into your cheeks,

you would ram your head against the wall of your bedroom
like a bull penned too long in his moody pen—

If one of those children came toward me with both hands
in the air, fire rising along both elbows,
I would suddenly go back to my animal brain,
I would drop on all fours screaming,
my vocal chords would turn blue, so would yours,
it would be two days before I could play with my own children
again.

I read parts of that poem, not because I want to, but because if we are
going to be healed we are going to have to go back into what we did in
Vietnam. The Germans after the Second World War went into their ac-
tions and they didn't. They healed and they didn't heal. Now, I think, if
we are going to heal we have to take two public acts. The first is public
mourning. The American people elected Carter and Reagan on a secret
agreement that the two men would never make us face the Vietnam War.
But when we avoid facing anything we get sick. When someone close to
us dies, it is important to mourn. A young man came up to me the other
day and said, "I wanted to weep at my father's funeral, but I couldn't.
What do you think about that?" We all get ill if we don't mourn. Lincoln
was not a boy, and I believe that if Lincoln were president now the first
thing he would do would be to call for a national day of mourning. He
would say: "Please nobody go to work today. We are going to mourn for
the Vietnam War today and mourn for the damage it has caused to us and
to others. We are going to think about the rupture of faith between young
and old men, and the rupture of faith between men and women." I think
he would begin then with a deep cry, on national television—something
like the old women who mourn at Greek funerals. Aaaaaaaaah-
hhhhhhhhaaaaaaaahhhhhhhh. The sound would induce weeping. Lin-
coln might keep that up for a whole hour because he had the ability to
mourn—as you can see by looking at his face.

Walt Rostow will soon give his major address and he will lie to us
again in his cool dry way. There will be no grief in his voice. That doesn't
bother me. What bothers me is that you, the audience, may comment and
ask him questions in the same cool voice. What worries me is that, flat-
tered by having a celebrity in the room, not one of you will say no to him.

The second public act I think essential is this: that the older men pub-
licly apologize to the younger men. General Kinnard owes the younger
men an apology in public, and I did feel some apology in the private talk
he gave here yesterday. I think the Bundys should apologize. I think that
McNamara should apologize. I hear that he had trouble sleeping after the
war, but he has never talked about that in public. The young veterans
now consider themselves crazy. The old men's apology and admission of
their craziness could help bring the older and younger men together. I

174

would say that extreme mourning in the service of human union is no vice.

I am going to leave the Vietnam War subject now and recite a recent poem that suggests the way I feel now. One of the gifts given as one gets older is being able to grieve more.

What is sorrow for? It is a storehouse far
in the north for wheat, barley, corn and tears.
One steps to the door on a round stone.
The storehouse feeds all the kinds of sorrow.
And I say to myself: Will you have
sorrow at last? Go on, be cheerful in autumn;
be stoic, yes, be tranquil, calm,
or in the valley of sorrows spread your wings.

JEANNE BLAKE

No Houses, No Gardens

By now, parts of the story of the Hmong are well known: the secret war in Laos; the recruitment of Hmong by the CIA; their heroism as guerrilla fighters along the veins of the "Ho Chi Minh" trail; the promise to take care of them should American forces be defeated. Part of the tragic results of those efforts are also well known: the fall of Laos and Vietnam in 1975; mass refugee movements into Thailand; idle years in refugee camps; acceptance of over fifty thousand Hmong into the United States; appearance of women in sarongs carrying babies on their backs on the streets of major American cities; and, now, the upsweep of the Hmong in the newest cycle of backlash against immigrants, inevitable in hard economic times.

Some important parts of the Hmong story are not so well known: their origin in the basin of the Yang-tze River in northern China; their existence in Chinese records as a distinct ethnic group as early as the tenth century; their seven hundred year history of warfare with the Chinese, with occasional spectacular victories interspersed with hundreds of years of persecution; their flight from the Yunnan and Kwangsi provinces of southern China into the Golden Triangle area beginning in the 1800s and continuing, though much reduced, even today. The history of Hmong as refugees is not a short one.

Over a million Hmong remain in China, recognized today as one of fifty-five official minorities by the government of the Chinese People's Republic. Grandfather Txia puts it this way:

They [Chinese Hmong] don't speak the same language as we do [Lao Hmong]. We cannot understand them because they speak Chinese. We had to give up our clothes and our language so that the Chinese wouldn't recognize us as Hmong. But their ritual practices are the same as ours. And their faces. Those are the ways we know they are Hmong.

The Hmong are often said to have been peaceful people, before the interference of the American CIA, leading an idyllic, independent existence atop their mountains. As Hmong men tell it, however, Hmong have always been fighting a war of some kind. Great-grandfathers remember fighting for or against the Japanese in World War II. Grandfathers remember fighting for or against the French in the postwar years. And every father remembers fighting for the Americans in the second Indochina conflict.

Hmong were not a monolithic force, united under the leadership of the great general, Vang Pao, fighting for the cause of Americans and freedom. Significant numbers of Hmong also fought on the side of the Pathet Lao, under the leadership of Fay Dang Lao. Splinter groups, some of them traditional Hmong messianic movements, were characterized as crazy and attacked by both sides.

Elements of the "peaceful life" theory *are* close to the truth. Hmong are the largest of twenty-plus recognized minority ethnic groups in Laos. High in the mountains, Hmong practice the slash-and-burn agriculture common throughout Southeast Asia. They raise staple foods like dry rice, corn, vegetables, oranges, bananas, and hot peppers, and, in the old days, opium, their cash crop, sold in the spring to Chinese merchants. Hmong are animists; their world is full of spirits, good and bad. Many of the spirits are dead relatives, who remain close to their earthly houses. A goodly fraction of a Hmong life is devoted to the spirits and their rituals.

THE INTERVIEWS

The narratives in this chapter are excerpts of conversations, held specifically for this project, with eight Hmong people in Saint Paul, Minnesota, during January and February 1987. The conversations centered around the themes of making the decision to come to the United States, comparing the old life with the new, connections to the old life, and exploring the components of a successful life, old and new. They are reflections of people's expectations, hopes, and fears about the future; the story of their lives in America; and changes in traditions and cultural elements. They are also assessments of what we can learn from each other.

The conversations took place in people's homes, often with several other listeners present. Six of the eight conversations were conducted in Hmong; two in English. The longest was conducted via an exchange of cassette tapes and long distance telephone calls with Father Tong in California. The names of the participants have been changed at their request. The relationship terms are those by which I, as the daughter of Tong, would address each person, modified by age relationships. Biographical information has been altered slightly to preserve the privacy of specific individuals. As much as possible, allowing for translation and extensive condensation (over fifteen hours of conversations were recorded), the narratives are told in people's own words.

There is nothing scientific, nor particularly scholarly, about the interviews. I simply tapped some of my friends for help. These are people I know well. Our lives are entwined in a number of ways. It was a trade, as any trade among friends. I was expected to—and did—repay the favor and the time. This is not the "Hmong story." There is no "Hmong story," only a collection of individual stories, each a product of a particular personal history and a unique human spirit.

Several of the people interviewed seemed to have a strong focus, an anchor, in their lives. For Grandfather Txia, it is a form of prayer, "asking the sky." For Colonel Vang, it is winning the American dream. For Son Cher, it is helping his people, especially the old. For Grandmother Xia, it is joining her children. For Aunt Mai, it is making friends. For Daughter Pang, it is getting an education. Others, like Uncle Fai, seemed to speak about no such anchor. Tong, my close friend and beloved father, also seems to have no anchor, except, sadly, his anger.

THE TITLE

After the theme of "we have no country," probably the most common theme that Hmong people bring up about their life in the United States is that of not owning anything, of nothing being truly their own. This is often expressed as "we have no houses and no gardens" and "the houses belong to others." There is a meaning to this idea that goes beyond the loss of material possessions and even beyond the loss of independence that having to rent houses brings. The owned house is the basis of nearly all Hmong religious practices. Without a house of your own, these practices make no sense. How can you call a spirit to help you protect a house that belongs to someone else? Inevitably, when one asks an old man or woman what Hmong ceremonies have been changed or abandoned, the answer will be a short description of the changes, closed by, "We cannot do those things here. We have no houses, no gardens." Hmong often say of themselves, "We are a people without houses, without gardens. We are nothing."

Who are these people whom we remember from wartime broadcasts as the "fierce Meo tribesmen," whose "black pajamas" turned out to be just clothes? What are the effects of the near extinction of two generations of men on the "hearts and minds" of a people? Of a people who fled war for fifteen years in their own country, living on "rice that dropped from the sky"?[1] Of a people who killed their children to keep them quiet on the

180

desperate road to Thailand? Of a people half of whose population are simply "lost in Laos"? Of a people who lived idly for five years or more in refugee camps, forbidden, as Aunt Mai says, "to step one foot outside or they'd shoot you"? Of a people who boarded a plane and crossed an ocean so broad it will separate them forever from their country, from "the place where you 'fit' "? Of a people being "dropped into America," where literacy and technical skills and money are what keep you alive? Of a people who realize, now, that most Americans, even though they don't know them, wish they would go home?

COLONEL VANG

(Thirty-seven years old; from the Long Cheng area of central Laos; high-ranking officer in the Royal Lao Army under General Vang Pao; living with wife and five children; small business owner; full-time engineering student; emigrated to Thailand in 1975 and to the United States in the same year.)

The main problems for middle-aged Hmong are money, jobs, and language. Especially hard hit are families who came with only small children. These people must depend entirely on welfare. They've never had education or jobs; they don't know the language. They rely entirely on the good will of agency social workers. It's easier for those whose children had some education in Laos. They can continue their education and, in a short time, can provide for their families.

But this country is not easy. The old and the uneducated live in constant worry. They think, "If my money is cut today, then today is the day I will starve to death." Even those who work fear the loss of their jobs. They know that, when you lose your job and cannot find another one within a month, you'll have to move somewhere else where you've heard there is work.

Relationships have been turned upside down in this country. Many who had always been poor in Laos have come here and achieved a good life. Former leaders, those who were prosperous and powerful in the old country, those who led "with their strength and their brains," have fallen backward. The work is different here and they cannot provide for themselves. If they get jobs in factories, the wages are small and they must work with many former commoners. Once they were the leaders and now they have become children, the led; the "children" have become the leaders. The poor have improved and the prosperous have become poor. The former rich are burdened in heart about their loss of status. They don't want the once-poor people to see their reduced state. We Asians don't think, like you do, that both the stupid and the smart should succeed.

Younger people, like myself, who have a chance for a good education, have no problems. I was a government soldier[2] for ten years. I never wanted to be an average person. I wanted to be one who has more than others: better work, higher education. Now I want to be a leader, to be equal to Americans. I already have a house, money, education. The only thing I haven't done is to be an official. But this, I think, you can only do in your own land. Even if it is held in the palm of another's hand, you have to have your own land. Then you'll have equal rights with others.

This country is not so easy for those who have no education. The old people see something good and want to have it. Cars, for example. They see other people driving cars and they want them, too. But they don't see the problems that they're getting along with the car: insurance, license, driving laws, speeding tickets. All these problems eventually come back upon us young people. The old people are very upset. They say, "No matter what you do, you don't have freedom. Americans say this is a free country, but *this* is freedom?" They don't understand that control is necessary for progress. In our country, there was no planning for the future. There was no thinking about "How will we improve next year?" or "What do we have to do this year to prepare?" Ten years in the future one's life would be exactly as it was today. Here, the government makes budgets and plans five, ten years ahead. But Hmong hearts are suited to the old ways.

The youth have only one problem: they don't listen to their parents. They want to imitate others, but they don't imitate the worthwhile. They follow foolish fads like dyed hair, ragged clothes, wrist chains. Our children see other children wearing these ragged, dirty clothes and think that's the thing to wear. They say, "Oh, you parents! You don't know anything. You're too old-fashioned. You're just talking about your old culture. That's too old-fashioned for us." We're very concerned about this.

To the children close to me, I use the example of the University of Minnesota. I tell them that, out of thirty or forty thousand students, the ones who dress like that are as few as your fingers. The rest wash their faces, comb their hair, and wear, if not fancy, at least clean clothes. The ones with the crazy clothes and painted faces are from poor parents. Americans know that people who look like this are worthless; the worthwhile dress well. Why do we Hmong, as poor as we are, choose these things to imitate? If we do this, others will hate us. We'll never prosper. We must change. We must make our children follow the worthwhile paths.

Old people miss the old country, the old houses up on the mountains, the old fields, the old friends, and the Hmong New Year, the biggest of our celebrations. They think that, in ten to fifteen years, after they're gone, the young people will have lost the Hmong customs. The old people see that Americans are interested in and respect others' customs and cultures. So they have come up with the idea of forming an association and getting funding for preserving our culture.

First, we must preserve our funeral customs. Then, our wedding customs and all the wedding songs.[3] Then the rest of our spiritual practices. Every word, every detail must be recorded, from beginning to end. They should also be translated into English so others can learn about them.

Funerals were a big problem for us until about 1982. Funeral homes didn't understand our customs. The pipes[4] and the drum,[5] all those people crying and wailing made too much noise. The funeral homes were open only a few hours during the day.[6] This "darkened the eyes" of the old people. They scolded their children. "You just brought me here to die like this. I, the older, who gave birth to you, if I die and this is all you do for me, you and your children will be no good." But since 1982, some American funeral homes have realized that what we are doing is part of our culture. Since they don't understand our language, it must seem strange to them, so many people coming and going, talking, drinking.[7] It must look like we are just having fun. But this is our way of grieving, of loving the dead.

The old people ask me every day to try to get funding for a cultural center so they can practice the Hmong customs and teach them to the young. And so when they die, they can have a full Hmong funeral and not have to enter those "carpeted funeral homes."[8]

These are the things that make us keep talking about winning our country back. And saying that, if we can't, we must send our bones back to be re-covered with Lao earth. But going back is mostly a dream. The chances are 99 percent that we'll stay in this country.

What will our future be like? How will we prosper? We must follow the example of the Chinese, the Japanese, and the Koreans. Even our faces are like theirs! These people have succeeded, become prosperous. They did this through education and business. The Chinese, for example, started food businesses. Business also holds the way of prosperity for the Hmong: grocery stores, manufacturing, sewing, whatever looks profitable. We've been here ten years and it's time for us to start our businesses.

The three most important things, then, for our future are: to preserve our funeral, wedding, and spiritual customs; to get education; and to succeed in business.

GRANDFATHER TXIA

(Seventy years old; father of Son Cher; came to the U.S. late in 1980; living with his wife, son, daughter-in-law, and four grandchildren; originally from the Xieng Khouang area of central Laos; later from Long Cheng, the Hmong military headquarters in the later years of the war and an area of extremely heavy combat; follower of a messianic movement rejected by both pro-CIA and the Pathet Lao.)

The sky[9] created all people, each with their own language and customs. And the sky divided the earth's people, each to their own land. The sky causes all things. It caused the Japanese and the French to make war in our country and our country to fall. After the fall of Laos, we fled to Thailand, where we lived for nine months. The Thai hated us. Hmong turned on other Hmong. The poor killed the rich. Our entire family decided to go to America.

Many old people say they didn't want to come to the U.S., that it was too hard. What did you think?

I thought that, too. Our country had already fallen, so I knew in the end we would leave. But we were born on that land. And when we die, we must return there once more. We still regret the loss of our country.

I asked the sky, "King Sky, you created us. Now the rulers have lost the country. Are we to go to the United States and, if we go, will we ever come back? If we are to go and never to come back, we'll lift our hearts to go. If you, King Sky, say there'll be a way to come back, I'll go, and no matter how many years I have to live there, I'll come back. But if you say that, if we go we will never return, then I'll come back another day to ask you whether our lives will prosper. If our lives will be good, we'll go. But if we will go to live like slaves, we won't go."

And the sky answered, "It is well that you go. You will certainly return, but it will take a long time." I thought and thought about whether the sky had spoken the truth or only an illusion. I didn't truly believe. But I remembered something I'd seen years before, in 1962 in Xieng Khouang, when we'd been completely surrounded by Vietnamese forces, almost completely destroyed, and, through the action of the sky, had miraculously escaped. I knew then that the sky didn't lie.

Back then I'd asked the sky, "Why are you spilling out our lives like this? Is it to destroy us completely?" And the sky answered, "This war came from me. When I created you, I gave you the crossbow. I didn't give you guns and knives. I didn't create you to make war, to kill each other. I created you to love each other. But you haven't learned how. If you see someone with money, you kill him to get his money. If you see someone with a beautiful wife, you kill him to get his wife. You fight over land and forget that the land is big enough for everyone. I already divided you each to his own place, each to eat from his own land. I created enough land for everyone to have a place. And there are multitudes of women, enough for everyone to have a wife. Why do you keep on killing each other? I've brought on this trouble purposely, to make you suffer and learn. I am the creator. No one of you can create a fish—only I can. No one of you can create a tree—only I can. If you change your ways, do not kill, do not steal, do not take others' wives, then I'll stop the war." And for three years, there was no war near us. Until we went back to the old, evil ways.

The way of war is not the way of riches. People die on both sides, everyone dies, just the same. The leaders just want to live a free life. There is not a single person who can create a fish. Not a single person who can say, "Oh, now I've made a tree." No matter how hard he tries. In the end, we have to return to pray to the sky.

Do you think your life will be successful, prosperous in the future?

I don't know. It will be as it was in Laos. You [Americans] will take care of the goodhearted, the industrious. The lazy, evil ones, you won't. I've seen that in your country, the leaders love the good and not the bad. The sky gives such a heart to the leaders. Hmong, Americans, all races, all have good and all have bad. It's like the trees: some bear sweet fruit and some bear bitter fruit.

What Hmong customs have changed (will change) in the United States?

In ordinary customs, we'll imitate your ways. But religious customs, each race of people has its own. It depends on the sky. We'll have to see what the sky teaches us. Whether the sky will teach us a new way or will have us go back to the old ways.

We'll have to ask the sky. Asking the sky is like asking people. You don't just sit and wait for people to volunteer information. You have to ask specific questions in order to get it. And that's the way you must deal with the sky. With people, you have to explain something from the root up and ask for an answer. They listen and, if it's a worthwhile matter, they'll give you a worthwhile answer. The sky is the same. It answers specific questions.

Are you worried and sad like some of the old people?

I'm not troubled in any way. I'm just upset and ashamed that we lost our country. Some bad people, young people here revile us because we lost our country. But the good ones speak gently, teach us, give us clothes, food. If you Americans weren't good, we wouldn't all be fat!

How much of the Hmong customs do you still use here? You still shaman, don't you?

We've abandoned a lot. I still shaman[10] to ask the spirits about all kinds of problems, like people getting sick because their spirits have been taken from their bodies and people having trouble because they owe money from past lives.[11] People thought that by coming to America, they could escape the spirits, but HA! There are more spirits here than in the old country! The spirits like a rich country, too!

185

What about the wedding songs?

We cannot sing the long wedding songs here because people have much more work to do here than they did in Laos. Everyone has a job and they cannot be absent or they will lose it. So we've had to abandon these. In our country, we had enough money, enough crops, and enough time for these, but here we've had to give them up.

Also, here we only rent our houses. Our houses and gardens are not our own. They're small, rented houses with room for only a few. They aren't suited for inviting large numbers of people. In our country, if your house was so full it broke, it didn't matter. We could have two-, three-, four-day weddings.

Some old people say they are unhappy about dying here and not having a proper funeral and burial. What do you think about that?

There are good things and bad things about those big Hmong customs. Funeral customs are things that *people* thought up. The old people just did whatever their hearts wanted. If people had not created them, then everyone would do them exactly the same way. The important thing is to follow the ways the sky has taught.

What about your own death, if your sons do not have proper funeral clothes or a proper Hmong funeral for you?

I'll tell the truth: if one cannot have these things, one's heart will be unsatisfied. I'd be satisfied with just three sets of funeral clothes.[12] It's not good to die naked. The rich should wear rich clothes and the poor should wear poor clothes. Then the soul will be happy.

Would you go back to Laos if you had the chance? Why?

Yes, absolutely, I'd go back. The sky gave us a certain piece of land as our own and so we must go back. All land is the sky's land, that's true. But the sky divided it among the people of the world. Each one can only truly live on his own land. The sky created it, people didn't. The sky gave us the land and told us to take care of it. If you work a land, you must go to see it. When you live in another's country, all you see is others' land, not your own.

What Hmong customs do you think your children must preserve?

Nothing. Like I said before, if the sky directs us to follow a new way, new customs, we'll follow the new way. If the sky doesn't so direct, we'll follow the old ways without giving anything up. Except the parts that give offense [in the new country]. Our children must study the arts and sciences. But about religious practices, it's up to them. I wouldn't force them to do any particular thing.

Will you teach Hmong ritual practices to your children?

If they want to follow our spiritual customs, I'll teach them. If they don't, I won't.

What would you like us to learn from Hmong?

Whatever you would like to learn. If you want to learn about shamanism, we'll teach you. Or about our New Year. Whatever suits you.

What would you change if you went back to Laos?

If the sky tells us to change things, we'll change them. If not, we won't. The sky is the one who created us. The old ways were taught to us by the sky.

What things are these? The rodents and the birds each have their own cry. Each kind of people speaks its own language. The sky taught each to make its own kind of house. The sky taught the doves to bore holes in trees and use leaves to make their beautiful houses. The sky taught others to live in holes in the ground, so that's where they build their nests. Others, the sky told to live in caves and, no matter how far away they go, they always come back to sleep in the caves. We are all created by the sky. Everything else we have thought up ourselves.

Everything depends on your ideas, on your brains. The lives of the lazy and the satisfied will come to nothing. We must learn from and imitate the energetic, the worthwhile. All customs and ways of life are correct. There are no mistakes.

SON CHER

(Twenty-five years old; youngest son of Grandfather Txia; single; six years of education in Laos; two years of college in the U.S.; caseworker for a multi-ethnic social service agency; emigrated to Thailand in 1975 and to the U.S. in 1980. Interview conducted in English.)

When I left the refugee camp, I was happy because I had the chance to go to the United States. But halfway to Bangkok,[13] and getting on the plane, I started to worry. I couldn't get a clear picture. It was like trying to break through the world and see the other side. I didn't know what my life would be like in the United States. I didn't know what I'd add up to, who would be my friend. I got out my book and wrote the story of everything that happened along the way.

One Cambodian woman got stuck in the plane's bathroom for over seven hours. I thought about that lady, about all our people. We didn't know anything, even something as simple as that. How would we ever make a life in the United States?

The first year I was sure we had made the wrong choice. I was put into ninth grade for half a year. Math was easy for me because I'd already studied simple algebra and geometry in Laos. Everything was easy until they put me into a literature class. We had a quiz on the first day. I just pushed my paper away because I didn't know what I was supposed to do. I really felt awful during that first half year.

After that, I began to understand much, much more. I picked up a lot of things. All my friends were American. Not having anybody around me to speak Hmong to, I had to force myself to speak English. Also, in a small town, people are very friendly. Everybody wants to talk to you. So I did alright during the second year, when I went to a half year of tenth grade and a half year of eleventh grade. I didn't get very good grades, but I did okay.

That first year, I had to help my family a lot. I was the only one who could speak a little English. I had to take them everywhere: for physical check-ups, to the dentist, to the hospital. And there was so much paperwork! I had to handle anything that required English. That made me feel proud of myself. I'd had a lot of problems in the beginning but I was beginning to understand the language and the system. I was getting better every day.

My older brother[14] has always been the leader of the family. In a lot of ways, I still feel that he can lead, that he should be the one to make the decisions. But a lot of things have changed. The language, the laws, the systems in the United States are different. I don't want to say that I know more, but I think I might have a better, clearer understanding than he does. He knows a lot, though, and he is my older brother. We say that the person who saw the sun and the moon before you will know more than you. And it's true.

The old people always talk about how much they miss our old country. It's because they grew up and did so many good things there. They think, "Oh, I lived in this house. When I lived there, I did this and this and this. I went fishing here in this river, farmed in this field, hunted in this forest." When they think about all that detail, they miss their old country very much. Wherever you grow up, you will miss the place. If the Hmong people who were born here and grew up in this culture went to Laos, they would miss Minnesota. They'd say, "Oh, I miss the zoo."

There are many things about our culture that should be kept. The ceremonies, the musical instruments, the social events. Our old ritual practices should still be done once in a while, maybe in a little different way. It would be too hard to just cut them off completely. But once the old people are gone . . . it's very hard to study to become a shaman; it would be impossible. If those things were lost, it wouldn't bother me personally very much. But it would be a loss to the whole people, the Hmong.

Our language, though, is a very important issue. People are already starting to worry that their children do not know how to speak their own language, only English. It would not be good to let our language get lost. We must think of some way to teach our children the language.

My hopes for my life are still in the dark. Right now, education is probably the most important step that I need to take. And, later, to get a better job. If my way is the right way, I want to try to get my people to understand what steps they have to take in order to make a new life. I feel that if you try really hard, whether your English is good or not, if you really try to improve your life, you can do it in this country. But you must work hard. It's very important to me to help my people. I'm not really doing that right now. To do that, you have to be a person that others know and respect, which I'm not.

I sometimes think I have a double life. We have to think about where we came from, what kind of people we are, what language we are speaking, what we look like. We have to remember the old, but we also have to face the new.

I would say my true home is somewhere in the middle of nowhere. Right now, I'm in the United States. I'm working. I have a house. I'm very comfortable. This is my house. This is my place. This is my village. This is where I belong. But if I think about it . . . I wasn't born here. I came from another country. I came as a refugee. I don't know how long I'm going to be here. Most people my age would say the same thing. We really don't know where we're going to be in the future. We've been here just long enough to feel comfortable but not long enough to feel that this is our home.

I think that you have to be comfortable wherever you are, to try to adjust to where you are. Things will go much easier that way than if you think about it too much. The Lao have a saying, "If you've fallen in with pigs, you have to be a pig. If you've fallen in with buffalos, you have to be a buffalo." Whether you're a cow or anything else, when you're with others you must feel that you're a part of them. You need to make yourself comfortable and think about what you should do to be self-sufficient at this moment instead of saying, "I'll wait here until the grass is greener on the other side, and then I'll jump over."

UNCLE FAI

(About fifty years old; husband of Grandmother Xia; living with wife and three children; from Nong Het region of southern Laos, near the Vietnam border; emigrated to Thailand in 1983 and to the U.S. in late 1984. Uncle Fai is able to describe life in Laos after the fall.)

We Hmong have always had war. When my parents were eight or nine

189

years old, it was war with the Chinese. In our country, there were two opposing groups: the "Democrats"[15] under Souvanna Phouma, and the "Vietnamese"[16] under Souphanouvong. Hmong were divided, too: Democrats under Tou Bee Lee Fong and Vang Pao, and *nyaj laj*[17] under Fay Dang Lao and Tou Thao Yang. Fay Dang's side got help from the Chinese and the Vietnamese; Vang Pao's side got money and assistance from the Americans. That's how we got the name "American soldiers." We all fought, the young and the old alike. Neither side could defeat the other and vast numbers were killed as the victory went back and forth. Finally, they told us to quit fighting. They said that we were all Lao, all brothers. They said that we would tell all foreigners, the Chinese, the Americans, the Vietnamese, to go back to their own countries and that we Lao would embrace each other as brothers. They said that Lao had not made war on Lao; that outside countries had enticed us to do this. They promised to restore the country, the economy, education. We believed they'd be able to do this so we ended the war. Vang Pao, having been on the American side, left with the Americans. The Vietnamese came in and collected all our guns. They led people away to "study the new ways" but it was really to jail and to death. They said that it had not been a negotiated settlement but that they'd won a military victory. They took all those who had been army officials away and killed them.

We were afraid we'd be killed, too, so we took up the fighting again. But it was only a peasant war, one without leaders. Vang Pao had fled. We asked the Thai for help many times but were refused. There was no answer from America. In the end, we decided to follow our leaders and flee to Thailand.

In Laos, we had land and houses. We built them ourselves, we rented nothing. The land actually belonged to the government, but anyone could claim it as his own and build his house on it. We still miss our old life very much. Whatever we did, no one had anything to say about it. Whatever we liked to do, we did.

In Thailand, we were not allowed to do anything. We only lived on begged food. We ate the UN's rice[18] and lived on whatever other countries donated. We decided that, since it was the Americans who had led us into war, we should go to America.

Here in the United States, the leaders love us.[19] Those who have no houses or no land request assistance from the government[20] for food, housing, and school. The Hmong are very grateful for that. But we are still bereft of something: we have no houses or gardens like in our own country. We have no houses of our own. We have no land of our own. We have no place where we can raise animals. This makes us sad. We worry every day about our lives. What will happen to us? Will someone find work for us to do? If not, we will be very poor.

Why did you come? What were your feelings when you got on the airplane to come to this country?

In Laos, the Vietnamese leaders were afraid of anyone who was smart. They were afraid that these people would find a way to enlist the aid of other countries or collect a group of soldiers and resume the war. So they took them all away and killed them. Only the stupid ones were left. We saw that the only way we could live was by becoming stupid, believing and following whatever anyone else told us. If you made any answer, they would know you weren't stupid and one day they would come for you and kill you.

So we went to Thailand. We thought we'd stay there, but our Hmong leaders had no power to help us. So we thought, with no one to help us, we'd better come to the United States. We came to learn why you knew how to love and lead your country, to love all races and never make war. We came to discover your ideas, what you were taught that made you so good. Now we're here and we see that it is true: your people, young and old, men and women, listen and obey. You are not evil to each other, you do not kill each other, you do not have war. If, in the future, we get our country back, we'll follow these American customs. We'll have our government teach our citizens as yours teaches you.

Would you go back if you had the chance?

If all of our family would go back, then I'd go. If I could take my wife and all my children along, I'd go so I could return to the use of all of our old customs.

Do you think the women would go back to Laos?

Some would go and some wouldn't. In the United States, women's lives have improved. In Laos, the men had all the money. A single woman couldn't make a living. Here people can earn their own money and they don't have to rely on anyone else. Women's lives have definitely improved.

Some men say they are not happy about the rights women have in this country. What do you think about that?

In this country, women go to work and meet other men whom they think are richer or better than their husbands. Then they abandon their husbands. We men don't like this. A much better idea would be to find work that both husband and wife could do together, like we did in Laos. Separation just causes problems.

What Hmong customs do you still use in the United States?

We still use shamanism and call the spirits. We still consult with the relatives of a couple in cases of household problems. We still do not want married couples to divorce. If they stay together, each side gets a new group of relatives. But if they divorce, both the husband and the wife become poor again.

Some Hmong have become Christians. They did this in Laos, too, but it was mostly people who had some problems or guilt they wanted to escape. In the United States, the Christian Hmong want everyone to convert. We spiritists[21] think Christianity is fine, but that it is not truly our tradition. It is an American and European tradition. Our traditions were given to us by Shao,[22] the original creator, and we've preserved them ever since.

It's very hard. Our young people go to school, marry, move far away, but they know nothing. They just convert because it's easy. They don't listen to their parents.

What do the old people think about these customs?

All such customs are equally good. If the young want to learn the old ways, the old will teach them. But if they don't, then they should just follow the new ways.

The old people are a little sad. When Hmong die, the survivors must burn paper money[23] so that the dead person's spirit will be rich in the afterlife. Christians do not do this. Their spirits will be poor and hungry and will return to cause trouble.

Are you sad about the small funerals Hmong have in this country?

Yes, I am. I'm afraid those spirits will be poor in the afterlife. But the young and the old don't agree. I don't know what to say. I prefer the old ways. If your funeral homes would allow it, we would do exactly as we did in Laos.

What do you think your future will be like?

We'll be a little poor. We won't be able to get jobs. In Laos, the illiterate were better off than the literate. The literate did only a single job, for wages. The illiterate did all kinds of things: farming, trading, raising animals. In this country, the illiterate have fallen behind. There are no jobs for us.

How do you feel about being here?

It's the same as it would have been if I had stayed in Laos. In Laos, I was worried about being killed in war or by some rule of law. Here, I'm worried about the problems I'll have in the future, about having no work. My heart is equally heavy, just about different things.

GRANDMOTHER XIA

(Sixty-six years old; wife of Uncle Fai; living with husband and three children; from Nong Het region of southern Laos, near the Vietnam border; from a well-educated family, closely related to influential members of the former Pathet Lao; emigrated to Thailand in 1983 and to the U.S. in late 1984. Several of Grandmother Xia's sons and close nephews went to Thailand as early as 1975. Some remain in Thailand; others came as single men to the U.S. in 1979.)

I'm very happy to have come here. All my children came before me and now I can live as my heart wishes. It's good to live in a prosperous country where they provide for you, even if you are living on their land. I'm a little upset about one thing, though. We are a people who have lost our country. When you live in another's country, there is no land you can call your own, or your people's own. You have to rent the house of others, their gardens. It seems like you are the only ones without a country.

This country is much better than Laos. Laos is very poor; you have only your strength to eat on. Your back feeds you. In the good years you eat and in the bad years you starve. Here machines and capable people do the work.

Why did you decide to interview[24] so quickly and come to the United States, instead of remaining in Thailand like your relatives?

We started out from Laos with the intention of coming to the United States. We never planned to do more than rest a while in Thailand. All our children were already here. We needed to join them.

Would you go back to Laos if you had the chance?

I'm old and good for nothing. I wouldn't go back without my children. My sons grew up here. They are your people. They can work and provide for me. Most of me would say stay here; only a little part of me would say go back.

We old people think we will die here and this makes us very sad. We came here to join our children, it's true, but we left our parents and our relatives behind. But it doesn't matter. We've already seen enough poverty and misery in our own country. To live and eat with one's children is good enough.

Our children will grow up and go to school with your children. It remains to be seen whether they will ever see their country of Laos again.

How do you feel about your children losing Hmong customs and language?

We're a unique race, but after we, the old, are gone, our children will know nothing of the old rituals. They'll have to become your people. I wouldn't say this if we had a country and still used all of the old ways. But if we cannot go back, if we have to live in this big country, after this generation our children will be your people. Those who have been here six or seven years are already Americans. But we who have come recently still follow most of the old ways.

How much of the old Hmong ways do you still use?

Exactly like in the past. Shamans still practice, we still call spirits, tie strings around our wrists.[25] The Hmong who go to church don't do these things. They don't even have Hmong weddings; they have church weddings. But our group of relatives still practices the old ways.

The Hmong who have converted to Christianity are constantly preaching at us to convert. The Christian Hmong say that when our generation is gone, everyone must become Christian and that Hmong must give up the *qeej*,[26] give up the Hmong funeral songs. The young seek the easy way; they become Christians.

How does this make you feel?

My son-in-law has been here for twelve years and he explained the truth to us about Christianity. Only the surface is different from our ways. The Bible is just like our funeral song, the "Advice to the Survivors."[27] You bury the dead in a casket; we carry them on logs to be buried. But our "Opening the Way"[28] song and the prayers from the Bible are the same. Before meals, Christians pray to heaven; we Hmong invite our parents and ancestors to eat with us. It's the same. People who have been Christians a long time know the truth. It's just those who have converted recently who say all kinds of things.

What is your life like here?

I'm worried about how I will live. There is no land to work, no opportunity for us to earn money. We stupid old people, no one wants to hire us because we don't know the language. How will I eat? I've fallen back on my children. But my children help me. They have jobs. Each one adds what he can and, together, we all get by.

I'm upset with myself because I don't know a single word of English. My children can all talk with Americans. Even my husband has learned enough to talk on the telephone. The only stupid one around here is me. No matter how much I want to talk to our teachers, I can't. When Americans come to our house, I want to be polite and invite them in, but I'm afraid to open my mouth for fear of making a mistake.

It's not that I haven't studied. We've had a tutor one evening a week for a year. But I'm old and cannot remember what she teaches. I've had so many children and so much suffering in my life that my brain is no good. I don't see very well and I can hardly write at all. Ai! I'm just old and can do nothing! I do know how to dial the telephone and can recognize all the numbers and letters. So I can recognize house numbers and street names.

What do you do every day?

Watch the grandchildren, clean the house, do the dishes. Just live. We old people, all we know how to do is stay at home. When my sons and daughters-in-law have a big meal,[29] they invite me. And when I have to prepare a big meal, they come to help. I have no worries.

Except this problem with my daughter. She's just gotten married and I miss her terribly. She was so industrious. She did most of the work around here. I'm very worried about her life and her happiness. She doesn't know these people very well and now they've taken her far away.[30] I can't watch out for her so far away. After a few months, when I'm sure she's happy with them and they really love her, I won't worry so much. But she just left today and this is still a new hurt for me so I'm very, very sad and lonely right now.

As you live every day, what feelings are in your heart?

Except for this problem with my daughter, I'm not sad about anything. When I lived on the other side of the world, my children were far away and I cried every day. But I have come here, we are all together and, for these two years, there have been no problems.

Our own country has been destroyed. We must resolve to live here with our children. Wherever my children live, that's where I'll live. Whatever they do, I'll accept it. Whatever they cannot do and must, therefore, be provided by others, it'll be enough for me. I'll live and raise and educate my children and they'll be able to provide for me and I won't be poor any more.

AUNT MAI

(Forty-six years old; mother of Pang; living with her husband and three teenage children; from Luang Prabang area of northern Laos, the least educated and most rural region; emigrated to Thailand in 1975 and to the U.S. in 1980. Aunt Mai is one of the most enterprising Hmong women in the city. She's first on the scene for opportunities like garden plots, flea markets, craft sales. She's the behind-the-scenes organizer of a group of her husband's relatives, many of whom have arrived only recently.)

We lived six years in Thailand. We thought about it long and hard, about things like "We'd never again have a country" and "We have no way to

set one foot out of this camp" and "We only have what others donate."
They locked us in that camp with a fence. We were so poor. We knew
we'd never have a country again. So we decided, for good or for bad, to
come to America. If we never got our country back, we'd never see it
again and that would be that. If we did get it back, the American rulers
would probably let us go back. So in 1980 we interviewed and came to the
United States.

As we started out, we were worried sick. But we were also happy
because all of us, even our grandparents,[31] were going together. Good or
bad, at least we'd be together. Even as we got up into the airplane, we
were so sad we began to die inside. I had left my parents behind, all my
relatives, my country. We knew we would never come back and see our
country again.

Your country is a fine one. But how can I ever describe those first three
months! We were desperately poor. We slept and ate on the floor, all
from one pot. We didn't even have any dishes! No one knew a single
word of the language. For almost a year we cried. We thought we'd made
a terrible mistake by coming.

Shortly after we arrived, my daughter went to the hospital to have a
baby. I didn't even know how to get there to take food to her. The first
night I stayed until they wouldn't let me stay any later and then a nurse
had to take me home! Once when I was visiting her, I just walked out of
the door of the hospital and waited there for the bus. I didn't know the
bus only stopped in certain places. At our house, it stopped right outside
the door. Oh, so stupid! And one time I got on the bus and rode and rode
until I suddenly realized everyone else had gotten off the bus. My son-in-
law, who had come a little before us and knew a few words of English,
told the bus driver we wanted to get off downtown. The bus driver said
he was at the end of the line but not to get off, that he'd take us back
downtown and show us where to get off. He even wrote a little note
telling us how to take the bus to the hospital. Oh, we were so poor and
miserable! We thought we'd certainly not be able to live here.

Even now when I think about it I cry. I'd left my mother and father
behind and come to a strange country. My daughter moved away with
her husband and I missed her terribly. I became like a crazy person. I got
sick all the time. I had to go to the hospital almost every week. Eventual-
ly, welfare sent out a social worker to find out what was wrong. She
discovered my extreme sadness and talked with me about it. She gave me
a bicycle to ride. By that time I knew some of the Hmong people in our
building.[32] I started going outside more. After about half a year, I learned
to walk to the grocery store. Pao's mother and Lia's mother[33] took me
everywhere with them. We started school together. Finally 1982 was
over. It wasn't quite so hard. But I was still sad and heavy in heart. I
thought that, if life were going to be as hard as this, I might as well make
up my mind to die.

What was it like in 1983-84?

All of us were in school. The children grew up a little and learned a little English. It wasn't as hard. I got very motivated to go to school. I was upset that I was already old and it was so hard to learn. I wanted to learn enough to help myself. In 1983 and '84, I wasn't so miserable as before. By 1985, my son could fill out forms[34] for us. We didn't have to rely on other people for help. Finally, in 1986, we resigned ourselves to living here. If we ever get our country back and they *make* us go back, we'll probably go back. But, as long as we don't have a country, we'll just live here.

The most important thing was that I had American friends to help me with things I didn't know. Wherever I've lived, I've always had many friends. In Thailand, I befriended a Thai couple who came to buy our embroideries.[35] Through them, I became the one who organized the handcraft business[36] in the camp. I was good friends with all the Hmong Thai[37] women in the market. Nowadays, I have many American friends. Whatever they tell me to do, I do. Wherever they tell me to go, I go. As long as they take me, I go. I've gone lots of places and done lots of things. You go someplace, you learn something.

You were one of the first Hmong women who learned to drive. Why was that?

My husband told me to hurry up and get my permit and learn to drive because all we knew how to do was sit at home. We don't have small children, and soon they'd probably make both of us go to work. One person wouldn't be able to take both of us to work. So I hurried up and got my permit and practiced driving. And it wasn't so hard after all! I took the test and got my license in 1982. Then, whenever I needed to go anywhere, I could. But it was still very hard. When you don't know the language, you can only go places you're familiar with. If you end up in a strange place, you get lost and can't find your way home!

You're the one who always knows about everything first. Why is that?

That's true. It's like this: I go around and see new things and think, "Oh, I'm not so old. I'll have to practice this so I can do it well." No one can do anything well the first time. Everyone has to practice and learn. So I make up my mind to practice things until I can do them.

Some people say that Hmong men are upset that in this country, women have rights. What do you think about that?

Oh, that's a lot of nothing. You have to remember that long ago when you were very young and getting married, your own mother and father told you that you had to think of your husband as higher than you; that, as a wife, you must never "go above your husband's head." That way others would respect him. You have to remember that they paid a lot of money to get you[38] and you have no money at all. So you must never "exceed" your husband, never use the law or custom against your family. Otherwise everyone will talk about it and your life will be ruined. You have your husband's relatives to be afraid of on one hand and your own on the other. And you must remember that your children are old enough to be embarrassed by what you do. That's what I think. Those people who say, "Oh, I'll go to America where I'll have rights!" What do they think they will be able to DO with those rights!

What Hmong customs do you think must be preserved?

We cannot follow the old customs, even if we try. We are a people who have nothing. We have no houses so we cannot see the way clear to do any of the old rituals. All the houses are others' houses. We have no way to follow the spirits' ways.

What Hmong ways do you think your children should preserve?

For those who are still trying to follow the way of the spirits, the most important thing is to remember how your ancestors performed those rituals and teach them exactly that way to your children. For those who have become Christian, the most important thing is to teach your children to observe the food taboos[39] after childbirth.

What if your children forget the Hmong language?

As long as the old people are still alive, we must teach our children to speak Hmong so they will remember. After we old people have died, it won't matter. We won't know. All our children will have become Americans.

What if they not only forget how to speak Hmong, but forget everything, clothes, celebrations . . .?

As long as we're dead, it won't matter. Let them all change into Americans.

And if the name "Hmong" is completely lost?

If we can't go back to our country, it doesn't matter. Let everyone be children of this government. Only if we go back will it be important to remember our customs.

What do you think will help you in the future?

I'm very worried about my future. We old people, who are unable to find or do work, are very worried. Our children have gone to school and, later on, they'll be able to find work. But they'll have their own families to provide for. How will we old people eat? Right now the children are still young and we're able to provide for them. But in the future . . . if we had a little work to do, we'd have a little money to live on and we wouldn't have to worry so much. If I hadn't been so sick, once our children are all grown up, both my husband and I could get jobs and that would be enough to provide for us. But I've been sick and had surgery . . . you have to realize that, when you can no longer work, it's all over.

Would you go back to Laos if you had the chance?

Oh, I think I wouldn't be able to provide for myself any more. I think I wouldn't go back. I've already told my mother and father that I've had surgery and many illnesses and could not farm or provide for myself and so I won't go back. All my children are grown. My daughters have married and I have several nearly grown sons. If they were not to permit the Hmong to live in this country, we'd have to go back. But as long as they allow us to live here, we won't go back.

DAUGHTER PANG

(Sixteen years old; sophomore in high school; daughter of Aunt Mai; living with her parents and two brothers; emigrated to Thailand in 1975 and to the U.S. in 1980. Interview conducted in English.)

What courses are you taking this year, Pang?

All the required courses: biology, math, geometry—that's pretty hard. And gym, because it's required. I'm interested in taking pictures, like pictures of viruses or of someone who is very sick to study about them. So I'm taking a photography class, learning to develop film and print pictures.

And I'm taking a Lao language class. My mom and dad say it's important for me. So in case we do get to go back to Laos, I won't need an interpreter. If you were in business, or were a doctor or a nurse, and someday we have a chance to go back, and people come to you, you wouldn't know how to talk to them and you'd have to find an interpreter. So I thought maybe it was a good idea. And even though we might not have a chance to go back, I'm interested in it anyway because a lot of the letters we get have Lao words in them and no one in this family understands them.

Lao will be my fourth language: my own (Hmong), English, and last summer I took Chinese at Highland High School in a program for talented youth. They have a Chinese class at Highland right now. I really want to go there to continue because someday I want to go to China. I want to see the Great Wall, Hong Kong, all the interesting places. I just want to explore for a while.

What would a successful life be like?

At my age, I'm too young to be a real success. It would be to have a real career, to buy a house so that you can live in your own house and do anything you want in it, to get married, to have kids. I guess that would be a success.

What is the most important thing for you to do to be a success?

Education is very important right now. Everything requires an education. If you have no education, you have no way. All my friends have the same feelings about education. Some people, though, just decide to start their life early, to get married early. But not the people I go around with. The only friends I know think education is important.

What advice would you give American students?

If they were my friends and didn't study, I'd tell them to study and not fool around. If they smoked or drank, I'd tell them not to do that. But that would be like telling them what to do, and I know people don't like to be told what to do. I would tell them to think about it, that those things are bad for you.

And I'd encourage people who are thinking about dropping out of school to stay in school. I have a friend who's dropping out of school. He's a senior and he only has four credits left. I tell him every day that, if he got his diploma, his education, he could get a much better job. But some people have different feelings about their education, and they're going to do whatever they want to do.

Was it a good idea for your parents to have come to the United States?

Oh yes, a very good idea. You hear on the news about people still back there, how they're being punished. And you think they should all be here, in a nice, safe place.

What would you tell your cousins who are still in Thailand about life here?

I'd tell them that it's really nice here; that if they came, they could go to school and learn a lot; that it's better than in Thailand. I'd tell them that you can have a nice life if you have a good education, a good background.

When you're with your Hmong friends, do you speak mostly Hmong or mostly English?

Mostly English. We only speak Hmong a little, like when we don't know the English word for something. Or if someone has just arrived, we'll speak Hmong to them.

Do you understand the old people when they speak Hmong?

Yes, those things that I've heard before. But the things I've never heard before, I don't understand.

What Hmong customs do you think you'll use in the future?

I don't think I'll use any. I want to be a Christian; I'm already baptized. The old ways cost too much money. If you're Christian, you just say a prayer and you really get what you ask for without paying any money.

If you had a chance to go back to Laos, would you go or stay?

I'd like to stay here. I could always go for a visit.

Do you think you will change into an American?

I think I'll be two things. I'll keep my culture and also become an American citizen. I think it's not good if you change completely into an American and forget your own culture. But if you live in someone else's country, and just keep on doing things your own way, that's not good either. I'll have to be two things.

FATHER TONG

(Forty-six years old; widower; six living children, two married; from the Luang Prabang region of central Laos; soldier in the Royal Lao Army; emigrated to Thailand in 1975 and to the U.S. in 1979. Father Tong was interviewed by cassette and telephone. He responded in a traditional mode of speaking about one topic at a time. He addressed a total of twenty-nine subjects. I've selected four subjects relating to parts of the American social system: parent/child rights, law enforcement, court cases, and welfare. I've also selected some material expressed in the beautiful metaphors that permeate the language of the Hmong.)

This "new life." I don't know anything about a "new life." We thought we'd see the light but it is completely dark before our eyes. We old people are completely blind. All we can do is beg for food and drink and wait until we die for it all to be ended.

In our country, we had fields of rice and corn, gardens and houses that were truly ours. There were no charges or bills for anything. Not for medical care, not even for the government. Now we have fallen into the country of others and have become wanderers, migrants, hobos. We have no houses, no gardens in which to live. We're like dogs in the mountain caves, living a few days here and a few days there. For what reason should we think our lives will be good?

One of the concerns for us, the old people, is raising our children in your country. We can't escape this problem; it's like having someone riding on the back of our necks! Our parental rights have been taken away from us. When we chastise our children, they call the police. We old people don't know English and, when the police come, our children lie to them. The police believe the children and not the parents. They arrest us and press charges against us. This has happened to us many times. Our hearts have gone crazy with worrying. To raise children properly, parents must have rights. Parents spank children to make them worthwhile; parents don't beat children to kill them! Parents should have the right to slap or spank their children to make them grow up worthwhile. If parents beat their children severely, make their children's blood flow, of course that is not right. Parents must not beat up children like that. But if parents take a small switch and switch their children a little to make them worthwhile, then just let the parents take care of things. We ask that the American leaders investigate this matter. Don't simply arrest the old people who cannot speak English. To believe the children and jail the parents is the communist way! This has made the old people so angry that some have even committed suicide over it. But we Hmong are a people with no land and no country, so we can do nothing.

Why do you Americans run your system of law enforcement the way you do? Why is it that, when a burglar breaks into your home, your system helps the burglar and not the homeowner? Why is it that, even if you call the police *while* the burglar is stealing your things, they don't come? Much later, after the robber has already stolen the money, property, everything, and escaped far away, they send that car crying "veeoo, veeoo," coming so slowly that the robber doesn't even see it! "Next time, call us," the police say. We wish that, when someone calls the police, they would come immediately, arrest the burglar, and jail him for real. This is the correct way. Help the homeowner, not the thief. We wish the American system could be changed like this.

In the American legal system, one can keep on talking for ten years, maybe a hundred years, and still matters have no end. The American legal system actually prevents problems from coming to a final conclusion. It's just a way of enticing people to spend money. If I have a little money, I go out and hire a lawyer; if you have a little money, you go out and hire a lawyer. People spy on each other, look for problems, create new ones. The original problem has no way of coming to an end. We wish that this could be changed. When you bring matters to court, they should be settled once and for all. Elders[40] should investigate and determine who is truly guilty. The innocent should be declared innocent, once and for all. The winner should really win and the loser should really lose. This is how legal matters and court cases should be handled.

If Americans love us, they should love us effectively. The way things are, with one hand people stroke our heads and with the other they pinch our asses. They give us a little money and then turn around and curse us for it. They say, "Oh, Hmong are lazy. They just live on welfare, they don't work." We're not lazy. We'd work if we could. But we don't know the language, anything it takes to get and keep work. The consonants, we do not know. The vowels, we do not know. People see our foreign faces and do not want to hire us. We can help you but you must help us first. No one can know what he hasn't been taught. Is there an American who, having never learned, can farm like we farmed? Try it. Get a field and we'll plant rice and see whether the American would know how to weed. See whether he'd know which were the weeds and which were the rice. The American would probably pull up some of the rice! You must teach us so that we truly know the language, the things that are important. Then our children will grow up to be productive citizens of your country.

Each race of people should follow its own customs. Americans should follow American customs, Hmong should follow Hmong customs. This is the better way. We Hmong should continue to do such things as calling spirits and, in cases of sickness or weakness, restoring the spirit, the soul. These are not things you can see, but when you call the spirits of your family, they are healthy and live well. Hmong should not be made to go to church. If some want to go voluntarily, that's fine. But it is much better to follow the old customs.

If we could have what our hearts most desire, we would like an area of land, even if it is in your country, to live on. Then we could all go there and feed ourselves. Everyone would have a house and property of his own. We would never have to beg for the government's welfare money. We would be able to provide for ourselves. We could stop living like dogs in caves. Our old people could stop being so heavy-hearted.

We cannot go back. The sky is too high. The ocean is too wide. We have no airplanes. We have no money. Please love us as you love your children. Then we will be able to live with you, to be your servants. If you do not love us, we cannot serve you, follow your wishes. Whatever some of us may be like, please give us a little food to eat. Whoever is poor, please help him so that, whatever he tries, he will succeed. Help children go to college and, those who cannot, help them find work so that they can put food into their own mouths. For those who work, please do not deduct so much from their wages that the money is not enough to live on. If you do not do this, in the end, our people will die out. Americans do not need to use guns to kill us, they can use food.

Who will love us Hmong? We are so stupid. We are like a herd of animals, like cows or horses or buffalo, with no owner to watch over us.

203

We are a people with no houses and no owners. We're a people like the bat. Every night we just hang by our feet up in the trees, our bodies hanging down under the branches. If we try to go live among the birds, the birds don't accept us. If we try to go live among the mice, the mice don't accept us either. If we Hmong try to speak English, it's not true English. If we try to speak Lao, the Lao don't accept us either. We are a people with no country, like the animals in the forest with no owner. We old Hmong people think that, in the end, the seed of the Hmong people will die out.

The Twenty-nine Subjects

1. Our old, independent, isolated way of life
2. The beginning of the war, in-country refugees
3. American medicine, hospitals
4. No houses and no gardens
5. The old people are blind and cannot learn
6. "Eating" American money
7. Raising children
8. The behavior of some women
9. Children and pornography
10. Autopsies
11. Each should follow their own customs
12. Living on welfare
13. The American way of teaching
14. A people of wanderers
15. No leaders, no place
16. The American law enforcement system
17. The American legal system
18. Opium addiction
19. We are your servants
20. How to truly help the Hmong
21. Keeping our names out of the courts
22. Create an area for us
23. Why Hmong move from city to city
24. History of the war in Laos
25. Why we came to the United States
26. Medical examinations; birth control
27. We can help you in the future
28. Hmong should not be social workers
29. Hmong lie about their customs

1. Rice dropped from aircraft to Hmong and other hill tribes isolated in temporary relocation sites in Laos during the war. Sources estimate that, in 1971, up to fifty tons per day of rice was dropped at 120 sites. See D. P. Whitaker, et al., *Laos: A Country Study* (Washington, D.C.: Foreign Area Studies, American University, 1971).

2. A member of the Lao Royal Armed Forces.

3. Long chants which are sung by the two representatives of each family (the *mej koob*) at various points throughout the several days of negotiation and ceremony. These songs describe the origins and meaning of Hmong wedding customs.

4. A reed instrument *(qeej)* constructed of bamboo tubes inserted in a body containing the reeds. It is a "talking" instrument through which the player sings words, though to the untrained ear it sounds rather like a bagpipe. The pipes and the drums (see note 5) are the two instruments played at funerals. Hour after hour, the *qeej* player sings the funeral songs through the pipes, accompanied by the hypnotic beat of the funeral drum.

5. A special drum made of cowhide stretched across a large, hollowed-out log, used only at funerals. It is beaten in certain rhythms throughout the playing of the funeral songs in the pipes. In Hmong villages, the eerie "ba-ba-BUM, ba-ba-BUM" of the drum provides the first notice of a death.

6. The Hmong funeral goes on constantly for several days and nights. The "Advice to the Survivors" (see note 27), for example, should be sung during the night before the burial. The corpse should never be left unattended. The limited hours of business of American funeral homes makes these practices impossible.

7. While s/he lies in state, the dead person is offered food three times a day just as s/he was in life. Liquor is sometimes offered as well.

8. The Hmong worry that their funeral practices of killing chickens, eating, drinking, etc., will disturb the cleanliness of American funeral homes.

9. The "sky" *(lub ntuj)* is the protector, the creator, the powerful all-seer, the avenger of evil. The "sky" is less personalized than the Christian "god"; it is sometimes translated as "god."

10. Hmong shamans are chosen by "teacher spirits" to perform rituals which cure spiritually-caused illnesses and other difficulties.

11. Most Hmong who have not been converted to Christianity subscribe to the belief in reincarnation common throughout Asia. People who die as creditors are likely to return in future lives as children, friends, or animals to collect the debts owed them.

12. Special burial clothing prepared by a wife for herself and her husband during their lifetimes. Funeral clothing is different from, and much more elaborate than, ordinary clothing.

13. The first leg of a refugee's journey to a third country is a twelve-hour bus ride from the refugee camp to a transit center near Bangkok. Before about 1981, people spent only a few days in this center for medical evaluation. Later refugees took a six-month literacy and cultural orientation program before coming to the United States.

14. Even though the patriarch (the father of these two brothers) of this family was still living, the oldest son (Son Cher's older brother) had taken over family leadership, possibly because of his younger age, his position in the army, and the heavy concentration of the father with messianic affairs.

15. The (former) Royal Lao Government, ruled from Vientiane as a constitutional monarchy.

16. The communist-dominated Lao Patriotic Front (also called the Neo Lao

Hak Sat), "under the direction of the People's Party of Laos, a semi-secret organization that was under strong North Vietnamese in political, economic and military matters." See D. P. Whitaker, et al., *Laos: A Country Study*.

17. The Hmong term for "Vietnamese." It has a somewhat generic meaning, being applied to anyone who fought against the Royal Lao Government, including people who were actually Lao and Hmong.

18. The United Nations High Commissioner on Refugees oversees the operation and distribution of relief supplies in the Hmong refugee camps in Thailand.

19. In addition to the idea of romantic love, the Hmong word *hlub* conveys the meaning of parental love, loving care, charity, empathy, and concern.

20. Various forms of public assistance for which refugees, as other disadvantaged Americans, are eligible.

21. Traditionally, Hmong believe in the presence of numerous spirits in the world. Examples include household spirits, jungle spirits, spirit tigers, and spirits associated with specific localities.

22. A legendary Hmong spirit, sometimes said to be an all-powerful creator and judge, giver and teacher of all the Hmong rituals and customs, and other times characterized as an advice-giver or sage.

23. Special golden or silver-colored paper which is said to be the money used by spirits. The smoke produced from burning the paper carries the money to the spirit world.

24. The several interviews, conducted under the auspices of the American embassy and the U.S. Department of Immigration, to determine the eligibility of refugees for resettlement in the United States.

25. Strings tied on the wrists of a person in some curing ceremonies to assure the indwelling of his/her soul. Some people say that this custom was borrowed, in their lifetime, from the Lao.

26. See note 4.

27. A long funeral chant, sung on the night before the burial, instructing the survivors how to behave now that they have no mother or father to guide them. The song takes an entire night to finish.

28. A long funeral chant which tells the person that s/he, indeed, has died and gives his/her spirit directions for finding its way back to the house in which it was born, reclaiming its "velvet coat" (its placenta, considered clothing in the spirit world), and, after much further sojourn, being reborn into the earthly world.

29. Most Hmong ceremonies require that a large, festive meal be served to a crowd of relatives and friends. Meals are served not only at major occasions such as weddings and funerals but at a host of minor ceremonies such as a shaman's diagnosis or cure or the calling of a newborn's spirit.

30. After marriage, a Hmong woman goes to live in her husband's household. Grandmother Xia's new son-in-law's family lived more than a thousand miles away from her.

31. These were, in fact, her husband's parents. After marriage, a Hmong woman changes the terms by which she calls relatives, calling her husband's relatives by those terms she formerly used for her natal relatives. Hmong women also commonly call relatives by the terms their children would use.

32. Hmong often gradually fill up an entire apartment building, the first families informing others, especially their relatives, as units become vacant.

33. Two other Hmong women living in the building. These middle-aged women were divorced wives of cousins. Left as they were to fend for themselves, they had been forced to get out and about the community quickly.

34. The numerous forms required by schools, hospitals, clinics, and public assistance agencies. The ability to complete these complex and difficult forms is

often cited as high praise for someone's accomplishment at learning English.

35. Hmong needlework (called *paj ntaub*, or "flower cloth") of reverse appliqué, embroidery, or cross-stitch. Originally done to produce parts of Hmong clothing, Hmong have recently begun making decorative pieces for sale in countries in which they have resettled.

36. Hmong needlework, as well as the handcrafts of other hill tribes, is sold in tourist shops and cultural centers in Thailand. Hmong Thai women often act as intermediaries, coming to the camps to buy both new and traditional pieces at extremely low prices. Various relief agencies in the refugee camps have also set up programs to buy and export Hmong needlework, providing some refugees with a meager source of income.

37. Approximately sixty thousand Hmong people live as free Thai citizens in the highlands of northern Thailand. Hmong Thai are not refugees as are Hmong who flee into Thailand from Laos.

38. The family of the groom pays a bride price to the family of the bride to compensate for the cost of raising her and the loss of her labor and reproductive contribution to her parents' household (since, after marriage, she will go to live with her husband's family and contribute all of her labor to them).

39. Hmong have very strong food taboos during the month following childbirth. In general, the new mother must abstain from eating or drinking anything cold. During the first week or ten days, she should only eat rice, chicken, and chicken broth. Some people say that she must eat only these things for the entire month. Others say that, after about ten days, some warm, boiled vegetables and broth are allowed. If these taboos are not followed, the woman will be subject to many illnesses, such as coughing and arthritis, in her old age. These taboos are still followed—to the confusion of American health care providers!

40. In Hmong villages, a group of elders, the important and knowledgeable older men of the village, settled problems which could not be settled within the family and were consulted on most major decisions involving the village.

RECOMMENDED READING

N. Chindarsi, *The Religion of the Hmong Njua*. Bangkok: Siam Society, 1976.

C. Johnson and S. Yang, *Myths, Legends and Folk Tales from the Hmong of Laos*. Saint Paul, Minnesota: Macalester College, 1985.

Paul Lewis and Elaine Lewis, *Peoples of the Golden Triangle*. London: Thames and Hudson, 1984.

J. Mottin, *History of the Hmong*. Bangkok: Odeon Store Ltd., 1980.

T. D. Roberts, et al., *Area Handbook for Laos*. Washington, D.C.: Foreign Area Studies, American University, 1967.

M. Stuart-Fox, *Contemporary Laos: Studies in the Politics and Society of the Lao People's Democratic Republic*. Saint Lucia and London: University of Queensland Press, 1982.

"UNHCR in Thailand," United Nations High Commissioner on Refugees, 1980.

D. P. Whitaker, et al., *Laos: A Country Study*. Washington, D.C.: Foreign Area Studies, American University, 1971.

H.-M. Wong, "Peoples of China's Far Provinces." *National Geographic* (March 1984).

Terry Allen, *CHINA NIGHT*, 1985, installation detail: Snow White. Photo: Michael Tilden, courtesy of the artist.

Terry Allen's "Youth in Asia" Series[1]

Deracinated, shredded, misted, triaged, bagged. The war in Vietnam, its disruptions and contradictions, its incompetence and irresolution are difficult to talk about. But since 1983, Terry Allen has been doing an admirable job of just that. He has been talking about the war and the war's physical and psychological devastation in a group of works called the "Youth in Asia" Series.[2] The works in this new cycle are about death and, what was often worse, survival. They are about the eternal return. Allen examines the war from multiple points of view and, by so doing, recaptures a considerable part of the Vietnam era's complexity. Homecoming and the inability to readjust to civilian life after the experiences of battle, the physical and emotional ruin, personal despair and self-destruction, drug dependence and crime—these are some of Allen's themes. Each work in the "Youth in Asia" Series functions as a kind of episode or chapter in a larger and more complex narrative—one that turns back on itself again and again.

THE FIRST DAY (Back in the World) can serve as a paradigm for Allen's general working method. The piece is part painting, part sculpture, and part assemblage. It deals with the disconnectedness and emotional confusion involved in returning to the World (the slang among Vietnam soldiers for the United States) with little or no preparation. Transport planes carried the dead, the wounded, and the living back from Vietnam with breathtaking swiftness. Soldiers could be engaged in pitched battles in the middle of jungles in Southeast Asia and then, in almost no time, be sitting in their living rooms half-a-world away.[3] Such abrupt homecomings were often overwhelming, as unbearable as the combat. Indeed, they were often more unbearable: many young men preferred returning to the war zone for a second and sometimes a third tour of duty over dealing with life back in the States. Among the war's greatest self-contradictions was its capacity for producing emotional states in which the battlefields of Southeast Asia seemed somehow less life-threatening than home sweet home.

The main support for THE FIRST DAY is a wall construction covered with sheet lead, a material that Allen has been using for several years, but perhaps never more effectively than in the "Youth in Asia" Series. He says that lead was an obvious medium for these works for several reasons. The surface of lead tarnishes quickly and stays in flux, depending on such things as humidity; it has a beautiful and rapidly changing patina. It is soft, easily malleable, ductile, and has, in Allen's words, a "weird, flesh-like quality, very different from other metals." Most important, lead is poisonous and one of the main constituents of bullets.[4]

THE FIRST DAY is accompanied by a poetic text that is divided into three parts: "Morning," "Afternoon," and "Evening." These sections are contained within smaller framed panels hanging on the larger support like pictures; the panels are covered with plexiglass and the inch-and-a-half frame allows Allen enough room to attach fairly large objects to the surfaces underneath the plexiglass. The panels are thus shallow display cases as well as pictures. The plexiglass also provides him with a surface for attaching objects and allows him to layer his images. On the surface of the lead around the "Morning" part of the poem, there are small tufts of dog hair attached with small strips of lead that look like pieces of tape; there are also three matchbooks, a white piece of crumpled paper, and a red swatch of cloth. At the right edge of this panel, there is a smaller framed photograph of a burning fire. A feather is taped onto the surface of the plexiglass. A stuffed bird, a Derby (Kiskadee) Flycatcher, sits on top of the panel.[5]

The "Afternoon" section of the poem in the central panel has oriental brushes attached to the surface around it, each ending with a bright dab of color—red, yellow, blue. Just below the text, the word "pistol" is stamped directly into the surface of the lead with letter punches. In the lower right corner, there is a postcard photograph taken in the late 1950s or early 1960s of the Club Cafe in Santa Rosa, New Mexico. Among the cars parked outside are a '59 T-Bird, a '57 Plymouth, and a '56 Chevy. On the right-hand side of the central panel, there is a smaller panel with bright red paint splashed over the word "windshield" and a representation of a bright blue T-shirt or upper torso.

The "Evening" section of the poem is mounted on black paper in the panel on the right-hand side of the main support. A small replica of a screen door overlaps the text of the poem. Above this panel, the word "home" is imprinted in the lead. Above the main support itself are two small framed panels. In the one that is somewhat off to itself on the right, the crescent moon floats behind small lead clouds attached to the surface of the plexiglass. The small panel near the center has the words "In Memoriam" and then the title of the piece stamped into its surface. At the bottom, there is a rising star taken from an old American flag; it is over-lapped by two twigs. The images and objects used in THE FIRST DAY begin to make sense when they are considered in relation to the text. The twigs overlapping the star, for example, refer to the irrational actions of the soldier described in the "Evening" section of the poem. He tapes twigs over his eyes and then looks up at the sky.

As in the other works in the "Youth in Asia" Series, the visual and literary parts of THE FIRST DAY act in concert. But more than this, they link up with other pieces in the series. The individual elements of the various works, acting alone and together, set up a multidimensional manifold of narrative pathways, or rather, points of departure. Marcia Tucker describes Allen's general working method in her discussion of his earlier cycle of works, the RING. In terms that apply equally well to the "Youth in Asia" Series, she points out that:

> What makes Allen's work so jolting in its effect despite the familiar-ity of its images is its structure, which has no linear plot develop-ment in the usual narrative sense; there is no beginning, middle or end . . ., no specific point of reference or critical locus. Its fugue-like quality, in which repetitions and variations on a theme create a kind of hallucinatory feeling, as though we had just seen something and turned to find it gone, and the sense of dislocation, akin to seeing oneself from behind reflected fleetingly in a mirror, are also a result of the circularity of Allen's work.[6]

Each fragment of THE FIRST DAY is deeply suggestive; each recalls some component of the war and its devastation. The storylines in the piece are perpendicular and keep folding up into themselves. The various souve-nirs scattered across its surfaces encourage personal reflection.[7] On the left-hand edge of the main support, again stamped directly into the lead sheeting, is a list of Vietnam military abbreviations, acronyms, and slang: "AK-47, AK-50, Angel Track, AOD, APC, APL, AR, ARVN, Bandoliers, Big Boys, Boonies, Bouncing Betty, Bravo, CA, Camies, Chicom Mine, Chopper, Claymores, Cobra, CP, CP Pills, Dust Off, EOD, FDC, Fire Base, FO, Fours, Grids, Grunt, HALO, Lager, Lego, Loach, LRRP, LST, LZ, M-16, M-60, MACV, MOS, NCO, NPD, NVA, OR, Point, RPD, RPG, RTO, Salvo, SF, Slick, SOP, Spooky, TAC, Tango Boat, TOC, Track, USARV, VC, WC, etc."[8] A second list comes down across the surface near the center. Some of the places in North Vietnam and South Vietnam that were important during the war are hallmarked into the lead: "Hoa Binh, Nam Dinh, Hanoi, Thanh Hoa, Vinh, Dien Bien Phu, Ha Tinh, Haiphong, Dong Hoi, Happy Valley, Bong Son, Pleiku, Kin Son, Tuy Hoa, Phnom Penh, Mekong Delta, Saigon, Cam Ranh Bay, Nha Trang, Qui Nhon, Kontum, Da Nang, Hue, Loc Ninh, An Loc, Bien Hoa, Di An, Lai Khe, Khe Sanh, Can Tho, Long Xuyen, My Tho, Da Lat, Ban Me

Terry Allen, THE PRISONER SONG, 1984, lead and mixed media, 46¾ x 46¾".
Photo: John Dean, courtesy of the artist.

Thuot, Quang Ngai, Quang Tri." Each of these terms and names gener-
ates a dense field of associations. Their meaning depends on who we are
and where we have been.

The poetic text used in THE FIRST DAY intensifies the piece's many
resonances; it talks about coming home to Santa Rosa, New Mexico, to
the supposed normalcy of the World. It speaks of loss and fragmentation
and engenders the personal desolation of the war by talking about the
panic parts of the day-to-day. It deals with returning from the fighting to
find home changed beyond recognition, turned inside-out by one's own
loss of innocence and a kind of dread so penetrating that it changes basic
brain chemistry. The poem combines the processes of rising, of coming
awake, with ritualized, unreasonable behaviors involving both prosthesis
and camouflage. It reads as follows:

Morning

Waking up . . . being still
Listening to the radio
Turning it off
Looking at breasts, at eyes closed
Sitting up
Looking in the mirror
Looking at sleep-withered penis
Standing and walking across the room
Opening the closet
Getting inside and turning
Looking out at the bed
Looking at the sleeping woman
Finding something soft
Scotch taping it to the bottom of the stomach so that it falls over
    the penis
Leaving the closet
Opening the drawer
Leaving the room
Going outside
Picking up doghair
Scotch taping it to both arms
Being very still, listening for birds
Imitating birds with a whistle
Picking up twelve leaves (each as different as possible)
Scotch taping the leaves to different parts of the face
Going inside
Turning around slowly in the doorway
Walking backward to the kitchen
Finding matches
Turning on gas at the stove
Lighting the burners
Getting a pan for each burner
Filling each pan with water and placing it on a burner
Getting a slice of bread
Tearing it in half
Scotch taping one half to the top of each foot
Going back to the stove
Waiting for the water to boil
Getting a knife
Scotch taping the knife to the left thigh
Waiting for the water to boil
Looking at all the pans of boiling water one at a time
Finding a book
Bringing the book back to the kitchen

Tearing one page at a time out of the book and dropping it into
   the boiling water
Tearing and dropping until the book is gone
Turning off the burners
Listening to the bubbling of the boiling water
Imitating the sound of the water using your lips until it stops

Afternoon

Standing by the car
Looking at the lonely road
Opening the trunk
Taking out the paint
Painting the windshield red
Writing "WINDSHIELD" on the lonely road
Humming a familiar tune
Putting the paint on the side of the lonely road behind a bush
Getting the pistol from under the front seat
Crossing the lonely road
Painting the pistol green
Tying the pistol to your right thigh
Crossing the lonely road
Taking off your top
Crossing the lonely road
Painting your torso blue
Walking toward the sun
Walking back
Painting your boots yellow
Crossing the lonely road with the yellow brush
Painting a bush yellow until the bush is covered or the paint is
   gone
Crossing the lonely road
Tying the yellow brush to the top of your face
Getting in the car
Driving on the shoulder to Santa Rosa
Parking in the parking lot at the Club Cafe
Putting the car in neutral
Finding a large rock
Placing the large rock on the accelerator
Turning on the radio
Dialing it full volume on static
Turning on the headlights
Opening the glove compartment
Opening the ashtrays
Opening the windows
Opening the vents

Getting out of the car
Opening the hood
Opening the trunk
Getting out the spare tire
Rolling the spare tire as far as it will go away from the Club Cafe

Evening

Walking outside
Looking at the moon
Walking inside
Taking off your clothes
Walking outside naked
Looking at the closest star to the moon
Squatting on the ground
Picking up two sticks
Taping one over each eye
Standing up
Looking at the moon
Looking at the closest star
Following that star until daylight rubs it out

In a work called THE BOX, Allen tells the story of a young man perhaps less, perhaps more, fortunate than the soldier described in THE FIRST DAY. Rather than returning home to stare with crazy eyes out of closets or to paint unintelligible messages on highways, he returns dead. The text for THE BOX is crazy enough to be true. It is about a young man, a former New Mexico high school track star, who is killed in a mine explosion in Vietnam. It is said that, already in high school, he had very crazy eyes. Because he had been described by a local sports writer as a "high-stepping Chaparral," he had gone to Juarez to have pictures of roadrunners tattooed on the backs of his calves.

The story of the roadrunner is told by a survivor, one of his friends who goes to visit the dead man's mother and father, both of whom have been driven over some strange brink by their loss. The grieving mother hands the visitor a small wooden box filled with various mementos of her son and his death in Vietnam, including an ominous green envelope. The narrator explains:

I opened it real careful and pulled out some notebook paper like from a school binder . . . when I unfolded it the polaroids fell out . . . three of them . . . two were just of him you know . . . with a bunch of guys standing in the jungle with guns and knives and bullets and **censored** with their shirts off . . . the other one was of his legs off just above the knee and laying in a cardboard box about the size toilet paper rolls come in at the supermarket. I . . . uhhh . . . his folks just sat there looking at me . . . not saying a word . . .

her not blinking a blink, him just rubbing the legs of his pants . . .
but her SMILE is what really ahhh weirded me out . . . CHRIST I
didn't know what to do . . . to say . . . but **censored** I must have
said something . . . **censored** or JESUS or something . . . it was all so
SLOW . . . like I was in a dream or a carwreck, you know . . . that
kind of slow motion that is so clear and real, but crazy as bat **cen-
sored.** That's the closest I can get to explaining it . . . that . . . the
living room was like being right in the center of a wreck, slide be-
fore the crash . . . I felt cold as a mackerel . . . just kept lookin' at
those legs in that cardboard box . . . those big Juarez roadrunners
all covered with goo and stuff . . . granted, very tore up, but NO
WAY you didn't know whose they were . . .[9]

The story goes on to tell about the sense of surreality involved in sitting in
such a completely insane living room. It tells about reading a letter from
the dead man's Vietnam buddies, men crazy enough themselves to send
pictures of amputated legs to the parents of their friend, their friend
whose proto-crazy, high-school eyes had been made totally crazy by the
war.[10] All this craziness might somehow distance the story, make it unbe-
lievable, if it were not so fully possible. Without knowing that just such
things, and worse, happened during the war, were caused by the war,
we might not believe the story.[11] But we do believe it.

The narrative of *THE BOX* goes on to explain that the roadrunner had
been walking point during a patrol and had tripped the wire of a Bounc-
ing Betty mine, a type of booby trap that consisted of one charge that
threw a second up into the air to explode about waist high.[12] Walking
point in Vietnam was one of the most completely terrifying experiences
ever invented. Having crazy eyes and parents who were inclined toward
the capacity for keeping wooden boxes and polaroids were perhaps use-
ful prerequisites—but then, maybe all that was really necessary was bad
luck and a sense of responsibility.

The personal loss of the war, something that was repeated in
thousands of variations in thousands of homes, is evoked by Allen in a
work called *Poem*. The text for this piece consists of just a few lines:

SP4 AR
17 JAN 43
19 SEPT 67
PANEL 26 E
LINE #93

POEM for Stanley

This straightforward message tells how to find a name on the Vietnam
War memorial in Washington, D.C. It locates the name of one of Allen's
close friends—the best man at his wedding. The image that goes along

with the text is austere—a black landscape, a hill, a mountain, a monumental wedge. A dark rainbow arcs across the painting, and the broken stock of a shotgun is attached near the bottom of the panel.[13]

The disruptions of the Vietnam War involved death and survival, and often some never never land in between. In a piece called THE END OF THE WORLD . . . JUST PRIOR TO THE BATTLE OF SANTA ROSA, Allen explores the consequences of a young soldier coming home alive, but dying on the inside:

twilight

Sneak up on it

deep now, into the neighborhood
the old block . . . and finally,
the third house on the left

Go slow
Be careful
Move along the sidewalk to that turn and turn
Stop
Sniff the air for killers
Move on . . . inch at a time
Crush every final crack of childhood all the way up to the front
    porch

break your mother's back
cave in her heart

Stop
Then step up
And step up
And step up again

a cross, the 3 stations of the door

And stop
Face it
No sweat
Fire a cigarette at a shrub
Make the fist

it's groovey time

Knock on the door
KNOCK the deep empty
    make-a-hole become everything that can never be in
    there again
KNOCK the lousey limp wish-thud . . . and finally

KNOCK the sweep simple,
   piss on all of it forever

No sweat
Empty house and some hard fucking knocks

the ancient battle cry

This poem is part of a triptych covered with sheet lead. Openings, or windows in the lead, frame a tranquil suburban scene. In the central panel, steps and a porch lead up to the open front door of a house. A corner of the house is seen in the left panel; the front yard in the right panel. Just below, there are several tufts of hair. The title of the work is hammered directly into the lead above the house. Small lead triangles labeled Hill Alpha, Hill Bravo, Hill Charlie, and Hill Delta are spaced here and there around the three panels. The house and yard are rendered in a very colorful, divisionist painting technique, which is a reference to youth and lost innocence—the patches of color are derived from a bubblegum metaphor that figures prominently in the entire "Youth in Asia" Series. Allen explains that he had carried a large cellophane wrapped mass of bubblegum pieces—something like a Salvo Detergent tablet—around with him since the mid-sixties.[14] The multicolored chunks of "H.I.P." gum were labeled "Psychedelic." In the painting, the pointillism suggests that the world of innocence, with its suburban house and yard, has been blown into a million colorful pieces. At the bottom of the windows in the left and right panels are the words "Sigh" and "Gone."

In art historical terms, the divisionist brushstrokes recall French Neo-Impressionism, and, although Allen says he was not "trying to be French,"[15] it is difficult not to see the pointillism as a reference to the French colonialism that is so important to understanding the background of the Vietnam conflict.[16] The French conquest of Southeast Asia was completed during the same years that Seurat was painting his masterpieces, and it provided part of the economic base on which he and other artists of his time depended.[17] With this in mind, Allen is ironically connecting his artistic images, and one major thread of modernism, with the socioeconomic aspects of the war.

The story of the soldier's homecoming and his breakdown under the exigencies of maintaining is continued in the next piece in the series: *THE BATTLE OF SANTA ROSA*. The structure of the text for this piece is quite similar to that in *THE FIRST DAY* and reads as follows:

I

Wake up
Awaken to the fact
Listen to the radio

Look at a hair
Smell around
Listen to the weather
Old Hendrix
Turn it off
Get up
Walk naked into the living room
Past the pictures
To the kitchen
The bottle
Take 4 pills
Light a joint
Smoke it
Pour some whiskey
Drink it
4 more
Walk back to the living room
Wonder why they call it that
Past the pictures
Some Indians
The ribbons
A star
Hear a siren . . . a bird
Pull the couch out from the wall
Get back in there
Squat
Keep low
Stare at the stucco
Fix on the stains
Some zen
A million colors
The insides of friends
Old Hendrix
Her breasts
Rub the penis
Look right through the wall
See the sleepy dog

burn him down

II

Stand by the car
Be young
Cross the street
Chew gum
Past the pictures

Some Indians
The ribbons
A star
Enter the Kitty Kat Klub
Drink wine
Shoot pool
Talk to Jesus
Squeeze the waitress
Pull her tits
Drop the 8
Kill some fucker . . . and
Get off

cool and trippy
just light him up

an didi mau

III

walk outside
look at the sun

walk inside
take off your clothes

get a knife
cut off hair

sit in a shadow
eat soup with a fork

walk outside naked
pick up a stick

punch holes in the air
pick up a stone

hit the stone with the stick
set up a rhythm

look at the sun

stand on one leg . . . and
hum a little tune

til hell freezes over

The returning vet, insane, unable to adjust, aftermathed, divided, subtracted, is embattled in his old neighborhood, surrounded by enemies on every side. The piece itself is a long, complex tableau. It is the domestic scene from *THE END OF THE WORLD* . . . tilted crazily up onto its psychological edges. The work consists of three sections of wall and floor, each slightly different in size, placed against a longer running wall. In the first section, there is a minimal couch pulled out from the wall providing a place to hide; above the couch, there is a tilted photograph of a bedroom in Southeast Asia with debris flying around on its surface. The first part of the poem is framed and hung behind the couch.

The conflate teeter-totter between the boonies of the World, the radical transitions and displacements from Indochina to Indo-America, are symbolized in the second section of the *BATTLE OF SANTA ROSA* by a statue of the Buddha, leaning, slipped, de-foundationed on a miniature pool table—the mythic arena of adolescent conflict and escape, much favored by American youths prior to their battles—a place to drop the eight before killing some enemy. We look at the back of the Buddha; it looks at a cross made from chewed-up wads of bubblegum stuck on the wall. The second part of the poem is just above this section; inside its frame, there is a tuft of hair, a detail from the Club Cafe postcard (showing the '59 T-Bird), a wad of chewing gum, a detail from a postcard showing an Indian crushing corn, and a Mexican Day-of-the-Dead skull.[18]

In the right-hand section of the piece, the house in Santa Rosa is turned up on its edge, the three steps to the crucifixion are off to themselves. The words "Stop to Shoot Little Girl" are stamped into the roof of the minimal house. Above this section, there is a tilted, framed picture with a star from an American flag; lead hills and lead clouds float in front of it. The word "seige" is stamped into its surface. A small framed

Terry Allen, *Storm on the Ghost Train . . . Laos, New Mexico,* 1984, lead and mixed media, three panels, 22½ x 47½" overall. Photo: John Dean, courtesy of the artist.

222

panel with the third section of the poem is hung on the wall just behind it. Phrases are embedded into the fabric of the three sections, first in Vietnamese, then in Spanish, and finally in English: "can cuoc, identificacion, I.D. card; khong biet, no comprende, I don't know; lai day, venir, come; que lam, peon, backward person; chieu hoi, abri brazo, open arms," among others.[19] There are lead triangles here and there with such designations as "Hill Secured," "Hill Ignored," "Hill Overrun," "Hill Reinforced," and "Hill Abandoned."

The ritual in THE BATTLE OF SANTA ROSA, and the terror, is symbolized by tufts of hair taped down by lead strips in little bunches all over the surfaces of the three sections. Horripilating, these bits and pieces change from dog hair in the first, to cat hair in the second, and finally, in the third, to human hair—hair's breadth, hair-raising, hair-triggered; hair that is clipped and carried as a remembrance of things past, little souvenirs; pieces of hair that is dead, locked, part of some person or animal. Allen uses fragments of hair in the majority of the "Youth in Asia" pieces; somehow they pull out the basic fiber and meaning of the phrase that he uses in his poem for THE BATTLE OF SANTA ROSA: "didi mau"—Vietnamese for "run away, fast."

A large number of veterans came back from the war fundamentally unable to readjust. Many of them, far too many, committed serious crimes after their return and were thrown into jail or prison. Joe Klein, in his book *Payback: Five Marines after Vietnam*, points out that "by 1980, more Vietnam veterans had died since they came home than had been killed in the war. They comprised 30 percent of the nation's prison population (about 70,000)."[20] In many cases, their sociopathic behaviors were drug related. Allen explores these aspects of coming home from Vietnam in a work called THE PRISONER SONG.

Chemical escapes were a way of life in Vietnam and, as responses to the fear and loneliness of battle, they were nothing new. John Keegan, in his general study of warfare, *The Face of Battle*, points out that alcohol has always been part of armed conflict: it "depresses the self-protective reflexes, and so induces the appearance and feeling of courage. Other drugs reproduce this effect, notably marijuana; the American army's widespread addiction to it in Vietnam . . . may therefore be seen if not as a natural, certainly as a time-honoured response to the uncertainties with which battle racks the soldiers. The choice of that particular army, moreover, had local precedents: the pirates of the South China Sea traditionally dosed themselves with marijuana before attacking European ships."[21] The Vietnam War was fought by soldiers who depended on drugs. Even conservative estimates suggest that forty to fifty thousand veterans returned from the war seriously addicted, and perhaps a quarter-million men, or more, had used hard drugs during their tours in Vietnam.[22]

The drugs made the war . . . what? Less unbearable. Less absurd. More colorful. They just added to the picture. One young soldier told

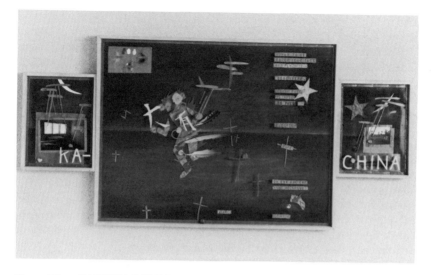

Terry Allen, *KACHINA FIELDS*, 1984, lead and mixed media, three panels, 22½ x 47½" overall. Photo: John Dean, courtesy of the artist.

Myra MacPherson this: "I wasn't on nothin' when I went there, but in Vietnam you had a choice: getting high on hard drugs or hard liquor. Heroin was plentiful, falling out of trees. You see someone get blown away and, hey, you smoke some OJs [opium joints] and, hey, man, that's cool." And another: "Where did I get hooked? Nam. Why Nam? Cheap stuff, good stuff. Why Nam? I'll give you one word: 'despair.' Now that's a big word, it's damn near the biggest word I know. I got hooked for jollies, to ward off the despair."[23]

THE PRISONER SONG is a square format work covered with sheet lead. There is a window in the center of the panel opening onto a pointillist landscape showing a body of water with trees along the shoreline. The painting was done after a postcard photograph of the "Blue Hole," a supposedly bottomless lake not too far from Santa Rosa, New Mexico. There are long, horizontal strips of lead representing musical staffs attached to the surface of the plexiglass in front of the landscape; small red flames take the place of notes, as if the lines were, at those points, on fire.

The surface of the panel is like a jailhouse wall, gouged, scarred, and covered with graffiti. Thin one-two-three-four-fives made out of lead strips are distributed over the surface, marking time. Some are scratched into the surface. A feather is attached to the wall on the left; there are some pencils attached along the bottom; wads of chewed bubblegum are stuck on in various places. "Hue, Gia Ho, Citadel, River of Perfume, Saigon" are stamped into the surface of the lead to remind us of the war

and to bring back to memory its overwhelming ruin in cities like Hue and Saigon.

There are four drawings taped onto the surface of the panel. These works were done in a Gallup, New Mexico jail by Navajo veterans. One of the drawings shows an Indian smoking a pipe and holding a bottle of liquor. The small drawing next to it shows a kind of eagle's head and parachute. The draftsman has written a note to his wife on the drawing: "Honey, see if you can find a ball point pen and send it to me in your next letter." The large drawing at the top of the panel shows an Indian capturing an eagle. The smaller work next to it shows an Indian dressed as a cavalry scout looking toward a bottle of liquor sitting out on a frozen lake. Most of the drawings were done on the backs of police reports, among the only scraps of paper available to the prisoners. Allen obtained this suite of drawings from one of his cousins who had been thrown into jail along with the Indians for disturbing the peace. This cousin was also a veteran and deeply troubled by his war experiences.[24]

The poetic text for THE PRISONER SONG is stamped into the lead on the right-hand side of the panel. It talks about disorientation, disillusionment, crime, and drug use:

Start dead center
Rob a Toot 'n' Totem
Run to the lake

Shoot up and dance

HA YA YA YA
HA YA YA YA

Fuck the cops
Flip them the bird

Go to jail
Draw some pictures

HA YA YA YA
HA YA YA YA

Look at the window
Look out the world

Write her a letter
Put gum on the wall

HA YA YA YA
HA YA YA YA . . . then

Tear off your dick

HA YA YA YA . . . and

Gouge out your eyes

HA YA YA YA
HA YA YA YA
HA YA YA YA
HA YA YA YA

Sweeten the fields of fire

The prospect of "sweetening the fields of fire"—a kind of activity that was one thing in Quang Tri and another in Santa Rosa, or Lubbock, or Gallup. The young Indian who has returned from the banks of the Perfume River to the banks of the Blue Hole has had his fields of vision fundamentally altered by what he has seen—something that is suggested by the dual meaning of the phrase "fields of fire." It describes not only a land where fire is planted and grown—but also the degrees of azimuth gun emplacements can "see."

The text of THE PRISONER SONG vents something about a displacement that is well understood by Native Americans, but only dimly perceived by most whites. For the Indians who went to the war, the fragmentation of the Vietnam experience was a kind of redoubling. Roxy Gordon, in his discussion of Allen's work, points out that "many [Vietnam veterans] still haven't recovered. They want, they say, for America to welcome them home. Which America is that? There is another America, not nearly so well-lit, not nearly so clean, not anywhere near so ordered, where . . . the future was never a sparkling urban freeway, but instead some dirty old dirt road that winds off into the desert among generations of empty beer cans. That America hardly noticed they were gone."[25]

In several of the works in the "Youth in Asia" Series, the disenfranchisement of American Indians in the Southwest is made to parallel the deprivations of peoples in Southeast Asia. "Run to the Lake. Shoot up and Dance. HA YA YA YA." In Allen's work, that cry in Hopi or Navajo blends into Mnong Gar, the dance shifts hemispheres, and, to the white man, the sounds are equally alien. Allen puts the two worlds together; he conflates the American Southwest and Southeast Asia by symbolically superimposing such things as Chinese characters over images of the deserts of New Mexico. In a letter to Ron Gleason, he explained that the Chinese language "might as well be Martian to most Americans . . . and Vietnam seemed to me like it was pretty Martian (or Navajo) and the people who came back were up against even more Mars when they got back (only difference being that if they had been on the Red Planet more people would have probably talked to them)."[26]

One of the key works in the "Youth in Asia" Series is a piece called BEARING STRAIGHT AT THE CLUB CAFE (The Mexican Shepard Boy). It too overlays images and ideas about the American Southwest and Southeast Asia in order to intricate their common grounds. In another letter to Ron

Gleason, Allen discusses some of the things he had in mind while working on this piece:

> . . . America and Asia . . . connected at the Bering Strait. A follow-up on the theory of that being a connection at one time . . . I guess the "voice" in this writing (maybe all the writing) is partially American Indian . . . Navajo. I was thinking about Asians centuries ago, leaving Vietnam (what is now Vietnam) and walking to America and settling in New Mexico to become Indians . . . and years later "trekking" back at the expense of Uncle Sam to fight Uncle Ho . . . then back again, crazy and not even Indians anymore. . . .[27]

The main panel in *BEARING STRAIGHT AT THE CLUB CAFE* is covered with sheet lead; its central image shows a pointillist rendition of the world map. Coming down across North America, right through the Southwest, and seeming to emanate from another Mexican Day-of-the-Dead skull, is the text of a poem:

Sit in booth
Drink coffee

listen

Look at peas
Tiny dead eyes

eat them

Light cigarette
Break match

smoke

Watch salt
Behind it

wait

Smell cordite
Don't blink

see jumping demons

Open pants
Get under table
see gum

Hear song
Hold penis

sing along

flyin purple
people
eater

On the right side of the large panel, a small window opens onto a small landscape painting of mesa formations in the Southwest; it has a fork mounted on top of it. On the left, the postcard photograph of the Club Cafe that we saw in THE FIRST DAY appears again. The name Santa Rosa is incised into the lead below it. The cafe is one of those generic night spots off some godforsaken highway out in the deserts of America (here Route 66). The piece is a way of saying again what has been said many times before—of saying things that cannot be said.

Dave Hickey accurately points out that Allen's works have always operated in areas where "questions of cause-and-effect, possibility-and-probability were adjustable to taste":

The indeterminacy of perception and the unreliability of mediation were acknowledged. The relativity of time and space was presumed and their interchangeability allowed. So the artist, if he wished to preclude the elements of story, history and causation from his artistic universe, could substitute space for time and transform his tale into a "room," or in order to structure temporal duration without story logic, substitute musical organization for narrative organization. To delimit or specialize the function of language in a piece, he could deploy an alternative graphic, plastic, tonal, or temporal information system wherever he felt language could or should not go.[28]

In BEARING STRAIGHT AT THE CAFE CLUB, clubs (as in spades) float around the picture postcard and the text of a conversation that might have been overheard inside the cafe:

. . . wives run off an leave em . . . lotta boys get back to find out, sides screwin everything stickin out, the little lady's also turned into some brassiere burnin type an moved up to Santa Fe. Happens everywhere, I know . . . but this is also god's truth about New Mexico.

Statistically they says a big percent of em join these groups where men ain't allowed . . . have secret meetings like shriners an cathlics an get rooms with one another . . . this way they can swap lies bout how tough it is an experiment with bein lesbians . . . some pretty little things too.

. . . just a faze though . . . they just kind of peter out an the gals wind up over at the La Fonda havin mixed drinks an showin their tits lookin for some rich sugar daddy. . . . no wonder there's so much trouble on the weekends.

Course the boys are mad as hell an go lookin for em . . . ready to kill em . . . an believe me, some do just that . . . but mostly, they just end up sayin to hell with em and go try to find a job, but now . . . what's a kid like that who ain't done nothin but play ball or eye girls an listen to nigger music down at the Sonic his whole life . . . that an the Asia thing . . . what's he gonna work at? Probably bein Indian or Mex to boot?

I knew one kid . . . fine little Mex fellow . . . he was gone two years an in all kinds of deep shit . . . lots of medals an things . . . well, he got back real nutty . . . went out an became a shepard boy over near Tucumcari. Didn't want to be around nobody. He told me sheep don't mess with his head . . . I hear he's turned into a drug fiend though.

Lotta time they just went on back . . . easier to face that crap than no job an a shitty woman, I guess.

They're awful young.

Along the left-hand edge of the main panel are the names of places in Vietnam: Hoi An, Kontum, Pleiku, Qui Nhon, Ban Me Thuot, Nha Trang. Below the main lead panel, there is a black relief sculpture of the booths in the restaurant. Wads of brightly colored bubblegum are stuck, or perhaps crucified, under the T-shaped cross-sections of the tables. In a small panel off to itself on the right, there is a drawing of the Mexican shepherd boy; Christ-like, he carries a lamb with halo. The ewe, also with halo, looks up adoringly at the shepherd boy. But these sheep are easily lost, easily led astray, easily burned down.

The general theme of overlaying Southeast Asia and the American Southwest is continued in *Storm on the Ghost Train . . . Laos, New Mexico*. This work is a sheet lead triptych with one large rectangular panel in the center and two smaller panels abutting it on either side, each slightly offset. The title of the triptych is stamped into the lead along the bottom of the three panels, and five framed scenes jounce across their surfaces like windows in a train or openings in the soul. They look out on badlands—purple table mesas and then, in the distance, red peaks. In the left panel of the triptych, a crescent moon cut out of lead hangs in the sky. In the right panel, a red hammer and sickle counterbalances the moon. Lead storm clouds float on the plexiglass that covers the panels. One of these clouds overlaps a Mexican Day-of-the-Dead skull. Near the bottom of the central panel there is a capsule containing a white powder—some generalized nepenthe. A Laotian flute, an instrument called a "can" that produces a very eerie sound, is attached to the surface of the central panel.[29] Hear that lonesome whistle blow.[30]

The strange but somehow inescapable logic of "Laos, New Mexico" is continued in a work called *Kachina Fields*. This piece is another triptych and uses the same size panels as *Storm on the Ghost Train . . . Laos, New Mexico*. *Kachina Fields* shows a distant landscape seen from a great height.

On the left and right panels are the words "Ka-" and "China." The words are separated by the central panel and thus have a dual meaning. They can be read as either "Ka" and "China" or "Kachina." On the surfaces of each of the three panels, there are lead storm clouds over small crescent moons and a few wads of bubblegum. There are feathers attached to both side panels. In the left panel, there is a photograph of a bedroom interior taken by Allen while he was in Thailand in late 1983 and early 1984.[31] In the right, another image shows a derelict American transport plane, an old DC-3. Allen took this photograph at a kind of aircraft graveyard near Ulom where some of the last planes out of Saigon had been piled. In a letter to Ron Gleason, Allen explained that the "photo is at sunset in the jungle . . . and one of the saddest feelings and strange-strongest images I got on that trip. Beautiful horrible."[32]

In the central panel, there is a Kachina plunging from the sky with flames shooting from it. It is cut out of sheet lead; one severed foot falls through the air by itself on the right-hand side of the panel. There are three feathers attached to the Kachina, but they seem ineffectual. On the plexiglass in front of the figure, there are the Chinese characters from the *I Ching* for "Possession in Great Measure." The commentaries in the *I Ching* explain this image in the following terms: "Fire in heaven above: The image of Possession in Great Measure. Thus the superior man curbs evil and furthers good, and thereby obeys the benevolent will of heaven."[33] A backward "Z," indicating sleep, and small crosses are attached to the surface around the falling spirit being. In the upper left, there is a small lead rectangle with three dabs of color and three locks of hair. On the right, there is a red swatch of cloth and a white star from an old American flag. Another white star, but painted red, is off to the side in the right panel. There is a short poem coming down across the right-hand side of the central panel:

> Human raise
> Color your face
> And fly in it . . .
>
> Somewhere.
>
> Human race
> Painted
> To fall in
>
> Sleeping
>
> Fire
> On the ancient
> Hunting Ground
>
> Of Asia

Kachinas are much more than the dolls that are familiar to most white Americans.[34] Even the term "doll" is misleading: Kachina dolls are not toys; they are *tithu*, objects of reverence that incorporate women and children into the Kachina ceremonies. Kachinas are spirit beings, rain beings, who take on the character of human beings; they become the people who wear their costumes and the people become them; the Kachinas represent the thunder, the clouds, the animals and plants, the birds, the fire and the ashes, the principles of birth and death. They represent the eternal cycles of planting and harvesting; they are the corn without which the people would die.

The Kachina rituals and dances and the other ceremonies of the Pueblo Indians make life itself possible. They are fundamentally tied to the land and its fertility. For half of the year, the Kachinas live in the sacred mountains that are near the cuestas and mesas where the Indians build their pueblos. They are part of the earth and the sky. At the winter solstice, they come into the world through the holes, the *sipapus*, in the floors of the kivas. After the summer solstice, they return again through these ceremonial passageways back to the Underworld. It is said that the people themselves came into the world through a hole in the ground at the beginning of time; and when the people die, their souls or "breath bodies" return as mist to the Underworld and join the other supernatural beings there.

The Kachinas are sacred to the Hopi and the Zuni and the other Indian peoples of the American Southwest, and they are not unlike the spirits who animate the religions of the Far East. The Hopis worship their ancestors and so do many of the peoples of Southeast Asia.[35] The religious beliefs of both the Indians and the Indochinese are tied to cyclical systems in which the supernatural is fundamentally tied to the activities of the here and now. Frances FitzGerald, in her excellent book on Vietnam, *Fire in the Lake*, points out that "until the arrival of the European missionaries there was never such a thing as a church in Vietnam":

> Shaped by a millenium of Chinese rule and another of independence within the framework of Southeast Asia, the "Vietnamese religion" was a blend of Confucianism, Taoism, and Buddhism sunken into a background of animism. More than a "religion" in any Western sense, it was the authority for, and the confirmation of, an entire way of life—an agriculture, a social structure, a political system. Its supernatural resembled one of those strange metaphysical puzzles of Jorge Luis Borges: an entire community imagines another one which, though magical and otherworldly, looks, detail for detail, like itself.[36]

With only a few modifications, this passage could describe the religions of the Hopi or the Navajo. The Southwest American Indian and the Southeast Asian systems are distorted mirror images of one another. They reflect imperfectly, each in their own ways, mankind's relationship with time and the land and the sky.

The general theme of *Kachina Fields* has been picked up and elaborated in the most ambitious work in the "Youth in Asia" Series to date—a large installation called the *CHINA NIGHT*. This work simulates one of the generic bars that are found in small towns in the Southwest—that somewhat amorphous area in North America that includes northern Old Mexico and large parts of the United States (southern Colorado, New Mexico and Arizona, West Texas, parts of California). The neon sign in the window of the dilapidated saloon reads "Kachina Night," but the "Ka" is short-circuited and buzzes on and off so that it reads two ways: "Kachina" and then "China" Night.

The *CHINA NIGHT* installation consists of a small rectangular building (about three-quarter scale) with a yard surrounded by fencing topped with a guard rack of barbed wire leaning inward. On the wall opposite the front of the fence there is a neon sign that reads "Don't Mean Nothin'"—a phrase that was often repeated in Vietnam.[37] The sand in the yard has an old discarded tire and rim (an H78 x 14), some beer bottles and cans, crushed cigarette packages and butts, cups, a comb, one empty pill bottle, boot prints, a wet stain, a pair of dice. Near the front part of the enclosure there is a strange blue and white plaster Madonna surrounded by a mandorla-like shell—our lady risen from the sea, like Venus Anadyomene. She is treading on a green snake.

Terry Allen, *CHINA NIGHT*, 1985, mixed media installation. Photo: Michael Tilden, courtesy of the artist.

An·American flag hangs like a curtain in the window of the bar. We cannot see in. There is a comb and a key on the sill, along with a small Buddha and a bust of John F. Kennedy. There are also two Mexican apotropaic candles—one a black cross, the other a red skull and cross-bones. There is one soldier card from the Mexican game Loteria stuck into the side of the window. A Vietnamese toy—a small skeleton—hangs in front of the flag on the right. Graffiti, "Saigon '68," is written on the upper framing. Nineteen sixty-eight was the year of the Tet offensive; it was the year of the battles of Hue and Khe Sanh; it was the year heavy fighting came to large urban centers like Saigon; it was the year 14,521 American soldiers died in Vietnam.[38]

The old, too-small door with "BAR" written above it seems permanently shut, despite the dirty hand prints near its handle. The stucco exterior is painted blue-white and resembles the sky. Five realistically painted Kachinas seem to float around the door and the window.[39] On the upper left is Kokopell' Mana, the Assassin Fly Girl; on the lower right is her male counterpart, Kokopelli, the Assassin Fly Kachina; in the center emerging from behind the door is Hemis Kachin' Mana, the Yellow Corn Girl; on the lower left is Ahote; and in the lower center is Umtoina-ka, the Making-thunder Kachina. On the left side wall of the building, there is a large painting of an Indian's face. On the right side wall, there is a profile of an Indian wearing a feathered headdress. A large diamondback rattlesnake curls around the outside edge of the wall enframing hand-lettered advertisements that read: "COLD BEER" and "SEE SNAKES LIVE."

From the back side of the installation, we can look through the wire fencing into the interior of the small bar. On the wall opposite is a neon sign that reads: "Never happen"—a basic form of denial in Vietnam.[40] In the guard rack above the fence, the coils of barbed wire have been re-placed by straight wire, glimmering nonetheless with the associations of battlefields like German razor wire.[41] Inside, there are no bar fixtures as we might have expected after reading the signs on the outside, and there are no snakes, at least none that are visible. Rather, the room seems to be a metaphor for the general topsy-turvy of the Vietnam era. It is an upside-down bedroom with austere, minimal furniture; a bed, chair, and end table with blue porcelain lamp hanging from the ceiling. A blue and red glow emanates from behind the bed and chair. The lamp light is green. Standing on the dirt floor/ceiling of the upside-down room are plaster statues of Snow White (painted white) and the Seven Dwarfs (painted with yellow faces and hands), little Vietcong. Happy, Grumpy, Dopey, Sneezy, Bashful, Sleepy, Doc. Disneyland East.[42] In the dirt in front of them is a neon sign that reads: "There it is."

"There it is"—another cryptic phrase that was used constantly in Viet-nam, untranslatable, empty, but mainly it means death.[43] Here, in the piece, it indicates something about the subject and the territory of the CHINA NIGHT. The installation exposes some of the personal demons that were created during the Vietnam War. It calls up those evil spirits that were forced into the psychological spaces of the men and women who experienced the conflict first hand and also, to some lesser degree, into those who experienced it second hand. The madness ran very deep in Vietnam. Even in the beginning, the Vietnam War was not very clear, except perhaps in youthful reasons for going, and as it progressed, it became increasingly murky. It was a dreamland filled with dark clouds where all remnants of youth, all remaining Disney ideas were soon shattered and twisted beyond recognition. It was a place where friendly dwarfs transmogrified into VC and NVA; where Snow White, ashen, was washed with fire.

The CHINA NIGHT installation is accompanied by a soundtrack that consists of the poetry and stories associated with the earlier works in the "Youth in Asia" Series—writings that were read aloud by Allen and two of his friends, Ron Gleason and Roxy Gordon. Their strong interpretations, made even more compelling by their Texas accents (New Mexican in Gleason's case) are intermixed with fragments of music that seem particularly meaningful in the context of the Vietnam War: Jimi Hendrix asks if we are experienced or if we have ever been experienced. Creedence Clearwater Revival sings Born on the Bayou. Bo Diddley gives us Roadrunner, and George Jones sings Things Have Gone to Pieces. Lowell George and Little Feat sing Willing, and Townes Van Zandt Poncho and Lefty. Lydia Mendoza sings Mi Problema and No Es Culpa Mia; Violetta Parrar sings El Albertio. Perhaps most strange, the voices of Montagnard tribesmen from the Central Highlands of Vietnam sound like American Indians, Navajo or Hopi.[44] Ha Ya Ya Ya. Together, the poetry and the music embed the CHINA NIGHT in a rich network of iconographic associations.

The dark cantina is engauded with the debris of wasted time and wasted dreams. It seems to exude an intangible sense that something bad has happened. Like Allen's earlier works, the CHINA NIGHT installation fuses art and life—it seems too close for comfort. The old bar glows with an alien light like the beauty in fire fights. Snow White, pure and beautiful, stands there aghast. In the books of children, the evil is clearly demarcated with hood and poisoned apple. But fairy tales are wrong; their vision is blank, not filled-in. The most dreadful thing may be innocence, terrifying because it involves ignorance of the things on the inside. The greatest terror may be self-delusion, perhaps because it involves some real necessity, some biological limit to any individual's ability to know themselves.

The recursion seems complete. It echoes into the far past, it reverberates into the far future. It is woven into the basic fabric of being. It is predicated on millions of evolutionary choices that have made us smart about death—but not smart enough. There are times when you want to return to childhood, to the remembered scene of things resolvable. Then, the things that were not right had solutions; the evil there, in those Dis-

Terry Allen, *CHINA NIGHT*, 1985, installation detail: the Seven Dwarfs. Photo: Michael Tilden, courtesy of the artist.

ney simplifications, was black and hooded. Terry Allen: "I'm not sure but what Snow White isn't the most frightening figure I've ever made."[45]

The candles in the window of the *CHINA NIGHT* are apotropaic. They're meant to ward off evil, but they're not going to work. The evil is in the fiber. It's in the weave of being. There are spaces where the interiors are upside-down, where madness is part of the general thing. It's in the fabric. My country 'tis of thee, sweet land of liberty. The demons are shut in, but they're alright, it's airtight. The Kachina nights are eternal. It's the recursion; they return again and again, wearing white, self-proclaiming, innocent, self-deluded; it's built into the basic fabric of being. It's in the fabric of the flag, bearing straight to China, Ka Ka Ka, Ka-China.

Part of what you know lies, buried in a cortical area of no return, eternal return. The war was fought little brother against little brother, bearing straight to some serdab in an adobe mastaba out in Laos, New Mexico, built by a despotism grounded in making things grow, in the corn, the wheat, the rice.[46] In Allen's space, there are eternal demons equipped with everything they need—well provisioned for an afterlife, especially for the joy of survival, the luck of the drawing, the draftsmanship, the luck of the draft, the loteria, the art of delusion, the euthanasia, the youth in asia. The conjoining of the common places, the overlays, the interpenetrations, the conjunctions, the blockages. Turning off the pain, turning off the paint, drugs for erasure. Sports, football, track—metaphors for the cosmic oversimplifications. Never happen. Don't mean nothin'. There it is. You can only speak of these things through your own perplexity.

The replacements were most disruptive, the insidious metaphors. Snow White and the Seven Dwarfs among the demons of the American Southwest, ancestral Vietcong, the all-night cantina, source for cannon fodder. The fertile soil, the fertile sky. It grows the plaster and neon, it floats the Kachinas. The white man's America, the repatriated Amerindian's China. But that's not the point, the point has more to do with displacement: replacement. The Dwarfs = the Vietcong. Interdiction = search and destroy. Pacification = killing and burning villages. Those were the metaphors, the tricks of words, but the actualities were absurd, ruptured.

Allen's works deal with re-seeing, re-looking, over-looking. Fly, bird, soul. Fly. Assassin Flies. Float, Kachinas. Enter the space of the building—a three-manifold with boundary. Like a chunk of some non-Euclidean sky, in no-Space. The deeply ramified structure of the pun breaks the normal codes of discourse. Dis-course. Dis-curse. Circle. Verbal circle. Nietzsche's Eternal Return—a mirror flush with the surface of another mirror. A space/time intersection. A hypothetical continuum of concerns.

All of Allen's works are interrelated. The various installations depict aspects of the same world. The interior and exterior landscapes are elemental slices of a tesseract that has unfolded and then refolded back up into itself. The warp and weave is interdimensional. The fabric unravels, its thread bare. Don't tread on me. The Devil's Condo is where the soldier lives.[47] He goes to drink at the China Night. The soldier doesn't like peas. He walks through a Santa Rosa tableau. The country-western rockabilly in the background sings of those spaces in the American Southwest where there is cheap cannon fodder as well as cheap dreams. Time/short circuit. Death.

The recursion is spatial as well as temporal. Re-curse. Shun. It's locked into the things that return from every place there is. But basically it's about betrayal, the promise of survival in some better sense that trips on its own low self—some balled-up thing. Allen's rooms tend to have incandescent glows. The paint, the materials of construction, tend to be brimstoned; they re-call the presence of the devil. His condo looks like the Billingsgate Motel, looks like the Vietnam scenes.[48] Allen's entire oeuvre turns back on itself again and again, a complex system of visual and verbal puns.

The pun is linguistiche, an overlay, an interpenetration of sounds and associations, poetic resonances, reverberations, like the sound of the guitar in Thailand bands, in Laos, New Mexico. Texican, Mexican, sailed across the Taoscean blue, across the waves of pain and remorse and the images that won't go away ever go away stay in the brain shattered by the light in the images, inverted, in the perspective piercing behind the I-balls like peas, like rotten peas, dead from the revelation, from the being alive in the dead zone, the free fire zone, the DMZ, the LZ. Terry Allen: "Yell low."

Works like BEARING STRAIGHT AT THE CLUB CAFE and the CHINA NIGHT installation recall the war's devastation. Like the art, the war itself is folded back into itself again and again. It comes back at you. The essential tragedy reduplicates—in spades, in clubs. The bed chairs, the minimal forms, the nature, the non-nature, the disruption, the camaraderie are masks for the impossibility of getting it said. You say it every way you can think of. It remains unsaid. God in the machines. The machines were filled with things you know about, but you know they will never let you say it; so much of it you have forgotten and will again before the clarity arrives—it never will. You sense that the addition cannot really help, but you also cannot see any reason why the silence should be maintained, since only you could care and you do already. The risk cannot be any greater and the caring is displaced too and no one here handles it convincingly. Still, the worry about the space has as much to do with personal interiors as the act of making the art. But it was the route. Sometimes mapped by good brains.

It is the recursion that is so frightening. It is so enormously ancient. The Chinese who walked across the Bering Strait to the all-night honky-tonk cafe and back again through drug-filled visions that could not really see very far anyway through the mists of self-delusion incorporated by the eternal recursions into the fabric of life, into the double helix, twined into itself, codon after codon for hatred and self-proclaiming innocence. The whiteness is an illusion. It fills the span of time and the reach of evolution. To be self-blind, to blind one's self, to dissemble, to disassemble, to not eat peas because there is a vision of eyeballs turned green from decay. White light—the flash of fire that smashes through the brain before the sound arrives.

Take time frozen in the art. Congealed. Like sand, stoned, only it flows like time, and remolds itself eternally into the same shapes and patterns—the death and sorrow of humanness—the same for the Cro-Magnon and the Crow Indian. The Kachina in Cochin-China. Umtoinaka, making thunder. Ka Ka Ka Caw Caw Caw Ha Ya Ya Ya—a chant from an Indian ceremony that becomes Vietnamese. It's the basic antimony. Call it dialectical. The little sign (semi-idiotic) blinks its dual message through a short circuit. Like meaning charged with the faulty current. A kind of buzz, the connect that comes in and out of thought, creates a new thought, fades. Hermeneutical. Herman-Nautical. Sailed across the sea. She left. Had a party. He returned, found she was gone. And went back to Laos from Taos. The mapping held. The basic impossibility of maintaining any kind of hold on it with the distance from the Fire Zone to the Mountain Time Zone less than twenty-four hours by available transport. The jets dropped into the bizarre in both hemispheres.

237

Homeland, Thailand, you can't go home again. Birds, fly, escape, bearing straight to the Club Cafe. All Nights in China. Kachina nights. Hybrids. Like everything growing around Lubbock and Amarillo, the concepts and the creatures in Terry Allen's work take on blended significance. Crows flying over wheat fields. Slicks flying over rice fields.[49] Birds of prey. Carrion birds. Carrying on. The slicks, the snakes—they CA'd men into hot LZs.[50] CA. CA. CA. Ka/China. Birds of prayer. Shaman. Fly up into the sky at the Club Cafe. Fly straight, bearing north, frozen in the wastes of ice. Looking for the rice, frozen in time, slowed to a crawl of desperation. The need for bigger brains that cannot possibly arrive in time. The oblivion, the stupid perceivers looking through systems of vision that contain their own betrayal. The silver-sheened lining of the mind, mirror-coated with its own design and the recursion of the light, back and forth through the interstices of time, surfaced with coatings that will not reflect the events of significance; they flash past too bright and too swift, with the dead silence of ablation.

Terry Allen: "Raven. Rave on. Rave on."

Never happen. Don't mean nothin'. There it is.

NOTES

1. An earlier version of this essay appeared in *Arts Magazine* 60 (April 1986): 50-59; see also my essay "Youth in Asia: Ka/China Night," in *China Night: Terry Allen*, exhibition catalogue (Tallahassee: Florida State University Fine Arts Gallery, 1986), pp. 4-56.

2. Much of what follows is based on conversations with Terry Allen (October and December 1985, January 1986). I would like to thank Mr. Allen for his cooperation and for the many courtesies he has extended me during the preparation of this essay. The following are among the books about Vietnam that I have found most useful (many of them recommended to me by Terry Allen): Michael Herr, *Dispatches* (New York: Knopf, 1977); Ronald J. Glasser, *365 Days* (New York: Braziller, 1971); Frances FitzGerald, *Fire in the Lake: The Vietnamese and the American in Vietnam* (Boston: Little, Brown and Company, 1972); Philip Caputo, *A Rumor of War* (New York: Ballantine Books, 1977); Tim O'Brien, *Going After Cacciato* (New York: Delacorte Press/Seymour Lawrence, 1978); James Webb, *Fields of Fire* (Englewood Cliffs, N.J.: Prentice-Hall, 1978); C.D.B. Bryan, *Friendly Fire* (New York: G. P. Putnam's Sons, 1976); Al Santoli, *Everything We Had: An Oral History of the Vietnam War by Thirty-Three American Soldiers Who Fought It* (New York: Random House, 1981); Al Santoli, *To Bear Any Burden: The Vietnam War and Its Aftermath in the Words of Americans and Southeast Asians* (New York: Dutton, 1985); John M. Del Vecchio, *The 13th Valley* (New York: Bantam Books, 1982); Mark Baker, *Nam: The Vietnam War in the Words of the Men and Women Who Fought There* (New York: William Morrow, 1981); Joe Klein, *Payback: Five Marines After Vietnam* (New York: Knopf, 1984); Myra MacPherson, *Long Time Passing: Vietnam and the Haunted Generation* (Garden City, N.Y.: Doubleday, 1984); Douglas Kinnard, *The War Managers* (Hanover, N.H.: University Press of New England, 1977).

3. See, for example, Myra MacPherson, *Long Time Passing*, pp. 53-54: "Unlike other wars, they came home not on troop ships where they could wind down, decompress, be together. They went alone and came home alone. And with the

mind-wrenching suddenness of jet-age from here-to-there, from Nam to the world. From firefight to front porch in thirty-six hours. After all these years, many veterans still shudder at the unbelievable suddenness of it all. 'I was killing gooks in the Delta and seventy-two hours later I'm in bed with my wife—and she wonders why I was different,' says one warrant officer. No one bothered to examine the incredible psychological trauma this jet return to civilization often created."

4. Conversations with Terry Allen, December 1985.

5. Allen obtained this particular object in a trade with a Vietnam veteran (conversations, December 1985).

6. Marcia Tucker, "The Ring: 'A Story which Swallows Its Own Tale,'" in *Ring: Terry Allen*, exhibition catalogue (Kansas City: Nelson Gallery/Atkins Museum, 1981), p. 70. See also, Marcia Tucker, "Terry Allen (On Everything)," *Artforum* 19 (October 1980): pp. 42-49.

7. In the two most extensive essays that have been written about the "Youth in Asia" Series to date, Roxy Gordon and Ron Gleason (both friends of Terry Allen) make very effective use of their own personal voices. Gordon is part Choctaw Indian; his essay, "Making Sense: The Magic, the Art, the Artist," appears in Terry Allen, *China Night*, pp. 51-59. Gleason is a Vietnam veteran; his essay, "Smoke and Mirrors," appears in *Terry Allen: Visual and Aural Mythologies*, exhibition catalogue (Calgary, Alberta: Alberta College of Art Gallery, 1985), pp. 9-18.

8. Most of these terms are included in the glossary of Ronald Glasser's *365 Days*, pp. 289-292.

9. The "censored" indications in this passage are part of Allen's original. For the complete text of the story, see Terry Allen, *China Night*, pp. 13-19.

10. The war's effect on sanity is well described by Michael Herr in *Dispatches*, p. 59ff.

11. See Herr, pp. 82-83.

12. For the physical ruin caused by stepping on a mine, see Glasser, *365 Days*, pp. 57-59.

13. Shotguns were used as assault weapons in Vietnam.

14. Conversations with Terry Allen, December 1985.

15. Ibid.

16. See Frances FitzGerald, *Fire in the Lake*, pp. 50-71 and passim; see also her comments in *Many Reasons Why: The American Involvement in Vietnam*, by Michael Charlton and Anthony Moncrieff (London: Scholar Press, 1978), pp. 157-160; see also Bernard Fall, *Street Without Joy: Insurgency in Indochina, 1946-63*, 3d rev. ed. (Harrisburg, Pa.: Stackpole, 1963); Bernard Fall, *Viet-Nam Witness* (New York: Praeger, 1966); also useful are Jean Lacouture, *Vietnam: Between Two Truces*, trans. Konrad Kellen and Joel Carmichael (New York: Random House, 1966); Jean Lacouture, *Ho Chi Minh: A Political Biography*, trans. Peter Wiles (New York: Random House, 1968).

17. FitzGerald, *Fire in the Lake*, p. 53.

18. For the Day of the Dead (November 1), see Malcolm Lowry's *Under the Volcano* (Harmondsworth: Penguin, 1962; originally published 1947); see also Sergei Eisenstein, *The Film Sense*, trans. and ed. Jay Leyda (London: Faber & Faber, 1948), pp. 197-198.

19. Most of these terms can be found in the glossary of James Webb's *Fields of Fire*, pp. 341-344.

20. Joe Klein, *Payback*, p. 6.

21. John Keegan, *The Face of Battle* (New York: Viking, 1976), p. 326.

22. MacPherson, *Long Time Passing*, pp. 53, 572-575.

23. Ibid., p. 53.

24. Conversations with Terry Allen, January 1986. For his cousin's story, see Gleason, "Smoke and Mirrors," pp. 16-17.

25. Gordon, "Making Sense," pp. 51-52.

26. Gleason, "Smoke and Mirrors," p. 13.

27. Ibid., p. 12.

28. Dave Hickey, "A Few People Dead," in *Rooms and Stories: Recent Work by Terry Allen,* exhibition catalogue (San Diego: La Jolla Museum of Contemporary Art, 1983), p. 77.

29. Conversations with Terry Allen, December 1985; see also Dave Hickey, "The Lights of Lubbock," *Xtra Magazine* (June 1985): 13.

30. It is perhaps worth mentioning something here about the symbolism of trains: Freud, in *The Interpretation of Dreams,* Standard Edition, vol. 5, p. 385, points out that "dreams of missing a train . . . are dreams of consolation for another kind of anxiety felt in sleep—the fear of dying. 'Departing' on a journey is one of the commonest and best authenticated symbols of death."

31. An important impetus for the "Youth in Asia" Series occurred in 1982 when Allen was presented with the opportunity of working on the soundtrack for a German documentary film by Wolf-Eckart Buhler entitled *Amerasia,* about Amerasian children and American veterans who had stayed in Indochina, mainly in Thailand, after the Vietnam War ended, or who had returned there after being unable to readjust to life in the United States. Allen began work on the "Youth in Asia" Series in 1983 and then, in December 1983 and January 1984, spent six weeks in Thailand with the film crew. While involved with the film, Allen worked with a Thai band called "Caravan," toured and played with them, and, since neither he spoke Thai nor the band members English, communicated with them largely through music and drawings. Together with Surachai Jantimatorn, the leader of the Thai band, Allen produced *Let Freedom Ring,* a rendition of *My Country 'Tis of Thee.* In their interpretation, this familiar old work becomes both country-western anthem and Mon-Khmer dirge. Allen's distinctive, West Texas voice, Jantimatorn's verses in Thai, and the plaintive sounds of traditional Southeast Asian instruments combine to transform the song from something completely worn out into something completely renewed and unforgettable. It recalls the war in Vietnam and its many inconsistencies as strongly as anything can.

32. Gleason, "Smoke and Mirrors," p. 18.

33. *The I Ching or Book of Changes,* trans. Richard Wilhelm and Cary F. Baynes (New York: Pantheon Books, 1950), p. 96.

34. See Harold S. Colton, *Hopi Kachina Dolls with a Key to their Identification* (Albuquerque: University of New Mexico Press, 1959); Edwin Earle and Edward A. Kennard, *Hopi Kachinas* (New York: Museum of the American Indian, Heye Foundation, 1971); John Walter Fewkes, *Hopi Katcinas Drawn by Native Artists,* Smithsonian Institution, Bureau of American Ethnology Annual Report (Washington, D.C.: Government Printing Office, 1903); Dorothy K. Washburn, ed., *Hopi Kachina: Spirit of Life* (Seattle: University of Washington Press, 1980); Barton Wright, *Kachinas: A Hopi Artist's Documentary* (Flagstaff and Phoenix: Northland Press and Heard Museum, 1973); Tyrone Stewart, Frederick Dockstader, and Barton Wright, *The Year of the Hopi: Paintings and Photographs of Joseph Mora, 1904-06* (New York: Rizzoli, 1982).

35. For a number of interesting parallels, see Jesse Walter Fewkes, *Ancestor Worship of the Hopi Indians,* Smithsonian Annual Report (Washington, D.C.: Government Printing Office, 1923), pp. 485-506; and Leopold Cadière, *Croyances et pratiques religieuses des vietnamiens,* 3 vols. (Saigon: École Française d'Extrême Orient, 1955-1958).

36. Frances FitzGerald, *Fire in the Lake*, p. 14.

37. The following passage from John del Vecchio's *The 13th Valley*, p. 580, suggests how the term was used:

Cool wind rushes through the open sides of the helicopter.

"Where in the fuck did the gooks come from?" Thomaston cries. "They were right on the knoll with us."

Jackson too is crying. His face is distorted, ugly. "We left 'em there," he screams. "We left 'em there. Egan woant dead."

El Paso vomits.

Pop is dazed.

Cherry is cold, breathing hard. He looks at Jax. He says at him, a smirk on his face, "Fuck it." He bursts out laughing. "Don't mean nothin'."

38. See Clark Dugan, Stephen Weiss, and the editors of the Boston Publishing Company, *Nineteen Sixty-Eight*, The Vietnam Experience Series (Boston: Boston Publishing Co., 1982), p. 185.

39. See the works cited in note 33 above; Allen's source for his Kachina paintings is Barton Wright, *Hopi Kachinas: The Complete Guide to Collecting Kachina Dolls* (Flagstaff: Northland Press, 1977).

40. As an example, Michael Herr, *Dispatches*, p. 26, reports the following story told by a young soldier: "We had this lieutenant, honest to Christ he was about the biggest dipshit fool of all time, all time. We called him Lieutenant Gladly 'cause he was always going like, 'Men . . . Men, I won't never ask you to do nothing I wouldn't do myself gladly,' what an asshole. We was on 1338 and he goes to me, 'Take a little run up to the ridge and report to me,' and I goes like, 'Never happen, Sir.' So he does, he goes up there himself and damned if the fucker didn't get zapped. He said we was gonna have a real serious talk when he come back, too. Sorry 'bout that."

41. Barbed wire was sometimes placed *behind* troops in Vietnam. One marine who was at Khe Sanh remembered it this way: "What happened initially, because of the concern that we might be overrun, was that barbed-wire barricades were built behind the troops on the front lines. Behind us. Behind the marines. Although there was barbed wire in front of us, because they also put barbed wire behind us, we felt cut off and isolated from the pogues [soldiers in the rear] behind us. It was psychological, too; we were not only cut off from those behind us, but from those back in the United States. This was something that I had never seen, not even in a John Wayne movie. You don't isolate your troops that way. . . . The reason we were so upset by them putting the barbed wire behind us was that we felt that they were writing us off. It was clear: 'You're the first priority to die. You go first.'" This story is told in Heather Brandon's *Casualties: Death in Viet Nam; Anguish and Survival in America* (New York: St. Martin's Press, 1984), p. 77.

42. "Disneyland East" was the name of a bar row and red-light district in An Khe, but the term has more universal applicability. References to Disneyland and Disney characters abound in the literature. As a counterpart to Allen's examination of lost innocence, Ron Gleason, "Smoke and Mirrors," p. 18, cites the following story by Thomas Hargrove, an American expatriot living in Southeast Asia: "During Tet, when many units moved from fighting in the countryside to fighting in the cities, he found himself moving from building to building in the center of town. He entered a two story building and moved slowly up the stairs. It was at night, dark and the stairway was dimly lit. He came to the first door, hesitated, took a few careful, deep breaths, kicked the door open and moved in fast. The room was pitch black and though he couldn't see, he sensed something in the back of the room, turned fast, pointed his M-16 at the spot and pulled his finger

against the trigger. It was a short burst and the figure was blown apart. When he stopped firing, the form in the back of the room began to take shape. As his eyes acclimated to the darkness he began to recognize the still figure. It was Donald Duck. A shredded poster of Donald Duck was hanging on the back wall of the room. Fucking Donald Duck. And he had blown him away."

43. Michael Herr, *Dispatches*, p. 254, has perhaps come closest: *"There It Is*, the grunts said, like this: sitting by a road with some infantry when a deuce-and-a-half rattled past with four dead in the back. The tailgate was half lowered as a platform to hold their legs and the boots that seemed to weigh a hundred pounds apiece now. Everyone was completely quiet as the truck hit a bad bump and the legs jerked up high and landed hard on the gate. 'How about that shit,' someone said, and 'Just like the motherfucker,' and 'There it is.' Pure essence of Vietnam, not even stepped on once, you could spin it out into visions of laughing lucent skulls or call it just another body in a bag, say that it cut you in half for the harvest or came and took you under like a lover, nothing ever made the taste less strong; the moment of initiation where you get down and bite off the tongue of the corpse."

44. The Vietnamese sources are "Ly Che Huong" ("Song of the Rose"), from *Folksongs of Viet Nam* (Folkways Records); "Noo Toong Toong" (Montagnard songs), from *Musique Mnong Gar du Vietnam* (Ocora Radio-France); and "Noo Nyiim Khot" (Montagnard funeral lamentations), from *Musique Mnong Gar du Vietnam* (Ocora Radio-France).

45. Conversations with Terry Allen, October 1985.

46. I am thinking of Karl Wittfogel's *Oriental Despotism: A Comparative Study of Total Power* (New Haven: Yale University Press, 1957).

47. For Allen's earlier installation *ORNITHOPERA (The Devil's Condo)*, see *Rooms and Stories*, pp. 18-23.

48. For *BILLINGSGATE (A Motel)*, see ibid., pp. 24-49.

49. "Slicks" are the Huey helicopters that were used to transport combat troops in Vietnam.

50. "Snakes" are Cobra gunships. The acronym CA, used as a verb in Vietnam, means "combat assault."

Women and Vietnam:
Remembering in the 1980s

The Vietnam War, like every war, has endless consequences and victims. In the 1980s women have continued to write about the effects of the war both on the veterans and the people who stayed home. It is often overlooked that there were several thousand American women in Vietnam during the war, and that they are veterans. They have begun to tell their stories about Vietnam and the profound and disturbing effects that their experience continues to have on their lives. The families of all veterans will live with the war forever, and women writers are also giving form to their experience in fiction and poetry.

There are two recent books that give accounts of the experience of American women in Vietnam: *Home Before Morning: The Story of an Army Nurse in Vietnam* by Lynda Van Devanter, and *A Piece of My Heart: The Stories of Twenty-Six American Women Who Served in Vietnam*, edited by Keith Walker. Both of these are moving and vivid first hand accounts. Amongst the women veterans, Lynda Van Devanter has been particularly outspoken and has played a crucial role in getting recognition for the contribution women made in Vietnam. *Home Before Morning* is her frank, personal narrative of how one year in Vietnam changed her life. Starting out as a typically idealistic and naive young girl, but with a spirit of adventure and feistiness and a patriotic father without sons who regretted that he could not fight in World War II, she volunteered to go to Vietnam as a nurse, believing in her country but totally unprepared in every way for what she would have to face. The myth that women are not in any physical danger in war, that they are confined to safe zones, was immediately shattered for her, as the day she arrived a nurse had been killed in a rocket attack on the hospital compound where she was to work. Van Devanter then sees that in Vietnam the war was everywhere. Immediately thrown into the war, she is forced to work hours, sometimes days on end, going far beyond her nurse's training, and she is suddenly immersed in death. The traditional camaraderie of war and her own strong spirit helped her cope, and after a few months the extreme numbing that is required set in. The legacy of these experiences will stay with her for many years: the sense of importance and purpose can never be repeated and the emotional repression will turn into an inability to feel, and difficulty in understanding what she does feel. Both of these intense experiences were unconsciously working their way into her and will only become fully clear years later.

There are two things that stand out strongly in her story, and in all the stories of women in Vietnam: on the one hand, their experience is very much like that of the male veterans, but they go completely unrecognized; on the other, as women, their experience has unique aspects. They do suffer the same post-traumatic stress as the men often do and their lives are also often similarly riddled with the same emotional and work-related problems, nightmares, flashbacks, and physical problems possibly related to Agent Orange. However the women have been ignored even more than the male Vietnam veterans. There are many male veterans who were not in combat but who also suffer in these ways; they are still seen as veterans. But women are traditionally not viewed as part of war, even when they are participating. The general ambivalence toward women in the military is expressed even more strongly in the case of Vietnam. The female veterans have suffered the hostility and lack of recognition that all the Vietnam vets have had to endure, and in addition it has been a struggle for them to receive recognition from the veteran's organizations.

Van Devanter describes how a fellow nurse insists on going back into a burning helicopter to get a wounded veteran when everyone else has given up. Defying the crew chief's "He's going to die anyway," she refuses to listen and saves the soldier, who survives. This kind of courageous action is not fully recognized; when her Bronze Star arrives it is missing the V for valor: "Nurses are not awarded things like that." Returning to the States, the women in Vietnam are abandoned just as all the male vets are, once they leave the army plane, without even any transportation. Van Devanter tells of her shock and hurt as she waits for hours trying to hitchhike to the next airport to get home, while people driving by see her uniform and hurl both insults and objects at her. When she tells people she was in Vietnam, she is consistently treated with hostility; consequently, like most of the women who were in Vietnam, she hides her past, never mentioning that she was in the war. It is clear from all these accounts that the damage of repression continues to take its toll; the emotional repression required to get through in Vietnam is then doubled by the necessity to be silent at home.

244

Like many of the men who were in Vietnam, the women also had to confront the betrayal of their ideals about their country. Young, patriotic people who had volunteered to go to Vietnam, they could not overlook that something was terribly wrong with what their country was doing there, and they could not deny that lies were being told back home. They had to face the possibility that all the death and destruction they witnessed was in no way justified. Van Devanter tells how, in the midst of her nightmares and her difficulty working as a nurse with limited duties in the U.S., she hears about a protest march organized by the Vietnam Veterans Against the War. But her attempt to express some of her sorrow and rage about Vietnam is again thwarted when the male veterans tell her that women can't march, veterans or not, because "Nixon and the network news reporters might think we're swelling the ranks with non-vets." Lacking the strength to argue, Van Devanter and the women leave, silenced again.

It is only years later, after a great deal of lonely suffering, that Van Devanter coincidentally makes another connection which leads her out of this paralyzed isolation. Attending interviews her husband is conducting with veterans for a documentary he is making, she starts crying and tells them she is a veteran, too. "Women veterans. We forgot all about women." The male veterans insisted that she be included in the film, *Coming Home, Again,* and this marks the beginning of her coming to terms with her war experience. It is only through talking about her experience and taking action for other women veterans that she can restore herself, and she goes on to organize the Vietnam Women's Veteran Project, to get therapeutic help for herself, and to reach out to other women who have suffered in silence the way she had for years.

But what also stands out in the women's reports of their time in Vietnam is that their experience was also a particular one for them as women. Their work as nurses, Red Cross workers, entertainers, intelligence experts, etc., also included being women, playing women, and white "round-eyed" women for the American men in Vietnam; they had to play the roles of mothers, girlfriends, and sisters for all the men and do the emotional work that women traditionally do, that always goes unrecognized and remains invisible. The extreme contradiction between the numbing that was required to work and live in Vietnam and the role of nurturer and caretaker caused an excruciating strain and a lot of guilt that persists through the years. The constant tension between getting involved and staying remote has left these women with unforgettable images. The nurses had to have this kind of relationship with hundreds of patients, watching them all leave, never knowing whether they lived or died:

I don't remember his last name—his first name was John. He was twenty-one. He'd gotten married just before he came to Vietnam. And he was shot in his face. He absolutely lost his entire face from

245

ear to ear. He had no nose. He was blind. It didn't matter, I guess, because he was absolutely a vegetable. He was alive and breathing; tubes and machines were keeping him alive . . . I just . . . I couldn't handle it . . . His wife's life was completely changed, his parents, his friends, me—it affected me too. And all because of one split second. I got to realizing how vulnerable everybody was. And how vulnerable I was. I took care of him for a week. They finally shipped him to Japan, and I never heard from him again. I don't know if he's dead or alive. I don't know how his wife or his family are doing. I don't know how he's doing. It seems like every patient on that ward, when they left, took a piece of me with them. They came in, we would treat them for a few hours or a few days, and then we'd send them off and never hear a word. I had this real need to see one GI who'd survived the war after an injury, because I never saw them—never heard from them again.[1]

This is another severe kind of loss that was added to the actual deaths observed, the patients lost; war causes many different kinds of losses and in some way each of these men was experienced as yet another bereavement. Many of the women report that they were haunted for years by certain faces, and desperately want to know what happened to these people. Some of them feel some emotional recovery and healing only years later when they meet some veterans who thank them for saving their lives and their friends' lives. Van Devanter recounts her gruesome recurring nightmares:

I walked through the double doors of the OR in Pleiku and saw thousands of soldiers packed in like cattle. They were all bleeding, some with their guts hanging out, others with their arms blown off, still others without heads. Two were playing catch with a bloody foot that had fallen from a comrade's leg. As I tried to back out the door, I felt a hand grab my arm. When I turned I saw a young man with his face blown away. In his other hand he was holding a picture. On it was written, "Gene and Katie, May 1968."[2]

Gene was a soldier who died, leaving his high school picture behind, and it is only when Van Devanter meets a Vietnam veteran who has survived after having had his face completely mutilated that she begins to resolve some of these feelings and to free herself of some of these tormenting visions. When she sees and hears that one of the men who suffered this extreme kind of damage has survived, with one of the most disturbing wounds since faces seem to be so central to being human, she finds some strength to go on.

In any life or death situation, the people around feel there is something they should have done that might have made a difference, that might have prevented the death, and the nurses are burdened with a tremendous guilt of this kind. Did they do something wrong because they weren't trained well enough? Were they kind enough with those young boys when they had to remain detached to be able to keep going? They didn't have to fight, they only had to pick up the pieces. Why were they in a safer place, and why were they surviving in Vietnam? They too suffered some of the same survivor guilt that Robert Jay Lifton describes that the veterans who saw their friends and fellow soldiers die suffer so acutely. And in some of the most pathetic cases, women live for years plagued by guilt when men went out of their way for their sake, performing some chivalrous act only to get killed:

> I had just turned twenty-one and had met this buck sergeant with the 199th. Ski and I were becoming closer all the time. In August, he and his buddy, Rowdy, and another guy came to pick us up, and that night I was the only woman who could make it. The three of us were riding in the back, drinking Wild Turkey and joking around when Ski had to go to the bathroom. The truck stopped and he jumped down and started to jog into the bushes. He stepped on a mine . . . He was gone . . . All we could do was continue on and report it—someone with detectors would have to come and get him. I remember we got back in the truck, and Rowdy took a drink from the bottle, passed it to me, and quietly said, "I gotta stop making friends over here." I was filled with guilt; I was the only woman on the truck. He wouldn't have gone into the bushes if I hadn't been there . . . I never told anyone about that . . . not anyone. For twelve years I believed it was my fault that Ski was dead. Now I know I didn't kill Ski . . . The war did. The war got Rowdy too, about a week later during their next outing. Except for R&R and coming home, I never left the Long Binh compound again.[3]

These memories don't go away, they are locked in, and for years no one wanted to listen. There was no organized way for these women to talk to people who had the same experience, something they sorely needed, but for many it was too painful to verbalize the memories they could not escape. It is only years later that some of them have made connections with each other, worked in veterans groups, sought out the therapy they needed, and begun to free themselves from their ordeal in Vietnam.

But there were also American women in Vietnam who did not volunteer to go. Some went as wives. These women, while in danger at times in the attacks that occurred everywhere, were at a further remove from the war. Completely ignorant of the Vietnamese culture, they were unprepared for the daily, mutually incomprehensible contact with the Vietnamese. Powerless observers, nonparticipants, they fumbled around senselessly in their ambiguous roles, increasingly alienated. Once again, the numbness to what was really going on again took over, interrupted only by moments of physical danger and fear and a silent horror at the contradictions in the U.S. presence in Vietnam.

Wendy Wilder Larsen went to Vietnam with her husband, a journalist for *Time* magazine. Years later she has written the extraordinary *Shallow Graves*, with a Vietnamese woman, Tran Thi Nga. Larsen has transformed Nga's reminiscences into prose poems, staying as close to the memories as possible. Nga, working for Larsen's husband's office as a bookkeeper, provided guidance for Larsen during her time in Vietnam. Years later they meet again when Nga is trying to adjust to life in the U.S. *Shallow Graves* is unique in bringing the voices of an American and a Vietnamese woman together, and the great beauty of this book lies partly in the relationship between these women who have had such different lives, linked by the war in Vietnam. But it also lies in the economy of the prose: in the form of simple and elegantly written prose poems, the book condenses Larsen's experience in Vietnam and Nga's awesome life story. Focusing on the details of everyday life and events, Larsen makes each image resonate with layers of political and personal meaning, bringing out the profound contrast between the American and Vietnamese cultures and the consequences of the war for those who are not on the battlefront.

In Vietnam, Larsen quickly learns a crucial lesson from Nga: the importance to the Vietnamese of saving face; and Nga guides her through the intimidating markets. Looking back, Larsen shows an acute awareness of her lack of understanding of the Vietnamese and the extreme ironies in the conjunction of the American and Vietnamese worlds. Teaching English, she uses Shakespeare and she observes with humor the mistranslations between herself and her students, the play between literal and metaphorical meaning:

Star-Crossed

They stood when I entered the classroom,
called me Ba Larsen,

which means "Mrs." or "Lady"
a sign of respect.

I concentrated on appearance
and reality, textual analysis of *Romeo and Juliet*

Late one afternoon Miss Hoa
came to the apartment on Le Thanh Ton.

I remember her white dress
black hair to her waist.

She had never been in an elevator before.

She said she was in love with her cousin
had been since she was thirteen

explained that many Vietnamese love their cousins,
the extended family.

Such love was forbidden by the church.
Should she kill herself like Juliet?

She drank the Coke I offered.

From the balcony we watched
magnesium flares fall beyond the harbor[4]

Exams

During examination week
there was a demonstration
in the more radical
School of Science.

I decided to hold my orals anyway.

I was asking Mr. Phuc
to explain the role of the witches in *Macbeth*
when we heard an explosion
and both dived under my desk.

He pointed to the book in his hand.
Through tear-gassed eyes,
I read the title dimly:
Shakespeare Without Tears.

We held on to each other
under my desk
our cheeks wet
with laughing and crying.[5]

Shallow Graves is pervaded with an awareness that our languages, and
our cultures, do not translate; it is difficult for a Western ear to pick up the
tonalities in Vietnamese that make one word mean many different
things. In the military interpreter's handbook, "birthday suit" was trans-
lated as "nude as a worm in a cocoon," "send to Siberia" as "where the
monkeys cough and the flamingos sing." But there is the shared bastard
language of war with its own vocabulary. As Larsen puts it: "we learned
it all and we couldn't speak to anyone when we got home." Those out-
side the war will never speak it, and those who were in the war will never
be able to make it understood. This is part of the legacy to the women in
the U.S. who could not understand the veterans who returned to them.
They do not understand the language of the war, and they do not under-
stand, cannot embrace what the experience was.

Shallow Graves summarizes in this poignant form so many of the eco-
nomic and cultural discrepancies between the U.S. and Vietnam. The

immense economic gap is illustrated again and again: our litter became houses saying Coca Cola and 7-Up on their sides, weapons, artifacts. The American women in Vietnam admired the beauty of the material culture and rushed to acquire things for decoration in their homes in the U.S. Larsen reveals her own insensitive desire for one of these crafted objects, perfectly contrasting the excessive luxury of American life with the basic economic needs of the Vietnamese; in the most simple way, she gives us a metaphor for the U.S. in Vietnam, juxtaposing a poem from Larsen's perspective and one from Nga's:

The Noodle Cart

My friends sent back rain drums from Laos,
lacquered trays with goldfish, ceramic elephants.
Once I knew we were leaving
I wanted a noodle cart

the old kind,
like the one I passed each morning on Le Thanh Ton,
with the stained-glass panels
of dragons and oceans and mythic sword fights.

I loved the giant ladies
the blue-and-white bowls in racks
the pots of boiling soup
over the charcoal braziers
the tiny stools on the street.

I loved the way the vendor
knew his clients
knew their favorite noodles
what they liked on top
like a waitress knowing you like your eggs
"sunny-side up" in an American coffee shop.

I asked Mrs. Nga to help me find a noodle cart.
After a month she said she had.
To buy one, she had to talk a family out of theirs.
The son was all in favor, but not the father
who was dead against selling the family business.

Now the noodle cart stands
on my brother's porch in California
stocked with little green bottles of Perrier water
Mr. and Mrs. T's Bloody Mary Mix.[6]

The Noodle Cart

My boss's wife was educated.
She taught English literature at the university.
She called the office and asked questions,
"Why is Chi Phuc crying?
Why don't Vietnamese eat cheese?"
One day she asked me to find a noodle cart
to take home to the United States.
She was my boss's wife. Of course I would do it.

It took me three weeks of searching.
I would go from cart to cart
asking where to buy one.
No one would tell me.
I got Bao to drive me through Cholon
way out to the countryside to PhuLam
where I had never been.

Every week I went to the same noodle man
pretending I went for noodles.
Soon he knew what I liked
and we started talking.
He asked if I wanted to start a business.
I explained my boss's wife
wanted the cart as a souvenir.
He said the Chinese would never sell
except to another Chinese.
After 14 bowls, he told me where to go look.

Bao said I was spending too much time on the project.
I said I had made a promise and I would keep it.
I would go by cyclo if he would not take me.
One Saturday we drove round and round for two hours
to a place where there were few houses.

Far away, all lined up in a field, we saw the noodle carts.
There were only Chinese there.
They said no carts would be ready for six months.

Finally I found a man in Saigon
who wanted to sell his cart.
He had a second wife in Can Tho
and wanted to move down with her.
The father and son fought.
The father refused to sell.
The son said he had to. The father cried.
The son told me to sneak back in the evening

and take the cart.
I had to find people to push it to the warehouse.

My boss's wife was pleased with the noodle cart.
"It's perfect," she said.
She had it shipped home to the United States.[7]

Larsen shows in many of these moments the contrast between the conditions of life for the American and Vietnamese women: while Larsen and other American women in Vietnam are in their consciousness-raising group discussing why pink is for girls, blue for boys, a Vietnamese woman, forced into the city by the war, lies in the street outside with her baby. When one of Larsen's household workers, a twenty-seven-year-old woman, is dying from her eighth pregnancy, Larsen takes her from her home where her deserter husband hides behind a chest covered with *Playboy* covers, and at the hospital the young woman shrugs when she appears in Larsen's missing silk underpants. When we reach Nga's story, we are deluged with her life as a female in Vietnamese society, spanning time that seems to go from something almost medieval to modern times. In addition to living through numerous wars and exiles, Nga has lived in a world of arranged marriages and polygamy, where she had to fight to get educated and to work. Nga advanced by virtue of her own personal power, as she is stopped over and over again. But she does not give up. Born in China in 1927, she was the daughter of an official in French colonial Vietnam; she charts her life as her family moves back to Vietnam, and the brutal situation for her family when the French are defeated, the chaos of war:

Muc

One night, caught in the fighting
between the French and the Viet Minh
we were forced to run.
I was carrying my little brother.
Our dog followed us from house to house, barking.
The neighbors yelled, "Kill him. Kill him.
Otherwise he will get us all killed
with his barking."

My second brother had to shut his eyes
and stab Muc with a knife.
Muc, our trusting dog,
his hair bright and black as velvet.
The look in his eyes
as he opened them wide
just before my brother stabbed him,

so helpless, so pitiful—
it followed me for years.[8]

Nga lives through the Chinese occupation, a famine when bodies are piled outside her family's door, the decision to leave the north for the south, the hostility of the southerners toward the northerners, continuing war, and after her father dies, her departure from Vietnam for the U.S., but without her mother:

Packing

I packed strange things
sandalwood soap from Hong Kong,
12 of my best ao dai,
my collection of tiny perfume bottles.

We all wanted to bring our mothers.
None of us could.
We had so many false starts
I never said goodbye to her.

One morning I made an incense offering
on my father's altar.

"You going today?" Mother asked.
"No," I said. "I just missed him
dreamt about him
wanted him to wish us luck."

I left my mother in our house on the street
that had been named General de Gaulle,
then Cong Ly, or Justice Street,
and then Cach Mang, Revolution Street.

I left my money on the outside porch
and never saw her again.[9]

Nga's personal story again confronts the Western reader with the cultural differences: she is forced to marry a Chinese general who kidnaps her father until she agrees, she arrives in China to find out she is a second wife, has two children, but returns to Vietnam when her husband is killed. There she becomes the second wife of the man she originally wanted to marry, who is now married to her sister. She has two children and is forbidden to work by both her husband and father . Through sheer determination she manages to get away and gets herself to England to study; on her return to Vietnam she stops in Rangoon and finds her husband there who forces her to remain with him and to again function only as a wife. When they are sent back to Vietnam, she leaves for the U.S.

where more culture shock must be faced and adjustment has to be made, where she must watch her children become Americans and reject the Vietnamese traditions she tries to maintain:

Blue Cable

Washington D.C. accepted my application.
My mother had a chance to come to America.
My heart sang.
Back from work, I shared the news with my family.

Everyone wanted her.
We agreed she would stay three months with each group.
We carried our happiness everywhere
even in our dreams.

Late April I was in the backyard in the garden
admiring my new red tulips.
The postman had me sign a blue cable.

"Mother died. March 26. Funeral Saturday."

My mother dead for one month.
My mother so far away
did our relatives perform the ceremony?
Did they dig her tomb deep?

O my country!

O my countrymen
so many of you left in shallow graves
in time of war
your souls wandering ceaselessly.[10]

Nga's story, given form in Larsen's prose poems, is the story of Vietnam through years of invasions, and testimony not only to Nga's remarkable individual strength but to the Vietnamese spirit. The Vietnamese women have shown incredible survival abilities and, despite the submissiveness demanded of them, women still rose to leadership positions in defense of their country (including Nga's favorite aunt, who was tortured and killed for political work).

In the closing poem of the book, Nga and Larsen go to the Museum of Natural History in New York together:

In the American Museum of Natural History (excerpt)

We find the Hall of Asian Peoples
just past the elephants.
Finding Vietnam is more difficult;

one small window
buried between India and China.
Black-and-white drawings show
a traditional wedding procession,
a typical farmer plowing with a water buffalo,
rice growing in a Vietnamese landscape,
four Vietnamese faces.
The only statue is a grinning Money God.
Its caption says
small change is dropped in his back for good luck.

Leaving the Hall of Asian Peoples,
Mrs. Nga smiles as she says,
"I think your country wants to forget about mine."

I picture us, Ba Larsen and Madame Nga,
arm in arm walking through the skeleton
of the dinosaur upstairs.
She has a flute and I a drum.
We carry no flags
and we make a sad song
as we pluck on the bones
dancing over the sides of the universe
past the bison and the bear
and the five-clawed dragon
and its burning pearls of wisdom.[11]

But *Shallow Graves* is a contribution that will not let us forget. Overcoming the barriers of culture and war, Nga and Larsen have made a painful but exquisite statement of remembering.

For the women who lost husbands, brothers, sons, and friends to the war, forgetting is impossible. The losses are varied and are experienced in many different ways. Bobbie Ann Mason and Jayne Anne Phillips are two of the women writers who have recently given expression to the continuing repercussions of the war.

Bobbie Ann Mason's *In Country* is told completely, and seamlessly, from the point of view of a teenage girl, Sam, whose father was killed in Vietnam. Years later, her mother is off with a new husband and a new baby and Sam lives with her uncle Emmett, a Vietnam veteran who seems to be living the war constantly, a casualty. The book embodies the obsession with the war not only for some of the veterans and the people who lived through that time, but in the mind of this girl who cannot understand, cannot know what surrounds her, what has determined her life. She is one of the children of Vietnam who will never know her father, lost to her before she is born. Her dilemma is the inability to know, to understand the event that has shaped everyone significant in her life. No one will talk about Vietnam with her; least of all her veteran uncle who is the central figure in her life. Completely dependent on each other, Sam reaches the age to decide whether to go away to college, whether to get married, and she cannot move: until she knows her uncle will be all right, and until she can know something of her father, she cannot move on. Mason skillfully describes a teenager who is beginning to reflect on life; emerging from her childlike concerns, she is developing a consciousness that demands to know more. Sam will not relent; hounded by what she hears about Agent Orange, she forces her uncle to go to a VA doctor, pressures him about why he does not work and why he gave up his attractive girlfriend. She is infected with the feeling that gripped many people during the war and especially those returning from the war: ordinary, everyday life seems meaningless, and she is increasingly alienated from her friends and their trivial interests. Losing interest in her young boyfriend, Sam pursues an older Vietnam veteran, trying to get closer to Vietnam through him; his impotence only puzzles and worries her more. Then she confronts her mother and Emmett's ex-girlfriend, hoping that women will somehow make her understand, know something. You don't want to know, says Emmett's girlfriend; I barely remember your father, says her mother. "Women weren't in Vietnam," says Emmett, "so they can't really understand." Sam knows that there were women in Vietnam as nurses, but that does not seem to matter. Women are cut off from the experience and from the veterans; they have no knowledge that satisfies her and they find the veterans just as unreachable:

> She thought of all the lives wasted by the war. She wanted to cry, but then she wanted to yell and scream and kick. She could imagine fighting, but only against war. All the boys getting killed, on both sides. And boys getting mutilated. And then not being allowed to grow up. That was it—they didn't get to grow up and become regular people. They had to stand outside, playing games, fooling around, acting like kids who couldn't get girlfriends. It was absurd.[12]

When Sam finally gets to read her father's war diary, she is horrified by his reference to the Vietnamese as "gooks" and his unfeeling, offhand report of killing a "VC." Suddenly the war begins to become more real to her and, desperate to wallow in something like her father's experience in Vietnam, she runs away to the dangerous swamp, the only treacherous place she knows, the place that causes Emmett's flashbacks, nightmares, fear. At dawn, when a scared and worried Emmett finds her there, he at last begins to break down: "His cry grew louder, as loud as the wail of a peacock. She watched in awe. In his diary, her father seemed to whimper, but Emmett's sorrow was full-blown, as though it had grown over the years into something monstrous and fantastic."[13] When Emmett starts to remember out loud, freeing himself of some of the pain, he also helps to liberate her from her loneliness and isolation, giving her something of her father and of the people who lived through that time, many silent and speechless victims of Vietnam.

Bobbie Ann Mason again shows her feeling for the devastating effects of war on the wives and children of veterans in her short story, "Big Bertha Stories." Donald, a veteran, and Jeannette marry, but a few years later Jeannette finds that her husband, who she expects to provide for her and their son, begins to be increasingly crippled by memories and nightmares of Vietnam. He is one of the veterans who suffered the tremendous conflict of loving Vietnam, "its landscape and its people," while having to believe in the project of destroying it all. Haunted by this, his mind wavers wildly between thoughts of Vietnam's lush beauty and the grace of the seemingly fragile Vietnamese women and explosive images of total devastation.

Instead of children's stories, Donald channels these obsessions into Big Bertha stories, filling his son with tales of the all-powerful giant strip mining machine he works with, when he is capable of working. His son joins in, and he dreams, talks, and draws Big Bertha stories of power and ruin. The child loves his father, wants to emulate him, and incorporates his father into himself, taking whatever he can get, another child of Vietnam.

In this story, Mason captures the male infatuation with machines and the belief in technological power that has proved false in Vietnam. Anger about this failure is mixed with guilt and sorrow, and her character continually moves from combativeness to appreciation in a flash:

> If we could have had tanks over there as big as Big Bertha, we wouldn't have lost the war. Strip mining is just like what we were doing over there. We were stripping off the top. The topsoil is like the culture and the people, the best part of the land and the country. America was just stripping off the top, the best. We ruined it.[14]

America also stripped the land, but Donald aches for the people; Jeannette is alienated and mystified by his preoccupation with Vietnam. Frustrated that Donald cannot play his role as husband and father, she resists listening ("Wasn't that a long time ago?") and she screens out parts that fit into her neutral frame of reference. But she refuses to enter his. Inexorably, he ends up in a psychiatric ward and in a moment of epiphany she realizes that she has not thought of him "as himself," as more than fulfilling that traditional role, and with this shift she is destined to join her husband and son in morbid fixation, as she dreams of "jumping on soft moss" that turns into a "springy pile of dead bodies."

Bobbie Ann Mason's story captures what it takes to continue to love a veteran, and how difficult it is to help. The problem is not only understanding an unimaginable experience. For to love someone is to internalize something of them, and the resistance to taking in the extreme horrors of the war stands between these women and the Vietnam veterans.

Beginning with the title, Jayne Anne Phillips's *Machine Dreams* works with images of the machines and nightmares that are part of war. On one level it is a story of a small town family, Mitch and Jean and their daughter Danner and son Billy. On another, it is a dirge for the many losses of the Vietnam War period. With its sensual prose, *Machine Dreams* flows in between dreams and through time, drawing the reader in like a drug, subtly foreshadowing death and a mourning that will not end. From the beginning there is a dislocation in her parent's memories of the World War II years; things do not seem right, and there is an inexorable feeling that nothing can be done to change their direction. The lives are not easy in *Machine Dreams*; there are financial and emotional struggles throughout and the parents are at odds. Mitch resents his wife's working and advancing, making money, while his career slides further down. The tension and distance between the parents links the children closer together in a quiet, unquestioned bond, prefiguring the enormity of the loss when, inevitably, Billy goes to war in his time.

His father is still haunted by his experiences in World War II in nightmares:

The smell was bad, horrible and terrible and full of death, he couldn't think of a word to say what the smell was, it rose up underneath and around him and he turned to get away. Behind the smell someone kept crying, weeping like a child on and on as the smell broke in the heat, ten in the morning and hot, already hot as hell and the sky a searing bright blue mass over the dried rust red of the bodies. A twisted khaki of limbs and more he didn't want to see clearly opened flat and mashed and rumpled, oh, the smell, like a deadness of shit and live things rotted, some gigantic fetid woman sick to death between her legs had bled out her limitless guts on this sandy field flattening to the green of Ora Bay. Nothing to do but go ahead, hot metal seat of the dozer against his hips, vibration of motor thrumming, and that kid still crying, some island kid, get a detail over there to keep those kids away got to get pits dug and doze this mess.[15]

With this machine dream we begin to feel the inevitability of the small town son following his father into war. But the Vietnam War is different; more machines, more destruction, and more senselessness. Phillips captures the way the war seemed to shatter all the given values, rendering all the customary things unstable. For the young men who were destined to go to war, the impending moment hung over them as they awaited the lottery; in *Machine Dreams*, Billy drops out of college, breaks up with his girlfriend, reunites with her in an unspoken, intense, possibly last farewell. Danner tries to convince her younger brother to go to Canada, but she meets with their father's patriotism and her brother's abdication, and the inevitable day arrives: "Dad, Billy is missing, he's not dead." The army provides neither solace nor information, and a veteran father must fight with the government to learn anything about his son, echoing the powerlessness of the American people in the face of their government. Each alone in their pain, Danner tries to get as close to Vietnam as she can get. Obsessed like Sam in *In Country*, she pursues all the veterans she meets, immersing herself in Vietnam to try to experience something of her brother. At home, her mother keeps her son's room intact, untouched, for when he might return. *Machine Dreams* is a meditation on loss, the unresolvable loss of unfulfilled lives, of a family amputated by a loss that cannot be named. Billy went down in a plane, one of the machines of war, and for his sister the irresolution of the missing goes on forever:

> Danner and Billy are walking in the deep dark forest. Billy makes airplane sounds. Danner, oblivious to her brother's play, is stalking the magic horse. There are no cloven tracks, but the dust on the path is disturbed and the horse seems to be circling. Occasionally Danner looks over her shoulder and sees the animal watching them through thick leaves. The mare's eyes are large and certain. Certain of what? Billy pays no attention and seems to have followed his sister here almost accidentally. They walk on, and finally it is so dark that Danner can't see Billy at all. She can only hear him, farther and farther behind her, imitating with a careful and private energy the engine sounds of a plane that is going down. War-movie sounds. *EEEE-yoww, ack-ack-ack.* So gentle it sounds like a song, and the song goes on softly as the plane falls, year after year, to earth.[16]

The story of women and Vietnam is one of invisibility, of the women who worked in Vietnam who have suffered no recognition of their contribution and their experience, the women who walked through it with husbands, watching powerlessly, and the many women who have suffered the loss of relationship with the dead, the missing, and the living. None can forget, but remembering can help heal and give us some strength to prevent the atrocity of war.

NOTES

1. Keith Walker, ed., *A Piece of My Heart: The Stories of Twenty-Six American Women Who Served in Vietnam* (Novato, Calif.: Presidio Press, 1985), p. 78.

2. Lynda Van Devanter, with Christopher Morgan, *Home Before Morning: The Story of an Army Nurse in Vietnam* (New York: Beaufort Books, Inc., 1983), p. 280.

3. *A Piece of My Heart*, p. 25.

4. Wendy Wilder Larsen and Tran Thi Nga, *Shallow Graves: Two Women and Vietnam* (New York: Random House, 1986), p. 20.

5. Ibid., p. 92.

6. Ibid., p. 95.

7. Ibid., p. 220.

8. Ibid., p. 153.

9. Ibid., p. 232.

10. Ibid., p. 269.
11. Ibid., pp. 277-278.
12. Bobbie Ann Mason, *In Country* (New York: Harper & Row, 1985), p. 140.
13. Ibid., p. 224.
14. See Bobbie Ann Mason, "Big Bertha Stories," in this collection.
15. Jayne Anne Phillips, *Machine Dreams* (New York: E. P. Dutton/Seymour Lawrence, 1984), pp. 59-60.
16. Ibid., p. 331.

RECOMMENDED READING

Arthur Egendorf, *Healing From the War.* Boston: Shambhala Publications, Inc., 1986.

Wendy Wilder Larsen and Tran Thi Nga, *Shallow Graves: Two Women and Vietnam.* New York: Random House, 1986.

Robert Jay Lifton, *Home From the War: Vietnam Veterans: Neither Victims Nor Executioners.* New York: Simon & Schuster, 1973.

Bobbie Ann Mason, *In Country.* New York: Harper & Row, 1985.

Jayne Anne Phillips, *Machine Dreams.* New York: E.P. Dutton/Seymour Lawrence, 1984.

Lynda Van Devanter, with Christopher Morgan, *Home Before Morning: The Story of an Army Nurse in Vietnam.* New York: Beaufort Books, Inc., 1983.

Keith Walker, ed., *A Piece of My Heart: The Stories of Twenty-Six American Women Who Served in Vietnam.* Novato, Calif.: Presidio Press, 1985.

VARD M RUDITYS
ALL · TIMOTHY J H
Y JOHNSON · ADA
NGUS W McALLIS
MARVIN L POSPIS
OBERT L SHIRODA
OR · WAYNE L THO
F GRIFFIN · CLARI
T BATCHELOR Jr ·
KINGHAM · MICH
CLIFFORD D CO
DONALDSON · SA

ELIZABETH HESS

Vietnam: Memorials of Misfortune

PART I: 1983

War memorials may be too important to leave simply to artists and architects.

—Congressman Henry J. Hyde

Advocates of modernism and realism often have difficulty appreciating each other. The conflict between these two points of view has been elevated to a new stage—the nation's capital—where two memorials for Vietnam veterans, one abstract and the other realistic, will soon be permanently at war with each other. The bitter Washington debate surrounding the erection of these two monuments has itself been warlike. What began as a clearly defined project to memorialize Americans who died in Vietnam has become, during the past two years, a battlefield echoing with the same rhetoric once heard at Kent State. So far there have been no casualties in this art war, only compromises.

Original plans had called for a single memorial to be built on Washington's prestigious mall between the Lincoln Memorial and the Washington Monument. Its design was to be selected by a jury of specialists from participants in a nationwide competition. In May of 1981 the judges unanimously chose Maya Ying Lin, a twenty-one-year-old Yale undergraduate, as their $20,000 winner. But soon after Lin's design for a simple, V-shaped wall was made public, the protests began. A small group of influential men—some in government and some private citizens—

launched a noisy, finally unsuccessful campaign to block construction of Lin's memorial. In spite of their efforts, ground was broken in March of 1982 and seven months later the memorial was on its site.

But Lin's opponents did not admit defeat; though they could not prevent the erection of her monument, they did manage to arrange for the addition of a second memorial. A larger-than-lifesize realistic statue of three GIs in battle dress, designed by Frederick Hart, a figurative sculptor from Washington, D.C., is presently under construction. Accompanied by a fifty-foot flagpole, Hart's statue (which has thus far only been seen in maquette form) will be placed on the memorial site by Veterans Day, 1983.

The story of the two memorials begins with Jan Scruggs, who was born in Washington, D.C., graduated from high school, and went straight to Vietnam. Half of his company, the U.S. Army Light Infantry Brigade, was killed or wounded between 1969 and 1970, and Scruggs himself landed in the hospital for two months. Upon his return to the U.S., Scruggs enrolled at American University and became deeply involved in the problems of the demobilized Vietnam troops. Eventually attending graduate school, he completed a study on the psychological adjustments facing Vietnam veterans, and in 1976 presented his findings to a Senate subcommittee. Scruggs's sincere if somewhat naive aspiration was to replace the veteran's nightmare with the American Dream.

In 1979, Scruggs incorporated the Vietnam Veterans Memorial Fund (VVMF) of which he remains president. Its specific and only purpose was to erect a national monument honoring those who had died in the war. According to a press release issued by the Fund, the monument was to be "without political content," and it was to be funded by contributions from private sources. That year legislation was introduced in Congress to allocate land for the planned memorial and the project was eventually signed into law by President Carter in 1980. As is usual in such matters, all considerations for the memorial—design, landscape, planning, aesthetics— would have to be approved by the National Capital Planning Commission (NCPC), the Commission of Fine Arts (CFA), and the Department of the Interior. (Those familiar with the process of trying to get anything built in the District of Columbia know that at best it is an extremely arduous procedure.)

The VVMF decided to select a design by holding a juried competition open to all American citizens over eighteen, even though the Fund would thereby lose control over the final result. Advised by landscape architect Paul Spreiregen, the VVMF placed the decision in the hands of eight men: landscape architects Hideo Sasaki and Garrett Eckbo; architects Harry Weese and Pietro Belluschi; sculptors Costantino Nivola, James Rosati, and Richard H. Hunt; and Grady Clay, editor of *Landscape Architecture*. The seed money to launch the contest was provided by Texas computer millionaire H. Ross Perot. (Ironically, Perot would later be among those who would attempt to dismantle the entire competition process.)

There were two design requirements stipulated by the VVMF that severely limited all entries. First, the names of the 57,939 Americans who died, or are still missing, in Vietnam had to be engraved somewhere on the memorial. Second, contestants were required to be sensitive to the Washington Monument and the Lincoln Memorial, which would bracket the site. Constitution Gardens, as the area is called, is the president's backyard—it's sacred territory. These considerations pretty much ruled out a vertical monument, and a wall of some sort would obviously be necessary for the names.

The competition, which was announced in October 1980, received 1,421 entries, a surprisingly large response. In accord with contest rules, no names were attached to any of the proposals. Thus, when Maya Lin's design was selected in May of the following year, everyone was astonished to find that the winner was female, Chinese-American, and an undergraduate. Lin's competition-winning design was a combination minimalist sculpture-earthwork. It consisted of two walls—each 250 feet long and made of 140 panels—which met at a 125-degree angle; beginning at ground level at each extreme, both walls gradually rose to a height of ten feet at the monument's center, or the apex of the angle. Working within and taking full advantage of the Fund's guidelines, Lin made some innovational decisions: she chose polished black granite as her material, thus turning the walls into mirrors; and she decided to list the 57,939 Vietnam casualties not alphabetically, as is customary, but in the order in which they were killed. ("I wanted to return the vets to the time-frame of the war," Lin explains, "and in the process, I wanted them to see their own reflection in the names.") Furthermore, rather than simply setting the two walls on top of the ground, Lin's design proposed to build them into a rise in the landscape, with only their inscribed sides visible. The spectator, walking downward along the length of either wall, would thus have the dramatic sensation of descending into the earth. In view of the response that Lin's walls would later provoke, it is amusing to speculate that initially her design was chosen because of its utter modesty—its simple, straight lines, its unobtrusive character. The jurors may well have thought that Lin's proposal was least likely to make waves in the ultra-sensitive District of Columbia.

On October 13, 1981, Lin attended one of the regular monthly meetings of the board of directors of the CFA, prepared to discuss granite samples. The CFA's chairman, J. Carter Brown, who has been called Washington's "arbiter of excellence," is also the director of the National Gallery. The commission, originally established by Congress in 1910, was created to give expert advice on works of art or architecture acquired or commissioned by the government. At an earlier meeting, Brown had already echoed the jurors' unanimous approval of Lin's design, and as a result everyone expected to discuss minor details of a largely site-specific character. All CFA monthly meetings are open to the public and transcripts were made of the proceedings for the record. No one was prepared for the arrival of Tom Carhart, a member of the VVMF and a former infantry platoon leader with two Purple Hearts. Carhart had helped raise funds for the memorial and, in his enthusiasm for the project, had even entered a design in the competition himself—the first art work he had ever attempted.

Carhart was not happy with Lin's design which he characterized as "the most insulting and demeaning memorial to our experience that was possible." He passionately argued that it was a memorial to "the war at home" rather than to the one in Southeast Asia: "When I came home from Vietnam in 1968," he said, "I was literally spat upon as I walked through the Chicago airport in my uniform by some girl in a band of hippies. That spit hurt." Carhart charged that Lin's design was geared to "those who would still spit," and he called the proposed monument a "degrading ditch." He was the first to publicly attack the color of the stone. "Black," he said, is "the universal color of shame, sorrow, and degradation in all races, all societies worldwide." Carhart demanded a white memorial.

Ross Perot in Texas was also unhappy with Lin's design. A legendary and somewhat enigmatic figure, even in a state known for its cowboy capitalists, Perot is notorious for meddling in political affairs. He once hired mercenaries who attempted, unsuccessfully, to bring POWs home from North Vietnam. On another occasion he financed a surveillance mission, also unsuccessful, into Iran during the hostage crisis. No one in Washington has been anxious to articulate Perot's exact role in the memorial controversy. Off the record, however, many people have targeted him as the organizer of the opposition to Lin's design. ("When powerful people are against you," Scruggs whispered to me over the phone, "it may not be in your interest to answer questions.") Perot, himself, was more than willing to talk to me about his side of the story in a telephone interview. To him, Lin's memorial was "a slap in the face." But he says he wasn't surprised that the memorial looked like a "tombstone" since "Maya did design it in a class on funereal architecture at Yale."

Rumor has it that when Perot's money talks, people listen. After contributing $160,000 towards funding the memorial, Perot may have expected to have some say in its final disposition. His strategy for overturning the decision of the jurors was to create the impression that the veterans themselves had rejected Lin's design. Scruggs believes that Perot flew in veterans from around the country to lobby against the jurors' choice. The Texan flatly denies this and says that all he did was "try to get the Fund off their ego trip long enough to remember their constituency of two million vets." To do so, he personally financed a poll of 587 POWs. According to Perot's poll, 67 percent of those polled disliked the original design; 70 percent thought the color of the memorial should be white; 96 percent thought the American flag should be prominently displayed on the memorial site. Though on the basis of Perot's statistics it seemed as if the majority of veterans were against the design, the memorial's supporters argue that, since POWs are more conservative than the average veteran, the survey was skewed. Moreover, Scruggs claims that when he had the poll checked by an expert, he was told that it wasn't worth the paper it was written on. Perot, on the other hand, brushes aside these objections, saying, "Losers always discredit the winners." He insists that the poll was sent to POWs only as a test mailing.

Meanwhile in Washington during the fall of 1981, Maya Lin was beginning to be viewed as a radical. Her work, which had initially been praised by the CFA because it was "apolitical," was now labeled subversive. James Webb, for example, a highly decorated marine and author of a Vietnam novel titled *Fields of Fire*, called it a "wailing wall for anti-draft demonstrators." In some quarters, the monument's V-shape was being interpreted as the symbol of the antiwar movement. Carhart had already referred to the black stone as a "black spot in American history." Although one critic described the listing of names in nonalphabetical order as "a profoundly metaphoric twist with universal implications," for Carhart it was a "malicious, random scattering . . . such that neither brother nor father nor lover nor friend could ever be found." The fact that it was possible from one vantage point to see the monument as sinking into the earth was interpreted by some commentators as an admission of guilt—an acknowledgement that we had committed crimes in Vietnam.

The VVMF, too, was under attack. Scruggs says, "The memorial's enemies are mostly members of the New Right" who were pressuring the Fund to compromise their original plan. According to the *Washington Post*, it was Senator Jeremiah Denton who led the fight against Lin's memorial on Capitol Hill, and the campaign picked up considerable steam on its way to the White House. Even Phyllis Schlafly became an art-critic-for-a-day, calling the memorial a "tribute to Jane Fonda" in the pages of the *Washington Inquirer*, the Moral Majority's weekly newspaper. As the flak got heavier, Scruggs admits that he began to suffer from battle fatigue. It seemed to him that if he wanted to dedicate the memorial by Veterans Day, 1982—then less than a year away—a compromise was the only way out.

It was clear to most observers that the battle over the memorial was being fought entirely with political ammunition. Attempting, as one senator ironically put it, "to neutralize this apolitical statement," the opponents of Lin's memorial could at most hope for additions to the site. They could not block completely construction or censor Lin's design without angering the press and the art world. It was also evident that James Watt, the secretary of the interior, held the final card, since his authorization was required before the VVMF could break ground. Watt, who would subsequently make his position clear in a carefully worded letter to the CFA, was refusing to grant permission until suitable additions to the memorial were agreed upon by the Fund, the CFA, and the National Capital Planning Commission.

By January 1982, the debate suddenly moved behind closed doors. A loosely organized committee, chaired by Senator John Warner and in-cluding, among other conservatives, Milton Copulos—a Vietnam veteran and currently an energy expert with the Heritage Foundation (a well-known right-wing think tank)—was formed; Scruggs was then invited to meet with them in face-to-face combat to settle the dispute. The press was not invited to this kangaroo court and no public record of proceedings exists. But according to a statement issued by the VVMF more than a year later, the group, which had convened on January 27, 1982, agreed, after a nasty fight, to support the addition to the memorial site of a sculpture and a flag, but "with no location specified." The opponents of Lin's memorial also agreed "to cease their political effort to block approval of the design and to allow the planned March groundbreaking to occur on schedule." A second meeting was planned to "consider various alterna-tive designs for the sculpture."

Now that the opponents of Lin's memorial had won their first major battle, they turned their attention to the strategic placement of the statue and the flag. According to members of the Fund, when Senator Warner's group reconvened in March of 1982 to discuss designs for the sculpture, it was Ross Perot who changed the committee's agenda. Realizing that placement of the sculpture would be a crucial issue, he urged the group to agree about it at once. When a vote was taken, the majority of those present wanted the flag placed on top of the memorial, at the vertex of the walls, and the sculpture placed on the ground below, at the middle of the V. According to the Fund's printed statement, this majority opinion was not surprising: "As at the prior meeting, the handful of VVMF repre-sentatives were far outnumbered by the group of opponents which Mr. Perot and others had organized to attend the meeting." But the votes taken at this meeting were not final. All decisions still had to go through Watt, the CFA, and the NCPC.

What was most significant about these meetings was that the VVMF had been convinced to sponsor the additional sculpture and flag. Realiz-ing that it was the only way to get Lin's piece built, Scruggs presented the VVMF's new proposal to the proper authorities, and in March work on the monument finally began. In April, without Maya Lin's knowledge, a sculpture panel was chosen by the VVMF to select an artist for the second memorial; it was comprised entirely of Vietnam veterans who had been involved in the dispute and included two people who supported Lin's memorial—Arthur Mosley and William Jayne—and two who opposed it—James Webb and Milton Copulos. In July, Frederick Hart was com-missioned by the VVMF (for a fee neither party will make public) to design a second Vietnam memorial, and by September Hart's maquette for the statue was unveiled.

The conservatives wanted a statue in the tradition of the Iwo Jima memorial, which was based on an actual photograph. But Hart knew that there were few heroic moments in the Vietnam War. (After all, one of the most memorable photographs in the entire Vietnam debacle was of the shot taken at point-blank range into a guerrilla's head by Nguyen Ngoc Loan, then chief of police in Saigon.) Hart's model is a competent homage to an abstraction called "vets"—as traditional as a Hallmark card. Three young men, one of whom is black, stand on a small base. All three look to their right, perhaps (depending on their final siting) towards Lin's walls. There is nothing to identify these soldiers specifically with Vietnam other than their uniforms; the realism lies in the details of their military garb, in the gun thrown over a shoulder, the ammunition around a waist. The facial expressions of these soldiers are somewhat peculiar; they look stunned—more bewildered than heroic.

When the maquette was made public last fall, its placement was still a matter of dispute. Members of Warner's committee who wanted the statue in the center of Lin's walls—penetrating her V—began to fight an extended battle over the location of the second memorial. The issue was not settled until February 1983, when, after a great deal of acrimonious debate, it was finally decided that both Hart's statue and the flag would be placed 120 feet from Lin's walls, near the entrance to the memorial site. Hart himself supported this decision, understanding quite well that the two works of art would clash if placed too close together.

The decision to add a second memorial to the site has not been popular everywhere in Washington. Some negative feelings were expressed at last October's meeting of the CFA, when many witnesses testified against acceptance of Hart's model. Among them was Paul Spreiregen, the Washington landscape architect who was advisor to the original contest: "Imagine Arlington Cemetery," Spreiregen said, "with groups of larger-than-life soldiers, in various combat outfits, winding their way through the trees, coming up on headstones." Robert Lawrence, president of the American Institute of Architects, called the compromise a "concerted effort . . . by a few individuals unhappy with the design," even though Lin's design had been "applauded almost unanimously." Indeed, what the rhetoric of the memorial controversy reflected was the difficulty of separating the issue of Lin's design from the politics of the war; the VVMF had mandated the impossible—a "neutral" memorial.

Throughout this period, the VVMF and Lin's supporters tried to prove that there was nothing radical about her design, but Lin's enemies continued to see red reflected in the memorial's slick black walls. The problem was not simply the fact that the monument was abstract and black. Lin's memorial ran counter to tradition in several other important ways: it appeared to be sinking into the ground rather than towering above the site; it had an unconventional system of listing names; it was completely unheroic, totally nonaggressive. It could, in fact, be read as a pacifist piece. To add insult to injury, the eight male jurors had chosen a memorial with a distinctly female character, placing at the base of Washington's giant phallus a wide V-shape surrounded by a grassy mound. The memorial was hardly a "black gash of shame," but it could indeed be read as a radical statement about the war, and even as the expression of a female sensibility. The vast number of names inscribed on the wall comes across as a powerful antiwar statement. As a woman standing in front of the memorial remarked, "What an unbelievable waste."

And facing the myriad names, it is difficult for anyone *not* to question the purpose of the war. The reawakening of old conflicts about Vietnam has inevitably disturbed members of the Reagan administration; these battle scars suggest parallels with our current involvements in, for example, El Salvador. Lin's memorial functions as a powerful reminder of the potential consequences of our current foreign policy.

Towards the end of the memorial battle, Benjamin Forgey in the *Washington Post* underlined the essentially nonaesthetic nature of the conflict. "Adding the sculpture and the flag," he wrote, "clearly was a political not an aesthetic necessity." Even those critics who argued that Lin's memorial was too abstract for popular taste were attacking it from a political perspective. Tom Wolfe, who published a well-timed article in the *Washington Post* on the same day that the CFA heard testimony on the proposed additions, is a case in point. Calling Lin's memorial "nonbourgeois art," or art "that baffled the general public," Wolfe compared Lin's experience to that of Carl Andre's in Hartford and Richard Serra's in downtown Manhattan. He concluded that her memorial, too, was abstract and elitist. Yet no one, including Wolfe, has actually been baffled by the memorial. While Wolfe predictably lambasted the "Mullahs of Modernism," he also used this occasion to add the antiwar movement to his enemy list. Having referred to the memorial as a "perverse prank," he ended his vituperative piece with the already familiar phrase, "A tribute to Jane Fonda!"

If Lin's memorial is a tribute to Fonda, then Hart's is a tribute to John Wayne. It salutes the military establishment—the representatives of the American Legion, the Marine Corps League, the Naval Association, and the Military Order of the Purple Heart—all of whom demanded an alternative to Lin's piece. What Hart's statue is not, however, is a tribute to the troops. In fact, no one has been anxious to hear from *them*. It is no secret that returning veterans were not welcomed home with open arms. There were no ticker-tape parades for an army that now has the highest suicide rate of any population of ex-GIs. "A few moments of honest conversation with any [veteran]," wrote critic Peter Marin in *The Nation*, "put to shame the versions of the war produced by our filmmakers, novelists and many journalists." The veterans are as divided as the rest of the population about Vietnam—and about the memorial. "I can't imagine anyone being proud of what we did over there," commented John Van-Zwieten, who returned home and joined the Vietnam Veterans Against the War. Although he now lives in Washington, VanZwieten doesn't even want to see the memorial—not because it's a tribute to Jane, but in fact for quite the opposite reason. As one veteran put it in *About Face*, a newspaper handed out at the dedication ceremony, "Buttering up Vietnam veterans as 'forgotten heroes' is a slap in the face directed at millions in this country who resisted the war."

Thanks to the battle over the Vietnam memorial, Constitution Gardens will present two very different interpretations of the war. Though initially Lin's memorial may have had a certain political ambiguity, its juxtaposition with Hart's conservative statue will clearly emphasize its radical edge. Scruggs's original contention that America owed the veterans was neither radical nor conservative. It was a centrist position shared by millions of Americans including the families of those who came home in body bags. These are the thousands who flooded Washington for last year's dedication: one monument was more than enough for them. Veterans have been weeping in front of Lin's black walls. Their families have been eager to touch a name or take a rubbing. Visitors have left flowers, clothes, snapshots, and personal treasures belonging to the dead. The reception to this cold, black, abstract object has in fact been overwhelmingly warm. As the *Washington Post* noted in its editorial column, "The argument over the memorial dissolves the moment you get there." When Hart's statue is in place, the two memorials will inevitably challenge each other with contrary points of view. But this is one confrontation that Maya Lin should easily win.

AN INTERVIEW WITH MAYA LIN (1983)

Certain people are outraged by your memorial. They read it as a statement against the Vietnam War.

The worst thing in the world would have been indifference to my piece. The monument may lack an American flag, but you're surrounded by America, by the Washington Monument and the Lincoln Memorial. I don't design pure objects like those. I work with the landscape, and I hope that the object and the land are equal players.

Is your piece political?

The piece itself is apolitical in the sense that it doesn't comment directly on the war—only on the men that died. For some people—especially right-wing politicians—that's political enough. It's like the emperor's new clothes: what people see, or don't see, is their own projection.

Were you involved in the antiwar movement?

No. But I think any war is pretty sad. People killing each other because they can't resolve their differences. I don't make judgments about the Vietnam War though, because I don't know enough about it.

Why do you think veterans like Tom Carhart dislike your memorial?

I haven't gotten one negative letter from a veteran. Most of them are not as conservative as Carhart. It's the administration that would like to remember Vietnam the same way it remembers other wars—through the heroes. Well, one of the things that made this war different is the fact that the veterans got screwed. They came back and their country called them "murderers." Nothing can make up for that. You can't pretend that this war was the same as others.

What do you think about the decision to add Hart's piece?

It was a coup. It was a power play. It had nothing to do with how many veterans liked or disliked my piece. Ross Perot has powerful friends who managed to get a compromise through. Even Jan Scruggs said, "We've been ambushed." The vice-president of the Fund called what happened a "rape" of my decision. I didn't even find out that they had made a "few modifications" until I saw it announced on TV! Perot flew in fifty people who hated the design from all over the country and they spread rumors in the White House that the designer was a leftist, that the jurors were all communists, and people believed it.

How has the memorial fund treated you?

The fund has always seen me as female—as a child. I went in there when I first won and their attitude was—okay, you did a good job, but now we're going to hire some big boys—boys—to take care of it. I said no! I wanted to help put together a team that knew about landscape, granite. Their basic attitude was I gave them the design and they could do what they wanted with it. They expected me to take the money [$20,000] and run.

271

How has the fund treated the veterans?

The fund has really gone show biz and it's upsetting a lot of vets. My attitude is that you shouldn't spend tons of money on the memorial—7 million has been spent so far. The money should be given to the vets who need it—like Agent Orange victims—because it's obvious that the government isn't going to help them out.

You haven't sat down with Hart to work something out?

No. But from what I gather, Hart thought a long time before accepting the commission. It wasn't necessarily going to be good for his reputation, but the price was right. They seem to be paying him twenty times what they paid me. He goes on and on about working with my piece rather than against it. But you can't really work with a piece if you don't have a dialogue with it. He claims that my memorial is "rude in its neglect of the human element." How can someone like that work with my design?

What do you think of Hart's sculpture?

Three men standing there before the world—it's trite. It's a generalization, a simplification. Hart gives you an image—he's illustrating a book.

But do you think the veterans will have an easier time relating to Hart's work?

No! I don't think the veterans are as unintelligent as some people would like to judge them.

Why did you choose black for the color of the stone?

Classical Greek temples were never white. They were highly colored. At some point much later, someone decided that white signified classical architecture. Black for me is a lot more peaceful and gentle than white. White marble may be very beautiful, but you can't read anything on it. I wanted something that would be soft on the eyes, and turn into a mirror if you polished it. The point is to see yourself reflected in the names. Also the mirror image doubles and triples the space. I thought black was a beautiful color and appropriate for the design.

Has this situation radicalized you in any way?

There were certain things I was aware of intellectually that I had never seen before. In the academic world where I grew up, my femaleness, the fact that I was Oriental, was never important. You didn't see prejudice. People treated you first as a human being. When I first came to Washington my biggest shock was that no one would listen to me because I had no power—no masculinity.

Do you think the memorial has a female sensibility?

In a world of phallic memorials that rise upwards, it certainly does. I didn't set out to conquer the earth, or overpower it, the way Western man usually does. I don't think I've made a passive piece, but neither is it a memorial to the idea of war.

AN INTERVIEW WITH FREDERICK HART (1983)

Can you describe your original submission to the competition?

Originally I had a circular wall with the names on it. There were two groups of soldiers on either side reaching out to each other. That was the whole idea—to reach back across a huge gap. I wasn't happy with it. In fact, I was astonished when I won the third prize.

At what point did you get back in the running?

People think I have been negotiating behind the scenes—that I've been wined and dined by Ross Perot—it's not true. When they [the Fund] eventually came back to me it made sense. Because I had entered the contest, I had already put a good deal of thought into the project. I was also the only figurative sculptor that had won a prize.

Certain critics think your sculpture portrays a stereotype.

I honestly thought that once people saw it, they would understand that what I was doing wasn't trite. The average age of the Vietnam combatant was nineteen years old and it was an excruciating kind of combat situation. What a burden to place on a nineteen-year-old child. I wanted to make people aware of these indignities. I wanted to use realism to give some sense of the youth and innocence of these kids. The figures do relate to the wall. I thought it was a good solution and that people would give me credit, but the situation was too politicized.

How did it get so politicized? How did Maya Lin come to represent the antiwar movement and Frederick hart the military establishment?

Well, I don't know how conscious Lin was about using the black stone to turn the memorial into a funeral piece, but unconsciously it appealed to many liberals as appropriate for a black moment in history. If the monument was meant as a Vietnam *War* Memorial—then even I couldn't argue with it because the war was a tragedy. But that wasn't what the memorial was supposed to be. It was supposed to give a little dignity to the people who fought the war—the nineteen-year-olds, not the generals. The piece rubbed them absolutely raw.

Is realism the only way to reach them?

No, not necessarily. All they wanted was for the memorial to be white! They didn't need a statue or anything else. The statue is just an awkward solution we came up with to save Lin's design. I think this whole thing is an art war. It takes a tremendous amount of egocentricity and arrogance for artists to feel that no one should interfere with their work—when it's for the public.

You mean Lin's memorial is purely art for art's sake?

I don't like blank canvases. Lin's memorial is intentionally not meaningful. It doesn't relate to ordinary people and I don't like art that is contemptuous of life. This event is a kind of Gettysburg for contemporary art—art that has isolated itself into a corner.

If Lin's piece is political, isn't yours political also?

Yes, but it's different. My position is humanist, not militaristic. I'm not trying to say there was anything good or bad about the war. I researched for three years—read everything. I became close friends with many vets, drank with them in the bars. Lin's piece is a serene exercise in contemporary art done in a vacuum with no knowledge of the subject. It's nihilistic—that's its appeal.

Were you involved in the antiwar movement?

I got gassed with everyone else, mostly out of peer pressure.

Weren't the competition's laws broken by your addition?

The Fund did what everybody does today. They relinquished their autonomy and handed it over to the so-called experts—the art mafia. Senator John Warner, James Watt—all those people who intervened didn't do it out of whimsy. They did it because their constituencies asked them to. Letters of protest went to the White House and they were handed over to Watt because the memorial is in his legal jurisdiction. It's his job. It was democracy in action, not totalitarianism, Stalinism, or fascism. Watt didn't simply say: I don't like this newfangled modern stuff and I'm gonna get rid of it.

Does the fact that Lin is a young Oriental woman have anything to do with this uproar?

There is nothing more powerful than an ingenue. If she had been a professional, the design would have been sacked. That's what happened with the Roosevelt memorial; the design went through. All the professionals and everybody else loved it—except for the Roosevelt family. They said no thanks, and that was it. Everybody is worked up about this poor little girl who is getting kicked around by the secretary of the interior. The press has turned her into a Cinderella.

Is there a war between the two monuments?

The collision is all about the fact that Maya Lin's design is elitist and mine is populist. People say you can bring what you want to Lin's memorial. But I call that brown bag aesthetics. I mean, you better bring something, because there ain't nothing being served.

Memories fade, and only official history remains.

—Noam Chomsky

All memorials are fictions ironically carved in stone. The story that Maya Ying Lin's modernist V tells is unusually radical for a public monument: It does not have a happy ending. Regardless, those vets who are not on the wall feel a magnetic attraction to it; thousands are traveling long distances to purge themselves of the Vietnam experience with almost bulimic compulsion. These same people are returning home and organizing local memorial projects across the country. In the five years since Lin and Hart's memorials were completed, approximately 150 new monuments have been dedicated to Vietnam veterans. Many others are in the planning stages.[1]

Not surprisingly, the military establishment continues to tailor the imaginations of those who are organizing these projects. For the most part it is Frederick Hart, rather than Maya Lin, who has managed to set (conservative) aesthetic and ideological precedents for the cloning of the Vietnam memorial. A strong desire to diminish, rather than engage the radical elements in Lin's design is evident in the majority of these new memorials. By necessity, most contain a wall for the names of KIAs, but the materials and shape have been altered; some have used white rather than black stone to brighten the surfaces and avoid any negative, or perhaps racial overtones.[2] Lin's choice of a V shape—particularly resonant for antiwar protestors—has been dropped, along with her innovative landscaping; sinking the stones into the earth, and turning the wall into a figurative gravestone. The new memorials tend to rise heroically above the spectator. American flags are *de rigeur* (Lin's original design did not include a flag) to insure that the monuments have a patriotic bottom line.

Realism—a la Norman Rockwell or Andrew Wyeth—is the dominant mode: in Wilmington, a bronze statue depicts a black soldier carrying a wounded white soldier; in Pittsburgh, bronze statues of vets are welcomed home by their bronze families; in Nashville, three armed soldiers watched over a wall; in Eufala, Alabama, a bronze eagle spreads its wings; in Little Rock, Arkansas, a combat soldier stands alone; in New Orleans, three bronze soldiers climb a hill carrying a wounded fourth; in Spokane, a bronze GI reads a letter from home.

The most controversial proposal is a bronze nurse, which the Vietnam Womens Memorial Project is attempting to add (separate but equal) to the D.C. site. There are only eight female names on Lin's wall, but more than ten thousand women[3] served in Vietnam, according to Diane Evans and Donna Marie Boulay, the co-directors of this project. "Hart's three men make the absence of women painfully visible," says Evans, who admits she would never have initiated this project had Lin's V stood alone. Evans and Boulay, both nurses who served in Vietnam, have won the approval of the military establishment (even the Veterans of Foreign Wars, which excluded women until 1976, sanctioned the addition after an acrimonious debate on their convention floor), Jan Scruggs, and significant members of Congress. They are currently touring three thirty-three-inch bronze maquettes across the country to raise $1 million for construction.

Except for their gender, Evans and Boulay are typical of those vets organizing memorial projects; they envision the memorials as apolitical statements: "I didn't support the war, only the men and women who fought it. We set our political opinions aside in Vietnam," says Evans, who wants the memorial to follow suit—particularly while the funds are being raised and they wade through the red tape that nearly strangled Jan Scruggs. But unlike the reception he received, according to Boulay, there has been no organized opposition to the bronze nurse thus far. This project is calculated to please conservatives such as William Westmoreland, who is helping to open doors for women vets.

The proposed statue, by Roger Brodin,[4] has dedication to the cause plastered all over her face; dressed in military fatigues and wearing a stethoscope, she stands alone, cradling her combat helmet like a bowl. Young, white, and asexual, her eyes are cast slightly upward under benevolently raised brows. As American as apple pie, she is ideal company for Hart's boys. Equal representation with men—with no distinction from their role in the war—is the single-minded goal of the Womens Memorial.

There are a few projects which have moved in a different aesthetic direction from traditional bronze, or at least have expanded their visions. In Neillsville, Wisconsin, a group is currently raising $300,000 for a hundred-acre memorial park which will include a museum for Vietnam artifacts and memorabilia (probably inspired by the fact that Lin's V has become a repository for these objects) and a memorial grove for Gold Star mothers; in Texas, H. Ross Perot's home state, $2.5 million is being raised for an elaborate park development. Some projects have buried time capsules on their sites containing information from the war; some have planted individual trees for KIAs which speak directly to the ecological destruction of Vietnam. But no project as original as Lin's V has yet surfaced. In part this is due to the fact that most communities have employed a democratic selection procedure governed by a jury.[5]

Still, the fact of erecting a popular monument dedicated to an unpopular war is implicitly controversial. More interesting than the monuments themselves are the struggles being waged to create them. In Circleville, Ohio, for example, city officials initially managed to ban every available public site for a Vietnam memorial. Their opposition to the project had little to do with this monument's design; the problem was their unwillingness to recognize the Vietnam War—or its veterans—at all.

This story begins with Leroy Stout, who graduated from high school in

1967 and tried to enlist in the army. As a result of misdemeanors on his record, Stout was rejected. But, much to his surprise, six months later his lucky number came up and he was drafted. After serving one year in Vietnam, this nineteen-year-old combat infantry sergeant came home to Circleville with a bronze star. "At the end I was cutting point into Cambodia," says Stout, unbeknownst to the American people, thanks to Richard Nixon.

The Circleville memorial, the largest of twelve others in the state, was one of the first to be erected after the D.C. battle. Stout raised $10,000 (the national monument cost $10 million), built the memorial himself with a small group of vets, and in the process almost lost his small heating and cooling business and his wife.

The controversy in Circleville centered around the memorial's placement, rather than its design. Initially, local vets and powerful civic groups such as the Knights of Columbus and the Rotary Club, were enthusiastic: "But all hell broke loose," Stout says, "when we proposed a site." "The Dirty Dozen," as he affectionately calls the group that completed the task, wanted the memorial prominently placed in front of the local courthouse. But city officials flatly refused and subsequently rejected each alternative site that was proposed.

In a surprise maneuver, Stout located a privately-owned piece of land (on the grounds of the Busy Bee Swim Club) that the owner, although not a vet, gladly donated for the memorial. At this point, according to Stout, the mayor, flanked by other officials, attempted to block construction by arbitrarily declaring the area in the public domain. After consulting with a lawyer, Stout gathered together a group of supporters, which included parents who had lost sons in Vietnam, at the site. "We put up posts and a fence around the area we considered ours and sat for hours waiting for a response." By the next morning they were surrounded by reporters all of whom helped to prove that Circleville officials had exceeded their authority. By the time Stout broke ground, popular opinion was in the memorial's favor; even the mayor attended the ceremony.

Notwithstanding, local veterans organizations remained aloof from the project. Only the Veterans of Foreign Wars, according to Stout, made a financial contribution—a meager $50. One of the problems in Circleville, and elsewhere, is the tension that exists between vets of different wars. Many of the memorials have been opposed because they distinguish Vietnam from World War I, World War II, and the Korean War. As a result, some organizers have capitulated and simply added Vietnam KIAs to a running list on other sites. Stout was determined to build a monument that exclusively conferred heroic status to Vietnam veterans.

What distinguishes the Circleville monument from many of the others is the fact that it was built exclusively by local vets. The key crew member was not an artist, landscape architect, or any other "expert," but a stone mason who was also a World War II vet. He was instrumental in creating a thirty-five-foot circular brick wall with a running bench around it that seats a hundred people; marble plaques with names of Pickaway county KIAs are mounted on the brick. (The marble was taken from old shower stalls and bathrooms from the nearby Chilliscothe VA hospital, which was being remodeled.) In the center, a brick pyramid rises up with sixteen steps (one for each year of the war between 1959 and 1975) that extends above the wall. From the top step, one can presumably see for miles. Stout describes this foxhole aesthetic as a "protective circle of strength" that refers not only to the town's name and ditches in Vietnam, but frontier days when settlers circled their wagons. Stout turned his memorial into a bunker—not a graveyard—ironically creating a warlike sanctuary for local vets.

With some exceptions like Circleville, throughout the memorial movement, realism has become a substitute for reality. These memorials project a bland image of a youthful, idealistic, and idealized combat soldier, the kind that fought first, and never dreamed he or she wouldn't live to ask questions later. Hart's fighting men and their clones emphasize survival—not the war. Ironically, violence is the one realistic element that is consistently absent, in stark contrast to the popular genre of Vietnam films.

By the standards of Reagan's America, Oliver Stone's *Platoon* is a liberal film; My Lai is depicted from the point of view of disgruntled vets, rather than the Rambo revisionists who, for instance, might consider the Phoenix program a lighthearted lark. The films, much more than the memorials, argue with each other and illustrate current ideological divisions on Vietnam. None of the bronze soldiers keeping watch across the country utter one word of protest.

As long as the administration continues to fight the same war in Central America, these mute soldiers strike a foolishly complacent pose. Their ironic task is to insure that the image of the war is "balanced" for posterity. The military establishment in particular hopes that despite the death toll, these heroic monuments will fall into their correct art historical place and convey a positive consensus on the outcome of the war. These memorials attempt to create the illusion that the White House is interested in coming to the aid of Vietnam vets—Agent Orange victims, for example. (How about a monument for them?) The problem is that the Vietnam generation—those who fought in, or against, the war, or those who did both—know, better than most, that the war wasn't merely a tragedy—but a crime.

NOTES

1. The Project on the Vietnam Generation, a nonprofit group in Washington, D.C., has completed a study on 143 Vietnam memorials across the country, not all of which are completed. But there are many that remain undocumented. In Alabama, for instance, the study lists seven memorials, while Steve Acai, an active

organizer there with whom I spoke, claims that there are 48 memorials in his state alone.

2. There are rumors that I was unable to track down for this article that a group of Black vets, who are not satisfied with their token representation in Hart's statue, are organizing to get a separate statue of a Black GI added to the D.C. site.

3. There are no accurate records of civilians, many of whom were female nurses, in Vietnam, with the exception of 1,800 Red Cross workers, 7,500 army nurses, 680 WACS, and 27 marines. According to an article in *Stars and Stripes*, 75 percent of the women in Vietnam witnessed combat.

4. Evans and Boulay failed to get in touch with Maya Lin before commissioning Brodin to create the bronze nurse. They never connected the fact that Lin is an Asian-American woman to the goals of their project, nor did they consider asking a female artist to create the memorial.

5. As far as I know, there is only one democratic competition underway which is attempting to select a design for a monument commemorating the students who died at Kent State. Many of the jurors are the same experts who participated on the panel that selected Lin. Needless to say, there is a potential controversy brewing.

W. D. EHRHART

The Invasion of Grenada

I didn't want a monument,
not even one as sober as that
vast black wall of broken lives.
I didn't want a postage stamp.
I didn't want a road beside the Delaware
River with a sign proclaiming:
"Vietnam Veterans Memorial Highway."

What I wanted was a simple recognition
of the limits of our power as a nation
to inflict our will on others.
What I wanted was an understanding
that the world is neither black-and-white
nor ours.

What I wanted
was an end to monuments.

CHARLES LITEKY

RENUNCIATION OF THE CONGRESSIONAL MEDAL OF HONOR
JULY 29, 1986
THE CAPITOL – WASHINGTON, D.C.

It is with great sadness that I renounce the Congressional Medal of Honor, but compassion for the victims of U.S. intervention in Central America says I must. I received the Medal of Honor in November of 1968 from President Lyndon Johnson in the East Wing of the White House. The award was given for saving lives under hostile fire in Vietnam.

At the outset of this statement I want to say that my renunciation of the Medal of Honor in no way represents disrespect for the medal itself or for the recipients of medals of valor throughout our history. My action is directed toward the inhumane foreign policies of my government, policies that cast shadows of shame over the heritage of this country and place the United States outside of the company of civilized nations, nations that respect international laws and universally accepted norms of morality.

I find it ironic that conscience calls me to renounce the Congressional Medal of Honor for the same basic reason I received it—trying to save lives. This time the lives are not young Americans, at least not yet. The lives are those of Central Americans of all ages: men, women, children, vulnerable innocents of the conflict.

I first became aware of atrocities funded by the American tax dollar by the victims of these atrocities: refugees from El Salvador and poor peasants in Nicaragua.

Their incredible stories of cruelty started me on a search for truth that has led me through book after book and report after report on the conditions of poverty and oppression in Central America and my government's response to these conditions.

The United States government has responded to the needs of oppressed people in El Salvador by supporting their oppressors, wealthy elites who control the lives of the poor through brutal military force.

In Nicaragua, the U.S. government response to the oppressed is the creation, direction, and support of a counterrevolutionary guerrilla army known as the contras. Winds of controversy whirl around the contras over the question of human rights abuse. In one of his speeches to the American people, President Reagan referred to contra atrocities as "much ado about nothing." In his most recent speech on aid to the contras, the president acknowledged the atrocities of the contras and assured us that contra human rights abuses would be corrected under U.S. direction, much the same as we have helped the Salvadoran army become respectful of human rights. This does not speak well for the future of the Nicaraguan poor. This makes me wonder if the president has read the human rights abuse record of the Salvadoran army for the year of 1985.

In a word, the policy of our government in Central America is primarily militaristic. It is devoid of creative, nonviolent conflict resolution, known as peaceful negotiation. The art of diplomacy has given way to the artless use of brute force, exercised judiciously on the weak and dependent. While the Latin American neighbors of Nicaragua patiently struggle in protracted nonviolent dialogue in a process known as Contadora, the U.S. pursues a "gunboat" diplomacy of military aid to the contras.

My dear fellow Americans, we have become a nation that arrogates to itself the right to impose its way of life on any country too weak to defend its independence. Nicaragua's fault is trying to break the pattern of Central American dependence on the United States.

She no longer wants to be a patch of grass in the mythical North American "backyard."

Lest anyone conclude that I have been duped by a slick Sandinista propaganda program, I want to say that I am not unaware of the human rights abuses of the Sandinista government. They exist. But they pale in comparison with the atrocities committed by the contras or the U.S.-backed military in El Salvador.

Let's take one of the State Department's favorite complaints against the Sandinistas, persecution of the church. In Nicaragua, the Catholic church radio has been silenced, ten to fifteen priests and a bishop have been expelled. Evangelical pastors have been harassed and a cardinal of the Catholic church has been censured.

In El Salvador, an archbishop has been murdered, his assassin still at large. Four American churchwomen have been brutally raped and murdered. Hundreds of priests, nuns, and lay catechists have been killed or disappeared.

Now why is our State Department so silent about persecution of the church in El Salvador and so vocal about persecution of the church in Nicaragua?

I am not a devotee of the Nicaraguan government. I don't have to be. I don't pay taxes in Nicaragua. I am, however, an advocate of the U.S. government. I am responsible for what it does in the name of America. If I am to be a true patriot, that is, a person who loves this country even when it's wrong, I must monitor and criticize its policies. It is my duty and my right.

On the basis of eighteen months of intense study of the history and nature of the problems in Central America, which includes two trips in the last year, I conclude that U.S. policy toward Nicaragua and El Salvador is grossly immoral, legally questionable, and highly irrational.

U.S. involvement in Central America is Vietnam all over again. Our advisors are there, our weapons are there, our logistical support is there, our money may soon be there in super abundance. Waiting in the wings for a cue from the president are U.S. combat troops.

The question is no longer, "Will Central America become another Vietnam?" Central America is another Vietnam and the time to demonstrate against it is now, not only to prevent the future loss of young American lives, but to stop the current killing of Nicaraguan and Salvadoran innocents.

I pledge to do everything within my power to foster nonviolent resistance to current U.S. policy in Central America. My conscience demands nothing less.

At the conclusion of this press conference my Medal of Honor will be placed in an envelope along with the statement I have just made and laid before the Vietnam Memorial Wall. The label on the envelope reads:

THIS ENVELOPE CONTAINS THE CONGRESSIONAL MEDAL OF HONOR
OF THE UNITED STATES OF AMERICA, AWARDED NOVEMBER 19, 1968
TO CHARLES J. LITEKY FOR VALOR IN VIETNAM. THE MEDAL WAS
RENOUNCED ON JULY 29, 1986 IN PROTEST OF UNITED STATES
INTERVENTION IN CENTRAL AMERICA, SEEN BY THE FORMER HOLDER
OF THIS MEDAL AS ANOTHER VIETNAM.

MY GOD!!!
IN SPITE OF THE NAMES ETCHED
ON THIS WALL, WE ARE DOING IT
AGAIN.
"WHEN WILL WE EVER LEARN?"
GOD FORGIVE US
AGAIN.

July 29, 1986

President Ronald Reagan
The White House
Washington, D.C.

Dear President Reagan:

The enclosed statement of my renunciation of the Congressional Medal of Honor and its associated benefits, represents my strongest public expression of opposition to U.S. military policies in Central America. You have been the champion of these brutal policies. I hold you most responsible for their origin and implementation.

You publicly stated your identification with some of the most ruthless cut-throats in Central American history when you said, "I'm a contra too." You insulted every American patriot when you referred to those killers of children, old men, and women as "freedom fighters," comparable to the founding fathers of our country.

In the name of freedom, national security, national interest, and anti-communism you have tried to justify crimes against humanity of the most heinous sort. You have made a global bully of the United States. You would not dare do to countries capable of defending themselves, what you have done to tiny nations like El Salvador, Nicaragua, and Honduras.

Mr. President, you are clearly set on a course of U.S. domination of Central America. There are a lot of us Americans who do not care to be counted among the oppressors of this world and we intend to let the government you lead know it by way of a series of nonviolent protests that will end when you stop the killing, the raping, the torturing, and the kidnapping of poor people in Central America.

You are not without company, Mr. President. There are other Americans who justify the murder of innocents in the same vigorous way that you do. You are polarizing this nation. One day you may have to repress your fellow Americans with the same kind of terror tactics you sanction in Central America.

I pray for your conversion, Mr. President. Some morning I hope you wake up and hear the cry of the poor riding on a southwest wind from Guatemala, Nicaragua, and El Salvador. They are crying STOP KILLING US.

I never met a Central American peasant who did not know your name.

Regretfully,

(Sgd.) Charles Liteky

Visions of Righteousness[1]

In one of his sermons on human rights, President Carter explained that we owe Vietnam no debt and have no responsibility to render it any assistance because "the destruction was mutual."[2] If words have meaning, this must stand among the most astonishing statements in diplomatic history. What is most interesting about this statement is the reaction to it among educated Americans: null. Furthermore, the occasional reference to it, and what it means, evokes no comment and no interest. It is considered neither appalling, nor even noteworthy, and is felt to have no bearing on Carter's standing as patron saint of human rights, any more than do his actions: dedicated support for Indonesian atrocities in Timor and the successful terrorist campaign undertaken in El Salvador to destroy the popular organizations that were defended by the assassinated archbishop; a huge increase in arms flow to Israel in parallel with its 1978 invasion of Lebanon, its subsequent large-scale bombing of civilians, and its rapid expansion into the occupied territories; etc. All of this is a tribute to the successes of a system of indoctrination that has few if any peers.

These successes permit the commissars to issue pronouncements of quite impressive audacity. Thus, Zbigniew Brzezinski thunders that the Soviet invasion of Afghanistan is

a classical foreign invasion, waged with Nazi-like brutality. Scorched villages, executed hostages, massive bombings, even chemical warfare . . . [with] several hundred thousand killed and maimed by Soviet military operations that qualify as genocidal in their intent and effect . . . It needs to be said directly, and over and over again, that Soviet policy in Afghanistan is the fourth greatest exercise in social holocaust of our contemporary age: it ranks only after Stalin's multimillion massacres; after Hitler's genocide of the European Jews and partially of the Slavs; and after Pol Pot's decimation of his own people; it is, moreover, happening right now.[3]

While the descriptive words are fair enough, when issuing from this source they merit all the admiration accorded similar pronouncements by Brzezinski's Soviet models with regard to American crimes, which he somehow seems to have overlooked in his ranking of atrocities of the modern age. To mention a few: the U.S. wars in Indochina, to which his condemnation applies in full except that there were *many millions* "killed and maimed" and the level of destruction was far greater; the Indonesian massacres of 1965 backed enthusiastically by the U.S. with half a million murdered; the Timor massacres conducted under Brzezinski's aegis with hundreds of thousands "killed and maimed" and the remnants left in the state of Biafra and the Thai-Cambodian border, an operation that is "happening right now" thanks to U.S. silence and support; the murder, often with hideous torture and mutilation, of over 100,000 people in El Salvador and Guatemala since 1978, operations carried out thanks to the support of the U.S. and its proxies, and most definitely "happening right now." But the readers of the *National Interest* will find nothing amiss in Brzezinski's presentation, since in Vietnam "the destruction was mutual" and the other cases, if known at all, have been easily assimilated into the preferred model of American benevolence. An auspicious opening for a new "conservative" journal of international affairs.

"It is scandalous," Brzezinski writes, "that so much of the conventionally liberal community, always so ready to embrace victims of American or Israeli or any other unfashionable 'imperialism,' is so reticent on the subject" of Afghanistan. Surely one might expect liberals in Congress or the press to desist from their ceaseless efforts on behalf of the PLO and the guerrillas in El Salvador long enough to notice Soviet crimes; perhaps they might even follow Brzezinski to the Khyber Pass so that they can strike heroic poses there before a camera crew. One should not, incidentally, dismiss this characterization of the "liberal community" on the grounds of its transparent absurdity. Rather, it should be understood as a typical example of a campaign carefully designed to eliminate even the limited critique of crimes by the U.S. and its clients that sometimes is voiced, a campaign that reflects the natural commitments of the totalitarian right, which regards anything less than full subservience as an intolerable deviation from political correctness.

Some feel that there was a debt but that it has been amply repaid. Under the headline "The Debt to the Indochinese Is Becoming a Fiscal Drain," Bernard Gwertzman of the *New York Times* quotes a State Department official who "said he believed the United States has now paid its moral debt for its involvement on the losing side in Indochina." The remark, which passed without comment, is illuminating: we owe no debt for mass slaughter and for leaving three countries in ruins, no debt to the millions of maimed and orphaned, to the peasants who still die today from unexploded ordnance. Rather, our moral debt results only from the fact that we did not win—or as the Party Line has it, that South Vietnam (namely, the client regime that we established as a cover for our attack against South Vietnam, which had as much legitimacy as the Afghan regime established by the USSR) lost the war to North Vietnam—the official enemy, since the U.S. attack against the south cannot be conceded. By this logic, if the Russians win in Afghanistan, they will have no moral debt at all. Proceeding further, how have we paid our moral debt for failing to win? By resettling Vietnamese refugees fleeing the lands we ravaged, "one of the largest, most dramatic humanitarian efforts in history" according to Roger Winter, director of the U.S. Committee for Refugees. But "despite the pride," Gwertzman reports, "some voices in the Reagan Administration and in Congress are once again asking whether the war debt has now been paid . . ."[4]

Invariably, the reader of the press who believes that the lowest depths have already been reached is proven wrong. In March 1968, as U.S. atrocities in South Vietnam were reaching their peak, the *Times* ran an item headed "Army Exhibit Bars Simulating Shooting at Vietnamese Hut," reporting an attempt by demonstrators to disrupt an exhibit in the Chicago Museum of Science and Industry: "Beginning today, visitors can no longer enter a helicopter for simulated firing of a machine gun at targets in a diorama of the Vietnam Central Highlands. The targets were a hut, two bridges and an ammunition dump, and a light flashed when a hit was scored." The *Times* is bitterly scornful of the peaceniks who demonstrated in protest at this amusing exhibit, which was such great fun for the kiddies, even öbjecting "to children being permitted to 'fire' at the hut, even though no people appear . . ." Citing this item at the time, I asked whether "what is needed in the United States is dissent—or denazification," a question that elicited much outrage; the question stands, however.[5]

To see how the moral level has improved since, we may turn to the *Times* sixteen years later, where we find a report on a new board game designed by a Princeton student called "Vietnam: 1965-1975." One player "takes the role of the United States and South Vietnam, and the other represents North Vietnam and the Vietcong." The inventor hopes the game will lead people to "experiment with new ideas, new approaches" to the war. We may ask another question: how would we react to a report in *Pravda* of a board game sold in Moscow, in which one player "takes the role of the USSR and Afghanistan, and the other represents Pakistan, the CIA, China, and the rebels," designed to lead people to "experiment with new ideas, new approaches" to the war—perhaps supplied with some accessory information concerning the "bandits terrorizing Afghanistan," who, according to Western sources, initiated their attacks from Pakistan with support from this U.S.-Chinese ally in 1973, six years before the USSR sent forces to "defend the legitimate government"?[6]

The American system of indoctrination is not satisfied with "mutual destruction" that effaces all responsibility for some of the major war crimes of the modern era. Rather, the perpetrator of the crimes must be seen as the injured party. We find headlines in the nation's press reading: "Vietnam, Trying to be Nicer, Still has a Long Way to Go."[7] "It's about time the Vietnamese demonstrated some good will," said Charles Printz of Human Rights Advocates International, referring to negotiations about Amerasian children who constitute a tiny fraction of the victims of the savage U.S. aggression in Indochina. Crossette adds that the Vietnamese have also not been sufficiently forthcoming on the matter of remains of American soldiers, though their behavior is improving somewhat: "There has been progress, albeit slow, on the missing Americans." The unresolved problem of the war is what they did to us. This point of view may be understood by invoking the terminology contributed by Adlai Stevenson—the hero of Brzezinski's "liberal community"—at the United Nations in May 1964, when he explained that we were in South Vietnam to combat "internal aggression," that is, the aggression of South Vietnamese peasants against U.S. military forces and their clients in South Vietnam. Since we were simply defending ourselves from aggression, it makes sense to consider ourselves the victims of the Vietnamese.[8]

This picture of aggrieved innocence, carefully crafted by the propaganda system and lovingly nurtured by the educated classes, must surely count as one of the most remarkable phenomena of the modern age. Its roots lie deep in the national culture. "The conquerors of America glorified the devastation they wrought in visions of righteousness," Francis Jennings observes, "and their descendants have been reluctant to peer through the aura."[9] No one who surveys the story of the conquest of the national territory, or the reaction to it over three and a half centuries, can doubt the accuracy of this indictment. In Memphis in 1831, Alexis de Tocqueville watched in "the middle of the winter" when the "cold was unusually severe" as "three or four thousand soldiers drive before them the wandering races of the aborigines," who "brought in their train the wounded and the sick, with children newly born and old men on the verge of death," a "solemn spectacle" that would never fade from his memory: "the triumphal march of civilization across the desert." They were the lucky ones, the ones who had escaped the ravages of Andrew Jackson who, years earlier, had urged his men to exterminate the "blood thirsty barbarians" and "cannibals" and to "distroy [sic] those deluded victims doomed to distruction [sic] by their own restless and savage conduct"—as they did, killing women and children, stripping the skin from the bodies of the dead for 'bridle reins, and cutting the tip of each dead Indian's nose to count the number of "savage dogs" who had been removed from the path of civilization. De Tocqueville was particularly impressed by the way the pioneers could deprive Indians of their rights and exterminate them "with singular felicity, tranquilly, legally, philanthropically, without shedding blood, and without violating a single great principle of morality in the eyes of the world." It was impossible to destroy people with "more respect for the laws of humanity." Still earlier, the Founding Fathers, in their bill of indictment in the Declaration of Independence, had accused the king of England of inciting against the suffering colonies "the merciless Indian Savages, whose known rule of warfare, is an undistinguished destruction of all ages, sexes and conditions"; they were referring to the response of the native population to the genocidal assaults launched against them by the saintly Puritans and other merciless European savages who had taught the Indians that warfare, European-style, is a program of mass extermination of women and children, a lesson that George Washington was soon to teach the Iroquois as he sent his forces to destroy their society and civilization, quite advanced by the standards of the era, in 1779. Rarely have hypocrisy and moral cowardice been so explicit, and admired with such awe for centuries.[10]

The story continues with no essential change in later years. The American conquest of the Philippines, led by men who had learned their craft in the Indian wars, ranks among the most barbaric episodes of modern history. In the island of Luzon alone, some 600,000 natives perished from the war or diseases caused by it. General Jacob Smith, who gave orders to turn the island of Samar into a "howling wilderness," to "kill and burn"—"the more you kill and burn the better you will please me"—was retired with no punishment by President Roosevelt, who made it clear that Smith's only sin was his "loose and violent talk." Roosevelt, who went on to receive the Nobel Peace Prize, explained that "I also heartily approve of the employment of the sternest measures necessary" against the cruel and treacherous savages who "disregard . . . the rules of civilized warfare," and who had furthermore "assailed our sovereignty" (President McKinley) in an earlier act of internal aggression. The director of all Presbyterian missions hailed the conquest as "a great step toward the civilization and evangelization of the world," while another missionary explained that the notorious "water cure" was not really "torture" because "the victim has it in his own power to stop the process" by divulging what he knows "before the operation has gone far enough to seriously hurt him," and a leading Episcopal bishop lauded General Smith's tactics as necessary "to purge the natives," who were "treacherous and barbarous," of the "evil effects" of "a degenerate form of Christianity." The press chimed in with similar sentiments. "Whether we like it or not," the *New York Criterion* explained, "we must go on slaughtering the natives in English fashion, and taking what muddy glory lies in the wholesale killing until they have learned to respect our arms. The more difficult task of getting them to respect our intentions will follow." Similar thoughts were expressed as we were slaughtering the natives of South Vietnam, and we hear them again today, often in almost these words, with regard to our current exploits in Central America. The reference of the "English fashion" will be understood by any student of American history.

For Theodore Roosevelt, the murderers in the Philippines were fighting "for the triumph of civilization over the black chaos of savagery and barbarism," while President Taft observed that "there never was a war conducted, whether against inferior races or not, in which there were more compassion and more restraint and more generosity" than in this campaign of wholesale slaughter and mass torture and terror. Stuart Chreighton Miller, who records these horrors and the reaction to them in some detail and observes that they have largely disappeared from history, assures the reader that "the American interventions both in Vietnam and in the Philippines were motivated in part by good intentions to elevate or to aid the victims"; Soviet scholars say the same about Afghanistan, with comparable justice.[11]

General Smith's subordinate Littleton Waller was acquitted in court-martial proceedings, since he had only been following orders: namely, to kill every male Filipino over the age of ten. He went on to become a major-general, and to take charge of Woodrow Wilson's atrocities as he celebrated his doctrine of self-determination by invading Haiti and the Dominican Republic, where his warriors murdered, raped, burned villages, established concentration camps that provided labor for U.S. companies, reinstituted virtual slavery, demolished the political system and any vestige of intellectual freedom, and generally reduced the countries to misery while enriching U.S. sugar companies. According to the approved version, these exploits not only illustrate the Wilsonian doctrine of self-determination to which we were dedicated as a matter of definition, but also serve as a notable example of how "the overall effect of American power on other societies was to further liberty, pluralism, and democracy." So we are informed by Harvard scholar Samuel Huntington, who adds that "No Dominican could doubt but that his country was a far, far better place to live in 1922 than it was in 1916," including those tortured by the benefactors and those whose families they murdered or whose villages they burned for the benefit of U.S. sugar companies.[12]

The record of U.S. intervention in Central America and the Caribbean, to the present day, adds further shameful chapters to the story of terror, torture, slavery, starvation, and repression, all conducted with the most touching innocence, and with endless benevolence—particularly with regard to the U.S. investors whose representatives design these admirable exercises. The worst period in this sordid history was initiated by the Kennedy administration, which established the basic structure of state terrorism that has since massacred tens of thousands as an integral part of the Alliance for Progress; this cynical program, devised in fear of "another Castro," fostered a form of "development" in which croplands were converted to export for the benefit of U.S. corporations and their local associates while the population sank into misery and starvation, necessitating an efficient system of state terror to ensure "stability" and "order." We can witness its achievements today, for example, in El Salvador, where presidents Carter and Reagan organized the slaughter of some 60,000 people, to mounting applause in the United States as the terror appeared to be showing signs of success. During the post-World War II period, as U.S. power greatly expanded, similar projects were undertaken over a much wider range, with massacres in Greece, Korea (prior to what we call "the Korean War," some 100,000 had been killed in South Korea, primarily in U.S.-run counterinsurgency campaigns undertaken as part of our successful effort to destroy the indigenous political system and install our chosen clients), Southeast Asia, and elsewhere, all with inspiring professions of noble intent and the enthusiastic acclaim of the educated classes, as long as violence appears to be successful.[13]

In brief, a major theme of our history from the earliest days has been a combination of hideous atrocities and protestations of awesome benevolence. It should come as no great surprise to students of American history that we are the injured party in Indochina.

Contrary to much illusion, there was little principled opposition to the Indochina war among the articulate intelligentsia. One detailed study undertaken in 1970, at the peak of antiwar protest, revealed that the "American intellectual elite" came to oppose the war for the same "pragmatic reasons" that had convinced business circles that this investment should be liquidated. Very few opposed the war on the grounds that led all to condemn the Soviet invasion of Czechoslovakia: not that it failed, or that it was too bloody, but that aggression is wrong. In striking contrast, as late as 1982—after years of unremitting propaganda with virtually no dissenting voice permitted expression to a large audience—over 70 percent of the general population (but far fewer "opinion leaders") still regarded the war as "fundamentally wrong and immoral," not merely "a mistake."[14]

The technical term for this failure of the indoctrination system is the "Vietnam Syndrome," a dread disease that spread over the population with such symptoms as distaste for aggression and massacre, what Norman Podhoretz calls the "sickly inhibitions against the use of military force," which he hopes are finally overcome with the grand triumph of American arms in Grenada.[15] The malady, however, persists, and continues to inhibit the state executive in Central America and elsewhere. The major U.S. defeat in Indochina was at home: much of the population rejected the approved stance of passivity, apathy, and obedience. Great efforts were made through the 1970s to overcome this "crisis of democracy," as it was called, but with less success than reliance on articulate opinion would suggest.

There was, to be sure, debate over the wisdom of the war. The hawks, such as Joseph Alsop, argued that with sufficient violence the U.S. could succeed in its aims, while the doves doubted this conclusion, though emphasizing that "we all pray that Mr. Alsop will be right" and that "we may all be saluting the wisdom and statesmanship of the American government" if it succeeds in subjugating Vietnam (what we would call: "liberating Vietnam") while leaving it "a land of ruin and wreck" (Arthur Schlesinger). Few would deny that the war began with "blundering efforts to do good" (Anthony Lewis) in "an excess of righteousness and disinterested benevolence" (John King Fairbank), that it was "a failed crusade" undertaken for motives that were "noble" though "illusory" and with the "loftiest intentions" (Stanley Karnow, in his best-selling history). These are the voices of the doves. As noted, much of the population rejected the hawkdove consensus of elite circles, a fact of lasting significance. It was that part of the population that concerned the planners in Washington, for example, Defense Secretary Robert McNamara, who asked in a secret memo of May 19, 1967 whether expansion of the American war might "polarize opinion to the extent that 'doves' in the US will get out of hand—massive refusals to serve, or to fight, or to cooperate, or worse?"[16]

It is worth recalling a few facts. The U.S. was deeply committed to the French effort to reconquer their former colony, recognizing throughout that the enemy was the nationalist movement of Vietnam. The death toll was about a half-million. When France withdrew, the U.S. dedicated itself at once to subverting the 1954 Geneva settlement, installing in the south a terrorist regime that had killed perhaps 70,000 "Viet Cong" by 1961, evoking resistance which, from 1959, was supported from the northern half of the country temporarily divided by the 1954 settlement that the U.S. had undermined. In 1961-62, President Kennedy launched a direct attack against rural South Vietnam with large-scale bombing and defoliation as part of a program designed to drive millions of people to camps where they would be "protected" by armed guards and barbed wire from the guerrillas whom, the U.S. conceded, they were willingly supporting. The U.S. maintained that it was invited in, but as the London *Economist* accurately observed, "an invader is an invader unless invited by a government with a claim to legitimacy." The U.S. never regarded the clients it installed has having any such claim, and in fact regularly replaced them when they failed to exhibit sufficient enthusiasm for the American attack or sought to implement the neutralist settlement that was advocated on all sides and was considered the prime danger by the aggressors, since it would undermine the basis for their war against South Vietnam. In short, the U.S. invaded South Vietnam, where it proceeded to compound the crime of aggression with numerous and quite appalling crimes against humanity throughout Indochina.

The *Economist*, of course, was not referring to Vietnam but to a similar Soviet fraud concerning Afghanistan. With regard to official enemies, Western intellectuals are able to perceive that $2 + 2 = 4$. Their Soviet counterparts have the same clear vision with regard to the United States.

From 1961 to 1965, the U.S. expanded the war against South Vietnam while fending off the threat of neutralization and political settlement, which was severe at the time. This was regarded as an intolerable prospect, since our "minnow" could not compete politically with their "whale," as explained by Douglas Pike, the leading government specialist on the National Liberation Front (in essence, the former Viet Minh, the anti-French resistance, "Viet Cong" in U.S. propaganda). Pike further explained that the NLF "maintained that its contest with the GVN [the U.S.-installed client regime] and the United States should be fought out at the political level and that the use of massed military might was in itself illegitimate" until forced by the United States "to use counter-force to survive." The aggressors succeeded in shifting the conflict from the political to the military arena, a major victory since it is in that arena alone that they reign supreme, while the propaganda system then exploited the use of "counter-force to survive" by the South Vietnamese enemy as proof that they were "terrorists" from whom we must defend South Vietnam by attacking and destroying it. Still more interestingly, this version of history is now close to received doctrine.

In 1965, the U.S. began the direct land invasion of South Vietnam, along with the bombing of the north, and, at three times the level, the systematic bombardment of the south, which bore the brunt of U.S. aggression throughout. By then, probably some 170,000 South Vietnamese had been killed, many of them "under the crushing weight of American armor, napalm, jet bombers and, finally, vomiting gases," in the words of the hawkish military historian Bernard Fall. The U.S. then escalated the war against the south, also extending it to Laos and Cambodia where perhaps another half-million to a million were killed, while the Vietnamese death toll may well have reached or passed 3 million, and the land was destroyed and the societies demolished in one of the major catastrophes of the modern era[17]—a respectable achievement in the days before we fell victim to the "sickly inhibitions against the use of military force."

The devastation that the United States left as its legacy has been quickly removed from consciousness here, and indeed, was little appreciated at the time. Its extent is worth recalling. In the south, 9,000 out of 15,000 hamlets were damaged or destroyed along with some 25 million acres of farmland and 12 million acres of forest; 1.5 million cattle were killed; and there are 1 million widows and some 800,000 orphans. In the north, all six industrial cities were damaged (three razed to the ground) along with 28 of 30 provincial towns (twelve completely destroyed), 96 of 116 district towns, and 4,000 of some 5,800 communes; 400,000 cattle were killed and over a million acres of farmland were damaged. Much of the land is a moonscape, where people live on the edge of famine with rice rations lower than Bangladesh. In a recent study unreported here in the mainstream, the respected Swiss-based environmental group IUCN (International Union for Conservation of Nature and Natural Resources) concluded that the ecology is not only refusing to heal but is worsening, so that a "catastrophe" may result unless billions of dollars are spent to "reconstruct" the land that has been destroyed, a "monumental" task that could be addressed only if the U.S. were to offer the reparations that it owes, a possibility that cannot be considered in a cultural climate as depraved and cowardly as ours. Forests have not recovered, fisheries remain reduced in variety and productivity, cropland productivity has not yet regained normal levels, and there is a great increase in toxin-related disease and cancer, with 4 million acres affected by the 19 million gallons of poisons dumped on cropland and forest in U.S. chemical warfare operations. Destruction of forests has increased the frequency of floods and droughts and aggravated the impact of typhoons, and war damage to dikes (some of which, in the south, were completely destroyed by U.S. bombardment) and other agricultural systems have yet to be repaired. The report notes that "humanitarian and conservationist groups, particularly in the United States, have encountered official resistance and red tape when requesting their governments' authorization to send assistance to Vietnam"—naturally enough, since the U.S. remains committed to ensure that its victory is not threatened by recovery of the countries it has destroyed.[18]

Throughout 1964, as the U.S. planned the extension of its aggression to North Vietnam, planners were aware that heightened U.S. military actions might lead to North Vietnamese "ground action in South Vietnam or Laos" in retaliation (William Bundy, November 1964). The U.S. later claimed that North Vietnamese troops began leaving for the south in October 1964, two months after the U.S. bombing of North Vietnam during the fabricated Tonkin Gulf incident. As late as July 1965, the Pentagon was still concerned over the "probability" that there might be North Vietnamese units in or near the south—five months after the regular bombing of North Vietnam, three months after the direct U.S. land invasion of the south, over three years after the beginning of U.S. bombing of the south, ten years after the U.S. subversion of the political accords that were to unify the country, and with the death toll in the south probably approaching 200,000. Thankfully, North Vietnamese units finally arrived as anticipated, thus making it possible for the propaganda system to shift from defense of South Vietnam against internal aggression to defense against North Vietnamese aggression. As late as the Tet offensive in January 1968, North Vietnamese troops appear to have been at about the level of the mercenary forces (Korean, Thai) brought in by the U.S. from January 1965 as part of the effort to subjugate South Vietnam, and according to the Pentagon there still were only South Vietnamese fighting in the Mekong Delta, where the most savage fighting took place at the time. U.S. military forces of course vastly exceeded all others in numbers, firepower, and atrocities.

The Party Line holds that "North Vietnam, not the Vietcong, was always the enemy," as John Corry observes in reporting the basic message of an NBC "White Paper" on the war.[19] This stand is conventional in the mainstream. Corry is particularly indignant that anyone should question this Higher Truth propounded by the state propaganda system. As proof of the absurdity of such "liberal mythology," he cites the battle of Ia Drang Valley in November 1965: "It was clear then that North Vietnam was in the war. Nonetheless, liberal mythology insisted that the war was being waged only by the Vietcong, mostly righteous peasants." Corry presents no example of anyone who denied that there were North Vietnamese troops in the south in November 1965, since there were none, even among the few opponents of the war, who at that time and for several years after included very few representatives of mainstream liberalism. As noted earlier, principled objection to the war was a highly marginal phenomenon among American intellectuals even at the height of opposition to it. Corry's argument for North Vietnamese aggression, however, is as impressive as any that has been presented.

The NBC "White Paper" was one of a rash of retrospectives on the tenth anniversary of the war's end, devoted to "The War that Went Wrong, The Lessons it Taught."[20] They present a sad picture of U.S. intellectual culture, a picture of dishonesty and moral cowardice. Their most striking feature is what is missing: the American wars in Indochina. It is a classic example of Hamlet without the Prince of Denmark. Apart from a few scattered sentences, the rare allusions to the war in these lengthy presentations are devoted to the suffering of the American invaders. The *Wall Street Journal*, for example, refers to "the $180 million in chemical companies' compensation to Agent Orange victims"—U.S. soldiers, not the South Vietnamese victims, whose suffering was and is vastly greater.[21] It is difficult to exaggerate the significance of these startling facts.

There is an occasional glimpse of reality. *Time* opens its inquiry by recalling the trauma of the American soldiers, facing an enemy that "dissolved by day into the villages, into the other Vietnamese. They maddened the Americans with the mystery of who they were—the unseen man who shot from the tree line, or laid a wire across the trail with a Claymore mine at the other end, the mama-san who did the wash, the child concealing a grenade." No doubt one could find similar complaints in the Nazi press about the Balkans.

The meaning of these facts is almost never perceived. *Time* goes so far as to claim that the "subversion" was "orchestrated" by Moscow, so that the U.S. had to send troops to "defend" South Vietnam, echoing the fantasies concocted in scholarship, for example, by Walt Rostow, who maintains that in his effort "to gain the balance of power in Eurasia," Stalin turned "to the East, to back Mao and to enflame the North Korean and Indochinese Communists."[22] Few can comprehend—surely not the editors of *Time*—the significance of the analysis by the military command and civilian officials of the aggressors:

The success of this unique system of war depends upon almost complete unity of action of the entire population. That such unity is

298

a fact is too obvious to admit of discussion: how it is brought about and maintained is not so plain. Intimidation has undoubtedly accomplished much to this end, but fear as the only motive is hardly sufficient to account for the united and apparently spontaneous action of several millions of people. . . . [The only collaborators are] intriguers, disreputable or ignorant, who we had rigged out with sometimes high ranks, which became tools in their hands for plundering the country without scruple. . . . Despised, they possessed neither the spiritual culture nor the moral fibre that would have allowed them to understand and carry out their task.

The words are those of General Arthur McArthur describing the Philippine war of national liberation in 1900 and the French resident-minister in Vietnam in 1897,[23] but they apply with considerable accuracy to the U.S. war against Vietnam, as the *Time* quote illustrates, in its own way.

Throughout, the familiar convenient innocence served admirably, as in the days when we were "slaughtering the natives" in the Philippines, Latin America, and elsewhere, preparing the way to "getting them to respect our intentions." In February 1965, the U.S. initiated the regular bombardment of North Vietnam, and more significantly, as Bernard Fall observed, began "to wage unlimited aerial warfare inside [South Vietnam] at the price of literally pounding the place to bits," the decision that "changed the character of the Vietnam war" more than any other.[24] These moves inspired the distinguished liberal commentator of the *New York Times*, James Reston, "to clarify America's present and future policy in Vietnam":

> The guiding principle of American foreign policy since 1945 has been that no state shall use military force or the threat of military force to achieve its political objectives. And the companion of this principle has been that the United States would use its influence and its power, when necessary and where it could be effective, against any state that defied this principle.

This is the principle that was "at stake in Vietnam," where "the United States is now challenging the Communist effort to seek power by the more cunning technique of military subversion" (the United States having blocked all efforts at political settlement because it knew the indigenous opposition would easily win a political contest, and after ten years of murderous repression and three years of U.S. Air Force bombing in the south).[25]

In November 1967, when Bernard Fall, long a committed advocate of U.S. support for the Saigon regime, pleaded for an end to the war because "Viet-Nam as a cultural and historic entity . . . is threatened with extinction . . . [as] . . . the countryside literally dies under the blows of the largest military machine ever unleashed on an area of this size," Reston explained that America is fighting a war now on the principle that military power shall not compel South Vietnam to do what it does not want to do, that man does not belong to the state. This is the deepest conviction of Western Civilization, and rests on the old doctrine that the individual belongs not to the state but to his Creator, and therefore, has "inalienable rights" as a person, which no magistrate or political force may violate.[26]

The same touching faith in American innocence and benevolence in Indochina—as elsewhere throughout our history—persists until today in any commentary that can reach a substantial audience, untroubled by the plain facts. Much of the population understood and still remembers the truth, though this too will pass as the system of indoctrination erases historical memories and establishes the "truths" that are deemed more satisfactory.

By 1967, popular protest had reached a significant scale, although elite groups remained loyal to the cause, apart from the bombing of North Vietnam, which was regarded as a potential threat to us since it might lead to a broader war drawing in China and the USSR, from which we might not be immune—the "toughest" question, according to the McNamara memo cited earlier, and the only serious question among "respectable" critics of the war. The massacre of innocents is a problem only among emotional or irresponsible types, or among the "aging adolescents on college faculties who found it rejuvenating to play 'revolution,'" in Stuart Chreighton Miller's words. Decent and respectable people remain silent and obedient, devoting themselves to personal gain, concerned only that we too might ultimately face unacceptable threat—a stance not without recent historical precedent elsewhere. In contrast to the war protestors, two commentators explain, "decent, patriotic Americans demanded—and in the person of Ronald Reagan have apparently achieved—a return to pride and patriotism, a reaffirmation of the values and virtues that have been trampled upon by the Vietnam-spawned counterculture,"[27] most crucially the virtues of marching in the parade chanting praises for their leaders as they conduct their necessary chores, as in Indochina and El Salvador.

The U.S. attack reached its peak of intensity and horror after the Tet offensive, with the post-Tet pacification campaigns—actually mass murder operations launched against defenseless civilians, as in Operation Speedy Express in the Mekong Delta—and mounting atrocities in Laos and Cambodia, called here "secret wars," a technical term referring to executive wars that the press does not expose though it has ample evidence concerning them, and that are later denounced with much outrage, when the proper time has come, and attributed to evil men whom we have sternly excluded from the body politic, another sign of our profound decency and honor. By 1970, if not before, it was becoming clear that U.S. policy would "create a situation in which, indeed, North Vietnam will necessarily dominate Indochina, for no other viable society will remain."[28] This predictable consequence of U.S. savagery would later be used as a post hoc justification for it, in another propaganda achievement that Goebbels would have admired.

It is a most revealing fact that there is no such event in history as the American attack against South Vietnam launched by Kennedy and escalated by his successors. Rather, history records only "a defense of freedom,"[29] a "failed crusade" (Stanley Karnow) that was perhaps unwise, the doves maintain. At a comparable level of integrity, Soviet party hacks extol the "defense of Afghanistan" against "bandits" and "terrorists" organized by the CIA. They, at least, can plead fear of totalitarian violence, while their Western counterparts can offer no such excuse for their servility.

The extent of this servility is revealed throughout the tenth anniversary retrospectives, not only by the omission of the war itself, but also by the interpretation provided. The *New York Times* writes sardonically of the "ignorance" of the American people, only 60 percent of whom are aware that the U.S. "sided with South Vietnam"[30]—as Nazi Germany sided with France, as the USSR now sides with Afghanistan. Given that we were defending South Vietnam, it must be that the critics of this noble if flawed enterprise sided with Hanoi, and that is indeed what the Party Line maintains; that opposition to American aggression entails no such support, just as opposition to Soviet aggression entails no support for either the feudalist forces of the Afghan resistance or Pakistan or the United States, is an elementary point that would not surpass the capacity of an intelligent ten-year-old, though it inevitably escapes the mind of the commissar. The *Times* alleges that North Vietnam was "portrayed by some American intellectuals as the repository of moral rectitude." No examples are given, nor is evidence presented to support these charges, and the actual record is, as always, scrupulously ignored. Critics of the antiwar movement are quoted on its "moral failure of terrifying proportions," but those who opposed U.S. atrocities are given no opportunity to explain the basis for their opposition to U.S. aggression and massacre or to assign these critics and the *New York Times* their proper place in history, including those who regard themselves as "doves" because of their occasional twitters of protest when the cost to us became too great. We learn that the opponents of the war "brandished moral principles and brushed aside complexity," but hear nothing of what they had to say—exactly as was the case throughout the war. A current pretense is that the mainstream media were open to principled critics of the war during these years, indeed that they dominated the media. In fact, they were almost entirely excluded, as is easily demonstrated, and now we are permitted to hear accounts of their alleged crimes, but not, of course, their actual words, exactly as one would expect in a properly functioning system of indoctrination.

The *Times* informs us that Vietnam "now stands exposed as the Prussia of Southeast Asia" because since 1975 they have "unleashed a series of pitiless attacks against their neighbors," referring to the Vietnamese invasion that overthrew the Pol Pot regime (after two years of border attacks from Cambodia), the regime that we now support despite pretenses to the contrary, emphasizing the "continuity" of the current Khmer Rouge-based coalition with the Pol Pot regime (see below). The Khmer Rouge receive "massive support" from our ally China, Nayan Chanda reports, while the U.S. has more than doubled its support to the coalition. Deng Xiaoping, expressing the Chinese stand (which we tacitly and materially support), states: "I do not understand why some want to remove Pol Pot. It is true that he made some mistakes in the past but now he is leading the fight against the Vietnamese aggressors."[31] As explained by the government's leading specialist on Indochinese communism, now director of the Indochina archives at the University of California, Pol Pot was the "charismatic" leader of a "bloody but successful peasant revolution with a substantial residue of popular support," under which "on a statistical basis, most [peasants] . . . did not experience much in the way of brutality."[32] Though the *Times* is outraged at the Prussian-style aggression that overthrew our current Khmer Rouge ally, and at the current Vietnamese insistence that a political settlement must exclude Pol Pot, the reader of its pages will find little factual material about any of these matters. There are, incidentally, countries that have "unleashed a series of pitiless attacks against their neighbors" in these years, for example, Israel, with its invasions of Lebanon in 1978 and 1982. But as an American client state, Israel inherits the right of aggression so that it does not merit the bitter criticism that Vietnam deserves for overthrowing Pol Pot; and in any event, its invasion of Lebanon was a "liberation," as the *Times* explained at the time, always carefully excluding Lebanese opinion on the matter as obviously irrelevant.[33]

The *Times* recognizes that the United States did suffer "shame" during its Indochina wars: "the shame of defeat." Victory, we are to assume, would not have been shameful, and the record of aggression and atrocities supported by the *Times* obviously evokes no shame. Rather, the United States thought it was "resisting" communists "when it intervened in Indochina"; how we "resist" the natives in their land, the *Times* does not explain.

That the U.S. lost the war in Indochina is "an inescapable fact" *(Wall Street Journal)*, repeated without question throughout the retrospectives and in American commentary generally. When some doctrine is universally proclaimed without qualification, a rational mind will at once inquire as to whether it is true. In this case, it is false, though to see why, it is necessary to escape the confines of the propaganda system and to investigate the rich documentary record that lays out the planning and motives for the American war against the Indochinese, which persisted for almost thirty years. Those who undertake this task will discover that a rather different conclusion is in order.

The U.S. did not achieve its maximal goals in Indochina, but it did gain a partial victory. Despite talk by Eisenhower and others about Vietnamese raw materials, the primary U.S. concern was not Indochina, but rather the "domino effect," the demonstration effect of successful independent development that might cause "the rot to spread" to Thailand and beyond, possibly ultimately drawing Japan into a "New Order" from which the U.S. would be excluded. This threat was averted. The countries of Indochina will be lucky to survive: they will not endanger global order by social and economic success in a framework that denies the West the freedom to exploit, infecting regions beyond, as had been feared. It might parenthetically be noted that although this interpretation of the American aggression is supported by substantial evidence, there is no hint of its existence, and surely no reference to the extensive documentation substantiating it, in the standard histories, since such facts do not conform to the required image of aggrieved benevolence. Again, we see here the operation of the Orwellian principle that Ignorance is Strength.

Meanwhile, the U.S. moved forcefully to buttress the second line of defense. In 1965, the U.S. backed a military coup in Indonesia (the most important "domino," short of Japan) while American liberals lauded the "dramatic changes" that took place there—the most dramatic being the massacre of hundreds of thousands of landless peasants—as a proof that we were right to defend South Vietnam by demolishing it, thus encouraging the Indonesian generals to prevent any rot from spreading there. In 1972, the U.S. backed the overthrow of Philippine democracy behind the "shield" provided by its successes in Indochina, thus averting the threat of national capitalism there with a terror-and-torture state on the preferred Latin American model. A move towards democracy in Thailand in 1973 evoked some concern, and a reduction in economic aid and increase in military aid in preparation for the military coup that took place with U.S. support in 1976. Thailand had a particularly important role in the U.S. regional system since 1954, when the National Security Council laid out a plan for subversion and eventual aggression throughout Southeast Asia in response to the Geneva Accords, with Thailand "as the focal point of U.S. covert and psychological operations," including "covert operations on a large and effective scale" throughout Indochina, with the explicit intention of "making more difficult the control by the Viet Minh of North Vietnam." Subsequently Thailand served as a major base for the U.S. attacks on Vietnam and Laos.[34]

In short, the U.S. won a regional victory, and even a substantial local victory in Indochina, left in ruins. That the U.S. suffered a "defeat" in Indochina is a natural perception on the part of those of limitless ambition, who understand "defeat" to mean the achievement only of major goals, while certain minor ones remain beyond our grasp.

Postwar U.S. policy has been designed to ensure that the victory is maintained by maximizing suffering and oppression in Indochina, which then evokes further joy and gloating here. Since "the destruction is mutual," as is readily demonstrated by a stroll through New York, Boston, Vinh, Quang Ngai Province, and the Plain of Jars, we are entitled to deny reparations, aid, and trade, and to block development funds. The extent of U.S. sadism is noteworthy, as is the (null) reaction to it. In 1977, when India tried to send a hundred buffalos to Vietnam to replenish the herds destroyed by U.S. violence, the U.S. threatened to cancel "food for peace" aid while the press featured photographs of peasants in Cambodia pulling plows as proof of communist barbarity; the photographs in this case turned out to be fabrications of Thai intelligence, but authentic ones could no doubt have been obtained, throughout Indochina. The Carter administration even denied rice to Laos (despite a cynical pretense to the contrary), where the agricultural system was destroyed by U.S. terror bombing. Oxfam America was not permitted to send ten solar pumps to Cambodia for irrigation in 1983; in 1981, the U.S. government sought to block a shipment of school supplies and educational kits to Cambodia by the Mennonite Church. Meanwhile, from the first days of the Khmer Rouge takeover in 1975, the West was consumed with horror over their atrocities, described as "genocide" at a time when deaths had reached the thousands in mid-1975. The Khmer Rouge may be responsible for a half-million to a million dead, so current scholarship indicates (in conformity to the estimates of U.S. intelligence at the time), primarily in 1978, when the worst atrocities took place, largely unknown to the West, in the context of the escalating war with Vietnam.[35]

The nature of the profound Western agony over Cambodia as a sociocultural phenomenon can be assessed by comparing it to the reaction to comparable and simultaneous atrocities in Timor. There, the U.S. bore primary responsibility, and the atrocities could have been terminated at once, as distinct from Cambodia, where nothing could be done but the blame could be placed on the official enemy. The excuses now produced for this shameful behavior are instructive. Thus, William Shawcross rejects the obvious (and obviously correct) interpretation of the comparative response to Timor and Cambodia in favor of a "more structurally serious explanation": "a comparative lack of sources" and lack of access to refugees.[36] Lisbon is a two-hour flight from London, and even Australia is not notably harder to reach than the Thai-Cambodia border, but the many Timorese refugees in Lisbon and Australia were ignored by the media, which preferred "facts" offered by State Department handouts and Indonesian generals. Similarly, the media ignored readily available refugee studies from sources at least as credible as those used as the basis for the impotent but ideologically serviceable outrage over the Khmer Rouge, and disregarded highly credible witnesses who reached New York and Washington along with additional evidence from church sources and others. The coverage of Timor actually declined sharply as massacres increased. The real reason for this difference in scope and character of coverage is not difficult to discern, though not very comfortable for Western opinion, and becomes still more obvious when a broader range of cases is considered.[37]

The latest piece of this tragicomedy is the current pretense, initiated by William Shawcross in an inspired agitprop achievement,[38] that there was relative silence in the West over the Khmer Rouge. This is a variant of the Brzezinski ploy concerning the "liberal community" noted earlier; in the real world, condemnations virtually unprecedented in their severity extended from mass circulation journals such as the *Reader's Digest* and *TV Guide* to the *New York Review of Books*, including the press quite generally (1976-early 1977). Furthermore, Shawcross argues, this "silence" was the result of "left-wing skepticism" so powerful that it silenced governments and journals throughout the West; even had such "skepticism" existed on the part of people systematically excluded from the media and mainstream discussion, the idea that this consequence could ensue is a construction of such audacity that one must admire its creators, Shawcross in particular.[39]

I do not, incidentally, exempt myself from this critique with regard to Cambodia and Timor. I condemned the "barbarity" and "brutal practice" of the Khmer Rouge in 1977,[40] long before speaking or writing a word on the U.S.-backed atrocities in Timor, which on moral grounds posed a far more serious issue for Westerners. It is difficult even for those who try to be alert to such matters to extricate themselves from a propaganda system of overwhelming efficiency and power.

Now, Western moralists remain silent as their governments provide the means for the Indonesian generals to consummate their massacres, while the U.S. backs the Democratic Kampuchea coalition, largely based on the Khmer Rouge, because of its "continuity" with the Pol Pot regime, so the State Department explains, adding that this Khmer Rouge-based coalition is "unquestionably" more representative of the Cambodian people than the resistance of the Timorese.[41] The reason for this stance was explained by our ally Deng Xiaoping: "It is wise for China to force the Vietnamese to stay in Kampuchea because that way they will suffer more and more . . ."[42] This makes good sense, since the prime motive is to "bleed Vietnam," to ensure that suffering and brutality reach the maximum possible level so that we can exult in our benevolence in undertaking our "noble crusade" in earlier years.

The elementary truths about these terrible years survive in the memories of those who opposed the U.S. war against South Vietnam, then all of Indochina, but there is no doubt that the approved version will sooner or later be established by the custodians of history, perhaps to be exposed by crusading intellectuals a century or two hence, if "Western civilization" endures that long.

As the earlier discussion indicated, the creation of convenient "visions of righteousness" is not an invention of the intellectuals of the Vietnam era; nor, of course, is the malady confined to the United States, though one might wonder how many others compare with us in its virulence. Each atrocity has been readily handled, either forgotten, or dismissed as an unfortunate error due to our naiveté, or revised to serve as a proof of the magnificence of our intentions. Furthermore, the record of historical fact is not permitted to disturb the basic principles of interpretation of U.S. foreign policy over quite a broad spectrum of mainstream opinion, even by those who recognize that something may be amiss. Thus, Norman Graebner, a historian of the "realist" school influenced by George Kennan, formulates as unquestioned fact the conventional doctrine that U.S. foreign policy has been guided by the "Wilsonian principles of peace and self-determination." But he notices—and this is unusual—that the United States "generally ignored the principles of self-determination in Asia and Africa [he excludes the most obvious case: Latin America] where it had some chance of success and promoted it behind the Iron and Bamboo curtains where it had no chance of success at all." That is, in regions where our influence and power might have led to the realization of our principles, we ignored them, while we proclaimed them with enthusiasm with regard to enemy terrain. His conclusion is that this is "ironic," but the facts do not shake the conviction that we are committed to the Wilsonian principle of self-determination.[43] That doctrine holds, even if refuted by the historical facts. If only natural scientists were permitted such convenient methods, how easy their tasks would be.

Commentators who keep to the Party Line have an easy task; they need not consider mere facts, always a great convenience for writers and political analysts. Thus, Charles Krauthammer asserts that "left isolationism" has become "the ideology of the Democratic Party": "There is no retreat from the grand Wilsonian commitment to the spread of American values," namely human rights and democracy, but these "isolationists" reject the use of force to achieve our noble objectives. In contrast, "right isolationism" (Irving Kristol, Caspar Weinberger and the Joint Chiefs, etc.) calls for "retreat from Wilsonian goals" in favor of defense of interests. He also speaks of "the selectivity of the fervor for reforming the world" among "left isolationists," who have an "obsessive" focus on the Philippines, El Salvador, Korea, and Taiwan, but, he would like us to believe, would never be heard voicing a criticism of the Soviet Union, Cuba, or Libya. The latter assertion might be considered too exotic to merit discussion among sane people, but, as noted earlier, that would miss the point, which is to eliminate even that margin of criticism that might constrain state violence, for example, the occasional peep of protest over U.S.-organized terror in El Salvador which, if truth be told, is comparable to that attributable to Pol Pot at the time when the chorus of condemnation was reaching an early peak of intensity in 1977. Crucially, it is unnecessary to establish that there is or ever was a "grand Wilsonian commitment," apart from rhetoric; that is a given, a premise for respectable discussion.

To take an example from the field of scholarship, consider the study of the "Vietnam trauma" by Paul Kattenburg, one of the few early dissenters on Vietnam within the U.S. government and now Jacobson Professor of Public Affairs at the University of South Carolina.[44] Kattenburg is concerned to identify the "salient features central to the American traditions and experience which have made the United States perform its superpower role in what we might term a particularistic way." He holds that "principles and ideals hold a cardinal place in the U.S. national ethos and crucially distinguish U.S. performance in the superpower role"—a standard view, commonly set forth in the United States, Britain, and elsewhere in scholarly work on modern history. These principles and ideals, he explains, were "laid down by the founding fathers, those pure geniuses of detached contemplation," and "refined by subsequent leading figures of thought and action" from John Adams to Theodore Roosevelt, Woodrow Wilson, and Franklin Roosevelt; such Kim Il Sungism with regard to the "pure geniuses," etc., is also far from rare. These principles, he continues, were "tested and retested in the process of settling the continent [as Indians, Blacks, Mexicans, immigrant workers, and others can testify], healing the North-South breach, developing the economy from the wilderness in the spirit of free enterprise, and fighting World Wars I and II, not so much for interests as for the survival of the very principles by which most Americans were guiding their lives."

It is this unique legacy that explains the way Americans act "in the superpower role." The Americans approached this role, "devoid of artifice or deception," with "the mind set of an emancipator":

> In such a mind set, one need not feel or act superior, or believe one is imposing one's ethos or values on others, since one senses naturally that others cannot doubt the emancipator's righteous cause anymore than his capacities. In this respect, the American role as superpower, particularly in the postwar years, is very analogous to the role that can be attributed to a professor, mentor, or other type of emancipator.

Thus, "the professor is obviously capable," and "he is clearly disinterested." "Moreover, like the American superpower, the professor does not control the lives or destinies of his students: they remain free to come or go," just like the peasants of South Vietnam or the Guazapa mountains in El Salvador. "It will help us understand America's performance and psychology as a superpower, and the whys and wherefores of its Indochina involvement, if we bear in mind this analogy of the American performance in the superpower role with that of the benevolent but clearly egocentric professor, dispensing emancipation through knowledge of both righteousness and the right way to the deprived students of the world."

The reader must bear in mind that this is not intended as irony or caricature, but is rather presented seriously, is taken seriously, and is not untypical of what we find in the literature, not at the lunatic fringe, but at the respectable and moderately dissident extreme of the mainstream spectrum.

The standard drivel about Wilsonian principles of self-determination—unaffected by Wilson's behavior, for example, in Hispaniola, or in succeeding to eliminate consideration of U.S. domination in the Americas from the Versailles deliberations—by no means stands alone. Kennedy's Camelot merits similar acclaim among the faithful. In a fairly critical study, Robert Packenham writes that Kennedy's policies toward Latin America in 1962-63 "utilized principally diplomatic techniques to promote liberal democratic rule," and cites with approval Arthur Schlesinger's comment that the Kennedy approach to development, based on designing aid for "take off" into self-sustaining economic growth, was "a very American effort to persuade the developing countries to base their revolutions on Locke rather than on Marx."[45] In the real world, the Kennedy administration succeeded in blocking capitalist democracy in Central America and the Caribbean and laying the basis for the establishment of a network of National Security States on the Nazi model throughout the hemisphere; and the aid program, as the facts of aid disbursement make clear, was designed largely to "improve the productivity of Central America's agricultural exporters and at the same time to advance the sales of American companies that manufacture pesticides and fertilizer," which is why nutritional levels declined in the course of "economic miracles" that—quite predictably—benefited U.S. agribusiness and their local associates.[46] Locke deserves better treatment than that. But these again are mere facts, not relevant to the higher domains of political commentary.

Open the latest issue of any major journal on U.S. foreign policy and one is likely to find something similar. Thus, the lead article in the current issue of *Foreign Affairs*, is by James Schlesinger, now at Georgetown University after having served as secretary of defense, director of central intelligence, and in other high positions.[47] He contrasts the U.S. and Russian stance over the years. "The American desire was to fulfill the promise of Wilsonian idealism, of the Four Freedoms. . . . The themes of realpolitik remain contrary to the spirit of American democracy," while the Russians, so unlike us, are guided by "deep-seated impulses never to flag in the quest for marginal advantages." The United States seeks all good things, but "almost inevitably, the Polands and the Afghanistans lead to confrontation, even if the Angolas and the Nicaraguas do not"—and most assuredly, the Guatemalas, Chiles, Vietnams, Irans, Lebanons, Dominican Republics, etc., do not have the same effect; indeed, the idea would not be comprehensible in these circles, given that in each such case the United States is acting in defense against internal aggression, and with intent so noble that words can barely express it.

True, one is not often treated to such delicacies as Huntington's ode to the Holy State cited earlier, but it is, nevertheless, not too far from the norm.

The official doctrine as propounded by government spokesmen, the U.S. media, and a broad range of scholarship is illustrated, for example, in the report of the National Bipartisan (Kissinger) Commission on Central America: "The international purposes of the United States in the late twentieth century are cooperation, not hegemony or domination; partnership, not confrontation; a decent life for all, not exploitation." Similarly, Irving Kristol informs us that the United States

> is not a "have" nation in the sense that it exercises or seeks to maintain any kind of "hegemony" over distant areas of the globe. Indeed, that very word, "hegemony," with all its deliberate vagueness and ambiguity, was appropriated by latter-day Marxists in order to give American foreign policy an "imperialist" substance it is supposed to have but does not.

Among these "Marxists," he fails to observe, are such figures as Samuel Huntington, who, accurately this time, describes the 1945-70 period as one in which "the U.S. was the hegemonic power in a system of world order."[48] And again, the idea that the U.S. does not exercise or seek any kind of "hegemony," alone among the great powers of history, requires no evidence and stands as a Truth irrespective of the historical facts.

Similar thoughts are familiar among the culturally colonized elites elsewhere. Thus, according to Michael Howard, Regius Professor of Modern History at Oxford, "For 200 years the United States has preserved almost unsullied the original ideals of the Enlightenment: the belief in the God-given rights of the individual, the inherent rights of free assembly and free speech, the blessings of free enterprise, the perfectibility of man, and, above all, the universality of these values." In this nearly ideal society, the influence of elites is "quite limited." The world, however, does not appreciate this magnificence: "the United States does not enjoy the place in the world that it should have earned through its achievements, its generosity, and its goodwill since World War II"—as illustrated in such contemporary paradises as Indochina, the Dominican Republic, El Salvador, and Guatemala, to mention a few of the many candidates, just as belief in the "God-given rights of the individual" and the universality of this doctrine for two hundred years is illustrated by a century of literal human slavery and effective disenfranchisement of Blacks for another century, genocidal assaults on the native population, the slaughter of hundreds of thousands of Filipinos at the turn of the century and millions of Indochinese, and a host of other examples.[49]

Such commentary, again, need not be burdened by evidence; it suffices to assert what people of power and privilege would like to believe, including those criticized, e.g., the "left isolationists" of Krauthammer's fancies, who are delighted to hear of their commitment to Wilsonian goals. Presupposed throughout, without argument or evidence, is that the United States has been committed to such goals as self-determination, human rights, democracy, economic development, and so on. It is considered unnecessary to demonstrate or even argue for these assumptions, in political commentary and much of scholarship, particularly what is intended for a general audience. These assumptions have the status of truths of doctrine, and it would be as pointless to face them with evidence as it is with doctrines of other religious faiths.

The evidence, in fact, shows with considerable clarity that the proclaimed ideals were not the goals of Woodrow Wilson, or his predecessors, or any of his successors.[50] A more accurate account of Wilson's actual goals is given by the interpretation of the Monroe Doctrine presented to him by his secretary of state, Robert Lansing, an argument which Wilson found "unanswerable" though he thought it would be "impolitic" to make it public:

> In its advocacy of the Monroe Doctrine the United States considers its own interests. The integrity of other American nations is an incident, not an end. While this may seem based on selfishness alone, the author of the Doctrine had no higher or more generous motive in its declaration.[51]

The category of those who function as "an incident, not an end" expanded along with U.S. power in subsequent years. How planners perceived the world, when they were not addressing the general public, is illustrated in a perceptive and typically acute analysis by George Kennan, one of the most thoughtful and humane of those who established the structure of the postwar world:

> . . . we have about 50% of the world's wealth, but only 6.3% of its population. . . . In this situation, we cannot fail to be the object of envy and resentment. Our real task in the coming period is to devise a pattern of relationships which will permit us to maintain this position of disparity without positive detriment to our national security. To do so, we will have to dispense with all sentimentality and day-dreaming; and our attention will have to be concentrated everywhere on our immediate national objectives. We need not deceive ourselves that we can afford today the luxury of altruism and world-benefaction. . . . We should cease to talk about vague and—for the Far East—unreal objectives such as human rights, the raising of the living standards, and democratization. The day is not far off when we are going to have to deal in straight power concepts. The less we are then hampered by idealistic slogans, the better.[52]

The subsequent historical record shows that Kennan's prescriptions proved close to the mark, though a closer analysis indicates that he understated the case, and that the U.S. did not simply disregard "human rights, the raising of the living standards, and democratization," but evinced a positive hostility towards them in much of the world, particularly democratization in any meaningful sense, any sense that would permit genuine participation of substantial parts of the population in the formation of public policy, since such tendencies would interfere with the form of freedom that really counts: the freedom to rob and to exploit. But again, these are only considerations of empirical fact, as little relevant to political theology as is the fact that the United States attacked South Vietnam.

Given these lasting and deep-seated features of the intellectual culture, it is less surprising perhaps—though still, it would seem, rather shocking—that the man who is criticized for his extreme devotion to human rights should say that we owe Vietnam no debt because "the destruction was mutual," without this evoking even a raised eyebrow.

The reasons for the rather general and probably quite unconscious subordination of large segments of the educated classes to the system of power and domination do not seem very difficult to discern. At any given stage, one is exposed to little that questions the basic doctrines of the faith: that the United States is unique in the contemporary world and in history in its devotion to such ideals as freedom and self-determination, that it is not an actor in world affairs but rather an "emancipator," responding to the hostile or brutal acts of other powers, but apart from that, seeking nothing but justice, human rights, and democracy. Intellectual laziness alone tends to induce acceptance of the doctrines that "everyone believes." There are no courses in "intellectual self-defense," where students are helped to find ways to protect themselves from the deluge of received opinion. Furthermore, it is convenient to conform: that way lies privilege and power, while the rational skeptic faces obloquy and marginalization—not death squads or psychiatric prison, as elsewhere all too often, but still a degree of unpleasantness, and very likely, exclusion from the guilds. The natural tendencies to conform are thus refined by institutional pressures that tend to exclude those who do not toe the line. In the sciences, critical thought and reasoned skepticism are values highly to be prized. Elsewhere, they are often considered heresies to be stamped out; obedience is what yields rewards. The structural basis for conformity is obvious enough, given the distribution of domestic power. Political power resides essentially in those groups that can mobilize the resources to shape affairs of state—in our society, primarily an elite of corporations, law firms that cater to their interests, financial institutions, and the like—and the same is true of power in the cultural domains. Those segments of the media that can reach a large audience are simply part of the system of concentrated economic-political power, and naturally enough, journals that are well funded and influential are those that appeal to the tastes and interest of those who own and manage the society. Similarly, to qualify as an "expert," as Henry Kissinger explained on the basis of his not inconsiderable experience in these matters, one must know how to serve power. The "expert has his constituency," Kissinger explained: "those who have a vested interest in commonly held opinions: elaborating and defining its consensus at a high level has, after all, made him an expert."[53] We need only proceed a step further, identifying those whose vested interest is operative within the social nexus.

311

The result is a system of principles that gives comfort to the powerful—though in private, they speak to one another in a different and more realistic voice, offering "unanswerable" arguments that it would be "impolitic" to make public—and is rarely subjected to challenge. There are departures, when segments of the normally quiescent population become organized in efforts to enter the political arena or influence public policy, giving rise to what elite groups call a "crisis of democracy," which must be combated so that order can be restored. We have recently passed through such a crisis, which led to an awakening on the part of much of the population to the realities of the world in which they live, and it predictably evoked great fear and concern, and a dedicated and committed effort to restore obedience. This is the source of the reactionary jingoism that has misappropriated the term "conservatism" in recent years, and of the general support for its major goals on the part of the mainstream of contemporary liberalism, now with a "neo" affixed. The purpose is to extirpate heresy and to restore domestic and international order for the benefit of the privileged and powerful. That the mainstream intelligentsia associate themselves with these tendencies while proclaiming their independence and integrity and adversarial stance vis à vis established power should hardly come as a surprise to people familiar with modern history and capable of reasoned and critical thought.

NOTES

1. Some of these remarks are adapted from my articles: "Dominoes," *Granta* 15 (1985): 129-133; and "Forgotten History of the War in Vietnam," *In These Times* 9, no. 24 (May 15-21, 1985): 11.

2. News conference, March 24, 1977; *New York Times,* March 25, 1977.

3. Zbigniew Brzezinski, "Afghanistan and Nicaragua," *The National Interest* 1 (Fall 1985): 48-51.

4. Bernard Gwertzman, "The Debt to the Indochinese Is Becoming a Fiscal Drain," *New York Times,* March 3, 1985.

5. *New York Times,* March 18, 1968; Chomsky, *American Power and the New Mandarins* (New York: Pantheon Books, 1969), p. 14.

6. "A Vietnam War Board Game Created by Princeton Senior," *New York Times,* April 1, 1984; Lawrence Lifschultz, "The Not-So-New Rebellion," *Far Eastern Economic Review,* January 30, 1981, pp. 32-33.

7. Barbara Crossette, *New York Times,* November 10, 1985.

8. For documentation and further discussion of the interesting concept "internal aggression" as developed by U.S. officials, see my *For Reasons of State* (New York: Pantheon Books, 1973), p. 114f.

9. Francis Jennings, *The Invasion of America* (Chapel Hill: University of North Carolina Press, 1975), p. 6.

10. Alexis de Tocqueville, *Democracy in America* (New York: Knopf, 1945), p. 1; General Andrew Jackson, General Orders, 1818; cited by Ronald Takaki, *Iron Cages* (New York: Knopf, 1979), pp. 80-81, 95-96. See Richard Drinnon, *Facing West: The Metaphysics of Indian-Hating and Empire-Building* (Minneapolis: University of Minnesota Press, 1980), for a penetrating discussion of these matters. For an upbeat and enthusiastic account of the destruction of the Iroquois civilization, see

Fairfax Downey, *Indian Wars of the U.S. Army* (Garden City, N.Y.: Doubleday, 1963), p. 32f.

11. Daniel Boone Schirmer, *Republic or Empire* (Cambridge, Mass.: Schenkman, 1972), p. 231; Stuart Chreighton Miller, *'Benevolent Assimilation'* (New Haven: Yale University Press, 1982), pp. 220, 255, 248f., 78, 213, 269; David Bain, *Sitting in Darkness* (Boston: Houghton Mifflin, 1984), p. 78.

12. Samuel Huntington, "American Ideals versus American Institutions," *Political Science Quarterly* 97, no. 1 (Spring 1982): 25; *Correspondence* 97, no. 4 (Winter 1982-1983): 753. On Wilson's achievements, see Lester Langley, *The Banana Wars* (Lexington: University of Kentucky Press, 1983); Bruce Calder, *The Impact of Intervention* (Austin: University of Texas Press, 1984).

13. For extensive discussion of these matters and their sources in U.S. planning, see my *Turning the Tide* (Boston: South End Press, 1985), and sources cited there.

14. For references to material not specifically cited, here and below, and discussion in a more general context, see my *Towards a New Cold War* (New York: Pantheon Books, 1982), *Turning the Tide*, and sources cited there.

15. Norman Podhoretz, "Proper Uses of Power," *New York Times*, October 30, 1983.

16. Mark McCain, *Boston Globe*, December 9, 1984; memo released during the Westmoreland-CBS libel trial.

17. Bernard Fall, "Viet Cong: The Unseen Enemy in Vietnam," *New Society* 22 (April 1965): 10-12; Paul Quinn-Judge, "The Confusion and Mystery Surrounding Vietnam's War Dead," *Far Eastern Economic Review*, October 1, 1984, p. 49.

18. Ton That Thien, "Vietnam's New Economic Policy," *Pacific Affairs* 56, no. 4 (Winter 1983-1984): 691-708; Chitra Subramaniam, *PNS*, November 15, 1985; both writing from Geneva. For detailed discussion of the effects of U.S. chemical and environmental warfare in Vietnam, unprecedented in scale and character, see SIPRI, *Ecological Consequences of the Second Indochina War* (Stockholm: Almqvist Wiskell, 1976), concluding that "the ecological debilitation from such attack is likely to be of long duration."

19. John Corry, *New York Times*, April 27, 1985.

20. *Time*, April 15, 1985, pp. 16-61.

21. *Wall Street Journal*, April 4, 1985. An exception was *Newsweek*, April 15, 1985, which devoted four pages of its thirty-three-page account to a report by Tony Clifton and Ron Moreau on the effects of the war on the "wounded land."

22. Walt W. Rostow, *The View from the Seventh Floor* (New York: Harper and Row, 1964), p. 244. On the facts concerning Indochina, see the documentation reviewed in *For Reasons of State*. Rostow's account of Mao and North Korea is also fanciful, as the record of serious scholarship shows.

23. Cited in *American Power and the New Mandarins*, pp. 253, 238.

24. "Vietnam Blitz: A Report on the Impersonal War," *New Republic*, October 9, 1965, p. 19.

25. James Reston, *New York Times*, February 26, 1965.

26. Bernard Fall, *Last Reflections on a War* (Garden City, N.Y.: Doubleday, 1967), pp. 33, 47; James Reston, *New York Times*, November 24, 1967.

27. Allan E. Goodman and Seth P. Tillman, *New York Times*, March 24, 1985.

28. Chomsky, *At War with Asia* (New York: Pantheon Books, 1970), p. 286.

29. Charles Krauthammer, "Isolationism, Left and Right," *New Republic*, March 4, 1985, pp. 18-25.

30. *New York Times*, March 31, 1985.

31. Nayan Chanda, "CIA No, US Aid Yes," "Sihanouk Stonewalled," *Far Eastern Economic Review*, August 16, 1984, pp. 16-18; November 1, 1984, p. 30.

32. Douglas Pike, *St. Louis Post-Dispatch,* November 19, 1979; *Christian Science Monitor,* December 4, 1979. Cited by Michael Vickery, *Cambodia* (Boston: South End Press, 1983), pp. 65-66.

33. On Lebanese opinion and the scandalous refusal of the media to consider it, and the general context, see my *Fateful Triangle* (Boston: South End Press, 1983).

34. Chomsky and Edward S. Herman, *The Political Economy of Human Rights,* Vol. 1 (Boston: South End Press, 1979), chapter 4.

35. The major scholarly study of the Pol Pot period, Vickery's *Cambodia,* has been widely and favorably reviewed in England, Australia, and elsewhere, but never here. The one major governmental study, by a Finnish Inquiry Commission, was also ignored here: Kimmo Kiljunen, ed., *Kampuchea: Decade of the Genocide* (London: Zed Books, 1984). See Kiljunen, "Power Politics and the Tragedy of Kampuchea in the '70s," *Bulletin of Concerned Asian Scholars* 17, no. 2 (April-June 1985): 49-64, for a brief account of the Finnish study, and my "Decade of Genocide in Review," *Inside Asia* 2 (February-March 1985): 31-34, for review of this and other material. Note that the Finnish study is entitled *Decade of the Genocide,* in recognition of the fact that killings during the U.S.-run war were roughly comparable to those under Pol Pot. The facts are of little interest in the U.S., where the Khmer Rouge have a specific role to play: namely, to provide a justification for U.S. atrocities.

36. Shawcross, in David Chandler and Ben Kiernan, eds., *Revolution and Its Aftermath in Kampuchea* (New Haven: Yale University Press, 1983); see my "Decade of Genocide" for further discussion.

37. See *Political Economy of Human Rights* and Edward S. Herman, *The Real Terror Network* (Boston: South End Press, 1982), for extensive evidence.

38. Shawcross, *Revolution and Its Aftermath in Kampuchea* and *Quality of Mercy* (New York: Simon and Schuster, 1984); see my "Decade of Genocide" for discussion. Perhaps I may take credit for suggesting this clever idea to him. In a 1978 essay (reprinted in *Towards a New Cold War;* see p. 95), I wrote that "It is not gratifying to the ego merely to march in a parade; therefore, those who join in ritual condemnation of an official enemy must show that they are engaged in a courageous struggle against powerful forces that defend it. Since these rarely exist, even on a meager scale [and in the case of the Khmer Rouge, were undetectable outside of marginal Maoist groups], they must be concocted; if nothing else is at hand, those who propose a minimal concern for fact will do. The system that has been constructed enables one to lie freely with regard to the crimes, real or alleged, of an official enemy, while suppressing the systematic involvement of one's own state in atrocities, repression, or aggression . . ." These comments accurately anticipate the subsequent antics.

39. On Shawcross's fabrication of evidence in support of his thesis, see my "Decade of Genocide" and Christopher Hitchens, "The Chorus and Cassandra: What Everyone Knows About Noam Chomsky," *Grand Street* 5, no. 1 (Autumn 1985): 106-131.

40. *The Nation,* June 25, 1977.

41. John Holdridge of the State Department, Hearing before the Subcommittee on Asian and Pacific Affairs of the Committee on Foreign Affairs, House of Representatives, 97th Congress, second session, September 14, 1982, p. 71.

42. Cited by Ben Kiernan, *Tribune* (Australia), March 20, 1985.

43. Norman A. Graebner, *Cold War Diplomacy* (New York: Van Nostrand Books, 1962).

44. Paul M. Kattenburg, *The Vietnam Trauma in American Foreign Policy, 1945-75* (New Brunswick, N.J.: Transaction Books, 1982), p. 69f.

45. Robert A. Packenham, *Liberal America and the Third World* (Princeton: Princeton University Press, 1973), pp. 156, 63.

46. Lester Langley, *Central America: The Real Stakes* (New York: Crown, 1985), p. 128; see *Turning the Tide* for discussion and further sources on these matters.

47. James Schlesinger, "The Eagle and the Bear: Ruminations on Forty Years of Superpower Relations," *Foreign Affairs* 63, no. 5 (Summer 1985): 938, 939, 940, 947.

48. Irving Kristol, "Foreign Policy in an Age of Ideology," *The National Interest* 1 (Fall 1985); Huntington, in M. J. Crozier, S. P. Huntington, and J. Watanuki, *The Crisis of Democracy* (New York: New York University Press, 1975).

49. Michael Howard, "The Bewildered American Raj," *Harper's* 270, no. 1618 (March 1985): 55-60.

50. For a review of the facts of the matter, see *Turning the Tide* and sources cited.

51. Gabriel Kolko, *Main Currents in American History* (New York: Pantheon Books, 1984), p. 47.

52. Policy Planning Study (PPS) 23, February 24, 1948, *FRUS 1948*, I (part 2); reprinted in part in Thomas Etzvold and John Lewis Gaddis, *Containment* (New York: Columbia University Press, 1978), p. 226f.

53. Henry Kissinger, *American Foreign Policy* (New York: Norton, 1969), p. 28.

RECOMMENDED READING

Noam Chomsky and Edward S. Herman, *The Political Economy of Human Rights*. 2 vols. Boston: South End Press, 1979.

Edward S. Herman and Frank Brodhead, *Demonstration Elections*. Boston: South End Press, 1984.

George Kahin, *Intervention*. New York: Knopf, 1986.

Gabriel Kolko, *Anatomy of a War*. New York: Pantheon, 1985.

William Appleman Williams, Thomas McCormick, Lloyd Gardner, and Walter LaFeber, *America in Vietnam*. Anchor Books, 1985.

"The Real War": Post-Vietnam
Low-Intensity Conflict

I

*If we ever reach the point of shooting it out with conventional Red Army forma-
tions, we already will have lost. What we are talking about here is real war.*

—John Michael Kelly,
Deputy Assistant Secretary, U.S. Air Force

*The U.S. logistical liability in South East Asia was compounded by a major mili-
tary mistake: determined dedication to a doctrine of strategic defense and tactical
offense. The U.S. played poker. The foe played go.*

—Lewis B. Tambs,
former U.S. ambassador to Costa Rica

Kelly's "real war" is happening today in various parts of the Third World.
It is unconventional and undeclared. The dirty little wars now unfolding
in Central America, the Philippines, and Angola are among its current
manifestations: the result of more than a decade of development of what
U.S. military strategists call "post-Vietnam counterinsurgency doctrine,"
or "low-intensity conflict." But though the United States is deadly serious
about winning this war, its real nature, as well as its origins, remain
largely invisible to the U.S. public.

Low-intensity conflict requires a radical departure from conventional
military thinking. Its name comes from its place on the "intensity spec-
trum" of warfare which ascends from civil disorders, through classical

wars, to nuclear holocaust. The traditional military defines low-intensity conflicts as those on the low end of the spectrum: conflicts which, for the United States, require fewer resources, less manpower, and cause fewer casualties than conventional war. But low-intensity conflict is not simply a scaled-down version of a conventional war. It is not less of the same thing, nor just a preliminary stage to "real" conflict.

"This kind of conflict is more accurately described as revolutionary and counterrevolutionary warfare," explains Colonel John Waghelstein, currently commander of the army's Seventh Special Forces. He warns that the term "low-intensity" is misleading, as it describes the level of violence strictly from a military viewpoint. In fact, Waghelstein argues, it involves "political, economic, and psychological warfare, with the military being a distant fourth in many cases." In perhaps the most candid definition given by a U.S. official, Waghelstein declares that low-intensity conflict "is total war at the grassroots level." For its victims in the Third World, this kind of war is hardly "low" in its intensity.

As a conceptual framework rather than just a new set of tactics, the idea requires far more emphasis on nonmilitary instruments of power and persuasion. "Low-intensity conflict is neither simple nor short-term," write U.S. Army majors Donald Morelli and Michael Ferguson. "It is a complex, multilevel, and multidimensional problem which has its roots in change . . . The initiative rests with those who can influence or exploit the process of change." A strategic study commissioned in 1983 by the Pentagon concluded that there is no such thing as victory by force of arms in a low-intensity conflict. Victory in such a context, the study suggests, can be better measured by "avoidance of certain outcomes, or by attitudinal changes in a target group."

Fundamental to this view is the understanding that military intervention is not enough to win in low-intensity situations and may, in fact, be counterproductive. "This does not imply," warn Morelli and Ferguson, "that we are incapable of conducting tactical operations in the low-intensity arena . . . the direct assistance of the United States may be required, and planning for that eventuality must be continuous and thorough. . . . However, if we·must commit U.S. forces to combat in a low-intensity situation, we have lost the strategic initiative."

Although the United States has been fighting low-intensity wars in the Third World, under different names, for decades, the total concept, enlarged and redefined, is finally catching on within the military itself, where "low-intensity conflict" is a term currently in vogue. The doctrine is gaining ground as a strategic framework for rethinking the nature of conflict in the Third World. In part, this is because of real changes taking place in the world; in part, it is because an assortment of powerful figures in the United States believe it to be the correct strategy to deal with those changes.

U.S. low-intensity conflict doctrine has evolved as a response to the growing challenge of popular movements in the Third World, which Defense Secretary Caspar Weinberger calls "the most immediate threat to free world security for the rest of the century." It assumes that revolutions are not purely military events. As U.S. Army secretary John Marsh explains, "The roots of insurgencies are not military in origin, nor will they be military in resolution."

Proponents of low-intensity conflict call for rethinking traditional tactics. Instead of relying on conventional armies to deal with unconventional and revolutionary conflicts, they advocate "total war" on a variety of fronts—economic, social, political, and psychological. The former head of the Defense Intelligence Agency, Lieutenant General Samuel Wilson, bluntly sums up the attitude of low-intensity conflict advocates:

> There is little likelihood of a strategic nuclear confrontation with the Soviets. It is almost as unlikely that Soviet Warsaw Pact forces will come tearing through the Fulda Gap in a conventional thrust. We live today with conflict of a different sort . . . and we had better get on with the ballgame.

II

For almost a decade, the accepted wisdom was that the U.S. military was transfixed by the ghosts of Vietnam, unable to look effectively to the future. In reality, though, the planners of U.S. military strategy in the Third World may have been less paralyzed by the past than those of us who opposed the war in Central America were by our conviction that history was bound to repeat itself. While we spoke of El Salvador as "another Vietnam," the Pentagon set about ensuring that it would not be.

To a large extent, the reading of the Central American crisis by the U.S. public, and the political response from opponents of the war, grew from the belief that the region was potentially "another Vietnam." A body of unexamined assumptions about the nature of that earlier war lay behind analysis of the situation in Central America. Many assumed that the U.S. buildup was the prelude to troop landings in El Salvador or a full-scale invasion of Nicaragua. They foresaw another war in which "our boys" would fight and die, with the United States becoming bogged down in a quagmire before eventually destroying the region or being forced into an ignominious withdrawal.

As the war in Central America becomes more difficult to understand in conventional terms, it seems that the public and the policy makers may have drawn two entirely different sets of conclusions about Vietnam. The lessons of Vietnam have informed the thinking of the U.S. national security establishment, and helped to bring about profound changes in their approach to military intervention.

Fears of "another Vietnam" in Central America stem from a failure to understand some of the key twists and turns in U.S. military strategy that took place during the war, and the important—if hidden—strategic debate that underlay them. Contrary to conventional wisdom, there was no single "hawk" view on Vietnam: the hawks took at least two key positions, which emerged during the earliest days of the war and have remained ever since. While the two camps may have coincided in some of their tactical recommendations, their strategic conceptions are quite different.

In the first view, war is essentially a *military* confrontation, a battle between two armies. Its goals are to capture and hold territory, and eventually to annihilate the enemy's main force units through air, sea, and ground operations, using superior force and firepower.

In the second view, war is fundamentally a *political* confrontation between two social systems ("democracy" and "communism"). Rather than simply destroying the largest number of enemy troops, it targets the civilian population with a combination of military force, economic pressures, psychological warfare, and other means, and attempts to destroy the enemy's political and social structures. This approach, labeled "counterinsurgency" in Vietnam, tends to be tactically flexible: it may use conventional military operations and/or guerrilla tactics. In this kind of war, winning means ensuring that the civilian population will accept a political and social alternative to the enemy's system.

Throughout the Vietnam War, these two hawk perspectives remained in conflict. CIA specialists who had served during the Kennedy era of counterinsurgency and special operations experts who had practiced unconventional warfare in Korea lined up against traditional army officers and Pentagon bureaucrats. Within the services, the Green Berets and the marines more often took a counterinsurgency approach, while regular army units tended to engage in conventional combat. Civilian agencies like AID and the CIA preferred "political warfare," while the military in general took the conventional approach of maximum firepower to devastating lengths.

In a 1983 article on marine "security assistance" and pacification operations, military historian John Hoyt Williams wrote:

> While Army and Saigon command continued to be obsessed with the numbers game, search-and-destroy missions, bombing and large-unit sweeps, the Marines kept stubbornly experimenting with local, small-unit tactics. . . . they lived in the hamlets, cooperated with the peasants, offered free medical and dental services, helped build schools and created a grassroots gendarmerie. In return, the villagers were to supply intelligence and finger VC cadre in their midst. The Marine operations were successful because they deescalated the war and guerrilla'd the guerrillas . . . recognizing that the Vietnamese peasant, rather than the Viet Cong, was the genuine goal of the war.

Under largely civilian direction, U.S. and South Vietnamese military units, the CIA, AID, and the United States Information Agency (USIA) were combined into CORDS (Civilian Operations and Revolutionary Development Support) to carry out similar programs: agricultural development, police training, psychological warfare, paramilitary operations in small units, and economic assistance to Vietnamese refugees and villages. CORDS operations took a comprehensive "carrot and stick" approach, ranging from "humanitarian relief" projects to the notorious Phoenix program, which identified and assassinated over twenty thousand suspected Vietcong cadre in 1969 with the help of "turned" guerrillas and local informers.

Meanwhile, neighboring Thailand and Laos saw similar attempts to build an infrastructure for the U.S. regional strategy, combining military operations with wide-ranging development programs to restructure local societies along lines that would benefit U.S. interests. Reflecting on the gamut of programs he had supervised in Indochina, former CIA chief of station Douglas Blaufarb noted that:

All of this was done under the formal rubric of refugee emergency assistance and resettlement, and of rural development, in order to conform to AID categories of approved activity. In actual fact, it constituted the civilian front of an unconventional war which could not have been prosecuted without the aid program.

The Vietnam generation of counterinsurgency experts offered a number of basic arguments about strategy. These were:

1. Pacification, or the "hearts and minds" approach, correctly targets *population*, not territory, as the strategic objective.

2. Military escalation is often counterproductive; overkill can win battles and lose wars. As former Vietnamese marshall Nguyen Ky admitted bitterly, "You cannot use a steamroller against a shadow."

3. Counterinsurgency fails where it does not take indigenous culture and history into account; successful operations need solid intelligence about local political, cultural, social, and economic conditions.

4. Counterrevolution can only succeed if it is combined with "nation-building"—the construction of an alternative social system. Nation-building combines "internal defense" (protection against insurgents) with economic assistance, in order to create a strong security apparatus, a manageable political community, and stable national institutions.

5. The United States cannot act alone; in fact, using U.S. combat troops is likely to significantly decrease the chance of victory. It is ultimately the role of local forces to win their own population. The United States should, however, train and "clean up" client forces so that abuses and corruption do not alienate the population from nation-building; and it should control and direct the nonmilitary aspects of the war.

6. The United States needs regional strategies to deal with regional conflicts. It must deny the enemy political and military sanctuary in

neighboring theaters, while "going to the source" of the regional conflict. It cannot allow itself to become bogged down in fighting on one subsidiary front while the enemy fights on several—an argument shared by analysts of conventional warfare.

7. The U.S. military establishment must overcome its own prejudices against conventional, "unmilitary" warfare; it must achieve greater coordination among the branches of the service as well as with civilian intelligence, aid, and development agencies.

8. This kind of warfare must seek to win the support of the U.S. population, as well as the foreign target population.

Yet even as the science of political warfare developed, men like General Maxwell Taylor, chairman of the Joint Chiefs of Staff, complained about "all this cloud of dust" from advocates of counterinsurgency who claimed to have a new model for warfare. Army commanders denounced Secretary of State Robert McNamara and his "Washington whiz kids" for "ignoring time-vindicated principles of military strategy," and for allowing civilian agencies to plan military programs. "I'll be damned," said one senior officer, "if I permit the United States Army, its institutions, its doctrine and its traditions to be destroyed just to win this lousy war."

This kind of opposition from conventionally minded strategists pushed aside the arguments of the advocates of counterinsurgency and nation-building. The new doctrine was never implemented comprehensively in Vietnam; it remained in the realm of small-scale, incomplete experiments. One of its supporters, Lieutenant Colonel James A. Taylor, later wrote,

> There are those who contend that this kind of effort did not work in Vietnam, and will not work elsewhere. The concept actually worked quite well in Vietnam. But it was not seen that way by those who were so busy with quantifiable activities that they failed to notice who controlled the countryside when the sun went down.

It was those in the Pentagon busy with "quantifiable activities" who held the upper hand in the Vietnam War. Under General William Westmoreland, they stepped up the military's traditional reliance on heavy units, massed firepower, high technology, and air power. And like Westmoreland, they argued that, "It takes the full strength of a tiger to kill a rabbit."

The United States lost that war, and a defeated U.S. military rushed to assign blame: the press lost the war, the public lost the war, the politicians lost the war, the South Vietnamese lost the war. Military officials who had killed a million Asians and turned half the Vietnamese countryside into scorched moonscape even claimed they had lost because they were "not allowed to fight."

In the sweeping revisions of history that followed, the general consensus was that "counterinsurgency didn't work" and was now irrelevant. It would take the next wave of Third World revolutionary movements, together with the rebirth of the U.S. Right, for the real lessons of Vietnam to be studied seriously.

III

The 1970s brought a new generation of revolutions in the Third World, and their impact was sweeping. In Zimbabwe and Nicaragua, indigenous revolutionary movements took power; in the former Portuguese territories of Africa, colonial rule crumbled; and in Iran, a different kind of radical nationalism swept away the Shah. The developed world began to take the concerns of the nonaligned nations seriously, and the axis of conflict, worldwide, began to shift from East-West to North-South.

U.S. strategy proved temporarily inadequate against such change. Certainly, attempts at controlling the Third World never ceased, and many of the elements of low-intensity conflict were adopted during the 1970s, albeit in a piecemeal fashion. Under Nixon, Washington decided to keep its own forces at home, supplying "friendly" regimes with the wherewithal to police their own countries, and limiting actual counter-revolutionary operations to the CIA. Under Carter, the Trilateralists attempted to implement "nation-building" and economic measures that co-opted the language of social reform. But a coherent, long-term strategy was absent.

After Vietnam, the military establishment had largely gone back to preparing for orthodox conflict in Europe and for nuclear war. Special Forces units were dismantled, counterinsurgency training declined precipitously, and the "political" conception of war was dismissed as a preoccupation of civilians who had betrayed the army. By the time of the Carter presidency, growing revelations of "dirty tricks" had even led to declining support for the CIA's paramilitary capability and the dismissal of hundreds of the agency's covert action experts.

During most of the 1970s most of the national security establishment assumed that the U.S. "backyard"—the Caribbean, Central and South America—was under control. U.S. assistance had engineered the death of "Che" Guevara in Bolivia in 1967 and destroyed the *foco* theory of guerrilla warfare. In Guatemala and Nicaragua, small local guerrilla forces met with serious reverses in 1967-68. Modest counterinsurgency and security assistance programs to repressive governments kept the lid on popular movements elsewhere, and with the help of the CIA, Allende's experiment in democratic socialism in Chile was over. Cuba, seen as the source for all revolutionary movements in Latin America, was generally assumed to be effectively "contained." U.S. Southern Command (SOUTHCOM) had no overall strategy; a country-by-country, haphazard array of old programs seemed enough to keep its domain quiet.

But the Sandinista triumph in Nicaragua in 1979 sounded alarm bells in Washington. For the Right, unprepared for "another Cuba" so close to home, it was a frightening new development. Coming just four months after Maurice Bishop's equally unexpected seizure of power in Grenada, the Sandinista revolution—an explosion of indigenous nationalism—signaled that the U.S. strategy for counterrevolution was in need of a thorough overhaul. Colonel John Waghelstein commented,

> The triumph of the Sandinistas in Nicaragua, the insurgency of El Salvador and Cuba's renewed efforts in the Caribbean Basin have conspired to force the Army to re-evaluate its priorities—and, like St. Paul on the road to Damascus, many have become converts and begun to reassess our capability.

Within the United States, the Right was in open rebellion. "After the disasters of the loss of Vietnam and the collapse of the Nixon presidency," charged Ray S. Cline, a right-wing policy advisor and former deputy director of the CIA, "the U.S. began to drift almost aimlessly in its strategic thinking." Dissident officials of the Nixon-Ford era like Fred Iklé had joined with Jeane Kirkpatrick and other neoconservative Democrats to form the Committee on the Present Danger and other think tanks and policy groups. Dozens of military and intelligence experts, dissatisfied with the direction of U.S. national security policy, flocked to older entities such as Georgetown University's Center for Strategic and International Studies (CSIS) and the National Strategy Information Center (NSIC). "We have done nothing but try to forget what we should have learned from our defeat," wrote one right-wing analyst. Bitter and determined, they began to study war some more.

Spearheaded by members of the intelligence community, the conservatives launched an all-out assault on the strategy of accommodation with the Soviet Union and its Third World "proxies." In its place, they called for a resumption of Cold War principles, but with a contemporary twist. Their perspective was not one of simple old-style militarism, and they had no objection to counterinsurgency as such. Rather, the Right lobbied against what it saw as an insufficiently anticommunist perspective by the Trilateralists and the Carter administration, which it blamed for the "loss" of a number of Third World countries.

The conservatives read an ominous trend in "Kremlin support for so-called wars of national liberation." U.S. national security, they argued, required not only a major buildup of conventional and nuclear forces, but the development of a new capability and an effective strategy for fighting revolutionary forces in the Third World.

The military itself was a relatively minor player in this emerging policy debate, although its reassessment of the Vietnam War did take on growing significance. The best-known critic of the United States' performance in Vietnam, Colonel Harry Summers, called for a return to the fundamental principles of warfare in his book, *On Strategy*. Summers charged that the U.S. military bureaucracy itself was responsible for the defeat in Vietnam. The internal bickering, failure to set and agree on goals, and lack of unity of command that had marred its performance in

Vietnam now left the United States "dangerously unprepared" to fight future Third World conflicts.

Though Summers explicitly rejected counterinsurgency as a U.S. Army mission, some of his criticisms fit the agenda of the resurgent Right. Vietnam-era "political warfare" hawks, in particular, identified with Summers's insistence on subordinating military means to political goals, and agreed that U.S. troops could not substitute for local forces engaged in counterinsurgency and nation-building. They counted on Summers's prestige at the Pentagon, where he was admired as a radical conservative, to give credibility to proposals for structural changes in the national security apparatus.

The low-intensity advocates neither expected nor wanted the Pentagon to abandon its NATO commitments or to scrap existing nuclear and conventional weapons programs. But hoping to gain some turf— probably in a Third World arena of lower priority—they lobbied incessantly for a new capability against "terrorism" and insurgency—fronts on which they claimed the United States was losing ground to communist forces. In promoting low-intensity conflict, they were practicing their own form of insurgency against the conventional military establishment: in the words of one advocate of the new approach, they were "using special operations on the system to make the system work."

IV

Today, the proponents of low-intensity conflict are enjoying a political climate in which their ideas can flourish. Even so, the doctrine is still an emerging one, and though it has made major advances, it has not been entirely accepted at the theoretical level—much less effectively implemented on the ground. Lewis Tambs, former U.S. ambassador to Costa Rica, complains that victory by means of low-intensity principles depends on winning "three battles—in the field, in the media, and in Washington within the Administration." Low-intensity conflict advocates still have some way to go on each front.

Bureaucratic inertia is the first obstacle. Like most large institutions, the Pentagon is not eager to embrace sudden change. Within the defense establishment, there is a bias against the disruption of the traditional patterns of command, career development, and procurement implied by a major doctrinal shift. The regular military has always resented "special" or elite forces from the other services, yet has resisted the introduction of "unconventional" perspectives within its own ranks. For civilian agencies such as the CIA, the State Department, and AID, coordinating operations between rival bureaucracies, and with the Pentagon, remains a major problem. On the ground, meanwhile, local forces trained for decades in conventional military science, and local leaders with their own national agendas, are often resistant to further *yanqui* interference.

Even before engaging the enemy in the Third World, then, the advocates of low-intensity conflict must convince the Pentagon bureaucracy, civilian officials, and other government agencies of their case. They must win over key decision makers—both political and military—in the security establishments of their foreign allies. And, increasingly, they must complement this internal debate and diplomacy with a full-scale effort to rally the U.S. public behind the policy.

By the end of 1986, it became clear that low-intensity proponents had been developing two tracks in their struggle. One—public outreach, bureaucratic politicking, and lobbying inside the Defense Department and Congress—continues overtly. The other track, carried out by men frustrated with the slowness and unresponsiveness of even the government itself, was a covert policy run by the National Security Council and a host of right-wing specialists in and out of government. Until it broke open with the Iran-contra arms scandal, advocates of this track simply set up their own parallel system, with its own intelligence, envoys, treasury, paramilitary forces, communications, and chain of command to engage in low-intensity conflicts. As Andy Messing, head of the National Defense Council, explained about his friend Lieutenant Colonel Oliver North, "Ollie was just trying to get things done." It is too soon to judge what impact the discovery of this scandal will have on low-intensity doctrine in its official form; it is unlikely, however, that advocates will abandon their plans, or retreat from the gains they have already been able to institutionalize within the system.

Low-intensity conflict is a radical concept partly because it calls for changes within the system itself. It means integrating military science with all other aspects of government policy, and implies new levels of interagency coordination. It involves securing the agreement of third parties—countries that include Israel, Taiwan, and South Korea—to act as reliable suppliers of hardware and training. And the new doctrine, as it has evolved since Vietnam, means enlisting the resources and ideological convictions of the private sector to aid the efforts of government.

Low-intensity conflict is also radical, however, in the comprehensiveness of its approach. It draws on a wide-ranging study of the different elements of conflict, few of which are strictly military. Researchers of think tanks and universities attempt to analyze and mimic the politico-military structure of revolutionary movements; others study the "backwards" tactics of guerrilla warfare, which invert traditional military rules of engagement, or delve into anthropology and social psychology; others still, like Britain's Brigadier General Frank Kitson, dwell on the British and French colonial experiences, and propose sophisticated police states as the means of preventing insurgencies.

The low-intensity conflict strategists have analyzed earlier U.S. experiments with conventional warfare behind enemy lines, such as the work of the Office of Strategic Services—forerunner of the CIA—during World War II. They have reassessed nation-building projects such as the

Alliance for Progress, and evaluated new economic assistance programs in terms of their potential contribution to internal security. Edward Lansdale, the legendary counterinsurgency expert whose exploits in the Kennedy era made him a hero to a new generation of low-intensity hawks, reviews his experiences with psychological warfare and covert operations in the Philippines and Southeast Asia. Says Lansdale, "I think they're going to listen to us this time."

The most visible manifestation of this new interest in low-intensity conflict has been the promotion of "special operations forces" (SOF), a concept that builds on the counterinsurgency capability of the U.S. Army Special Forces, Navy SEALS, and irregular units of the other services. Since 1981, old units have been revitalized and expanded by at least a third; special operations forces now number 14,900—or 32,000 including reserves. They have an important role to play in training, combat support, and "special operations" in a low-intensity context. Both the Army Civil Affairs and Psychological Operations battalions, based at Fort Bragg, North Carolina (home of the John F. Kennedy Special Warfare Center), played a vital part in the invasion of Grenada and the postinvasion "pacification" of the Grenadian population. Army Special Forces Mobile Training Teams (MTTs) are currently assigned to El Salvador, Honduras, Belize, and Costa Rica. Fifty-five SOF advisors in El Salvador are involved in most phases of the counterinsurgency war, and a battalion of Green Berets is permanently stationed in Fort Gulick in Panama.

This visible growth in SOF strength does not, however, suggest that elite U.S. commando units would take the lead in fighting a Central American war. Rather, they are conceived of as one element in a strategy of flexible response to a complex, multidimensional conflict situation. Though some doubts may linger about their usefulness in more conventional quarters of the Pentagon, the Special Operations Forces have become a convenient handle for addressing the issue of how the United States should build a low-intensity capability.

Another proposal to develop a "light infantry" is a compromise program with something for everyone: it is a further avenue for the creation of new combat units and training programs and for initiating research and development on counterrevolutionary warfare. Like the SOF, the "light infantry" concept offers low-intensity conflict advocates a new field for experimentation without threatening entrenched services, and a way of enlisting Pentagon support for low-intensity conflict. It also conveniently dovetails with the concerns of congressional proponents of "military reform."

While the military builds its unconventional warfare capability, the intelligence community has undergone a parallel expansion. The CIA has rehired hundreds of covert action experts lost during the Carter years, and strengthened its position within the national security establishment, recovering prestige as well as influence. The agency has also developed a virtual army of its own, a secret and unconventional force of soldiers and guerrilla warfare specialists. This vast expansion of the CIA's paramilitary assets, together with resources supplied by friendly third countries, has allowed the CIA to expand into areas that go far beyond traditional intelligence-gathering or limited tactical operations. The United States is now able to take the strategic initiative in low-intensity conflicts, and launch offensive guerrilla operations against established governments—the mining of Nicaragua's harbors being only the most striking example.

All these elements have now been combined into a new instrument aimed at reestablishing U.S. political control in the Third World. The 1980s have seen the birth of the so-called Reagan Doctrine, which proclaims a "global offensive against communism at the fringes of the Soviet Empire." This doctrine, outlined by the president and by Secretary of State George Shultz in 1984, places "Soviet imperialism" squarely behind instability and what the administration calls "terrorism" in the Third World. Rather than directly attack the Soviet Union in Eastern Europe, the doctrine singles out alleged embodiments of the Soviet/terrorist threat, such as Nicaragua, Angola, Kampuchea, and Afghanistan, as targets for "rollback" by the United States. As Elliott Abrams, Assistant Secretary of State for Inter-American Affairs, explains,

> We all believe that it would be morally justifiable to invade Poland for the same reasons that it was morally justifiable to invade Grenada. But it would be crazy to do it.

At the same time, the Reagan Doctrine provides a more subtle rationale for continued low-intensity intervention in the Third World. On the premise that the Soviet Union has initiated a global plan for low-intensity war in the developing world, the doctrine has the potential to convert conflicts in such places as the Philippines, Haiti, or Southern Africa into anticommunist and antiterrorist showdowns. The Reagan administration, facing a real decline in the United States' hegemony over a changing world, is determined to reassert itself by "projecting U.S. power" overseas, and stands ready to take direct control over a number of countries in crisis, both in Latin America and elsewhere in the Third World. Washington will block existing or potential models of independent development, and impose substitute models of its own—though these may not necessarily resemble the old autocracies blindly backed in the past. In fact, low-intensity hawks have been among the most ardent supporters of "reform" movements against right-wing dictators like Marcos, Pinochet, and Stroessner, arguing that crude repression merely fuels revolutionary movements.

The Reagan Doctrine attempts to blend older, often conflicting, approaches to Third World revolutionary movements into a new, integrated whole. Earlier administrations and their security advisors promoted differing interpretations of the origins of revolution. Some thought the causes were internal, lying in social and economic inequalities, poverty, lack of education and the absence of democratic political structures. Others insisted the causes were external, rooted in world communism and Soviet—or Soviet/Cuban—agitation.

Under President John F. Kennedy, the United States made its first stab at dealing with both aspects, combining the reforms of the Alliance for Progress with aggressive anticommunism on the military front. The counterinsurgency specialists of the Kennedy era argued for aid to civilians as well as for the development of the Green Berets to be "our own guerrilla force." But these solutions lacked any consistent ideological framework, and proved unable to cement the institutional support that is needed for multiagency programs to work effectively.

The synthesis offered by the Reagan administration begins, in a sense, where the Kennedy experiment left off, but with new urgency and coherence. It reiterates that revolution has both internal and external causes, and in the emerging doctrine of low-intensity conflict, it claims to have found a methodology that can deal with both. Regardless of its eventual success on the ground, the new doctrine does at least have the potential, in the present political climate, to become a truly bipartisan framework for approaching conflict in the Third World.

The Reagan Doctrine, while admittedly drawing on the experiments of the past, is qualitatively different from its predecessors. Reagan's innovation is to provide open backing for paramilitary insurgents or "freedom fighters" against a series of established Third World governments, at the same time as waging counterinsurgency campaigns against left-wing guerrilla movements. This gives an entirely new dimension to "political" warfare. In Reagan administration parlance, this is "revolutionary democracy," an ideological struggle designed to prove that the United States is capable of exporting counterrevolution, and that it has not only the means, but also the will and the moral and legal right to do so.

In the current right-wing political climate, there is more support than ever for restructuring parts of the U.S. military to conduct these conventional forms of warfare, and for expanding the "army" to include new institutional players from outside the Pentagon. But lobbying is not enough: the proponents of low-intensity conflict need to demonstrate the success of their theory on the ground. Each country in Central America— El Salvador, Nicaragua, Honduras, Costa Rica, and Guatemala, as well as Cuba and the island nations of the Caribbean—is a laboratory for what Colonel Waghelstein calls "total war at the grassroots level." And the outcome of these experiments in the Caribbean Basin will determine, to a large extent, the lasting impact of low-intensity conflict doctrine on U.S. strategy.

For U.S. strategists, the current war in Central America has become the most important laboratory for testing advanced models of low-intensity conflict. The countries of Central America and the Caribbean have always been central to U.S. ideas of empire; historically, Washington has used force in the region to meet any challenge to continued domination of its "backyard." And lingering post-Vietnam resentments give the Right a sense of mission: as Lewis Tambs wrote, "The continuing campaign to equate Central America with South-East Asia is an effort to influence the decision. But Central America is not South-East Asia. This time the logistics are on the U.S.'s side. The U.S., by supplying treasure, training and technology, can aid its allies . . . in conducting a protracted war of perhaps decades duration."

The war that the United States is fighting in Central America today indicates that old-fashioned military force is not enough to defeat a new generation of revolutionary movements. But Washington's ability to control events there, by force and/or by other means, is still perceived as crucial to the projection of U.S. power worldwide. If the United States can dominate Central America by using low-intensity strategies, the region could become a model for a world that is never really at "peace" again.

V

After 1982, signs of escalating low-intensity strategy against Central America were visible in the steady increase of the U.S. military presence, aid, and maneuvers in the region. These indicators did not mean, as some critics charged, that Washington was committed to a "military solution." They did, however, mean that there was a new will to win. In fact, the Reagan administration was now arming itself for a "political solution"—as defined in the uncompromising terms of low-intensity conflict. This solution would be based, as it was for an earlier generation of counterinsurgency theorists, on the recognition that the conflict was between two antagonistic social systems, not between two armies on the battlefield. As Bernard Fall wrote about Vietnam,

> It is important to understand that guerrilla warfare is nothing but a tactical appendage of a far vaster political contest and, that, no matter how expertly it is fought by competent and dedicated professionals, it cannot make up for the absence of a political rationale. A dead Special Forces sergeant is not spontaneously replaced by his own social environment. A dead revolutionary usually is.

U.S. strategists, therefore, would not expect to win by outfighting the enemy in battle. Instead, they would aim to separate the enemy from the civilian population, and neutralize enemy social structures—whether embryonic ones in FMLN zones of control, or the more institutionalized kind in revolutionary Nicaragua. The essential counterpart would be to hold the insurgent forces at bay while the United States constructed "democratic" regimes and alternative, *counterrevolutionary* institutions—political, economic, and social—for the region.

The low-intensity strategy for Central America was to combine both "active" and "preventive" measures: within each country, the choice would be determined, roughly speaking, by whether an armed in-

329

surgency already existed. The measures adopted in each country, whether active or preventive, were in turn designed to bear on the overall thrust of U.S. strategy at the regional level. At the same time, low-intensity strategists hoped that the terms of their doctrine, which explicitly favored keeping U.S. troops out of combat, would preempt public opposition to the war.

On the ground, the United States would seek the collapse of insurgent movements or revolutionary governments through a flexible combination of economic sabotage, political attacks, psychological warfare, and military pressure. Military tactics would emphasize the guerrilla nature of the war and would attempt to mirror the integrated politico-military approach of the revolutionaries. The influential low-intensity strategist Sam Sarkesian, arguing against "seeing conflicts through conventional lenses," urged the U.S. military to study its opponents' methods:

> The essence of success for revolutionary and counterrevolutionary systems is primarily contingent upon the commitment and skill of political cadre, political organization and psychological warfare— that is, by people on the ground in face-to-face contact with the indigenous population.

The United States' choice of methods, whether planning counterinsurgency or initiating insurgencies of their own against established governments, would depend not on vague moral constraints against the use of force, but on a careful assessment of the most effective combination of tactics to win particular battles. If the U.S. military has held back, since 1983, from using its full might in Central America, it is not because of any pacifist tendencies. "Frankly," said General Wallace Nutting, former SOUTHCOM commander and head of the U.S. Readiness Force, "all the talk about invading Nicaragua is counterproductive to the long-term coalition we ought to be building in the hemisphere." Victory, under the new strategy envisioned for the region, cannot be military: instead, it will require protracted and patient political struggle.

VI

To me, our most pressing problem is not in the Third World, but here at home in the struggle for the minds of people . . . Propaganda and organizations are not enough. We must have a purpose, and we must integrate the purpose of special operations, psychological operations, shows of military force, economic programs and all the rest. If we lose our own citizens we will not have much going for us anywhere else in the world.

—George Tanham, former president of the
Rand Corporation and counterinsurgency expert

At the heart of current U.S. strategy is the belief that winning low-intensity conflicts means changing the way that people think about the world. The "home front," as the military now sees it, was key to its defeat in Vietnam. In order to avoid a similar disaster, current strategists have focused an extraordinary amount of attention on winning the hearts and minds of their own people.

The Reagan administration has developed certain major themes and buzzwords—among them terrorism and humanitarian aid—designed to alter perceptions of the Central American war. These are part of an effort, on a global level, to redefine the "threat," the enemy, and the battle. As John Kelly, deputy assistant secretary of the U.S. Air Force, explained at a seminar on low-intensity conflict, "I think the most critical special operations mission we have today is to persuade the American people that the communists are out to get us. If we can win this war of ideas, we can win everywhere else."

Winning this war of ideas at home means mobilizing the U.S. public against both communism—the old enemy—and its new junior partner, the Third World. For low-intensity strategists faced with a prolonged war anywhere in the Third World, the task is to recreate the sense of a war-time situation within the United States—the only difference being that the war is not a conventional or declared one. Since the beginning of the first Reagan administration, a new vocabulary—inextricably linked to older anticommunist traditions—has emerged to justify the new forms of U.S. intervention.

When Secretary of State Alexander Haig declared in 1981 that "terrorism will replace human rights as the cornerstone of our foreign policy," he was laying the groundwork for "special operations" on a massive scale. The theme of terrorism has become a subtext in all discussions of U.S. foreign policy.

Ironically, even alarmists like Neil Livingstone, an ultraconservative "terrorism expert," admit that terrorist incidents have actually *declined* since the 1960s. Yet the issue has become a media staple, a topic for analysis in sensationalist headlines and sober university forums alike. The "war against terrorism" has given birth to an entire cottage industry of right-wing experts, many of them with direct access to administration policy making, who provide the intellectual rationale for placing public opinion on a war footing.

In this political climate, most U.S. citizens are more aware of—and more threatened by—the specter of terrorism than ever before, though few would be able to define it. "Terrorism" has become a label for virtually all forms of conflict that emanate from the real process of change in the Third World. These conflicts, whatever their true source and character, can be made to represent frightening and irrational forces. While Americans may not be moved by administration insistence that faraway revolutions represent a threat to their national security, terrorism personalizes the threat. And when "counterterrorism" is equated with "counterinsurgency," U.S. involvement in low-intensity conflict may come to appear a matter of self-defense, of immediate concern to ordinary citizens.

The war against terrorism has provided the excuse for advocates of low-intensity conflict to restructure special forces training and equipment programs within the Pentagon. It has helped launch new interagency programs such as the State Department Office for Counter-Terrorism and Planning, which in turn directs the Interdepartmental Group on Terrorism, made up of State, the National Security Council, the Drug Enforcement Administration (DEA), the FBI, CIA, and others. It has prompted proposals for legislation that would allow the attorney general to designate certain countries or organizations of its choice as "terrorist," and would allow for prosecution of U.S. citizens who support them.

Finally, it is serving to justify a new wave of counterinsurgency training of Third World police and military forces. In 1984, the Anti-Terrorism Assistance Program set up training programs with Central American governments; the administration is now arguing for an expanded Regional Counterterrorism Program to aid Central American police. Members of Congress who are hesitant to endorse aid to military dictatorships or repeal long-standing bans on U.S. police aid, are more willing to take a stand against "terrorism."

At a 1983 symposium on low-intensity conflict, J. Michael Kelly, assistant air force secretary, summed up the elements being discussed. He said,

> We have basically two tools with which to wage war: a carrot and a stick. The carrot is what is described under the rubric of civil affairs and economic assistance . . . the stick has been discussed at considerable length. . . . intelligence should tell us whether to apply the carrot or the stick. Psychological operations, ranging from public affairs on the one end, through black propaganda on the other end, is the advertising and marketing of our product.

The most powerful mechanism for making civilians the target of low-intensity operations is also the most difficult to understand as "warfare," and, like the issue of terrorism, has been a major theme in administration propaganda. It involves using food, clothing, and medical supplies to bolster U.S.-backed military forces on the ground, while publicly portraying such assistance as politically neutral "humanitarian" aid. Simultaneously, it uses material aid "relief" projects to manage the civilian population, under the guise of providing charitable assistance to needy refugees.

Humanitarian aid is now a familiar part of the Central American landscape, crucial to Washington both for its propaganda value and as a concrete means of advancing U.S. objectives. The most obvious example is the current program of assistance to the contras and their families in Honduras, which has virtually doubled the amount of direct aid to the contras annually. The Reagan administration has marketed the program—and most of Congress has endorsed it—as a compromise between a total cutoff of U.S. funding to the contras and continued support for military assistance channeled through the CIA.

In the context of a low-intensity conflict, however, the distinction between "military" and "nonmilitary" aid is totally superfluous. As the contras readily acknowledge, food, clothing, and medicine are as vital to their forces as guns and ammunition. These supplies provide direct logistical support to the civilian rearguard that sustains the contra army. Furthermore, if the contras hope to expand their political influence inside Nicaragua, they will need nonmilitary supplies to hand out to potential civilian sympathizers in situations where the carrot is seen as more effective than the stick. None of this means any appreciable lessening of U.S. command and control, since intelligence sharing between the CIA and the contras is specifically authorized as a form of humanitarian assistance. Even if Congress continues to deny explicitly military aid to the administration, "humanitarian assistance" allows it to make the contra war effective on the ground and more politically sustainable over time.

Under a similar program, the Pentagon has been supplying the Salvadoran army with food, medicine, and other "humanitarian" aid supplies for use in civic action projects in government-controlled rural areas. The administration has channeled this assistance through the U.S. military sales and grants program; AID provides additional resources for similar projects. The two aid channels are designed to be complementary. Pentagon resources are for "tactical civic action," permitting the army to gain a foothold in conflictive areas where civilian agencies cannot operate; AID funds are for "strategic civic action"—larger projects such as school and hospital construction, which require a degree of prior military control.

Humanitarian aid in Central America is inseparable from larger military purposes. Indeed, economic aid is often the more potent weapon. In effect, there is no more distinction between economic and military assistance than between M-1 and M-16 rifles; though the two weapons have different tactical functions, their end purpose is the same. "Humanitarian aid in a low-intensity conflict is as defense-oriented as the providing of training and technology," army lieutenant colonel James Taylor reminds his conventionally minded colleagues. "It is in no way soft."

Low-intensity conflict planners consider all aspects of social life as war fronts, with the population falling into three categories: it is either insurgent, a rearguard for insurgents, or in dispute—and thus a "target" to be won. As Douglas Blaufarb said of the aid and refugee programs he ran in Southeast Asia, they are "the civilian front of an unconventional war, which could not have been prosecuted without the aid program."

But the concept of humanitarian aid has also been a vital theme in the propaganda battle at home, and has had remarkable success in Congress. By posing false polarities between military aid and "nonlethal" economic and humanitarian assistance, the Reagan administration pretends that "war" uses only traditional weapons. It portrays its actions on the ground as a peaceful relief operation, and the real war as charity.

Army secretary John Marsh recognized both the psychological and the practical implications of private sector involvement in the war effort. "The twilight battlefield of low-intensity conflict," he said,

> . . . is an enormous area in which private sector resources can be used. We must find a way to incorporate into a grand strategy *the total resources of our society*. We live in a nation that has been the global pioneer in industrial development, marketing, advertising and communications. Now we must harness these resources in a common security endeavor.

In some instances, such as the expanded private component of "humanitarian" aid and development projects, religious and corporate involvement may have a significant economic impact. In others, marginal and "populist" right-wing groups like the Alabama-based Civilian Military Assistance and mercenaries from *Soldier of Fortune* magazine and other groups help divert attention from the more substantial direct involvement of U.S. forces. Citizen involvement is reinforced by the growing role of the National Guard in Central America and serves a long-range purpose for low-intensity strategists. Speaking at the American Enterprise Institute, Colonel John Waghelstein offered a graphic argument for new ways of enlisting civilian sympathies:

> I think we've also got to begin to do counterinsurgency training here in the U.S., not just on the military reservations where it's been for the last few years, but out in the countryside. We did it in the '60s and '70s in South Carolina in civilian areas, and I think we should start to do it again with U.S. units. . . . It's a good idea, it gets the populace familiar with this type of warfare.

Waghelstein went on,

> We should be able to set up two opposing teams, and have one of them be able to go in and recruit the preacher to their side, and recruit the editor of the local paper to their side. They should be able to capture the town without firing a single shot, so that when the other side comes in and the commander tries to talk to the people, he can't even get a glass of cold water. We've got to recondition our populace again, so that a soldier practicing for a war, for this type of war, is seen as a regular and necessary thing.

VII

For better or worse, American citizens are participants in the low-intensity war that is being played out in Central America. The public's ability to read the indicators of this kind of warfare may have a real effect on the nature, severity, and duration of the conflict. Much clearer analysis is needed of how U.S. military policy is formulated and executed. There is still inadequate research on how foreign policy is conceived, and then altered by its passage through the political bureaucracy of the administration of the day, as well as through the large and entrenched bureaucracies of the military itself, with all its branches and services. Questions of *intent* versus *ability* are key. In the absence of this research, it is difficult to grasp the extent to which any particular strategy is underway.

It is important to remember that advocates of low-intensity conflict are still a minority within the U.S. military establishment. Visionaries who understand the concept as a blueprint for global counterrevolution are even fewer; more common are those who see only a set of tactical innovations or a flashy new name for counterinsurgency. One former intelligence officer, contemptuous of the Pentagon's often faddish interest in the subject, decried the tendency to latch on to terms like "low-intensity conflict" without understanding them. "They'll probably start training their kitchen workers with courses like 'Low-Intensity Food Preparation,'" he said.

Even among those who agree on the principles of low-intensity conflict, there are significant differences over method. Conflicts remain between the range of U.S. institutions and agencies and their counterparts in other countries, as does the problem of translating ideas into practice. The sheer size and complexity of the U.S. apparatus may mean that it cannot effectively "mirror" the politico-military structures of revolutionary warfare. In frustration over the constraints imposed by a democratic society, Sarkesian writes:

> National leaders and the public must understand that low-intensity conflicts do not conform to democratic notions of strategy or tactics. Revolution and counterrevolution develop their own morality and ethics that justify any means to achieve success. Survival is the ultimate morality.

In Central America, Washington's intent to follow a low-intensity strategy is not always clear. Certainly, not every event in the war is a direct outgrowth of deliberate, centrally directed plans. Many apparently "low-intensity" practices are simply the continuation of older forms of political and economic control—what one Latin American economist calls "the maintenance system of imperialism." Low-intensity tactics do not in themselves mean that the overall direction of the war has become more sophisticated, although since 1983 they have reinforced and advanced the overall strategy.

Determining the extent to which a low-intensity strategy is underway means reading a set of indicators that are often confusing and contradictory. On the military front, various elements indicate a low-intensity approach. They include an emphasis on training local forces;

the use of U.S. special forces, National Guard, and reserve units; expanded intelligence and communications systems; offshore U.S. naval support available for mid-intensity levels; assistance from the armed forces and intelligence services of "friendly" third countries such as Israel and Taiwan; and the use of the military to channel economic and development aid to a target country.

In low-intensity conflict, the local armed forces begin to incorporate police and intelligence functions; the military talks more about reform and *much* less about body counts. Military hardware, in general, emphasizes high-tech surveillance and "antiterrorist" equipment. It is important to remember, though, that within the military establishment, the debate over correct tools and tactics for particular situations is very much alive, an integral part of the evolving body of knowledge on low-intensity conflict. Since this approach can also incorporate conventional tactics into its overall framework and respond flexibly on many levels of the intensity spectrum, the study of tactics alone can be misleading.

VIII

A low-intensity framework informs the way the U.S. thinks about using its military power. But, more importantly, it requires looking away from strictly military applications of power and towards the other tools that Washington employs in Third World conflicts. Low-intensity conflict is extreme: it is a science of warfare whose goal of controlling the qualitative aspects of human life merits the term totalitarian.

Campaigns limited to "cleaning up" the violence on a quantitative level do not touch on the fundamentally dirty character of this war. It penetrates into homes, families, the entire fabric of grassroots social relations; there are no "civilians" in a low-intensity conflict. The blurring of the military/civilian distinction means that any one of a number of operations may signify low-intensity conflict in action. The United States may work through its own military and reserves or local surrogate forces; third-country resources or local civilian government structures; the State Department, AID, the CIA, or private relief agencies.

The integrated character of the crisis in the Caribbean Basin raises further serious questions about whether Washington will be able to succeed with its regional strategy. What will be the impact on the thinking of the Salvadoran military on events in neighboring Guatemala, where the process of "nation-building" follows counterinsurgency operations rather than accompanying them? What are the dynamics of conflict between Honduras, chosen by Washington as the support base for its war against Nicaragua, and El Salvador? How can the Reagan administration manage "preventive" nation-building measures in Costa Rica while its "active" measures in support of contras on the Costa Rican/Nicaraguan border destabilize local society? What is the impact on the economic component of the low-intensity model as the Caribbean Basin Initiative fails as a viable example of economic nation-building in Grenada and other island countries? And what will be the larger consequences for conflict in the region of the broader Latin American debt crisis?

The Reagan administration may have learned from earlier U.S. mistakes, to the extent that it has avoided committing combat forces to Central America, and has refined some aspects of counterinsurgency theory. But even if Washington succeeds in implementing a more sophisticated, low-intensity strategy, events on the ground are still determined by many factors beyond U.S. control. The war in Central America cannot be reversed by theory alone, and already it may have progressed so far that it is too late for the United States to roll back the challenge of revolutionary nationalism. If that point has been reached, Washington may be capable of no more than inflicting pain—which, given the available options, may in itself become a goal of the low-intensity strategy.

Along with its redefinition of battlefields, the innovation of low-intensity doctrine has been its frightening redefinition of victory. Even if the United States is unable to win outright, it can try to cause enough physical destruction and political damage over a prolonged period to guarantee that the revolutionaries will not truly "win" either. It can settle for weakening its opponents to such a point that their political goals become unattainable. If their experiments can be aborted, the United States will be able to claim at least a partial victory.

The current low-intensity conflict in Central America is, as Morelli and Ferguson write, "neither simple nor short-term," and it remains to be seen whose side time is on. That unknown will be resolved in part by the impact of the war at home and the course of events within the United States.

IX

Opposition to administration policy embraces many different constituencies attempting to affect public and congressional opinion. They include the peace movement, anti-intervention and solidarity activists, sectors of the churches and the human rights community—a "movement" that is unified neither in its analysis nor its program of action. The impact of this opposition has been felt on some important levels: the human rights lobby and religious groups, for example, have altered some of the terms of the debate over Central America. At the same time, Congress has largely fallen in step behind the "compromise" option of low-intensity conflict offered by the administration. It is a difficult moment to plan a strategy for opposing the war in Central America.

One major risk is that opponents may organize to stop the wrong war—a rerun of Vietnam. For that is not what the U.S. military is fighting today, and the Reagan administration is quite sincere when it says it wants "no more Vietnams" in Central America. (Though it can be argued that Nicaragua could become "another Vietnam" in a different sense—

like today's Vietnam, ten years after its victory, still suffering from economic warfare, destabilizing contra operations on its borders, a political/diplomatic blockade, environmental destruction, and the grinding devastation of seemingly endless low-level conflict.)

In any case, a narrow focus on *conventional* military indicators can often misinterpret the course of a low-intensity conflict and make it hard to see the real war. This in turn makes it dangerously easy for the low-intensity strategists to appropriate the language of their opponents.

Without a context for their work, opponents of the war risk confusing tactics—or demands that apply to a specific moment—with principles. It is possible, for example, for Washington to "stop the bombing," or to claim it is providing "humanitarian aid." But these changes in tactics do not necessarily imply any shift in U.S. goals. Low-intensity conflict addresses every facet of policy and incorporates a wide range of means, few of which will be strictly military. Most, in fact, will attempt to *avoid* high levels of violence. It is much harder to oppose U.S. efforts to control Third World societies if they involve nonmilitary tactics, or forms of warfare that claim to promote economic development.

ECONOMIC AID NOT MILITARY AID
POLITICAL SOLUTIONS NOT MILITARY SOLUTIONS
TALKS NOT TROOPS

Many of these major themes started life as the slogans of peace activists; but they also express the principles by which U.S. low-intensity conflict strategists hope to win the war. They first emerged as valid responses to specific issues at particular moments. But the shift in the nature of the war challenges the peace movement to reexamine its assumptions, as the administration adopts the language of its opponents in an attempt to still their fears and seize the moral high ground.

Much of the U.S. public, and many Central Americans, maintain faith in genuine negotiations and political solutions to conflict. For the Reagan administration, however, negotiations are not an alternative to the war: they are simply another front in it. "The objective of negotiations is to protect our national security and our national interests," explains Lieutenant General Gordon Sumner:

> We are not going to negotiate away any of our interests in this area or those of our friends in Central America. We are not going to negotiate away political power in El Salvador. We are not going to accept the brutal communist regime in Nicaragua.

Calls for "talks not troops" fail to come to grips with the total, unconventional war now being fought in Central America. Instead, they lead to a false dichotomy between invasion and negotiations, at a time when Washington's real war has escalated in a manner designed precisely to avoid *both* talks and troops, both "giving in" and "going in." The new doctrine of war in the Third World challenges conventional opposition responses as well as conventional military wisdom. To frame the issues of war and peace as a contest between talks and troops can permit the United States to present its true strategy of low-intensity conflict as a moderate alternative, and allow the *real* war to be sold to the American public as a "third option," a compromise between the extremes of invasion or surrender.

RECOMMENDED READING

Frank Barnett, ed., *Special Operations in US Strategy*. Washington, D.C.: National Defense University Press, 1984.

Robert Taber, *War of the Flea*. Citadel Press, 1969.

Joaquin Villalobos, *The War in El Salvador*. San Francisco: Solidarity Publications, 1986.

Los Norteamericanos y Centroamerica

Quetzalina Yali is a four-year-old bundle of brown curls and laughter. Undaunted by the small fact that I cannot understand a word she is saying, she chatters away in Spanish, the language brought to her country four hundred years ago by the conquistadors. Pulling small pieces of cotton from a piñata made up to look like a rabbit, she pretends to fashion a beard and mustache for herself, but can't get the cotton to stay in place. I show her how to lick the cotton lightly, moistening it, so that it will stick wherever she wants it. Delighted with this new discovery, she plants a wad of cotton on the tip of my nose, then makes a goatee for herself.

We are on our way to San Jose de los Remates, a village of several thousand people in the mountains about ninety kilometers northeast of Managua, Nicaragua. Quetzalina's father, Flavio Galo, 28, is driving the Toyota Land Cruiser. Beside him are his wife, Carmen, 26, and Reverend David Funkhouser, 41, an Episcopal minister who is director of the Central America Organizing Project (CAOP), a community action group working out of West Philadelphia, Pennsylvania. David, a close friend of the Galos, has been to Nicaragua eight times since the 1979 revolution, and it is he who has arranged our trip. With Quetzalina and me in the back is Peter Morgan, 30, a freelance photographer.

The two-lane macadam road passes by a large Cuban-built sugar refinery, then skirts the edge of a brand new dam and reservoir guarded by Nicaraguan soldiers against potential terrorist attack by the U.S.-backed "contras," whom many Nicaraguans call "mercenaries." At the village of Teustepe, we leave the paved road and the flat plain around Managua, and head up into the mountains on a rough, one-lane dirt track heavily rutted by erosion. Five times our vehicles must ford streams because there are no bridges, and our progress is further impeded by regular encounters with small herds of cattle plodding along the road, each herd tended by a man or boy on horseback.

The bumpy, twisting dirt road between Teustepe and San Jose was built by the people of this region in 1974 with nothing more sophisticated than picks and shovels, ox-carts and mules. Prior to that time, a road connecting San Jose to the capital city and the government of Nicaragua simply did not exist. Once a day now, in the early morning, a bus leaves San Jose for the four-hour drive to Managua, returning late in the afternoon.

Peter offers a stick of gum to Quetzalina. Without hesitating, she takes the gum, tears it in half, and thrusts a piece over the front seat into her mother's mouth. Carmen Galo was raised in San Jose. During the revolution, she was a member of the "retroguard," building barricades, gathering information, and carrying intelligence and supplies to the Sandinista fighters. After "the triumph of the revolution," as she calls it, she became a Brigadista—a volunteer member of the Literacy Crusade. While working in the countryside, she met Flavio, who was then serving two years in the regular army. They were married in 1980, and Quetzalina arrived two years later.

Soon after we turn onto the dirt road, Quetzalina—whose name means "Queen of Birds"—curls up in my lap and falls asleep, impervious to the violent jostling we are being subjected to by the crude road surface. Her middle name, Yali, is the name of a town near which a close friend of Flavio and Carmen was killed fighting the contras. One of Flavio's brothers was also killed by contras while harvesting coffee in 1981. Neither Flavio nor Carmen have any doubts about the path their country has set itself upon: they feel they are building a future for their daughter.

Flavio's mother, Norma Galo, still lives in the Parish of San Pablo in Nicarao, a working-class barrio of Managua where Flavio and his brothers grew up. In 1966, when Flavio was eight, Norma and some other concerned adults organized a Base Christian Community with the help of the parish priest and a Maryknoll nun from the United States (one of four American women who would be raped and murdered by members of the Salvadoran army fourteen years later). Norma and the others wanted to do something to combat illiteracy, drug addiction among young people, and the general sense of hopelessness that pervaded the barrio.

"At first, the young people didn't want anything to do with Christianity," Norma told our group. "'Somoza and the bishops are the same thing,' they said. But we developed a program that finally got them interested." Listening to the young people's suggestions, they devised new rules for worship to make the mass less distant and alien: no cassocks for the priest, no kneeling during communion, face-to-face confession, and the mass said in Spanish rather than Latin. Soon, the active members of the parish, adults and young people alike, were involved in teaching others to read and write, and in attempting to bring minimal public health standards to the barrio.

By 1969, the parish had developed a popular peasant mass that included songs by the renowned Nicaraguan priest and poet Ernesto Cardinal (now minister of culture in the Sandinista government). Much of the mass was critical of the U.S.-backed Somoza dictatorship and the church hierarchy, Norma explained, taking the side of the peasants and the poor. "We had always been taught that poverty and suffering were virtues that would be rewarded in heaven," said Norma, "but we began to understand that the Kingdom of God must begin here on earth."

Taking advantage of their new-found literacy, for the first time the parishioners began to read the Bible for themselves. "We learned from the Bible that what God wants most is justice," said Norma. "It was not possible to separate religious consciousness from political consciousness. We began to study our own history. We began to see that Somoza and his generals had gotten rich from the suffering of our people, and that the exploitation of the poor went back all the way to colonial times. And we learned that the young people had been right all along: the church hierarchy has always acted in support of the status quo, reinforcing the system as it is."

Thus, it came as no surprise, Norma continued, when the church hierarchy and the Somoza regime together cracked down on the Base Christian Communities. The church forbade the peasant mass, and Somoza banned all "political activities," including efforts to improve literacy and public health. Still, the peasant mass was said in San Pablo, and the political organizing continued. "At times, I wondered if I was crazy to take such risks," Norma said, "but we couldn't do anything else. The repression was intolerable. We had to take risks because Jesus took risks."

In such an atmosphere, Flavio grew up. By this time, Norma explained, the Sandinista National Liberation Front (FSLN) was actively fighting Somoza's hated National Guard in the mountains. "We began to see that they were the only real possibility for change," she said. "They were fighting for justice, and so were we Christians." In 1972, Flavio, at fourteen already an accomplished guitarist, helped to found GRADAS, the first cultural-political organization of the FSLN. He was joined by the singer and composer Carlos Mejia Godoy and the young poet Rosario Murillo, who would later marry Daniel Ortega, now president of Nicaragua.

Together the members of GRADAS would sing their songs in parks and factories, on street corners and vacant lots, coupling their overt activities with covert political organizing. In 1974, Flavio was arrested and imprisoned by Somoza. In 1976, Godoy and Murillo went into foreign exile. Then in 1978, Flavio was arrested again, this time for organizing a strike of public workers. He was tortured continuously for fifteen days in a dark one-person cubicle in La Chiquita Prison. After his release, he finally took up arms, eventually becoming the leader of a 250-person guerrilla unit operating in and around Managua.

By this time, the resistance movement had erupted into mass insurrection, and Somoza's days were numbered. "Your president claims that Cuba and the Soviet Union helped us," Norma scoffed, "but that is not true. They gave us nothing. We made our own weapons." Norma made Molotov cocktails. Flavio's ten-year-old brother made contact mines. "Our fighters attacked the National Guard with these homemade weapons," she explained, "then they would capture the M-16s of the Guardsmen. Every time I was brought more captured weapons to hide, I would get down on my knees and thank God.

"I am a Catholic and a Christian," Norma said emphatically, "and I don't care what your president says—or the Pope, either. The revolution is an affirmation of our Christian faith because we are able to do things now that we were never able to do before. We didn't learn that from Marx and Lenin. We learned it from the Bible. The church is us. We have to fight for a better world. We don't want a new church. We want our own church to be reborn. All we ask is that the bishops, for the first time in history, walk by the side of the poor."

Not everyone, of course, perceives the Sandinista revolution as a Christian endeavor. During last spring's heated debate over the $100 million contra aid bill—which finally passed the House of Representatives by the slimmest of margins only weeks before our July 14, 1986, departure— Ronald Reagan said that the Sandinistas ought to be pushed "right back to Havana where they belong." The archbishops of Boston and New York have castigated the Nicaraguan government for its "attempts to violate the religious conscience of Nicaraguans." And a poster from the National Democratic Front (FDN), the largest of the U.S.-backed counterrevolutionary groups waging war against the Sandinistas, contains a portrait of a smiling Jesus, together with the words: "Christ is our liberator."

In fact, were one to take at face value the pronouncements of those who oppose the Sandinista government, one could only conclude that Nicaragua today is little more than a Third World version of the Soviet Union. Having lived through a combat tour as a marine volunteer in Vietnam, however, I have long since grown wary of bureaucrats and politicians who would have me believe that the world, or any part thereof, can be neatly divided into "freedom fighters" and "terrorists"—the freedom fighters, of course, always being on our side. After all, it is my tax dollars the contras are spending, and my own child may one day be asked or even ordered to fight in Nicaragua. And so I made up my mind to see Nicaragua for myself.

That, as it turns out, is surprisingly easy to do—at least for now. One need only hook up with any number of U.S.-based organizations like David Funkhouser's CAOP, plunk your money down (about $1,200 for a two-week trip), get on the airplane and go. For our trip, travel arrangements were made by a commercial travel agency in New York City in much the same manner as any tourist trip to England or the Bahamas. The Nicaraguan government issues tourist visas at the airport in Managua, and for now the U.S. government has been unable or politically unwilling to stop what has become a constant flow of U.S. citizens into Nicaragua, though it must surely be a major irritant for the Reagan administration.

Our two-week trip did not begin in Nicaragua, however, but rather in Honduras where, since the early 1980s, the U.S. has maintained a military presence fluctuating between 1,100 and over 5,000 soldiers. For three days, in the capital city of Tegucigalpa, at the U.S. base at Palmerola, and in the nearby town of Comayagua, we met with everyone from parish priests to peasant labor leaders, U.S. military personnel to opposition newspaper editors.

At the U.S. embassy in Tegucigalpa, we were told that the fifteen U.S. Marine guards assigned to the embassy are responsible only for internal security. External security, including the policy that no photographs may be taken of or near the embassy grounds, is entirely the responsibility of the Hondurans.

Only moments later, as we drove away from the embassy, I made the mistake of absentmindedly taking my camera from its pouch. Immediately, whistles began to blow all over the street, and we were flagged down by a Honduran security officer toting a shotgun. He thought I'd taken a picture and wanted to confiscate my camera. Two more armed officers arrived as I got out of the van, then two more. It was a tense situation. I was surrounded by five men armed with pistols, shotguns, and M-16s, but I refused to hand over my camera.

Finally, the Hondurans insisted that I accompany them back to the embassy. They took me straight to the U.S. Marine guard inside the front door, a junior enlisted man. "I give you my word as an ex-marine," I told the sentry, lifting my sleeve to reveal my USMC tattoo, "I did not take any photographs." With a single affirmative nod, the young corporal settled the matter like Solomon sitting in judgment, instantly countermanding the Honduran security officers supposedly responsible for external security.

At the embassy, we were told that Palmerola is a Honduran air force base, and that the approximately 1,000 U.S. military personnel stationed there were only "tenants." With its tin and plywood barracks, sandbagged bunkers, and rolls of coiled concertina wire, Palmerola, located sixty kilometers northeast of Tegucigalpa, looks very much like a typical U.S. battalion base camp in the earlier stages of the Vietnam War—and indeed, it turns out that Palmerola was built by the U.S. "for Honduras" with U.S. funds.

"We have no contact whatsoever with the contras," a regular U.S. Army lieutenant colonel stationed in Palmerola told us. "Furthermore, we are not allowed to train Honduran troops. We only engage in joint exercises with the Hondurans. We learn from each other." He went on to describe for us the various activities of U.S. personnel: medical and civic action programs, road building and other construction projects, signal intelligence. What he described sounded curiously like the strategy in Vietnam that was variously called "Rural Pacification," "Revolutionary Development," and "Winning Hearts and Minds," though he called it "low-intensity warfare." Who this low-intensity warfare is directed against is hard to determine since the only guerrilla forces currently operating in Honduras are the U.S.-supported Nicaraguan contras.

Later, a major in the Kansas National Guard assigned to Palmerola for thirty days explained enthusiastically that Honduras is a perfect place to train U.S. reserve forces "under realistic conditions." When I expressed my concern about deploying so many U.S. troops in an area of such international tension, the major replied that it may well be an attempt by the Reagan administration to create its own "Gulf of Tonkin incident." The analogy was the major's, not mine.

Dr. Jorge Arturo Reina is a leading politician in the progressive faction of the Honduran Liberal Party. He has presidential aspirations. "Because every Central American dictator has always called himself democratic," he told us, "people don't really know what democracy is. Democracy doesn't mean voting one day and dying of hunger the next. Democracy doesn't mean voting one day and losing your job the next. Democracy means voting one day so that your life will be better the next.

"This is not and never has been the case in Honduras," he continued. "Seventy-eight percent of our children are malnourished. Functional illiteracy is higher than 62 percent. The unemployment rate is 34 percent, with another 40 percent underemployed. The majority of our people live and die without ever turning on an electric light or using indoor plumbing or seeing a doctor or dentist or teacher. We don't want a revolution like Nicaragua or a war like El Salvador, but our problems must be addressed.

"U.S. aid to Honduras is a mirage," he insisted. "You saw the airport in Tegucigalpa. It is totally inadequate. The U.S. has built nine new airports in Honduras, but none of them is for the Hondurans. The U.S. says it is building roads for us, but the roads only connect one military base to another. There is no U.S. policy for Honduras except to use Honduras as a base of operations to achieve U.S. aims in Nicaragua and El Salvador, while the problems of Honduras only continue to get worse.

"Mr. Reagan's policy is like an elephant in a China closet chasing a rat. It creates greater problems than those it tries to resolve. Aid to the contras will not defeat the Sandinistas, but only radicalize them. And now the contras have more money than we do! Their presence in our country has created twelve thousand internal Honduran refugees who have been forced to flee contra-held territory in Honduras. Mr. Reagan's policy is leading Honduras closer and closer to war. God blinds those who do not love."

The Honduran political headquarters of the Nicaraguan contra group

FDN is located in a comfortable villa on the outskirts of Tegucigalpa. There, we met with Francisco Arana, director of central communications, and four of the FDN's eighteen regional field commanders. Most of the talking was done by Arana, a huge man who is a former banker, and Commandante Fernando, a former theological student who looked to be in his late twenties or early thirties. Two of the commandantes said nothing at all during the interview, but only sat motionless and glaring; it seemed to me that they did not like us very much.

"We wanted democracy and freedom," said Arana, "but the Sandinistas betrayed us."

I asked if it was true that the contras are really the remnants of Somoza's old National Guard. "We don't refuse anyone just because he was once a National Guardsman or a Sandinista," said Commandante Fernando, a member of the fundamentalist United Pentecostal Mission. "Those who have National Guard connections fight now for love of God and the liberation of Nicaragua. The FDN represents the true democratic aspirations of the Nicaraguan people, but the Sandinista propaganda machine has painted the opposite picture."

What about alleged atrocities committed by the contras against Honduran civilians? I asked. "That isn't possible," Arana replied. "All of the fighting is taking place inside Nicaragua. There are no permanent contra bases in Honduras. Honduran communists are committing these atrocities, and the FDN gets the blame. Believe me, the Sandinistas are financing all of the Honduran groups you've been talking with while you've been here."

David then asked about contra terrorist attacks within Nicaragua, citing the July 4, 1986, destruction of a civilian truck by a contact mine that killed thirty-four people, mostly women and children. "I see you are already one of the convinced," Arana replied with a shrug.

"You are a victim of propaganda," added Commandante Fernando. "The civilian dead are killed by the Sandinistas, not the FDN, but the Sandinistas lie. The Sandinistas dress up like the FDN, then commit these atrocities themselves."

What about the U.S. Government Accounting Office (GAO) report indicating that much of the aid already sent to the contras has been siphoned off without ever reaching the field? "That is Sandinista disinformation," Arana replied.

"You mean the GAO compiled its report from information received from the Sandinistas?" I asked incredulously.

"Our leaders are always with us," Commandante Fernando replied vehemently. "Even without material aid, God's love and our love for Nicaragua keep us going forward. We and the people of Nicaragua hope for the support of the government and the people of the United States. To compare Somoza with the Sandinistas, Sómoza would be an angel. The Sandinistas are Marxists, and Marxists are atheists. The Sandinistas are enemies of God. With God and patriotism, we will defeat communism and liberate Nicaragua, Central America, and the United States."

As we left the FDN villa with its beautiful rosebushes and manicured lawn, I happened to glance up at the hill behind the FDN compound. Perched precariously atop the hill and on its steep slopes were several dozen tin and cardboard squatters' shacks belonging to the poor of Honduras.

Roberto Flores Bermudez is director of foreign policy affairs for the Honduran Foreign Ministry. U.S. military activities in Honduras are beneficial, he explained, because they provide the Honduran army with equipment and training which will better enable Honduras to defend its territory and sovereignty—this despite the fact that U.S. officials at both the embassy and Palmerola told us explicitly that U.S. personnel are forbidden to train Honduran troops.

"Isn't it true," I asked, "that the Hondurans' traditional enemy is El Salvador?" (As recently as 1969, Honduras and El Salvador fought a brief but bloody war.) "How do you feel about the tremendous buildup of the Salvadoran army by the Reagan administration?"

"The internal situation in El Salvador requires it," he replied tersely.

"Doesn't the U.S. military presence in Honduras violate the Honduran constitution?" I asked.

"The U.S. presence is only temporary," he replied, echoing the assertions of U.S. officials.

"But we've been here for four years already. What would you call a permanent presence?"

"I wouldn't call Palmerola 'permanent,'" Bermudez responded. "It's only made of wood and tin."

"You mean, if it were made of concrete and steel, it would be permanent," I replied, "but since it's only wood and tin, it's temporary?"

Bermudez paused, smiling awkwardly: "Yes." As we left, I shook his hand and wished him and his country luck. "Thank you," he said quietly, "I think we will need it."

Given that U.S. embassy personnel in Honduras have told us that the Sandinistas wish to export communism and subversion to Honduras, it seems odd that Tan Sahsa, the Honduran airline, still maintains regular flights between Tegucigalpa and Managua. The young man who sat next to me is a medical doctor from Mexico. This was his third trip to Nicaragua since 1981, and he would be staying to work as a general practitioner for several months. "Why is Mr. Reagan so full of hate for these people?" he asked me. As the airplane touched down at Sandino Airport, he quietly said to himself, *"Nicaragua libre."*

The scene inside the airport was one of quiet pandemonium. It was two days before the seventh anniversary of the July 19, 1979 revolution, and the terminal was packed with incoming arrivals: Canadians, Swedes, Finns, French, Germans, Swiss, Israelis, and Americans—whom Latin Americans call *Norteamericanos.* ("We live in America, too," I was told by Maria Antonia de Alvarado of the Honduran Federation of Women's

347

Associations.) Because of the influx of people for the anniversary, security was especially tight, and our progress through customs was not helped by the grinding bureaucracy the Sandinistas have created. Every "t" had to be crossed, every "i" dotted on the visa applications. Bags had to be inspected. Names had to be checked and rechecked. But at last we cleared customs and headed into Managua.

The billboards in Nicaragua are not what I'd expected. Yes, there are the obligatory signs extolling the virtues of patriotism, the revolution, and the Sandinistas. But there are also billboards urging people to support one or another of the various opposition parties, along with advertisements for Pepsi and Coca-Cola, Ciba-Geigy products, local restaurants, and discotheques. Political graffiti of every stripe is everywhere, and there is even a McDonald's where one can buy a Big Mac and fried plantain cut to look like French fried potatoes.

Downtown Managua, however, is an eerie place. The capital was devastated by an earthquake in 1972, and the heart of the city was never rebuilt. Only the towering Bank of America building survived the quake, and now it looms up alone and forlorn amid overgrown vacant lots and the few remaining empty shells of other buildings, many inhabited by poor squatters. After the earthquake, the Somoza dictatorship received millions of dollars in international relief assistance. Instead of rebuilding the city, Somoza pocketed most of those funds.

Meals, we learned quickly, are always an adventure. On any given day, some restaurants haven't enough food to remain open. Others can offer only three or four entrees. In one restaurant, we are told that there is no fish or beef, but we may have chicken or pork. We order chicken. A half-hour later, we are told that there is no more chicken, but some fresh fish has just arrived. Food shortages are chronic, and tracking down one's favorite beverage—be it beer, orange soda, or Coke—can be a haphazard and frustrating affair.

On July 19, well before dawn, we joined a bus caravan from Managua to the northern city of Esteli for the commemoration of the seventh anniversary. Every intersection along the 150-kilometer route, every bridge and culvert was guarded by soldiers, and as the sun rose I could see other soldiers patrolling the high ground above the road. Clearly, great effort had been taken to see that the contras would not disrupt the ceremony. As we neared Esteli, two Soviet-built helicopter gunships darted low among the hills.

Later that night, I was having a beer at the hotel bar in Pochomil when a middle-aged Nicaraguan approached me. "Thank you for coming to Nicaragua," he said in English. "I love the U.S. I love the North American people. We don't want war. We want to be friends." His name, he told me, is Santos, and he explained that he left Nicaragua in the early 1960s to escape Somoza's repression. He has lived in San Francisco for twenty-three years, and since the revolution has worked as a Tur-Nica representative in the U.S. (Tur-Nica is the Nicaraguan state tourist agency.) As we talked further, we were joined by his friend, Ricardo. Their families have known each other since before Santos left Nicaragua.

"Are you a Sandinista, too?" I asked Ricardo, who manages a gas station.

"No!" he replied emphatically. "The Sandinistas have sold Nicaragua to the Cubans and the Russians. Things were better under Somoza. You could get anything then. Now everyone lives like shit."

"And you two guys are friends?" I asked Santos.

"Oh, sure!" Santos replied with a grin. "I don't agree with him, but he has his point of view, and it's important for you to hear it. In the United States, Reagan says that Nicaragua is totalitarian, but listen to Ricardo. He tells you what he thinks. Is that totalitarian? People should come to Nicaragua and see for themselves."

Sergio Murillo is a tractor driver on a private coffee farm in Carazo, a region between the Pacific coast and Managua. He earns 750 *cordobas* (about $.63) for an eight-hour shift, he told us during an impromptu interview amid rows of coffee plants, but if he wants to, he can work up to twelve shifts per week with doubletime on Sunday. Wages are set by the state. The owner of the hacienda spends most of his time in Miami, Sergio told us, but after the revolution he gave each worker a small piece of land for a family plot. Sergio built his own house on his plot, where he lives with his wife and two children.

Sergio belongs to the Sandinista Workers Confederation, a union which grew out of the revolution. He likes the union because it gives the workers clout with their employers, and because the union commissary offers clothing and other goods at reduced prices. "Our biggest problem is food distribution and rationing," he said. "Each person receives only four pounds of rice per month, which is not enough. Because of the war in the north"—the contra war—"many good farming areas can't be cultivated, and our fighters must have first priority on the food that's available. If there were a more peaceful dialogue between Nicaragua and the United States, everyone would benefit. Surely, there are hungry people in your country, too. This war is foolish."

Niquinohomo, just up the road from the coffee farm, is the town in which Augusto Cezar Sandino was born and lived. Sandino, namesake of the Sandinistas, is the greatest of all Nicaraguan heroes. His modest house is now a museum, but we arrived on Sunday afternoon, the house was locked, and no one seemed to know who had the key, so we had to settle for a stroll through the courtyard.

Being an ex-marine, I have a healthy respect for this carpenter's son who managed to fight the U.S. Marine Corps to a draw. The marines have a long history of involvement in Nicaragua, dating back almost to the turn of the century, including maintaining a permanent garrison there from 1912 to 1926 and again from 1927 to 1934. During those years, the marines ruled Nicaragua as an occupied country, acting to protect the interests of U.S. businesses. In 1935, the great Marine Corps general,

Smedley Butler, two-time winner of the Congressional Medal of Honor, wrote candidly and with evident regret of helping to "purify Nicaragua" for the international banking industry, and described himself as "a high class muscle man for Big Business, for Wall Street, and for the bankers—a racketeer for capitalism."

It is an aspect of U.S. history that most Nicaraguans know more about than do most Americans. Beginning in 1927, Sandino waged a guerrilla war against the marines that ended seven years later only when the United States agreed to withdraw the marines. In their place, however, the U.S. government created, trained, and equipped the Nicaraguan National Guard, which was placed under the command of a man named Anastasio Somoza Garcia.

Meanwhile, after the departure of the marines, Sandino emerged from the hills and reentered Nicaragua's political mainstream. Then one night in 1934, members of the National Guard kidnapped Sandino, took him out to the airport, and executed him. Shortly thereafter, Somoza used the National Guard to become dictator of Nicaragua. He and his two sons in succession ruled the country as a virtual family fiefdom for forty-three years, and not until the eleventh hour—when the Sandinista army was about to take Managua—did the U.S. finally withdraw its support from the Somoza dictatorship.

Companera Mercedes, 25, works in the Nicaraguan prison system for the Ministry of the Interior. She holds a degree in education science from the Autonomous National University of Nicaragua. She joined the Sandinistas in 1973, at age fourteen, and spent the next few years robbing banks to raise money for the revolution and doing clandestine political organizing in the poor barrios. During the revolution, she was an armed fighter. Her nineteen-year-old brother is now a militia lieutenant fighting "the mercenaries" in the north, and she has not seen him in over a year.

"I believe a majority of North Americans do not support Reagan's policies," she told me. "I urge them to work to change those policies before it is too late. We do not want war, but we will not give up what we have won. If the marines come again, they will die." I asked her about the Cuban and Soviet presence in Nicaragua. "The help they provide is help Nicaragua has not been able to get from any other country. Reagan has seen to that. He is waging war against us. We have a right to defend ourselves."

Later the same day, we stopped by a cluster of rundown shacks made of wood, cardboard, and tin. A dozen women and small children quickly clustered around us, eager to tell their stories. The land their crude houses stand on was given to them by the government after the revolution, and they receive what amounts to welfare as well, one woman explained, "but it was better before the revolution; things didn't cost so much."

"It doesn't matter what kind of government you have," added an older woman, "so long as you can eat. Now we can't make any money. We can't sell what we want. The government sets the prices and requires permits for everything. People come to Nicaragua and say how beautiful things are. Tell them we are hungry."

I asked them why they were willing to speak so freely. "This hungry child is what makes me speak out," said the first woman. "They may drag me around by the hair, but I don't care. *El hambre es mas hombre que un hombre* [Hunger is more of a man than any man]."

As the women talked, a sixteen-year-old girl with an infant suckling at her breast stood shyly off to one side. She was wearing a cheap bracelet with a pendant likeness of Lenin dangling from it. "Who is that man?" I asked her.

She fingered the pendant for a moment. "I don't know," she replied.

The barrio of Monimbo in the town of Masaya is the place where the final insurrection against Somoza began. The church in the center of town is still heavily pockmarked with bullet holes, and not far from the church is an eloquent statue of a human figure frozen in the act of hurling a paving stone. Paving stones, called *adoquinas,* are a symbol of the revolution.

Many of the roads and streets in Nicaragua are paved with *adoquinas.* After the 1972 earthquake, Somoza decreed that the roads be rebuilt with *adoquinas.* Somoza happened to own the only factory that manufactured *adoquinas.* Seven years later, the people of Nicaragua tore up the streets and built barricades with Somoza's *adoquinas,* from behind which the Sandinista fighters stopped the armored cars of Somoza's National Guard.

Down the street from the scarred church, Peter and I stopped in a small shop to buy some chewing gum. "How much?" Peter asked the teenaged girl who was minding the store.

"Four hundred *cordobas.*"

"That's expensive," said Peter.

"It's not expensive in dollars," she replied with a smile.

Don Alejandro is the local Sandinista representative and leader of a farming cooperative in San Juan de la Concepcion. He joined the FSLN in 1982, after his son was killed fighting the contras. He is a friend of the Galo family. To reach his house, a one-room structure made of rough planks, tin, and tile with a separate cooking shed, we had to drive many kilometers on a narrow dirt road, then walk another three kilometers on a dirt track impassable except for the sturdiest of off-road vehicles.

The land worked by the members of the co-op, Don Alejandro explained, used to belong to large landowners. Much of it went uncultivated while the peasants, working as wage laborers, went hungry. "Our priest told us that God will give us the answer, not the revolution," he said, "but our God is in the countryside. That's where we'll solve the problems. The only people here who are still hungry are those who are not willing to take the land and work it."

Each family in the co-op works its own piece of land, he explained,

351

though the members pool their resources for such things as fertilizer and marketing. As we shared a meal of corn pudding, meat, tortillas, and plantain, he explained that the co-op produces coffee, cotton, corn, pineapples, avocados, bananas, rice, mangos, oranges, and pitahaya. The co-op's biggest problems are the lack of tractors, and road-building and roofing materials.

"Some people think the mercenaries will come and solve all their problems for them," he continued. "They think government price controls are responsible for the food shortages. Here we just work all that much harder, even though our young men have to be away fighting in the north. With hard work, we will defeat those who are trying to undo the revolution. You know who is causing the war in the north, don't you?"

Miguel Vijil, a civil engineer with a degree from Catholic University in Washington, D.C., comes from an old and wealthy family. He used to earn a great deal of money in the petrochemical industry, he told us, but his Catholic beliefs made him uncomfortable about the poverty and suffering he saw all around him. He began doing religious charity work on a case by case basis, but soon came to the conclusion that the only real solution was a total reform of the system—a revolution. Now he is minister of housing and human settlement in the Nicaraguan government.

"There is little we can do for the squatters here in Managua," he told us. "The countryside must have priority because we don't have the resources to do everything at once. It is not really a problem of urban development, but rather the result of economic distortion endemic to all Central America. You saw Tegucigalpa; it is the same thing there. The way to solve the problem of urban squatters is to rebuild the rural areas, make it desirable for people to return to the land. We lack coffee workers in the countryside while thousands go unemployed here in Managua.

"Before the contra war began," he continued, "my ministry received 5 percent of the national budget. Now we receive only 2 percent. Yes, we receive aid from the Soviet Union, but that does not make Nicaragua a Soviet stooge. We are a poor country, and we need help. The United States has closed the door on us. Where else can be turn? Mr. Reagan is like the girl who won't dance with a certain boy, then gets angry when the boy dances with another girl."

"But surely the Soviets expect something in return for their aid," I pointed out.

"It is one thing what the Soviets expect in return," he laughed. "It's another thing what Nicaragua will do. Look, we are fighting for our survival. In the history of the world, there has never been a revolution without a counterrevolution. Look at your own revolution. One-third of all the people living in the American colonies left after your revolution; many were forcibly expelled. In Nicaragua, there *were* people who were comfortable under the old regime, and they are not going to be happy when changes are made, but they are a minority. Look at South Africa: if change comes there—and the whole world seems to think that it should—4 million people will be unhappy. But the 20 million oppressed have their rights, too. Of course, it is easy to understand South Africa because of the color of people's skin.

"Our only defense is the facts," he concluded, "but the propaganda process in the U.S. is highly professional. Whether our side gets heard in the U.S. media is out of our hands. I don't want a U.S. invasion. Many people will suffer. It is more than my love for Nicaragua and its people. It's my own self-interest that is speaking. I have six children. I want my family to live. We don't ask anything from the United States except to be left alone. That would be enough. It would be a dream come true."

At last we arrive in San Jose de los Remates where we will spend our last night. Peter and I will be staying with Mariano and Rosa Malespin. We are given a small room with two small cots, temporarily evicting ten-year-old Alberto and his eight-year-old cousin Eduardo. Mariano's father will sleep on the table in the front room, beneath a framed picture of Cyndi Lauper. The other seven members of the household will sleep in the main bedroom. Peter and I go out to explore the town.

The Malespins live at the edge of the grassy town plaza across from the Catholic church. Up the street is the local militia headquarters. Chickens, pigs, dogs, and cows wander through the narrow, rocky, unpaved streets amid houses made of mud and stone. Men on horseback dressed like cowboys ride by. Except for the dim streetlights on most corners, a black-and-white television se here and there, the town looks like something out of the nineteenth century.

Rigoberto Lopez is a cattle rancher, and rather well-to-do by San Jose's standards. He explains that most of the people in the region make their living as cattle ranchers or ranch hands, coffee growers, and small farmers. "San Jose," he tells us, "is the end of the line. It's the town everybody forgot. We were ignored by the Somoza regime, and we're ignored by the Sandinistas. It's been that way since time began.

"But you have to understand," he adds, "we don't have any big problems here, only little ones. Of course, we need more attention, but we're like St. Thomas: we'll believe it when we see it."

"Should the U.S. support the contras?" I ask.

Rigoberto thinks for a long time, slumping down in his chair, his arms crossed and his legs extended in front of him. "Well," he says at last, "I don't believe any country should stick its nose into another country's business."

Peter and I wander off in search of a beer. We've had a hard ride to San Jose, and we've both been dreaming about cold beer. Unfortunately, there doesn't seem to be a single beer left unopened in the whole town. At last, we find what passes for the local saloon—a room, attached to a private home, that contains two tables, half a dozen chairs, a radio blaring popular music in Spanish and English, and a framed poster of Elvis Presley. Three young men are seated at one of the tables drinking a bottle of rum, and they invite us to join them.

They are a farm worker, a teacher, and a dairy milker: 22, 20, and 16 respectively. All three say they are Sandinistas. Almost every young man in Nicaragua is eventually drafted, and we soon discover that the farm worker has just been released from his two-year stint. He spent most of those two years fighting the contras in the north. The fighting is very heavy, he tells us; six of his friends were killed there. As he talks, his eyes fill with tears.

"Presidente Reagan es muy loco," says the teacher, patting his friend on the back. Then he points to their sixteen-year-old companion. "He doesn't want to fight," he says with a laugh. "He's afraid he'll be killed."

"What about you?" I ask. "Will you go if you're called up?"

"Yes, I will go," the teacher replies. "I expect to be called any day now."

"Aren't you afraid of dying?"

"It doesn't matter if I die," he says. "Only the revolution matters."

Earlier in the afternoon, I had watched Quetzalina playing in the town plaza with a dozen of her San Jose friends, but by now she is fast asleep in her grandparents' house. It is late, and Flavio, Peter, David, and I are listening to the music of Flavio's friend, Carlos Godoy, on a record player at Rigoberto's. Tomorrow we will head down out of the mountains and return to the United States.

Over twenty years ago, a U.S. president told Americans that if we did not stop the communists in Vietnam, we'd have to fight them on the sands of Waikiki, and I believed him. Things didn't turn out quite the way most people expected, but the hotels along the beach in Honolulu seem to be doing fine just the same. Now we are being told by another U.S. president that if we don't stop the communists in Nicaragua, we'll have to fight them in the streets of Brownsville, Texas. As I sip rum and listen to the music, I find it hard to believe that the most powerful nation the world has ever known has much to fear from a poverty-stricken agrarian nation with a total population less than that of the city of Philadelphia. It is far easier to imagine that I might have something to fear from a government that tries to persuade me that we do.

"David tells me that you and your wife are expecting a child," says Flavio, interrupting my thoughts.

"Yes," I reply, "in December."

"You must be very happy."

"I'm happy, yes. But I'm also frightened. Your little Queen of Birds is a beautiful child. I hope that my child will never be sent to Nicaragua to wage war against her."

"Thank you, my friend," Flavio replies, "I hope that, too."

RECOMMENDED READING

Dee Brown, *Bury My Heart at Wounded Knee.* New York: Holt, Rinehart & Winston, 1971.

David Haward Bain, Sitting in Darkness. New York: Houghton Mifflin, 1984.

Michael Maclear, *The Ten Thousand Day War.* New York: St. Martin's Press, 1981.

Jonathan Kwitney, *Endless Enemies.* Harmondsworth: Penguin Books, 1985.

Walter LaFeber, *Inevitable Revolutions.* New York: W.W. Norton & Co., 1984.

In order as they appear, the books deal with the following:
  the U.S. war with Native Americans, 1854-1890;
  the U.S. war against the Philippines, 1900-1903;
  the Vietnam war for independence, 1946-1975;
  U.S. international economic policies since about 1960;
  the U.S. and Central America since about 1960.

MARILYN B. YOUNG

Teaching the War

I have been teaching about Vietnam for as long as I have been teaching. I began in 1969 in a basement room at the Residential College, University of Michigan and I continue now in a large-ish lecture hall at New York University. Someone born the year I taught that first seminar might now be in a class on the same subject. But differently. Then, the students and I lived together in a world made by that war. And it felt as if it would never end. The year was marked by the need to organize buses for Washington protest marches, solicit defense funds for jailed students, plan campus rallies. An analysis of the war meant having to analyze the ways in which the university participated not merely in the war but in creating the society which fought such wars. Fasting against the university's complicity in weapons research was fairly easy; trying to change the university so that it would better serve the needs of the society we hoped to create was quite another. We experimented with opening our classes to anyone in Ann Arbor who wanted to attend—no fees (but no credit either); we invited community leaders to join us in teaching classes (but no health benefits); we demonstrated (successfully) for increased black enrollment; joined graduate students in striking for collective bargaining rights; gave academic credit to students who *wrote up* their Venceremos Brigade experiences; and, after a while, began to meet those Vietnam veterans who cycled back into the educational system.

A significant minority of my students dropped out of school to attempt a more ambitious approach to ending the Vietnam War and bringing social justice not just to the University of Michigan but to the country as a whole. Unless there was a revolution here, in the belly of the beast, they argued, Vietnam would just happen again elsewhere, endlessly. By making revolution in America, they would let freedom ring everywhere. For a very small group this meant armed struggle in the ranks of a Third World vanguard. For a larger group it meant joining Detroit's industrial proletariat for the long hard struggle to raise consciousness—their own as well as their fellow workers.

And then the war was over and, to our surprise, so was the life of collective protest. Those people we had deemed literally guilty of war crimes—the Bundy brothers, Rostow, MacNamara, Kissinger, and all their underlings—went on to live and be well, which wasn't a surprise exactly but left some of us feeling empty and depressed. Like Gloria Emerson, I found it hard to celebrate in April 1975. I wanted vengeance.

Instead, Carter declared that the United States and Vietnam had suffered about equally and the effort to revise the history of the war began immediately after it was over. If, in Nazi Germany, the universal claim after the war was "I didn't know," in America it was going to be "that's not the way it happened." A German colleague and I began to teach a course on the Holocaust and the Vietnam War in an effort to understand the process of forgetting, or of remembering so as to forget. At times we felt like atrocity-mongers, punishing our class, and ourselves, with the sheer weight of past terribleness. At its best, the anger and energy of the course would be poured into current political protest. Sometimes, facing a student's stunned response to the course, we found ourselves trying to persuade them not to take it all *too* seriously. One earnest young man, of uncompromising integrity, quit school rather than remain in ROTC, which had been paying his way through Michigan. Efforts to get him to think about how to rip off the army were unavailing.

And all the time the war got longer ago and common points of memory harder to find. Even more, my students and I no longer shared very much. I had grown so much older than they—instead of babysitters for my children (as had occasionally happened in Michigan) these students were actually younger than mine. Last year the oldest students in my class had two vivid memories—people being airlifted off the American embassy in Saigon as the war ended and their own participation in the New York Vietnam Veterans Memorial March. Although I might still get a Vietnam veteran in class, returning late to school, more frequently I had the sons and daughters, nieces and nephews of veterans or antiwar protestors. At first I did not understand what this shift meant. I taught my Vietnam course as I always had, starting with the history of Vietnamese resistance to French colonialism, most effectively organized by the Indochinese Communist Party. A brief dip into the extraordinary life of Ho Chi Minh, a mostly doomed effort to sort out the complexities of joint Japanese and Vichy French rule, and then we were on our way, home so to speak, from U.S. funding of the French colonial war against the Viet Minh through the landing of the first marines at Danang. I braced myself for the anticipated response: guilt, confusion, anger, sorrow. This time, though, something new happened. One group of students, perhaps 15 percent of the class, protested—not exactly in defense of the war, but certainly in opposition to its condemnation. Frustrated and angry, they insisted that I had it all wrong, that it was my biased approach and not the war itself that explained how bad they felt after each class, for America had meant well in Vietnam, and had lost because of the peace movement and/or congressional betrayal and/or the misfortune of Watergate. Almost triumphantly they concluded that the current sorry state of Vietnam was abundant proof that the U.S. had been right all along. Animating their arguments was their sorrow and pity for Vietnam veterans. The vets had been spit at when they returned (the implication clear that it was people like me who had done the spitting); My Lai and the like were either aberrations or readily explicable by the fact that the Vietcong tied explosives around children and then blew them up in the face of GIs offering candy. Those who fought in Vietnam had been courageous and honorable; what the Vietnam War was *about* for these students was the mistreatment of veterans upon their return. When a veteran visited the class and bitterly denounced the war, this group of students dismissed his testimony.

Perhaps another 15 percent of the class suffered a kind of generation lag. They "missed" the sixties, in both senses of the word just as I, growing up, felt I had missed the thirties. They identified completely with the veterans of the antiwar movement and their sympathy for Vietnam War veterans was limited and abstract. Neither group had any sense of the complicated history of the relationship between soldiers and protestors, of the sanctuary movement, the GI coffeehouses, and antiwar newspapers.

Most of the students shifted uneasily between these two groups, trying to mediate when people got too angry, certain that the point was for us all to agree, deeply unhappy about the lines being drawn between different groups in the class. More significant, perhaps, was that they were all simply unused to having anything that happened in class *matter*. Whenever feelings ran very strong, the "mediators" would move forward in a phalanx, desperately trying to restore amity and detachment. But they didn't succeed because the issues did matter so very much. Occasionally there would be surprising defections. One man, who had stubbornly defended the decisions of each succeeding American administration in Vietnam, suddenly raised his hand in the midst of a passionate discussion of the morality of U.S. search-and-destroy tactics. He spoke softly, as much to himself as to the class. Search-and-destroy, he said, was wrong. More, it was wrong not because some other tactic would have been better but because in a war like Vietnam, it was the only *possible* tactic, which meant that the war *itself* was wrong. And if the war was wrong, then so was much of the way he had put America together in his head.

Some questions my students and I ask together, questions that simply did not arise in the same way (or at all) during the war itself. How to understand the nature of heroism in a bad cause? How is it that so many fled the revolution in power, including many who had helped to bring it to power? What principle of explanation can compass Pol Pot?

Some questions remain mostly mine, which students come to, if they do, in their own time. Can a family, a country, a class of undergraduates, look steadily in the face of 58,947 meaningless American deaths without fleeing for some sort of cover? Something, anything to hide the nakedness, to cover the shame with purpose or meaning, a piece of the flag, a shred of Benevolent Intentions. In the old days, during the war itself, students adamantly demanded to know *why* we were in Vietnam. It was very frustrating, for U.S. policy seemed to me peculiarly resistant to explanation. The means were simply incommensurable to any conceivable end. Unable to explain it rationally, I sometimes read to classes from Robert Bly's poetry to try to make the dark power of his vision a part of their understanding, as it was of mine. "We make war," Bly wrote, "like a man anointing himself." And I would read aloud from his anti-imperialist epic, "The Teeth Mother Naked At Last," as if saying penance. But this too was worrisome: one can get hooked on darkness and even come to admire if not like it. In 1969 one student thanked me for my excellent course on American imperialism: I had no idea we were so powerful, so mighty, he said with a broad smile. Still, less internal, daylight explanations could not then hold the truth of Vietnam.

These days I offer daylight explanations with far more confidence. Indeed, I insist on them: the war grew out of the necessities of maintaining a global capitalist system, of the daily specifics of decision making, of the requirements—individual and national—for "credibility" as defined by men who played zero sum games against a demonized communist Other. And for *these* reasons so many died. I have come to realize that the problem with my older notions of America the Dark, the Violent, the Satanic is that it implies its opposite, America the Light, the Good. This dichotomy is currently the favored organizing structure for literary and cultural critics of the war and appears in every major film on the war from the documentary *Hearts and Minds* (where high school football is the metaphor for America the Violent) to *Platoon* (where Light and Darkness are apportioned a sergeant each). There is much talk of the American Adam (the absence of Eve never noticed—was there an American Eve, or did she come from the Old Country?), the innocence lost never to be recovered. It is important to note that the idea of innocence operates in conservative as well as liberal recountings of the war. Guenther Lewy's *American in Vietnam*, the very first revisionist history, was explicitly dedicated to the task of recuperating the reputation of America the Good for a generation of young Americans who were under the impression that their country had committed war crimes in Indochina. More recently, a book in opposition to the war insists that "Americà must be for freedom, for dignity, for genuine democracy, or it is not America. It was not Amer-

359

ica in Vietnam. It runs the risk of forgetting how to be America." And a book on *The American Myth and the Legacy of Vietnam* concludes that however bad the war, America must not "draw back from the American frontier, from our own better dreams. . . . Perhaps from the landscape of our Vietnam failure we can find a new determination to brave the opening expanses." In each case America becomes reified, transhistorical, transcendental. Collectively innocent or collectively guilty, America still occupies the center of the world story, as omnipotent in its evil (or violence) as in its innocence (or benevolence).*

Ironically, my largest teaching task is actually an ancient Confucian one, as important to Vietnamese as to Chinese culture—the rectification of names, the proper naming of the world. I must try to get students to see naming as a problem. To see, for example, that while Kennedy and others may have named their behavior in Vietnam to themselves as necessary and benevolent in its intentions, the responsibility of students is to analyze how a culture can call the subversion of the Vietnamese revolution by the name of charity. I want to ponder with them the proper name for the moral reasoning of our representatives in Congress. Senator Daniel Inouye, for example, voting on military aid to El Salvador a few years ago, decided to support a compromise figure of $62 million, down $30 million from an original Reagan request: "You can kill less people with $62 million than with $92 million," he reflected. And to get them to question the ordinary naming they've learned in high school, I have to persuade them to an anterior query—about the Edenic world in which the American Adam roamed *before* Vietnam, littered as it was by apples he had already consumed (the overthrow of Mossadegh and Arbenz for example) or, alternatively, spit out before it was too late (China, Cuba).

The hardest thing to teach these days was a relatively easy task during the war. Then, with whatever misguided passion, students did not wonder why people would choose to make revolution, nor even that they might choose to dedicate themselves to a revolution led by communists. For my students, however, events in Indochina since 1978, combined with having spent their high school years entirely within the Reagan presidency, has made communism and communists totally remote and alien. Like so many of the recent books on the war, these students see the majority of Vietnamese (or Filippinos or Salvadorans or Guatemalans) as passive peasants anxious only to till their fields in peace whoever is in power. They find it extremely difficult to grant either agency or humanity to those who join communist-led or inspired revolutionary movements. This attitude is perfectly reflected in the words of an American mercenary

---

*Loren Baritz, *Backfire: A History of How American Culture Led Us Into Vietnam and Made Us Fight the Way We Did* (New York: William Morrow and Co., 1985), p. 341. John Hellman, *The American Myth and the Legacy of Vietnam* (New York: Columbia University Press, 1986).

fighting with the contras in Nicaragua who appeared in a recent TV documentary. "We're not down here fighting Nicaraguans," he insisted, "we're fighting the communists." In the press, among my students, and often my colleagues as well, communists appear as a race apart, members of some suprastate, bearers of an entirely separate culture. They appear in countries as widely distant from each other as the Philippines and Nicaragua and they may even take on the shape and guise of Filippinos or Nicaraguans, but this is misleading. By virtue of their ideology they deracinate themselves. You wouldn't want to be killing Nicaraguans, God knows, but killing communists is something else altogether.

Many days it feels like 1960 again. Advisors going into Central America, occasionally dying there: the lessons learned from Vietnam as wrongheaded as they are precise. Thus the *New York Times* reports that Army Reserve and National Guard troops are working on a major military road in Honduras that will facilitate matters if "Americans were sent to Honduras to fight the Sandinistas . . ." Why the guard and the reserve? The Reagan administration "seems to be trying to avoid what many military officers say was a mistake in Vietnam in the mid-1960s. Because President Johnson did not call up the reserves and guard, they argue, the public was not alerted early that the conflict was serious." The problem Reagan and the military face, however, is that much of the public is indeed alert. The governors of Maine, Massachusetts, Arizona, California, Washington, New Mexico, Vermont, and Nebraska are opposed to this use of the National Guard, and the governor of Minnesota has brought suit against the federal government. And when the state is caught lying—an almost daily event these days—there are people to point to its growing nose. This is essential, else one day we shall read not in Reagan's speeches but in some liberal rendering of America's goals in Central America that they were, in intention, benevolent, that through ignorance of a foreign culture, the wrong people were chosen as the instruments of that benevolence, that it was all most regrettable, but the damage, after all, was mutual and the crusade, on balance, noble.

During the war, and for a long time after, a rageful obsession with it was a sort of debt many of us felt we owed the Americans and Vietnamese who needlessly were killed and maimed there. Like a fetish, as I reflect on it now, our anger seemed protective, annealing. The Germans, appropriately, have a word for what we did in the period since the war, "trauerarbeit": the work of mourning. In the years I have been teaching the history of the Vietnam War, I have been, unconsciously or semiconsciously, doing that work. But in what Carl Oglesby once called "the ice age of imperialism," the work of mourning must be, as well, the ongoing work of protest.

RECOMMENDED READING

Gloria Emerson, *Winners and Losers: Battles, Retreats, Gains, Losses and Ruins from a Long War*. New York: Random House, 1976.

Seymour Hersh, *The Price of Power: Kissinger in the Nixon White House*. New York: Summit Books, 1983.

George McT. Kahin, *Intervention: How America Became Involved in Vietnam*. New York: Knopf, 1986.

David G. Marr, *Vietnamese Tradition on Trial: 1920-1945*. Berkeley: University of California Press, 1981.

Jonathan Schell, *The Military Half* and *The Village of Ben Suc* (soon to be reissued as a single volume with a new introduction by Pantheon Books).

After Our War

After our war, the dismembered bits
—all those pierced eyes, ear slivers, jaw splinters,
gouged lips, odd tibias, skin flaps, and toes—
came squinting, wobbling, jabbering back.
The genitals, of course, were the most bizarre,
inching along roads like glowworms and slugs.
The living wanted them back but good as new.
The dead, of course, had no use for them.
And the ghosts, the tens of thousands of abandoned souls
who had appeared like swamp fog in the city streets,
on the evening altars, and on doorsills of cratered homes,
also had no use for the scraps and bits
because, in their opinion, they looked good without them.
Since all things naturally return to their source,
these snags and tatters arrived, with immigrant uncertainty,
in the United States. It was almost home.
So, now one can sometimes see a friend or a famous man talking
with an extra pair of lips glued and yammering on his cheek,
and this is why handshakes are often unpleasant,
why it is better, sometimes, not to look another in the eye,
why, at your daughter's breast thickens a hard keloidal scar.
After the war, with such Cheshire cats grinning in our trees,
will the ancient tales still tell us new truths?
Will the myriad world surrender new metaphor?
After our war, how will love speak?

For Mrs. Cam, Whose Name Means "Printed Silk"

The ancients liked to write of natural beauty.

—Ho Chi Minh, "On Reading
The Ten Thousand Poets"

In Vietnam, poets brushed on printed silk
those poems about clouds, mountains, and love.
But now their poems are cased in steel.

You lived beyond the Pass of Clouds
along the Perfume River, in Hué,
whose name means "lily."

The war has blown away your past.
No poem can call it back.
How does one start over?

You raise your kids in southern California;
run a key punch from 9:00 to 5:00,
and walk the beach each evening,

marveling at curls broken bare in crushed shells,
at the sheen and cracks of laved, salted wood,
at the pearling blues of rock-stuck mussels

all broken, all beautiful, accidents
which remind you of your life, lost friends
and pieces of poems which made you whole.

In tidal pools, the pipers wade
on twiggy legs, stabbing for starfish
with scissoring, poking, needle bills.

The wide Pacific flares in sunset.
Somewhere over there was once your home.
You study the things which start from scratch.

Nicely like a pearl is a poem
begun with an accidental speck
from the ocean of the actual.

A grain, a grit, which once admitted
irritates the mantle of thought
and coats itself in lacquers of the mind.

Thoughts Before Dawn

For Mary Bui Thi Khuy, 1944-1969

The bare oaks rock and snowcrust tumbles down
while squirrels snug down in windy nests
swaying under stars above the frozen earth.
The creaking eave woke me, thinking of you
crushed by a truck thirteen years ago
when the drunk ARVN lost the wheel.

We brought to better care the nearly lost,
the boy burned by white phosphorus, chin
glued to his chest; the scalped girl;
the triple amputee from the road-mined bus;
the kid without a jaw; the one with no nose.
You never wept in front of them, but waited
until the gurney rolled them into surgery.
I guess that's what amazed me most.
Why didn't you fall apart or quit?

Once, we flew two patched kids home,
getting in by Army chopper,
a Huey Black Cat that skimmed the sea.
When the gunner opened up on a whale
you closed your eyes and covered your ears
and your small body shook in your silk ao dai.

Oh, Mary. In this arctic night, awake in my bed
I rehearse your smile, bright white teeth,
the funny way you rode your Honda 50, perched
so straight, silky hair bunned up in a brim hat,
front brim blown back, and dark glasses.
Brave woman, I hope you never saw the truck.

News Update

For Erhart, Gitelson, Flynn, and Stone,
happily dead and gone

Well, here I am in the *Centre Daily Times*
back to back with the page one refugees
fleeing the crossfire, pirates, starvation.
Familiar faces. We followed them
through defoliated forests, cratered fields,
past the blasted water buffalo,
the shredded tree lines, the human head
dropped on the dusty road, eyes open,
the dusty road which called you all to death.

One skims the memory like a moviola
editing out the candid shots: Sean Flynn
dropping his camera and grabbing a gun
to muster the charge and retake the hill.
"That boy," the black corporal said,
"do in real life what his daddy do in movies."
Dana Stone, in an odd moment of mercy,
sneaking off from Green Beret assassins
to the boy they left for dead in the jungle.
Afraid of the pistol's report, Stone shut his eyes
and collapsed the kid's throat with a bayonet.
Or, Erhart, sitting on his motorcycle

368

smiling and stoned in the Free Strike Zone
as he filmed the ammo explosion at Lai Khe.
It wasn't just a macho game. Marie-Laure de Decker
photographed the man aflame on the public lawn.
She wept and shook and cranked her Pentax
until a cop smashed it to the street. Then
there was the girl returned from captivity
with a steel comb fashioned from a melted-down tank,
or some such cliché, and engraved: "To Sandra
From the People's Fifth Battalion, Best Wishes."

Christ, most of them are long dead. Tim Page
wobbles around with a steel plate in his head.
Gitelson roamed the Delta in cut-away blue jeans
like a hippy Johnny Appleseed with a burlap sack
full of seeds and mimeographed tips for farmers
until we pulled him from the canal. His brains
leaked on my hands and knee. Or me, yours truly,
agape in the Burn Ward in Danang, a quonset hut,
a half a garbage can that smelled like Burger King,
listening to whimpers and nitrate fizzing on flesh
in a silence that simmered like a fly in a wound.

And here I am, ten years later,
written up in a local small town press
for popping a loud-mouth punk in the choppers.
Oh, big sighs. Windy sighs. And ghostly laughter.

Speak, Memory

1. THE BOOK AND THE LACQUERED BOX

So the Seal, that Drop, that Ray
Of the clear Fountain of Eternal Day,
Could it within the humane flow'r be seen.

—Andrew Marvell, "On a Drop of Dew"

The ink-specked sheets feel like cigar leaf;
its crackling spine flutters up a mildewed mast.
Unlike the lacquered box which dry-warp detonated
—shattering pearled poet, moon, and willow pond—
the book survived to beg us both go back
to the Bibliothèque in the Musée at the Jardin in Saigon,
where I would lean from ledges of high windows
to see the zoo's pond, isled with Chinese pavilion,
arched bridge where kids fed popcorn to gulping carp,
and shaded benches, where whores fanned their make-up,
at ease because a man who feeds the peacocks
can't be that much of a beast. A boatride,
a soda, a stroll through the flower beds.
On weekends the crowds could forget the war.
At night police tortured men in the bear pits,
one night a man held out the bag of his own guts,

which streamed and weighed in his open hands,
and offered them to a bear. Nearby, that night,
the moon was caught in willows by the pond,
shone scattered in droplets on the flat lotus pads,
each bead bright like the dew in Marvell's rose.

2. *THE OPIUM PILLOW*

A cool ceramic block, a brick
just larger than one's cheek,
cream-colored, bordered in blue.
a finely cracked glaze, but smooth,
a hollow bolster on which one lays
his face before it disappears
in curl of acrid opium fumes
slowly turning in the tropical room
lit by a lampwick's resinous light
which flickers on the floor and throws
shadows snaking up a wall.
The man who serves us with his pipes,
with nicotined and practiced hands,
works a heated wad of rosin
"cooked the color of a cockroach wing"
into the pinprick of the fat pipebowl.
He says, "Draw." One long draw
that pulls in combers of smoke rolling
down the lungs like the South China Sea,
crashing on the mind's frail shell
that rattles, then wallows and fills with sand.

I woke on wobbly legs to human cries.
Next door were Flynn and Stone
shouting and beating up an older man
they collared trying to steal their bikes.
Smith banged an M-16 against the fellow's ear
then struck him in the stomach with its butt.
He doubled up and wheezed for air;
they slammed him out and down the stairs
and, red and sweating, walked back in.
I stammered "no" but much too late;
my words were lifting up like bubbles
rocking off the ocean's floor.

Ten days later, they were dead. Flynn
and Stone, who dealt in clarities of force,
who motorcycled out to report war,
shot down together. Dead on Highway One.

Ten years now. Their only headrest,
this pillow of dreams and calmest sleep,
which once held echoes like a shell,
now sit upon my study shelf,
and ebbs out muffled echoes like a bell.

3. PRINCE BUU-HOI'S WATCH

A long story. Of love and perfidy
ticking away in an old Omega
with a cracked crystal and a dusty face,
which the Prince's English friend gave me
just after his heart attack and early death.
We sat in her home in the Villa Ségur.
"It's awful having it in the house," she said.
Above the mantle from which she took the watch
was a photograph of her taken years before
in sundress and shady hat, in Saigon,
with the Prince and Diem and Henry Cabot Lodge,
all cordial in their tropical white suits.
Lodge was smiling with tall, paternal grace
at the pudgy little man, earnest with good will,
whom we liked to call "the Churchill of Asia."
Diem would die the next day. Lodge already knew.
And Patricia and Prince Buu-Hoi, Minister of Health
and nearly the fixer of a separate peace, would flee
with sympathies from the French Ambassador.
One listens to the watch and sunlight shifts
as shadows shake through threshing palms,
through banyan and great sprays of Bougainvillea.
The time that it keeps best is past.

4. THE PERFUME VIAL

Its smooth shape fits easily in the palm
as one takes it from the shelf to see
the little mandarin with outstretched arms,
cap, queue, and courtly gown.
One simple question strikes me as I look:
The doves which flutter just above his hands
—are they flying to or from them?

In Celebration of Spring

Our Asian war is over; others have begun.
Our elders, who tried to mortgage lies,
are disgraced, or dead, and already
the brokers are picking their pockets
for the keys and the credit cards.

In delta swamp in a united Vietnam,
a Marine with a bullfrog for a face,
rots in equatorial heat. An eel
slides through the cage of his bared ribs.
At night, on the old battlefields, ghosts,
like patches of fog, lurk into villages
to maunder on doorsills of cratered homes,
while all across the U.S.A.
the wounded walk about and wonder where to go.

And today, in the simmer of lyric sunlight,
the chrysalis pulses in its mushy cocoon,
under the bark on a gnarled root of an elm.
In the brilliant creek, a minnow flashes
delirious with gnats. The turtle's heart
quickens its taps in the warm bank sludge.
As she chases a frisbee spinning in sunlight,
a girl's breasts bounce full and strong;
a boy's stomach, as he turns, is flat and strong.

Swear by the locust, by dragonflies on ferns,
by the minnow's flash, the tremble of a breast,
by the new earth spongy under our feet:
that as we grow old, we will not grow evil,
that although our garden seeps with sewage,
and our elders think it's up for auction—swear
by this dazzle that does not wish to leave us—
that we will be keepers of a garden, nonetheless.

For the Record

The clouds and the stars didn't wage this war
the brooks gave no information
if the mountain spewed stones of fire into the river
it was not taking sides
the raindrop faintly swaying under the leaf
had no political opinions

and if here or there a house
filled with backed-up raw sewage
or poisoned those who lived there
with slow fumes, over years
the houses were not at war
nor did the tinned-up buildings

intend to refuse shelter
to homeless old women and roaming children
they had no policy to keep them roaming
or dying, no, the cities were not the problem
the bridges were non-partisan
the freeways burned, but not with hatred

Even the miles of barbed wire
stretched around crouching temporary huts
designed to keep the unwanted
at a safe distance, out of sight

even the boards that had to absorb
year upon year, so many human sounds

so many depths of vomit, tears
slow-soaking blood
had not offered themselves for this
The trees didn't volunteer to be cut into boards
nor the thorns for tearing flesh
Look around at all of it

and ask whose signature
is stamped on the orders, traced
in the corner of the building plans
Ask where the illiterate, big-bellied
women were, the drunks and crazies,
the ones you fear most of all: ask where you were.

1983

North American Time

I
When my dreams showed signs
of becoming
politically correct
no unruly images
escaping beyond borders
when walking in the street I found my
themes cut out for me
knew what I would not report
for fear of enemies' usage
then I began to wonder

II
Everything we write
will be used against us
or against those we love.
These are the terms,
take them or leave them.
Poetry never stood a chance
of standing outside history.
One line typed twenty years ago
can be blazed on a wall in spraypaint
to glorify art as detachment
or torture of those we
did not love but also
did not want to kill

We move   but our words stand
become responsible
for more than we intended

and this is verbal privilege

III

Try sitting at a typewriter
one calm summer evening
at a table by a window
in the country, try pretending
your time does not exist
that you are simply you
that the imagination simply strays
like a great moth, unintentional
try telling yourself
you are not accountable
to the life of your tribe
the breath of your planet

IV

It doesn't matter what you think.
Words are found responsible
all you can do is choose them
or choose
to remain silent.   Or, you never had a choice,
which is why the words that do stand
are responsible

and this is verbal privilege

V

Suppose you want to write
of a woman braiding
another woman's hair—
straight down, or with beads and shells
in three-strand plaits or corn-rows—
you had better know the thickness
the length   the pattern
why she decides to braid her hair
how it is done to her
what country it happens in
what else happens in that country

You have to know these things

VI

Poet, sister: words—
whether we like it or not—
stand in a time of their own.
No use protesting   *I wrote that*
before Kollontai was exiled
Rosa Luxemburg, Malcolm,
Anna Mae Aquash, murdered,

before Treblinka, Birkenau,
Hiroshima, before Sharpville,
Biafra, Bangladesh, Boston,
Atlanta, Soweto, Beirut, Assam
—those faces, names of places
sheared from the almanac
of North American time

VII

I am thinking this in a country
where words are stolen out of mouths
as bread is stolen out of mouths
where poets don't go to jail
for being poets, but for being
dark-skinned, female, poor.
I am writing this in a time
when anything we write
can be used against those we love
where the context is never given
though we try to explain, over and over
For the sake of poetry at least
I need to know these things

VIII

Sometimes, gliding at night
in a plane over New York City
I have felt like some messenger
called to enter, called to engage
this field of light and darkness.
A grandiose idea, born of flying.
But underneath the grandiose idea
is the thought that what I must engage
after the plane has raged onto the tarmac
after climbing my old stairs, sitting down
at my old window
is meant to break my heart and reduce me to silence.

IX

In North America time stumbles on
without moving, only releasing
a certain North American pain.
Julia de Burgos wrote:
That my grandfather was a slave
is my grief;   had he been a master
that would have been my shame.
A poet's words, hung over a door
in North America, in the year

nineteen-eighty-three.
The almost-full moon rises
timelessly speaking of change
out of the Bronx, the Harlem River
the drowned towns of the Quabbin
the pilfered burial mounds
the toxic swamps, the testing-grounds

and I start to speak again

1983

In the Wake of Home

1.
You sleep in a room with bluegreen curtains
posters   a pile of animals on the bed
A woman and a man who love you
and each other   slip the door ajar
you are almost asleep   they crouch in turn
to stroke your hair   you never wake

This happens every night for years.
This never happened.

2.
Your lips   steady   never say
It should have been this way
That's not what you say
You   so carefully not asking, *Why?*
Your eyes   looking straight in mine
remind me of a woman's
auburn hair   my mother's hair
but you never saw that hair

That family coil   so twisted, tight and loose
anyone trying to leave
has to strafe the field
burn the premises down

3.

The home houses
mirages   memory fogs the kitchen panes
the rush-hour traffic outside
has the same old ebb and flow
Out on the darkening block
somebody calls you home
night after night   then never again
Useless for you to know
they tried to do what they could
before they left for good

4.

The voice that used to call you home
has gone off on the wind
beaten into thinnest air
whirling down other streets
or maybe the mouth was burnt to ash
maybe the tongue was torn out
brownlung has stolen the breath
or fear has stolen the breath
maybe under another name
it sings on AM radio:
And if you knew, what would you know?

5.

But you will be drawn to places
where generations lie
side by side with each other:
fathers, mothers and children
in the family prayerbook
or the country burying-ground
You will hack your way through the bush
to the Jodensavanne
where the gravestones are black with mould
You will stare at old family albums
with their smiles   their resemblances
You will want to believe that nobody
wandered off   became strange
no woman dropped her baby and ran
no father took off for the hills
no axe splintered the door
—that once at least it was all in order
and nobody came to grief

382

6.

Anytime you go back
where absence began
the kitchen faucet sticks in a way you know
you have to pull the basement door
in before drawing the bolt
the last porch-step is still loose
the water from the tap
is the old drink of water
Any time you go back
the familiar underpulse
will start its throbbing: *Home, home!*
and the hole torn and patched over
will gape unseen again

7.

Even where love has run thin
the child's soul musters strength
calling on dust-motes   song on the radio
closet-floor of galoshes
stray cat   piles of autumn leaves
whatever comes along
—the rush of purpose to make a life
worth living past abandonment
building the layers up again
over the torn hole   filling in

8.

And what of the stern and faithful aunt
the fierce grandmother   the anxious sister
the good teacher   the one
who stood at the crossing when you had to cross
the woman hired to love you
the skeleton who held out a crust
the breaker of rules   the one
who is neither a man nor a woman   the one
who warmed the liquid vein of life
and day after day whatever the need
handed it on to you?
You who did and had to do
so much for yourself   this was done for you
by someone who did what they could
when others left for good

9.
You imagine an alley   a little kingdom
where the mother-tongue is spoken
a village of shelters   woven
or sewn of hides   in a long-ago way
a shanty standing up
at the edge of sharecropped fields
a tenement where life is seized by the teeth
a farm battened down on snowswept plains
a porch with rubber-plant and glider
on a steep city street
You imagine the people would all be there
fathers mothers and children
the ones you were promised would all be there
eating   arguing   working
trying to get on with life
you imagine this used to be
for everyone   everywhere

10.
What if I told you your home
is this continent of the homeless
of children sold   taken by force
driven from their mothers' land
killed by their mothers to save from capture
—this continent of changed names and mixed-up blood
of languages tabooed
diasporas unrecorded
undocumented refugees
underground railroads   trails of tears
What if I tell you your home
is this planet of warworn children
women and children standing in line or milling
endlessly calling each others' names
What if I tell you, you are not different
it's the family albums that lie
—will any of this comfort you
and how should this comfort you?

11.
The child's soul carries on
in the wake of home
building a complicated house
a tree-house without a tree
finding places for everything
the song   the stray cat   the skeleton
The child's soul musters strength
where the holes were torn
but there are no miracles:
even children become exhausted
And how shall they comfort each other
who have come young to grief?
Who will number the grains of loss
and what would comfort be?

1983

Dreams Before Waking

Despair is the question.

—Elie Wiesel

Hasta tu país cambío. Lo has cambiado tú mismo.

—Nancy Morejón

Despair falls:
the shadow of a building
they are raising in the direct path
of your slender ray of sunlight
Slowly the steel girders grow
the skeletal framework rises
yet the western light still filters
through it all
still glances off the plastic sheeting
they wrap around it
for dead of winter

At the end of winter something changes
a faint subtraction
from consolations you expected
an innocent brilliance that does not come
though the flower shops set out

386

once again on the pavement
their pots of tight-budded sprays
the bunches of jonquils stiff with cold
and at such a price
though someone must buy them
you study those hues as if with hunger

Despair falls
like the day you come home
from work, a summer evening
transparent from rose-blue light
and see they are filling in
the framework
the girders are rising
beyond your window
that seriously you live
in a different place
though you have never moved

and will not move, not yet
but will give away
your potted plants to a friend
on the other side of town
along with the cut crystal flashing
in the window-frame
will forget the evenings
of watching the street, the sky
the planes in the feathered afterglow:
will learn to feel grateful simply for this foothold

where still you can manage
to go on paying rent
where still you can believe
it's the old neighborhood:
even the woman who sleeps at night
in the barred doorway—wasn't she always there?
and the man glancing, darting
for food in the supermarket trash—
when did his hunger come to this?
what made the difference?
what will make it for you?

What will make it for you?
You don't want to know the stages
and those who go through them don't want to tell
You have your four locks on the door
Your savings, your respectable past

your strangely querulous body, suffering
sicknesses of the city no one can name
You have your pride, your bitterness
your memories of sunset
you think you can make it straight through
if you don't speak of despair.

What would it mean to live
in a city whose people were changing
each other's despair into hope?—
You yourself must change it.—
what would it feel like to know
your country was changing?—
You yourself must change it.—
Though your life felt arduous
new and unmapped and strange
what would it mean to stand on the first
page of the end of despair?

1983

Brian Willson, Duncan Murphy, Charles Liteky and George Mizo.

"WHEN LEADERS ACT CONTRARY TO CONSCIENCE,
ME MUST ACT CONTRARY TO LEADERS"

AN OPEN LETTER TO THE AMERICAN PEOPLE

Dear fellow Americans,

We are four U.S. war veterans who are beginning a water-only fast for life.

On August 13, 1986 the United States Senate approved $100 million worth of killing power to assist an army called the contras whose aim is to overthrow the government of Nicaragua. The contras do not now, nor have they ever, received the support of the majority of the Nicaraguan people. It's no wonder. Ninety-five percent of the top leadership of the contras is made up of former members of Anastasio Somoza's National Guard, one of the most brutal armies in Central American history.

This band of thugs that the President of the United States calls "freedom fighters" has consistently used terrorism to intimidate and control the poor of Nicaragua. The contras' record of crimes against humanity are well documented in reports by Amnesty International and by Americas Watch. For arming, funding, training, and directing the contras, the United States recently was condemned by the World Court, whose jurisdiction we had accepted until Nicaragua filed its case.

We are here because we want to make it absolutely clear that if our government insists on supporting proxy killers, if it insists on violating the sovereignty and right to self-determination of other nations, if it insists on violating our own Constitution and international law, they are not going to do it in our name. In our fast for life, we want it known that our government does not speak for us. Nor does it speak for most Americans. Nationwide opinion polls taken over the past year have consistently indicated that a majority of the American people oppose aid to the contras. In the most recent poll, released just before the congressional vote on contra aid, a resounding 62 percent of the nation's citizens said "No!" to contra aid. It is inconceivable to us that a body of legislators could then so grossly depart from the expressed will of the people who elected them.

Clearly, there is no broad base of support in the United States for aid to the contras. There is no broad base of support in Nicaragua for the contras. And the memory of Vietnam reminds us that a war waged without the support of the people is doomed to failure.

We are so convinced of the immorality and illegality of this new Vietnam—this new undeclared war—that we now offer our lives in a statement of ultimate protest. Today, we begin a water-only fast that will end only when you, the American people, speak out loudly and clearly that you will not tolerate leaders that are willing to sacrifice the lives of the Nicaraguan people for questionable national interests.

We choose to act in a way that cannot be construed as being silent about or complicit with our government's illegal or immoral policies in Central America. We feel revulsion at our government's policies of death. We feel solidarity with the Nicaraguan victims of these policies. We feel an affirmation and love for life—all life. And we believe that the soul of our country needs to be awakened. Therefore, we plead with the people of our own country to connect passionately with the victims of our policies, and to search his or her conscience for a way to respond to their suffering.

We now offer our lives for the causes of truth, justice, and love. When the United States entered World War II and Vietnam, we offered ourselves to our country without question. But tragically, the pretext that got us into Vietnam turned out to be a lie. The Gulf of Tonkin incident was fabricated to seduce a reluctant Congress into supporting an immoral war. As veterans, we will not remain silent—we will not sit passively by—while timid politicians lead us into another Vietnam.

Invoking the Nuremberg principles, we veterans of two wars choose not to be a party to crimes against humanity committed in the name of the American people. When leaders act contrary to conscience, we must act contrary to leaders.

We will be praying for a change of the hearts and minds of our own people. We will patiently look for evidence that the North American people refuse to live in the silence of implied consent. We will wait prayerfully for a new commitment to peace, for an escalation of resistance to illegal, immoral, and insane government policies. And we will listen attentively to the voice of conscience for guidance. We ask you to heed the words of Mahatma Gandhi:

> If you want something really important to be done, you must not merely satisfy the reason. You must move the heart also. The appeal to reason is more to the head, but the penetration of the heart comes from suffering. It opens the inner understanding.

The principle goal of our prayer and fasting is to inspire the protest movement in this country to save lives—now. Nicaragua is in a crisis. A wider war is imminent. Its people fear for their survival as a nation. But they are resolute. They will never say, "Uncle" and thus surrender the dignity they gained by the revolution in 1979. We do not want to see anymore Nicaraguan children, women, and old men die before their time. Here are some of the ways you can help save Nicaraguan lives and ours too, since we have identified with the victims of the U.S. contras.

1. Pray and fast in solidarity with the goals of the Veterans Fast for Life. Namely: an end to U.S. militarism in Central America and the beginning of a new non-military approach to the resolution of conflict.

Write to us at the address below and tell us what you are doing. We promise to listen and respond and stop the water-only fast when we know there is hope for change within the not too distant future. Like the Nicaraguan people we do not want to die. We want to work with you as brothers and sisters for peace.

2. Give some thought and prayer to non-violent civil disobedience, civilian-based defense, and tax resistance. Tell us what you are doing or plan to do.

3. Stage rallies of peaceful protest.

4. Hold vigils.

5. Send us copies of the letters you send to your congresspeople.

6. Tell us about your own creative ways of protesting the immoral and illegal use of your tax money. For example: Some folks from San Francisco are building a 25ft. x 25ft. Central American Memorial Wall in a prominent place.

7. Pray for a conversion of heart for the contras and their supporters in Congress. There are 221 in the House of Representatives and 53 in the Senate. Find out who they are. Mention the ones from your district by name when you pray. Ask yourself if you want a contra voter representing your district or your state. If they don't have a change of heart by November, perhaps a change of occupation is in order.

The important thing is that you write to us and let us know what you are doing and how you have escalated the level of your protest. We will read your letters from the steps of the capitol where we intend to spend at least four hours a day and in due time, with the help of good volunteer support, we will answer you, tell you how the fast is going, tell you what others are doing, and ask you about some of the things you may be willing to do in protest.

You are the only hope for peace in Central America. If you show no interest in the suffering of our brothers and sisters there, we will continue fasting in solidarity with the victims of U.S. contra terrorism knowing that in our death we will have made known to the people of Nicaragua that we love liberty, justice, and them more than life itself.

We believe that a wave of support for "liberty and justice for all" will usher in a new day of truth and integrity for this nation, so that once again we can hold our heads high as a people of compassion.

Brian Willson
Duncan Murphy
George Mizo
Charlie Liteky

October 17, 1986
Washington, D.C.

THE FAST GOES ON – IN MANY NEW FORMS

"Is not this the fast that I choose: to loose the bonds of wickedness, to undo the thongs of the yoke, to let the oppressed go free, and to break every yoke?

—Isaiah 58:6

We risked starvation through our water-only fast in order to help bring about an end to our government's killing of the people of Nicaragua. Now thousands and thousands of you, people of faith and conscience— here and in Europe—are telling us that you have been moved to take action. We believe our shared faith and commitment to act will end this war. We are ending our water-only fast to *join with you* in the work ahead to reach our common goal of peace and justice.

We've felt your response through the thousands of letters we've received, from our many discussions with veterans, young people, congressional representatives, and the people we met on our numerous speaking tours, also, by the hundreds of telephone conversations we've each had, and in the stories you've shared as you came from all over the country to vigil with us on the steps of the Capitol.

What we heard over and over again was that you are taking *your own steps* to bring about an end to this war. How? By working to defeat congressional members who voted for contra aid, committing civil disobedience at military facilities, refusing to pay taxes, joining Nicaraguan harvest brigades, renouncing war medals; the list goes on and on. So many of you have told us you are taking action for the first time, while others say they are deepening a long-held commitment for justice and peace.

Such a groundswell of activity has now convinced us that by living we will do more to stop the war—than by our deaths. We choose to join with you in unrelenting nonviolent resistance to the war in Nicaragua. Our fast continues—we are merely changing the mode. Rather than deny ourselves nutrients we will deny ourselves "life as usual" in our efforts to stop the killing in our name.

We have received hundreds of suggestions of actions we might undertake. The following eight projects are some of those in which we see ourselves participating in the future. They are actions of faith and conscience, which demand that we risk our lives if we are to change the course of our government's foreign policy. This will be done through the continued use of fasting, praying, and biblical reflection as the spiritual basis from which we act. At some time in the future we, or others, may choose to return to an open-ended water fast to awaken hearts and to cry out for the oppressed.

1. Immediate sit-ins, vigils, and fasts at the home offices of the members of Congress, demanding: 1) a halt to aid to the contras; 2) a full-scale, bipartisan investigation of "Contragate," including any participation by governmental agencies or individuals in activities forbidden by Congress or otherwise in violation of U.S. and international law; 3) call for a special session of Congress shortly after the elections to accomplish these aims.

Work within the electoral system to get the North American contras out of Congress.

2. Develop and participate in an unarmed "Veterans Peace Action" to stand in cooperation with other unarmed citizens groups on the border between Nicaragua and the neighboring countries from which military actions are launched.

3. Develop and participate in a "Citizens Peace Action," which is a reserve of people who have committed themselves for specific periods of time in which they can be called upon to act in an organized, peacekeeping presence in areas of conflict, both domestically and internationally. Specifically, now, we may lay our bodies on the runways and block the sea lanes where arms are being shipped to supply the contras.

4. Work on campuses teaching and helping students to organize against the war.

5. Promote veteran participation in a broadening peace and justice movement. (Through this fast many veterans have found an opening into the peace movement for the first time.)

6. Promote people-to-government and people-to-people contacts and support. (Similar to *The People's Declaration*, calling for a U.S. support group for the Contadora process.)

7. Practice tax resistance so that we stop paying for war while we are working and praying for peace.

8. Maintain a prayer and fasting vigil on the steps of our nation's Capitol. Support the growing presence of groups of people who fast and pray together at military and war-making facilities.

Our peacemaking would not be possible without the many peacemakers who came before us—and those who are walking beside us. We are four men whose early lives were marked by the practice of violence as a means of conflict resolution, and we credit our conversions to the poor of the Third World—especially the people of Vietnam and Nicaragua. Our consciousness has been awakened by the Women's Movement, and we have been deeply influenced by Native Americans and other persons of color.

A recent caller said to us, "Thank you for your gift." Now it is we four veterans who are saying thanks. Together we will stop the killing!

May peace and justice prevail on earth,

Duncan Murphy
Veteran of World War II
Fayetteville, AR
Fasted: 33 days

Charlie Liteky
Veteran of Vietnam
San Francisco, CA
Fasted: 47 days

Brian Willson
Veteran of Vietnam
Chelsea, VT
Fasted: 33 days

George Mizo
Veteran of Vietnam
Boston, MA
Fasted: 47 days

JAN BARRY

From War to Peace:
Changing the Culture

The Vietnam War was a watershed in American history. It shattered lives and families, as all wars have, but in an unexpected turn of events it also shattered the American myth that our national good fortune and our future are built on war. Before Vietnam, it was taken for granted that when America went to war it was glorious and was going to be good for us. After Vietnam, a great many Americans are no longer so sure.

From deep-seated concerns about the threat of nuclear war to widespread insistence that the U.S. not get bogged down in "another Vietnam" in Central America, a great majority of Americans, public opinion polls have been consistently finding, are firmly expressing a new mood on matters of war and peace.

In a remarkable shift in national events, this new mood has grown despite the Reagan administration's commitment to expending the greatest military budget in history, characterizing the Soviet Union as the "Evil Empire" and source of all evil in the world to be challenged by American military might, and encouraging a hysterical torrent of anticommunist war films (from *Red Dawn* and *Rambo* to the ABC-TV fourteen-hour series *Amerika*) to gush out of Hollywood.

From the Civil War in the 1860s to Vietnam in the 1960s, such drum beats from the White House and from the purveyors of popular culture automatically awoke the awesome patriotic response of a nation preparing for battle. Spirited speeches and songs sent Americans willingly into war well into the age of movies, when the power of the silver screen was added to the power of the presidency to enflame the nation to embrace a military crusade.

Much as young men had marched eagerly off to the Civil War singing *The Battle Hymn of the Republic* and were spurred into battle by Lincoln's fiery challenge of the southern states' act of secession, young Americans rushed to fight in Vietnam with John F. Kennedy's bold challenge to battle communism ringing in their ears and visions of John Wayne's Hollywood war movie heroics gleaming behind their eyes.

In the wake of the Vietnam War, a new legacy has entered our culture, a legacy of public debates over issues of war and peace, a legacy of challenging the assumptions of military power in the nuclear age. This is a challenge which has grown despite President Reagan's formidable powers as a former Hollywood actor (who made movies for the military during World War II) and current commander-in-chief of the most powerful array of military forces in history.

This new, fragile legacy of debating the consequences of war has arisen because our military force has the power to destroy the world in a nuclear war, and because, in a limited war in Vietnam, our military force nearly destroyed itself and the people it was sent to save.

Today we have a new national holiday honoring, for the first time, an American who won the Nobel Peace Prize—a national leader who never served in the military, who left a legacy of nonviolent struggle for civil rights at home and a stinging condemnation of the violence in Vietnam. While Americans have been turning increasingly to honor the murdered leadership for peace and social justice of Reverend Dr. Martin Luther King, Jr., we have been inching away from our long tradition of militantly marching through our other national holidays—from Washington and Lincoln's birthdays to Veterans Day—waving the flag in a patriotic frenzy of war fever.

The new mood is evident across the country: from Washington, where Congress has created the U.S. Institute of Peace to help prepare generations of peacemakers, to Main Street—where many communities have been dedicating churches, schools, temples, YWCAs, and even city halls as community Peace Sites. It is a mood which coexists with the old flag-waving mood in surprising ways, such as the unexpected spectacle of a festive band of citizens marching amid the military bands in a 1980s' Fourth of July parade in Montclair, New Jersey, who carried off first prize and memories of an explosion of their neighbors' applause for a gigantic red, white, and blue banner stretched across the main street, which proclaimed "Peace is Patriotic."

This is quite a change from the traditional American attitude toward patriotism, summed up by Mark Twain in 1906: "To be a patriot, one had to say, and keep on saying,'Our Country, right or wrong,' and urge on the [latest] war." Indeed, Mark Twain would scarcely recognize the new mood in America toward war these days. After the Civil War and Indian Wars and the string of military campaigns in Cuba, China, and the Philippines at the turn of the twentieth century, the country's most celebrated humorist wrote a scathing "War Prayer" which he felt could never be published in his lifetime. "It was a time of great and exalting excitement. The country was up in arms, the war was on, in every breast burned the holy fire of patriotism . . . in the churches the pastors preached devotion to flag and country, and invoked the God of Battles," began Twain's tale of the carnage of battle that a real angel of heaven might add to a truthful war prayer.

O Lord, our God, help us to tear their soldiers to bloody shreds with our shells . . . help us to drown the thunder of the guns with the shrieks of their wounded, writhing in pain; help us to lay waste their humble homes with a hurricane of fire; help us to wring the hearts of their unoffending widows with unavailing grief; help us to turn them out roofless with their little children to wander un-friended the wastes of their desolated land in rags and hunger and thirst . . . We ask it, in the spirit of love. . . .

Twain also harpooned the reigning American attitude toward peace activists: ". . . and the half dozen rash spirits that ventured to disapprove of the war and cast doubt upon its righteousness straightaway got such a stern and angry warning that for their personal safety's sake they quickly shrank out of sight . . ."

Twain's "War Prayer" was a long-buried piece of antiwar poetry resur-rected by a few foolhardy protestors during the Vietnam War, when it was still a patriotic tradition for an American Catholic archbishop to jour-ney to the war zone and bless the machine guns.

Since the war in Vietnam, Catholics, Protestants, and many other religious groups have been in the forefront of the American peace movement—issuing bishops' joint statements denouncing the nuclear arms race, reintroducing the concept of Christ the peacemaker (a figure long obscured by the call to arms of many militant hymns, such as *Onward Christian Soldiers,* which Twain sought to satirize), declaring church-es and temples nuclear free zones, Peace Sites, and sanctuaries for Cen-tral American refugees fleeing war zones inflamed by U.S. military inter-vention.

Opposition to military support by the Reagan administration for var-ious forces fighting in El Salvador and Nicaragua has been a priority issue for many American Catholics—who see that the civilian victims of these wars are primarily other Catholics—and many other religious groups which have formed organizations such as Witness for Peace to travel to the war zones and work for nonviolent resolution to the region's social and political crises.

Parallel to the rise of the religious appeal to peace, voters in the 1980s have approved popular referendums in state after state calling for negotiation of a mutual, verifiable freeze of the nuclear arms race, "jobs with peace" actions by the federal government, and declaration of a num-ber of cities—from Takoma Park, Maryland to Chicago—as nuclear free zones. In a grassroots groundswell of citizen diplomacy, civic groups and local officials in some twelve hundred U.S. cities and towns have contacted citizens and officials in Soviet cities with messages of peace and intense interest in fostering steps to help prevent nuclear war.

Similar civic actions have been aimed toward Central America, with communities in the U.S. linking with communities in Nicaragua and El Salvador to provide peaceful people-to-people assistance, in defiance of the Reagan administration's support for military solutions to the region's grinding poverty and legacy of brutal social injustice.

Responding to these grassroots campaigns, military commanders in the Pentagon have warned the administration that the U.S. cannot fight any prolonged wars without public support. The Pentagon itself has engaged in little more than hit-and-run raids in Lebanon and Libya, and an overblown military assault on Grenada, an island with a population the size of a baseball stadium crowd. Congress has blown hot and cold on releasing funds to support military actions in Central America, and—in the teeth of Reagan administration hostility to the idea—in 1984 created the U.S. Institute of Peace to provide federal support for the development of peace education at colleges and universities across America.

With peace education courses, and even degree programs, already being offered by colleges from the Ivy League to the local community college level, federal legislation to lay the groundwork for creation of a national peace academy was strongly supported by a broad spectrum of Americans, from religious groups and labor unions to military leaders such as General Andrew J. Goodpaster, former NATO commander and superintendent of the U.S. Military Academy.

In the midst of this changing attitude toward war and peace sweeping across America, Mark Twain's "War Prayer" was presented as part of a television special, nearly eighty years after it was written in bleak despair of the American people ever entertaining its message: the need to reexamine our national love affair with war.

Yet, so much about war had been challenged as a result of the Vietnam era, so much in American attitudes had changed, that airing the "War Prayer" on television seemed unremarkable—just a few years after it had seemed so radical to be read in public in protest of the Vietnam War.

The contrast between American public attitudes toward war and peace in the 1960s and now in the 1980s is dramatic. A remarkable transformation—from rushing to war to seeking out the possibility of peaceful alternatives—has taken place in the time between the Gulf of Tonkin Resolution in 1964, authorizing military intervention in Vietnam, and Congress declaring Martin Luther King, Jr.'s birthday a national holiday in 1985. In those twenty-one years, America changed in ways so profound that it in turn has changed our history books.

Peacemakers, like King, are now portrayed alongside generals as having a profound effect on the course of events. The civil rights movement, women's rights movement, and the peace movement itself (which began at least with the opposition in New England to the War of 1812) are now portrayed in American history books as examples of nonviolent vehicles of social change, which in historic hindsight now characterize the era of the 1960s.

Despite Ronald Reagan's insistence that America put the "Vietnam Syndrome" behind us and get back to preparing to fight and win wars, a great many Americans have been listening to a different drummer.

"Look at what happened during the Vietnam War," Senator Claiborne Pell told a reporter early in 1986 after becoming the new chairman of the Senate Foreign Relations Committee. "We used words like 'negotiate' and 'peace.' They were dirty words. A Christmas card with a Picasso dove on it was a dirty thing to send out. That's all changed," he emphasized. "People saw that a great bolt from the God Jehovah did not knock you down for saying it might be possible to negotiate a way out."

Perhaps the most unexpected consequence of the Vietnam War is that it made working for peace respectable. Before Vietnam, Americans working for peace during wartime were jailed, assailed from the pulpit and from the White House as cowards and traitors. After Vietnam, working for peace began to take on the status of a public interest profession, one to which even generals and admirals began to aspire.

"I remember taking part in a [peace] demonstration with Senator Wayne Morse, of Oregon, one of the most outspoken opponents of the war," retired admiral Gene LaRocque recalled in a 1986 *New Yorker* profile. "It was when some of the Vietnam veterans against the war threw away their medals. I saw Morse marching along, and, on impulse, I stepped off the curb, joined him, and introduced myself. We walked along together, exchanging ideas and talking about how we all should be out there—senators, generals, and admirals—demonstrating and saving lives in Vietnam."

Few of the other peace marchers streaming through the streets of Washington that April day in 1971 knew that an admiral from the Pentagon had just joined them. But shortly afterwards, LaRocque retired from the navy and, with a group of other high-ranking retired military officers, founded the Center for Defense Information, an independent public affairs office in Washington which challenges Pentagon claims on nuclear weapons and other national security matters from a perspective of seeking to prevent wars, rather than promote them.

"From my office window in the E Ring [of the Pentagon], where the generals and admirals had their offices, I could look out toward Arlington Cemetery," LaRocque told the *New Yorker* reporter. "Sometimes I could see soldiers digging graves for the Vietnam dead. At the same time, the Pentagon wanted to send more men to Vietnam to get killed."

LaRocque had been to Vietnam in charge of a high-level study of the conduct of the war. "Fundamentally, I couldn't find anyone to tell me why the United States was in Vietnam and what it was we were trying to accomplish there . . . My group discovered that since nobody knew what the armed services were trying to do there it was impossible to find a way to do it," he later recalled.

"You know, in the United States we talk of going to war. In other countries, the war comes to them. But if there's a nuclear war it will come to us," LaRocque said of his decision to retire from the Pentagon and set up a counterbalancing institution dedicated to preventing war. "Einstein said, 'The unleashed power of the atom has changed everything except our way of thinking.' That is okay as far as it goes if it awakens understanding in mindful men, but I am convinced that we must do more: change our way of acting . . . Our actions must be adjusted to the nuclear age. Nuclear weapons have made the old rules obsolete."

The deputy director of the Center for Defense Information, Rear Admiral Eugene J. Carroll, Jr., is a retired aircraft carrier commander who served in units fighting in Vietnam for six years. "After retiring, in 1980, I accepted a position with a defense contractor," Carroll told the *New Yorker*. "In less than six months, I was totally disillusioned. Pursuit of contracts is ruthless and often unethical, if not illegal, and the exploitation of retired miltary officers is cynical in the extreme. When I notified the contractor of my plan to depart . . . there was general astonishment that I was going to the Center for Defense Information, at a substantial reduction in compensation, in order to do what I wanted to do—speak my mind and work for a measure of sanity in our national-security programs rather than just mindlessly promote more weapons just because there was a lot of money in it."

With the assistance of actor and actress Paul Newman and Joanne Woodward, a board of other retired military commanders, and income from foundation grants and nationwide fundraising letters, the Center has produced a series of thought-provoking films, conferences, and publications on how citizens can help in the campaign to prevent nuclear war.

Not far from the Center's offices in Washington, a peace group with a very different origin works to advance the same cause. Peace Links— Women Against Nuclear War was founded in 1982 by Betty Bumpers, the wife of Senator Dale Bumpers of Arkansas, after her nineteen-year-old daughter asked her where the family would meet again in the aftermath of a nuclear war.

"Well, honey, I guess back home in Arkansas," Mrs. Bumpers recalled in a 1983 interview in *McCall's* magazine. "Her daughter then asked, 'But what if Arkansas isn't there?' The question, Betty says, 'hit me hard, made me realize how we adults sweep our fear about possible extinction under the rug while our youngsters, who haven't yet developed these skills in concealing or rationalizing, they *live* with it.'"

With office space donated by Blue Cross/Blue Shield of Arkansas, Mrs. Bumpers founded Peace Links, which in a year grew to six thousand members with local coordinators in seventy-three of Arkansas' seventy-five counties. With the support of scores of other congressional wives and

403

women in such organizations as local PTAs and YWCAs, Peace Links rapidly spread across the country in a network of grassroots chapters and set up a national office in Washington.

In 1985, Peace Links hosted a visit by thirteen Soviet women in a historic tour of towns and cities across America. Accompanied by congressional wives, the Soviet visitors were welcomed in communities as diverse as Cleveland, Ohio, Nashville, Tennessee, and Salt Lake City, Utah.

"I believe we can turn this thing around," the former First Lady of Arkansas said in the *McCall's* interview. "But we have to talk about it. We have to face our own fears; that's the only way we can begin to change them . . . Our kids know more than we think they do. They need to be able to articulate their fears. If we start doing something to change things, then we can communicate that hope to them . . . If we put as much time, energy and money into peace as we do into war, there's no question but that we'd have peace. And I'm not alone in this hope. I'm just one vote in a great choir that's singing the same song."

Elsewhere in Washington are the national offices of Citizens Against Nuclear War, a lobbying coalition of some sixty national membership organizations, which was organized in 1982; the Coalition for a New Foreign and Military Policy, another lobby composed of some fifty national membership organizations; the National Peace Institute Foundation (formerly the National Peace Academy Campaign, founded in 1976), which mobilized grassroots and congressional support to create the U.S. Institute of Peace; and SANE, the Committee for a Sane Nuclear Policy, founded in 1958 and grown in recent years to well over a hundred thousand members nationwide.

The latest peace office to appear in Washington is called the Better World Society, founded in 1986 by cable TV pioneer Ted Turner and an international board of directors to promote the prevention of nuclear war, global overpopulation, and environmental poisoning through greater use of television. Through the use of Turner's cable TV network, WTBS, the Better World Society has been presenting a series of new films under the general title, "Ending the Nuclear Arms Race." After co-hosting the Goodwill Games in Moscow in the summer of 1986, Turner began negotiating with Soviet officials for an ongoing exchange of American and Soviet movies and television programs.

"We fully realize that the United States has not cornered the market on solutions to problems that directly affect the lives of people worldwide," Turner noted in a letter to prospective supporters. "For that reason, the Better World Society aims to become a genuinely international membership organization. We must recognize that no nation can impose its beliefs and solutions on others. We simply cannot go it alone."

Turner's remarks echoed the very similar perspective of another innovative organization, the International Physicians for the Prevention of Nuclear War, whose American and Soviet co-chairmen were presented the Nobel Peace Prize in 1985 for their efforts to educate both societies to the fact that nuclear war would be the "final epidemic," destroying doctors and hospitals as well as everything else.

The peace movement of the 1980s has grown far beyond the protests of the Vietnam War. It has grown from a few dozen peace groups thinly-scattered across the nation in 1967, the year the Vietnam peace movement mobilized its first massive march on Washington, to hundreds of peace groups able to turn out nearly a million marchers for a disarmament demonstration at the United Nations headquarters in New York in 1982, to some six thousand organizations estimated to be working for peace in 1986. It has grown from a focus of working for peace in one place to working for peace in the world.

Perhaps the most important, underreported news story of the 1980s is the geometric growth of a widespread, deep-rooted citizens' peace offensive. While the governments of the United States and the Soviet Union have been deadlocked in fruitless negotiations on nuclear arms control, millions of citizens in both nations have been seeking each other out in an extraordinary effort to prevent nuclear war and to make peace in bloody clashes involving the superpowers in Central America, the Middle East, and wherever Cold War tensions overheat.

Much of this citizen action has overwhelmed the ability of anyone in Washington, in the government or coalition peace offices, to keep track of it all. The *Boston Globe* in 1982 discovered over fifty peace organizations in the Boston area alone promoting national and international activities, including the headquarters of the Council for a Liveable World, Physicians for Social Responsibility, Educators for Social Responsibility, International Physicians for the Prevention of Nuclear War, and the Institute for Defense and Disarmament Studies, whose president and executive director, Randall Forsberg, was one of the founders of the nuclear freeze campaign.

The 1984 edition of the *Iowa Peace Directory* listed over a hundred peace groups active in the state, nearly twice the number listed in a 1982 directory prepared by the United Nations Association of Iowa. In an effort to provide means of communications among this explosion of peace groups, at least two national peace directories *(American Peace Directory* and *Grassroots Peace Directory)* and a computer network (PeaceNet) have been established, as well as the use by several groups of communications satellites to beam television programs on peace activities to universities and other organizations across the country with satellite receiver dishes.

To the peace action tactics of the 1960s of mass marches, sit-ins, and other public protests aimed at influencing policies in Washington, peace activists of the 1980s have added widespread use of mass media technology, linked with an extensive network of grassroots activities aimed at reaching out to people around the world.

Far from the foreign affairs offices of the State Department in Washington, local officials in scores of American communities have taken unprecedented actions to aid this citizens' peace campaign. In the early 1980s, in response to renewed federal plans for civil defense evacuation in the event of nuclear war, local officials and civic groups in cities from Cambridge, Massachusetts to San Francisco, California published and distributed booklets on the devastating effect nuclear warheads would have on their city, and steps that citizens could take to help prevent nuclear war.

"The terrible lesson of Hiroshima and Nagasaki is even more devastatingly clear today," San Francisco's mayor Dianne Feinstein wrote in the introduction to a fourteen-page booklet, *The Nuclear Threat to San Francisco*, mailed to every household in that city in 1983. After describing in detail how San Francisco would be destroyed if a one-megaton nuclear warhead exploded over city hall, the booklet urged voters to support a bilateral nuclear freeze with the Soviet Union and to "make sure those persons for whom you vote will do all in their power to promote peace and avoid nuclear war."

The San Francisco booklet, published by the city and county board of supervisors, was adapted from an earlier one mailed to residents of Cambridge, Massachusetts, by that city's government in 1981. The Cambridge booklet spawned "similar efforts in Toronto, London, Vermont and elsewhere," the Associated Press reported in a wire service story on this public education phenomenon.

In Boulder County, Colorado, the cities of Boulder, Louisville, and Longmont and the town of Jamestown joined the county commissioners in publishing the *Boulder County Nuclear War Education Booklet* after nearly twelve hundred residents jammed a public hearing to protest local participation in the Denver-Metro Crisis Relocation Plan, a nuclear war civil defense evacuation plan provided by the Federal Emergency Management Agency. The federal plan was unanimously rejected by the county commissioners, who declared in the booklet that they had "decided that County funds could be better spent informing the citizens of Boulder County of the consequences of a nuclear attack . . . and what we must do to prevent nuclear war."

By 1984, the list of local governments refusing to participate in the federal nuclear war crisis planning promulgated by the Reagan administration had grown to include Houston, New York City, and the states of California, Maryland, Massachusetts, New Mexico, and Washington. In Massachusetts, the state health department issued a booklet declaring nuclear war to be a public health hazard whose only cure is prevention, the same stand taken by Physicians for the Prevention of Nuclear War and other peace groups.

In New York City, after a council vote "to refuse all Federal funds for civil defense preparations for nuclear war," Councilwoman Ruth Messinger and the city chapter of Physicians for Social Responsibility published a colorful, cartoon-illustrated *New Yorker's Guide to Civil Defense*, full of compelling questions and suggestions for citizen action to prevent nuclear war. The New York booklet highlighted the nuclear freeze campaign, which had placed on the 1982 ballot a referendum question approved by a substantial majority of voters in eight out of nine states, as well as in the cities of Denver, Chicago, Philadelphia, Miami, and Washington, D.C.

Besides vividly demonstrating the strength of public opinion for an end to the nuclear arms race, the nuclear freeze referendum campaign provided another strong catalyst for peace groups and local government officials to work together—a partnership which blossomed across the country as relations between the White House and the Kremlin sharply deteriorated. Opposition from the Reagan administration only served to cement the new peace partnership.

"To me there isn't any other side to this issue," New Jersey governor Thomas Kean, a prominent Republican, told a strategy meeting of nuclear freeze workers in October 1982, just after President Reagan had blasted the freeze campaign as a Soviet KGB plot. "I am delighted to be here," said Kean, "and delighted to talk with you who are, after all, the troops without whom this movement is not going to be as successful as we all want it to be . . . For those who demean the efforts of people working in this movement, for people who say that somehow there are people who are anti-American . . . somehow in league with foreign powers or something, those people don't serve this country's cause at all."

With Governor Kean serving as honorary chairman, the New Jersey freeze referendum campaign organized a door-to-door voter education effort that reached deep into every legislative district and won the support of 66 percent of the state's voters. Two years later, the New Jersey legislature voted nearly unanimously to establish the nation's first state institute of peace and conflict resolution studies, as a spur to establishing the U.S. Institute of Peace.

Dissatisfied with the glacial pace of peace developments in Washington, government bodies in over forty of New Jersey's most populous cities and counties sent resolutions to Congress and President Reagan in 1985-86 urging that steps be taken to negotiate a comprehensive nuclear test ban treaty with the Soviet Union, then observing a unilateral moratorium on nuclear weapons tests, which the Reagan administration repeatedly refused to join. When lobbying Washington didn't bring direct results, local officials began taking their own actions to bury the hatchet with the Soviet Union.

On Veterans Day of 1986, in a dramatic development, the borough hall of Somerville, New Jersey, was dedicated as a Peace Site by unanimous action of the mayor and borough council. On December 7, Pearl Harbor Day, the city hall in Linden, in a neighboring county, was similarly dedicated as a Peace Site by the city council. Within weeks, the nearby communities of Cranford and Raritan declared their municipal buildings Peace Sites as well.

In a letter to fellow mayors in New Jersey, Somerville mayor Emanuel R. Luftglass urged the establishment of municipal government Peace Sites throughout the state. The Peace Site idea, he noted, was started in 1981 by Louis Kousin, a retired public relations executive in Cranford, New Jersey. In its first five years, the Peace Sites campaign spread rapidly across the U.S. as scores of churches, community centers, schools, synagogues, and social services agencies dedicated their buildings as Peace Sites to provide a more visible community focus on the effort to prevent nuclear war.

"We are concerned that the youth of Somerville may incorrectly fear that a nuclear holocaust is inevitable," Luftglass and the Somerville council stated in their Peace Site resolution, "and by this action we intend to help convince our youngsters that such an event is preventable." To the applause of members of the local American Legion post, the Somerville officials proposed sending a copy of their resolution to Soviet leader Mikhail Gorbachev, urging him "to ask towns in Russia to join with Somerville and declare government buildings as Peace Sites."

In contrast to the Vietnam era, when citizens' peace efforts often burst into bloom and quickly faded in discouragement in the face of the relentless war, grassroots peace actions in the 1980s more often have deeper roots which nourish each other. Even as Somerville's citizens were wondering how Russians would react to the idea of Peace Sites, residents of nearby communities were working to bring a delegation of Soviet citizens to New Jersey for a tour of the state and its work for nuclear war prevention, including an extensive network of community Peace Sites. Others in the state were working to arrange a visit by Soviet students and a rare performance by the Kirov Ballet, which added New Jersey to its first tour in the U.S. since the 1970s.

Similar intertwined peace action dramas have developed all across the nation. In Tucson, Arizona, a coalition of twenty-two Peace Sites has been created, which supports a very active network of religious groups involved in the Sanctuary movement on behalf of refugees fleeing the fighting in Central America. In Boise, Idaho, a group of citizens created a peace quilt which was sent to the Soviet Union, followed by a delegation of Idaho residents which included the lieutenant governor. In the Soviet Union, one of the groups they crossed paths with was a party of American religious and peace activists from the East Coast, which included a Catholic nun who brought the story of the Boise Peace Quilt back home to New Jersey.

In November 1986, nearly the entire national leadership of the YWCA of the U.S. gathered from across the country and traveled to Moscow to meet their counterparts in the Soviet Women's Committee. Early in 1987 a delegation of Soviet women came to the U.S. at the invitation of the YWCA, visiting its headquarters in New York City, a YWCA day care center in Ridgwood, New Jersey, and attending a meeting of the organization's National Board in Phoenix, Arizona. Among the information about the YWCA the Soviet visitors took home is that this international women's organization has dedicated YWCA Peace Sites all across America and in other nations from England to India, and that it wants to continue developing joint programs with Soviet women's groups.

The YWCA-Soviet Women's Committee exchange, as did the earlier exchange involving Peace Links and the Soviet visitors it hosted in cities across America, grew out of the efforts of a citizens' organization called US-USSR Bridges for Peace based in Norwich, Vermont. Headed by Clinton Gardner, a retired business executive, Bridges for Peace has organized over a dozen citizen exchange programs involving an overlapping array of American and Soviet citizens since 1983, when it began with a pioneer program in New England.

In a decision which was unexpectedly hard to make, in contrast to that which took me to Vietnam as a GI in the 1960s, I joined a Bridges for Peace delegation of New Jersey residents who went to the Soviet Union for two weeks in the fall of 1986. Unlike soldiering in Vietnam, and later joining the peace movement after resigning from a military career, flying to Moscow required facing squarely a lifetime of accepting with little question ingrained American attitudes of fear and ignorance, and self-righteous contempt, of Soviet communism. After traveling some four thousand miles across the USSR, it seems likely to me that the idea of community Peace Sites may well appeal to local governments and citizens in the Soviet Union—as a good idea for Americans. For their own society, I gather that they may consider it to be redundant.

From Leningrad to Volgograd, the memorials to 20 million Soviet citizens who died in World War II are often referred to by local tour guides as peace memorials. The first day of school in September across the Soviet Union is called "Peace Day," when World War II veterans and other adults visit to tell the students of their work to prevent another world war.

Gracing walls in airports and Intourist hotels, there are colorful, eye-catching posters in several languages proclaiming that tourism is another way of working for peace. Banners and billboards in city parks and on construction sites urge passersby to work for *miry mir*, world peace. In each city we visited, there are offices for the Soviet Peace Fund, a kind of United Way campaign to which some 90 million citizens were said to contribute annually, and local chapters of the Soviet Peace Committee and Soviet Women's Committee, which are supported by the peace fund. One of the largest sources of contributions to the Soviet Peace Fund was said to come from the Russian Orthodox Church, through collections among its national network of churches. Chaired by world chess champion Anatoly Karpov, the Soviet Peace Fund has 350,000 branches and local commissions across the USSR, according to a 1986 report on its work published in Moscow.

In Moscow, the headquarters of the Soviet Peace Committee, the organization that hosted our delegation, is located on a boulevard named Mira (Peace) Prospekt. On another Peace Boulevard, in Volgograd, the city that rose out of the ashes of Stalingrad, a rebuilt commercial building prominently displays a set of picturesque stained glass windows commemorating Volgograd's twelve sister cities around the world, including Coventry in England, and Hiroshima, Japan—two other cities substantially destroyed in World War II. Since 1983, Volgograd has hosted annual "Volga Peace Cruises" for American visitors who meet with Soviet residents in communities along the famed river through the Russian heartland.

In 1986, a companion "Mississippi Peace Cruise" took place on a paddlewheel river boat carrying fifty Soviet visitors who met with Americans in communities along the river from Minneapolis to St. Louis. In response to these citizen peace initiatives, our delegation was told that Volgograd officials were seeking to create a sister-city relationship with an American city.

Through a variety of contacts, a growing number of U.S. and USSR sister city ties have already been established. These include some surprising combinations, such as Trenton, New Jersey matched with the Lenin District of Moscow; Houston, Texas and Baku; Gainesville, Florida and Novorossiisk on the Black Sea. One day high in the foothills of the Caucasus Mountains in Soviet Georgia, our delegation was introduced to the mayor of a small wine-producing city called Telavi. "Do you know," the mayor said through an interpreter, "that we have a sister city in America? Fort Collins, Colorado!"

The mayor of Telavi's enthusiasm for linking with Americans at the grassroots was echoed back here in the States a few weeks later.

In a long editorial entitled "People to People" in the Gainesville, Florida *Sun* on January 18, 1987, it was noted with pride that

city commissioners can justifiably claim more diplomatic success . . . than even Ronald Reagan can boast. "I was quite pleased that we exchanged [holiday] messages with the mayor of Novorossiisk," Mayor Hill said last week. "President Reagan and Gorbachev couldn't even work that out."

And that's true. On December 30, the *Sun* printed a message of greetings from Georgi Khobotov, mayor of the Black Sea city of Novorossiisk, to the citizens of Gainesville. "We hold our contacts with Gainesville especially dear, for we are aware that the strengthening and promotion of our friendship might contribute to the improvement of Soviet-American relations on which the world's future depends to a great extent." A similar message from Gainesville found its way to Khobotov and his comrades.

That Gainesville should be maintaining diplomatic relations with a municipality in the land of that "other" superpower might seem surprising. But since 1982, when the commission voted to invite

410

citizens of Novorossiisk to initiate a "longstanding friendship and association," the two cities have maintained a formal "sister city" relationship . . .

Last week, Gainesville commissioners unanimously voted to extend another invitation of "friendship and association" to residents of a foreign city whose government has had stormy relations with Washington. And perhaps even more than its invitation to Novorossiisk, the commission's initiation of a sister city relationship with the city of Matagalpa, Nicaragua, represents an act of courage and goodwill.

Such acts of courage and good will have been happening in communities across America. The town where I live, Montclair, New Jersey, became a sister city with Pearl Lagoon, Nicaragua, in 1985 and sent a member of the township council to the Soviet Union on the Bridges for Peace delegation from New Jersey. The Essex County legislature voted unanimously to send me to Moscow carrying an enormous framed resolution of greetings and good will, and prepared to host a return visit by Soviet citizens despite an outcry from Eastern European emigré groups and other vocal anticommunists.

Indeed, when the Soviet delegation arrived, just days after the airing of ABC-TV's *Amerika* series depicting a Soviet military occupation of the United States, local officials in communities from one end of New Jersey to the other refused to be intimidated by the specter of being "dupes of the communist conspiracy" held out by members of the John Birch Society and a handful of other citizens who expressed outrage at anyone offering a hand in friendship to representatives of the Soviet Union.

As circumstances would have it, while the eleven-member delegation of Soviet visitors was being greeted by mayors and colleges, school classes and religious groups across New Jersey, a boatload of thirty-seven Soviet sailors was dramatically rescued from a sinking freighter by U.S. Coast Guard helicopters, flown to the nearest landfall, and put up in a motel near Atlantic City. President Reagan promptly invited the Soviet crew to the White House.

"In the past, I've often talked about what would happen if ordinary Americans and people from the Soviet Union could get together, get together as human beings, as men and women who breathe the same air, share the same concerns about making life better for themselves and their children," Reagan said in his welcoming remarks, widely reported by the news media. "And here we have a case where just this happened. I hope and pray that no matter how stormy international affairs, the leaders of the world can look and see what happened . . . between these fliers and sailors, and be duly inspired. After all, this good planet whirling through space isn't so very different from a ship upon the sea . . . We must reach out to each other in good will, for we have no other alternative," Reagan concluded, stating the case for making peace with the Soviet Union in clear-cut language for all the world to understand.

411

One of the tragedies of the Vietnam era is that Americans and Vietnamese were divided into warring camps by the reigning rhetoric of the day. In Vietnam, people had to be for us or against us, and if the latter they must be communists. In America, people had to be either for the war or against the war, a "hawk" or a "dove," patriotic or un-American. One had to have enemies. For the peace movement, "hawks" and GIs were supposed to be the enemy. For GIs, the peace movement and the Vietnamese who weren't our allies were supposed to be the enemy.

The savage disagreements during the Vietnam War divided Americans into bitter factions not only over the war but also over the basic images of American culture—the very basis for how we perceived ourselves. Supporters of the war wrapped themselves in the American flag, clung to social conventions, styles of speech, clothing, and haircuts carried over from the Eisenhower era of the 1950s, and proclaimed anyone who disagreed with them to be a traitor. Demonstrating their disdain for that vision of America, many war protestors trashed Old Glory, flaunted the counterculture's hallmarks of long hair, four-letter words, free sex, and the new hippie lifestyle, and proclaimed anyone who disagreed with them to be a fascist pig.

Not everyone in the peace movement acted that way, of course, but the news media and war supporters happily highlighted the hippie contingent as the essence of dissent. Families, friends, marriages were split apart by the near-civil war over what American image to project: self-righteous, militant, and conventional patriotism—or questioning, equally self-righteous, and militant rebellion on behalf of finding some new approach.

Into the middle of this cultural warfare, Vietnam veterans harboring a great range of feelings, including profound doubt and bitterness about the war, returned home from Indochina and found themselves running a gauntlet between the bitter lines of a national feud.

In the prevailing climate, some of us who came back from Vietnam and tried to talk sense with Congress and the American people began to see that we had much more in common with the hardpressed housewives, lawyers, teachers, religious leaders, and ordinary working people than we would ever have with the celebrated partisans of cultural welfare who commanded the national spotlight—busy trashing each other and tearing Americans apart—as the war raged on. Our patriotism being unimpeachable, even as we grew longer hair and supported the need for peace in Vietnam and sweeping social change in America, many Vietnam veterans began trying to bridge the bitter gulf between "hawks" and "doves," pacifists and GIs, Americans and Vietnamese. In concert with other concerned Americans, that was a great part of the patient, behind the scenes work toward national reconciliation and burying the hatchet with Vietnam that went on throughout the decade of the 1970s.

In the 1980s, many Americans began to realize the wisdom of Abraham Lincoln's observation that "the best way to destroy an enemy is make him a friend." These days, it's clear, it is not just peaceniks who are working for peace. The smog of self-righteous rhetoric has begun to clear. Ronald Reagan and Mikhail Gorbachev, on their better days, have begun to talk seriously about the necessity of building bridges of peace and eliminating the threat of nuclear war.

Thoughtful peace activists and news media managers have begun to question the limits of protest and harping on the fear of nuclear war, and have begun presenting creative programs on the positive developments of "transforming enemy images into friendly faces," in the words of a Fellowship of Reconciliation project which has won praise in both the U.S. and USSR. People and political leaders on both sides of the Cold War have begun to realize that we have to work together. The issue is no longer whether our view of the world will prevail, but whether the world will survive.

Our problem these days is that, while we are congratulating ourselves on becoming so wise, there is nothing assured about peace or preventing nuclear war unless we continue working to accomplish it.

First Peace Pagoda constructed by Nipponzan Myohoji in North America, located in Leverett, Massachusetts

To Embody Peace: The Building of Peace Pagodas Around the World

Civilization is neither having electric lights, nor having airplanes, nor man-ufacturing nuclear bombs. Civilization is not to kill human beings, not to destroy things, not to wage war; civilization is to become mutually amiable and respectful. What constitutes its foundation is not the establishment of a judicial system, but religious faith that seeks gentleness, peace, simplicity and uprightness.

—The Most Venerable Nichidatsu Fujii

A word such as "sanctity" comprises the core of spirituality, especially that of the religious and moral society. It is what gives life to such a society. There exists no religion or ethics without the concept of sanctity.

—The Most Venerable Nichidatsu Fujii

The Arising of the First Peace Pagoda in North America

In the lovely hills of western Massachusetts there now stands a beautiful "Peace Pagoda," initiated by the Buddhist order, Nipponzan Myohoji, and built by the volunteer labor and cooperation of hundreds of people, most of whom had never before met, drawn together only by their common desire to give of themselves for world peace.

In March of 1984, a handful of people began clearing the land; by October 5, 1985, thousands gathered for the inauguration of the completed Peace Pagoda. Since that time, the Peace Pagoda has become a special pilgrimage site for people of all backgrounds and circumstances—all ages, races, and creeds.

The Peace Pagoda is like a miraculous, living affirmation that the world is meant to be at peace—not doomed to endless war, culminating in nuclear holocaust. It radiates the preciousness, the sacredness of this world, and the purity and noble selflessness within the heart of humanity, within each one of us. And how we *do* need this purest and noblest treasure within us to be manifest in the world today.

Whenever I think of the Peace Pagoda, a great YES jumps up in me. Furthermore, this YES is always bright, as though it had just been made entirely new, in a great and original blooming . . . Thank you to all who helped get the Leverett Peace Pagoda built. We have put fear aside and built our love.

The Most Venerable Nichidatsu Fujii

The spiritual teacher who opened the way for building Peace Pagodas, believing they would shed light in these violent times, was the Buddhist monk, the Most Venerable Nichidatsu Fujii. He was the founder and teacher of the Buddhist order, Nipponzan Myohoji.

Ha Poong Kim, professor of philosophy at Eastern Illinois University, wrote of the Most Venerable Fujii:

When the Most Venerable Fujii died in 1985 at the age of ninety-nine, the world peace movement lost one of its great spiritual leaders. . . . The monks and nuns of the small order Nipponzan Myohoji, under his inspiration, have built over seventy Peace Pagodas in many parts of the world—recently one in London and another in Leverett, Massachusetts. They have walked around the globe, praying for tranquility and harmony in these violent times.

The Most Venerable Nichidatsu Fujii was born in a fertile farming area within a crater of an extinct volcano in Kyushu, Japan, on August 6, 1885. Although a Buddhist, the Most Venerable Fujii did not confine his aroused concern to any one people or group—truly his voice of compassionate awakening and encouragement belonged to all human beings alive today. Especially after the nightmare of World War II, culminating in the horror of the atomic bombing of hundreds of thousands of people in Hiroshima and Nagasaki, he tirelessly devoted himself, and urged his disciples' devotion, to the movement for worldwide disarmament and the necessary change of hearts and minds which would cause the renunciation of violence and the practice of "gentleness, simplicity and uprightness." It was at that time that the Most Venerable Fujii commenced building Peace Pagodas, believing that their presence in the world would be a powerful spiritual antidote to the violence and confusion of the nuclear age. Professor Kim writes:

The Most Venerable Fujii realized that the time had come when the Buddha's teaching of compassion and non-killing should be prac-

The Most Venerable Nichidatsu Fujii, August 6, 1885–January 9, 1985

ticed unconditionally, not just between individuals but between nations. He believed that the atomic age demanded nothing short of the universal salvation of all humanity.

The Building of Peace Pagodas: An Ancient Custom

The building of Peace Pagodas (traditionally referred to as "Stupas") dates back to the period immediately following the Parinirvana (physical death) of Lord Buddha (approximately twenty-five hundred years ago). After the sacred body of Lord Buddha was cremated, some of his disciples made a huge hemispherical mound of earth and stone with various adornments and crowned with a decorative "umbrella" to shade the relics of Buddha which were placed within the Stupa. This was done to express supreme reverence and gratitude for his life and teachings. This custom spread quickly, and Lord Buddha's relics were divided so that they could be enshrined within each Stupa (Peace Pagoda).

The building of Stupas was always associated with the enhancing of peace and happiness within human society. The preeminent example of this was King Ashoka (304 BC–233 BC), a king in India who waged terrible wars to gain land and power, causing great misery to the people. After one particularly bloody eight-year war against the Kalinga people, King Ashoka finally reached a point of repugnance towards violence and renounced thenceforth the waging of war. At that time he also adopted the teachings of Buddha, due to the influence of a Buddhist monk. Although a Buddhist, this spiritually rejuvenated king saw his role as promoting tolerance and harmony among the various religious and ethnic groups in his kingdom. He believed he should serve and care for the welfare of the people—a task to which he zealously devoted himself. He understood he needed to practice personal repentance and purification, which he did through fasting, making religious pilgrimages, and, again, actively working for the good of the people. King Ashoka, once called "Ashoka, the Wicked" by the people, became known as "Ashoka, Beloved of the Gods." Historical records indicate, too, that he was responsible for the construction of eighty-four thousand Stupas throughout many parts of Asia; he was also able to avert the invasion of Alexander the Great by sending messengers of peace. Through his benign influence, a period of human happiness and peace lasted for several centuries.

The Leverett Peace Pagoda and Beyond

As mentioned above, the Most Venerable Fujii believed this ancient custom of building Peace Pagodas was a great aid to awakening humanity's latent aspiration towards peace and selflessly working for the happiness of the whole human family.

This truly has been the experience in Leverett—both during the construction period, the inauguration, and the time since its completion.

The people who visit the Peace Pagoda leave with a message of hope, a feeling that we can create peace, and an enlightened community. The Peace Pagoda is a symbol of the seed of selflessness taking root in the midst of life-threatening destructive forces. The Pagoda is like the rising sun. It is a manifestation of our spiritual growth . . . a symbol of our spiritual nature taking root in America. May the spirit of unity of the monks, nuns and community who built the Peace Pagoda in Leverett spread everywhere.
(Venerable MahaGhosananda, Cambodian monk, founder of the Interreligious Task Force for Peace in Cambodia.)

As mentioned above, workers came from all quarters to help without remuneration—motivated just by the desire to give of themselves for world peace. All labor—professional, skilled, and unskilled—was voluntarily offered. Some materials were donated; when possible, recycled materials were used. When money was needed for materials it was offered without official "fundraising" drives; it was given spontaneously by those who were moved by the undertaking. Food was donated very generously also, from individuals, shopkeepers, and local companies. Venerable Kato, the monk who originally devoted himself to building a Peace Pagoda in New England, believed this was very auspicious, indicating that the Peace Pagoda was truly arising from the hearts of the American people.

Even though there is no advertising of the Peace Pagoda, numerous visitors come year round, even in inclement weather. Families, the elderly, handicapped, and infirm, students—all who come seem genuinely touched by the sight of the Peace Pagoda. Many groups of area school children have visited. Invariably the children write thank you notes and draw pictures indicating the inspiration they felt. Groups of local clergy have visited and invited monks to their churches; countless prayers of all faiths, formal and informal, have been offered there for peace.

All of this gives testimony to the belief of the Most Venerable Fujii that the Peace Pagoda could speak a universal spiritual truth for peace and righteousness. Michael Desherbinin, Peace Minister for the United Church of Christ in western Massachusetts, wrote of the Peace Pagoda:

> Our secular culture has seemed unable to act on the oft-repeated teaching of the pioneer of nuclear energy, Albert Einstein. Forty years ago he warned: ". . . there is no secret and there is no defense; there is no possibility of control except through the aroused understanding and insistence of the people of the world."
>
> . . . The Peace Pagoda holds the possibility of reaching the spirit and senses of a numbed world. The beauty of the Peace Pagoda and its surrounding site may allow each of us to experience a sense of love and nonviolence.
>
> Like the seventy-odd others already built, the Pagoda is grand in size, graceful in design and speaks softly of the mystery of human creativity guided by a loving deity.
>
> . . . It is up to us, the American people, to take the enlightenment it affords on to the next steps, in the worlds of our own religious congregations and in the complex realm of public policy.
> (From *The Amherst Bulletin*, October 2, 1985.)

A Peace Pagoda in Vietnam

> . . . The Peace Pagoda [in Leverett, Massachusetts] is for me the focus with which I found, and continue to find, direction. It has helped to remind me of my mission in life after my Vietnam War experience, filling me with hope, strength and resolve.
>
> I was honored to be allowed to share my physical and spiritual support, and I can only give my love in return. . . .
>
> It has been eighteen and a half years since I offered my life in war and took the lives of others. . . . I now offer my life to stop wars, to protect the lives and peace of others. . . .
> (Brian Emond, Vietnam veteran, Leverett Peace Pagoda worker.)

The building of the Leverett Peace Pagoda was an occasion for many previously unrelated people to meet and work together. One very auspicious linking arose between monks and U.S. war veterans, particularly Vietnam War veterans, who came to build the Peace Pagoda. This joining together has opened the way for future cooperation for peace, including a major proposal: to build a Peace Pagoda in Vietnam.

The carrying out of this aspiration would have a profound healing effect both for the Vietnamese and for the Americans. The proposal, although just in the preliminary stages, still to be developed and refined, can be stated as follows: Vietnam veterans, along with monks and nuns of Nipponzan Myohoji, would initiate the effort to build and take responsibility for the completion of a Peace Pagoda in Vietnam. This would be undertaken with the permission of the Vietnamese government, the approval of Buddhist clergy in Vietnam, and, hopefully, the good will of the general population in Vietnam. The necessary materials and funds would be donated from outside of Vietnam: the entire effort would be an offering to the people of that most devastated country.[1] Voluntary help would be welcome from all people, including those assisting in the construction; and, certainly, if Vietnamese people wished to join the effort in any way, it would be a cause for great happiness.

A Peace Pagoda: An Expression of America's True Heart to the People of Vietnam

A Peace Pagoda is conceived as a prayer for peace, a tangible structure that outwardly manifests the dedication of our lives to justice and peace and, in the case of Vietnam, a manifestation of a healing process.

In talking with Vietnam War veterans from around the country, it has been expressed time after time that they have been waiting years for some way to return to Vietnam to start that healing process both within themselves and within Vietnam, and feel that building a Peace Pagoda in Vietnam will help provide that way.

(George Mizo[2])

Vietnam veterans are a distinct group within the American population and even within the overall veteran population. The Veterans Administration has seemed unable to find medical treatment to heal the mental/spiritual wounds of veterans of that war. It is said that Vietnam veterans comprise one-quarter of the U.S. prison population, and that suicides since 1973 are estimated to be eighty thousand.

Many veterans point to the fact that they were deceived by their own government about the nature of the war, but realized this only after participating in the war. And the pain of being sent "to kill and be killed" in a distant country where the people were in no way an enemy was compounded by the stigmatizing process towards veterans upon their return to the U.S. The non-veteran population seemed willing to put anger and guilt upon veterans, with no awareness that the traditional teachings of society bid them to do their duty, and that the ultimate root of the war lay in the history of the U.S. from its inception, and the material way of life pursued by the American people as a whole.

In addition to this, after the war ended in 1975, the government would not squarely acknowledge that the veterans' extreme suffering came from carrying out the policies of the government; policies held in place through the deliberate deception of the American people.[3]

Also, by refusing to establish diplomatic relations with the new independent government of Vietnam in 1975, the U.S. government was in fact preventing any admission of its culpability for that war. On the popular level, all reflection about the war virtually ceased. A war so devastating—in which over 2 million Indochinese were killed and over fifty-six thousand Americans—a war which seemed to sear the conscience of the people so deeply . . . how could such a war seem to disappear from public consciousness almost overnight?

It is a most ancient and commonly held moral principle that when a wrong is done it must be acknowledged and repented. This is how humanity binds wounds and restores moral order within society. Because these steps have never been taken by the U.S. government or the people, the accumulation of the ill of that war is still within the heart and mind of the nation, eroding the moral sensibilities of the people unconsciously. It has left veterans, because they "can't forget," as the sole conscious carriers of the burden of the war. It has also inevitably lead the U.S. government to replicate the brutality of the Vietnam War in Central America and elsewhere. As retired major general Leonard V. Johnson of the Canadian Armed Forces writes, "The strategies and tactics of counterinsurgency [as used in Vietnam] were dusted off, rewritten, and renamed 'low-intensity conflict'" for use in Central America.

Thus, set against all the pain and suffering of the recent past (the people of Indochina, U.S. veterans) and the present (the people of Central America), the arising of a Peace Pagoda in Vietnam built by veterans stands out like a great beacon of healing light, an emergence of the true heart of the American people which desires peace and righteousness. For the first time in U.S. history, citizens—specifically, former soldiers—are taking responsibility for harm done in the name of "democracy" and "national interest."

The Vietnam War had many stepping stones leading to it: the near-genocide of indigenous people, enslavement of African peoples, wars of intervention, careless destruction of the environment, and the repeated use of nuclear weapons against humanity. All these were unacknowledged and unrepented acts of destruction leading to the Vietnam War. The veterans now desire to truly begin the healing process by building a Peace Pagoda in Vietnam: instead of guns, bombs, and napalm, this time an affirmation of the sacredness and inviolability of the people and land of Vietnam . . . and of all human life the world over. In a spirit of remorse for the war, we give the earnest labor of our hearts and hands purely to benefit the people of Vietnam. As the Peace Pagoda arises from the scorched earth of Vietnam, it is built invisibly within the hearts of the American people. And this certainly will strengthen and clarify our moral resolve to stop the U.S. war in Central America, and indeed change the way the United States relates to the rest of the world. George Mizo writes:

We as a nation need to ask for forgiveness from the people of Vietnam. . . .

Our government may be too shamed and guilt-ridden to ask forgiveness and start the process of reconciliation, but we as individuals must start that process of forgiveness and reconciliation for our own sake and for the sake of humanity.

Violence begets violence, and peace begets peace. Our government has used us to commit violence on the people and land of Vietnam and if they cannot or will not accept responsibility for that violence, and start the process of peace, then it is up to us as individuals to start that process for the sake of the Vietnamese people and for the sake of our own souls.

After stating the need of American people to ask forgiveness of the Vietnamese, George Mizo concludes the proposal with a positive affirmation of the benefit that the building of the Peace Pagoda can bring:

As in Hiroshima where a Peace Pagoda and Peace Park have arisen out of the ashes of nuclear holocaust, so do we believe that out of the ashes of napalm, Agent Orange, and other forms of destruction rained down upon Vietnam—some of which continue today—there can arise a symbol of hope and peace and cooperation among peoples of many nations, including those who at one time fought against one another.

We must, as a universal people, do everything within our power, through prayer and works of peace, to counteract the forces of evil which would destroy this planet, which would have the innocent killing the innocent, which puts the needs of the arms manufacturers and corporate interests above the interests of this planet and its people. A Peace Pagoda is a large step in that direction, and is a step by people towards people, and is a step by people towards faith and hope that the forces of evil will not ultimately triumph over the forces of good.

NOTES

1. Historian Howard Zinn, professor of history at Boston University, has called the U.S. war in Indochina "the most vicious full scale attack ever on a land and culture." Statistics published in the *Indochina Newsletter* (November-December 1982) convey some sense of this reality: 2,221,000 Indochinese dead, 3,200,000 Indochinese wounded, and 14,305,000 refugees as of 1975. *In South Vietnam alone:* 800,000 children lost one or both parents; 83,000 amputees; 200,000 prostitutes and 100,000 political prisoners under the U.S.-backed regime in Saigon.

It is important to note also the policy of the U.S. government towards Indochina since the end of the war. In the same edition of *Indochina Newsletter,* an interview with Noam Chomsky, professor of linguistics at the Massachusetts Institute of Technology, was published on this subject. Below is an excerpt:

Question: What is the current U.S. foreign policy toward Indochina?
Chomsky: Well, towards Indochina I think the main policy is what's called "bleeding Vietnam" . . . We fought the war to prevent Indochina from carrying out successful social and economic development. Well, I think the chances of that are very slight because of the devastation, the brutality of the war. But the U.S. wants to make sure it will continue. We refused [to send] aid. We try to block aid from other countries. We block aid from international institutions. I mean, sometimes it reaches a point of almost fanatic effort to make them suffer . . . For example, there was one point when the United States prevented the government of India from sending a hundred buffalo to Vietnam. (The buffalo stock in Vietnam had been decimated by American bombing.) We prevented them by threatening to cut off Food for Peace aid.

So, in every conceivable way the United States has tried to increase the harsh conditions of life in Indochina. And right now one of the main ways we're doing it is by supporting the Khmer Rouge on the Thai-Cambodian border.

2. George Mizo is one of the four veterans who participated in the Veterans Fast for Life in 1986, in which three Vietnam veterans and one World War II veteran undertook a public water-only fast on the Capitol steps to appeal to the people and the government that the U.S. policies of war and dominance in Central America must be renounced immediately: "No More Vietnams." George Mizo also helped construct the Peace Pagoda in Leverett and is actively working to see the Vietnam Peace Pagoda realized. He wrote a statement regarding the Vietnam Peace Pagoda, which is quoted several times in this article.

3. Professor Howard Zinn is quoted in *Indochina Newsletter:* "The *Pentagon Papers,* first published in the *New York Times,* clearly showed that the U.S. war was a deliberate war of aggression against an indigenous resistance movement in Indochina. And they showed that the government had deliberately deceived the public about the war. . . ."

RECOMMENDED READING

Shingo Shibata, ed., *Phoenix: Letters and Documents of Alice Herz.* Amsterdam: B. R. Grüner B.V., 1976.

426

MARTIN LUTHER KING JR.

A Time to Break Silence

(Dr. King delivered this historic address at a meeting of Clergy and Laity Concerned. The meeting was held at the Riverside Church in New York City on April 4, 1967, exactly a year before he was assassinated. Although this was not the first time he had expressed opposition to the Vietnam War, it was the first time he linked it to the civil rights movement.)

I come to this magnificent house of worship tonight because my conscience leaves me no other choice. I join with you in this meeting because I am in deepest agreement with the aims and work of the organization which has brought us together: Clergy and Laymen Concerned About Vietnam. The recent statement of your executive committee are the sentiments of my own heart and I found myself in full accord when I read its opening lines: "A times comes when silence is betrayal." That time has come for us in relation to Vietnam.

The truth of these words is beyond doubt but the mission to which they call us is a most difficult one. Even when pressed by the demands of inner truth, men do not easily assume the task of opposing their government's policy, especially in time of war. Nor does the human spirit move without great difficulty against all the apathy of conformist thought within one's own bosom and in the surrounding world. Moreover when the issues at hand seem as perplexed as they often do in the case of this dreadful conflict we are always on the verge of being mesmerized by uncertainty; but we must move on.

Some of us who have already begun to break the silence of the night have found that the calling to speak is often a vocation of agony, but we must speak. We must speak with all the humility that is appropriate to our limited vision, but we must speak. And we must rejoice as well, for surely this is the first time in our nation's history that a significant number of its religious leaders have chosen to move beyond the prophesying of smooth patriotism to the high grounds of a firm dissent based upon the mandates of conscience and the reading of history. Perhaps a new spirit is rising among us. If it is, let us trace its movement well and pray that our own inner being may be sensitive to its guidance, for we are deeply in need of a new way beyond the darkness that seems so close around us.

Over the past two years, as I have moved to break the betrayal of my own silences and to speak from the burnings of my own heart, as I have called for radical departures from the destruction of Vietnam, many persons have questioned me about the wisdom of my path. At the heart of their concerns this query has often loomed large and loud: Why are *you* speaking about war, Dr. King? Why are *you* joining the voices of dissent? Peace and civil rights don't mix, they say. Aren't you hurting the cause of your people, they ask? And when I hear them, though I often understand the source of their concern, I am nevertheless greatly saddened, for such questions mean that the inquirers have not really known me, my commitment, or my calling. Indeed, their questions suggest that they do not know the world in which they live.

In the light of such tragic misunderstandings, I deem it of signal importance to try to state clearly, and I trust concisely, why I believe that the path from Dexter Avenue Baptist Church—the church in Montgomery, Alabama, where I began my pastorate—leads clearly to this sanctuary tonight.

I come to this platform tonight to make a passionate plea to my beloved nation. This speech is not addressed to Hanoi or to the National Liberation Front. It is not addressed to China or to Russia.

Nor is it an attempt to overlook the ambiguity of the total situation and the need for a collective solution to the tragedy of Vietnam. Neither is it an attempt to make North Vietnam or the National Liberation Front paragons of virtue, nor to overlook the role they can play in a successful resolution of the problem. While they both may have justifiable reason to be suspicious of the good faith of the United States, life and history give eloquent testimony to the fact that conflicts are never resolved without trustful give and take on both sides.

Tonight, however, I wish not to speak with Hanoi and the NLF, but rather to my fellow Americans who, with me, bear the greatest responsibility in ending a conflict that has exacted a heavy price on both continents.

Importance of Vietnam

Since I am a preacher by trade, I suppose it is not surprising that I have seven major reasons for bringing Vietnam into the field of my moral vision. There is at the outset a very obvious and almost facile connection between the war in Vietnam and the struggle I, and others, have been waging in America. A few years ago there was a shining moment in that struggle. It seemed as if there was a real promise of hope for the poor—both black and white—through the poverty program. There were experiments, hopes, new beginnings. Then came the buildup in Vietnam and I watched the program broken and eviscerated as if it were some idle political plaything of a society gone mad on war, and I knew that America would never invest the necessary funds or energies in rehabilitation of its poor so long as adventures like Vietnam continued to draw men and skills and money like some demonic destructive suction tube. So I was increasingly compelled to see the war as an enemy of the poor and to attack it as such.

Perhaps the more tragic recognition of reality took place when it became clear to me that the war was doing far more than devastating the hopes of the poor at home. It was sending their sons and their brothers and their husbands to fight and to die in extraordinarily high proportions relative to the rest of the population. We were taking the black young men who had been crippled by our society and sending them eight thousand miles away to guarantee liberties in Southeast Asia which they had not found in southwest Georgia and East Harlem. So we have been repeatedly faced with the cruel irony of watching Negro and white boys on TV screens as they kill and die together for a nation that has been unable to seat them together in the same schools. So we watch them in brutal solidarity burning the huts of a poor village, but we realize that they would never live on the same block in Detroit. I could not be silent in the face of such cruel manipulation of the poor.

My third reason moves to an even deeper level of awareness, for it grows out of my experience in the ghettos of the North over the last three years—especially the last three summers. As I have walked among the desperate, rejected, and angry young men I have told them that Molotov cocktails and rifles would not solve their problems. I have tried to offer them my deepest compassion while maintaining my conviction that social change comes most meaningfully through nonviolent action. But they asked—and rightly so—what about Vietnam? they asked if our own nation wasn't using massive doses of violence to solve its problems, to bring about the changes it wanted. Their questions hit home, and I knew that I could never again raise my voice against the violence of the oppressed in the ghettos without having first spoken clearly to the greatest purveyor of violence in the world today—my own government. For the sake of those boys, for the sake of this government, for the sake of the hundreds of thousands trembling under our violence, I cannot be silent.

For those who ask the question, "Aren't you a civil rights leader?" and thereby mean to exclude me from the movement for peace, I have this further answer. In 1957 when a group of us formed the Southern Christian Leadership Conference, we chose as our motto: "To save the soul of

America." We were convinced that we could not limit our vision to certain rights for black people, but instead affirmed the conviction that America would never be free or saved from itself unless the descendants of its slaves were loosed completely from the shackles they still wear. In a way we were agreeing with Langston Hughes, that black bard of Harlem, who had written earlier:

O, yes,
I say it plain,
America never was America to me,
And yet I swear this oath—
America will be!

Now, it should be incandescently clear that no one who has any concern for the integrity and life of America today can ignore the present war. If America's soul becomes totally poisoned, part of the autopsy must read Vietnam. It can never be saved so long as it destroys the deepest hopes of men the world over. So it is that those of us who are yet determined that America *will* be are led down the path of protest and dissent, working for the health of our land.

As if the weight of such a commitment to the life and health of America were not enough, another burden of responsibility was placed upon me in 1964; and I cannot forget that the Nobel Prize for Peace was also a commission—a commission to work harder than I had ever worked before "the brotherhood of man." This is a calling that takes me beyond national allegiances, but even if it were not present I would yet have to live with the meaning of my commitment to the ministry of Jesus Christ. To me the relationship of this ministry to the making of peace is so obvious that I sometimes marvel at those who ask me why I am speaking against the war. Could it be that they do not know that the good news was meant for all men—for communist and capitalist, for their children and ours, for black and for white, for revolutionary and conservative? Have they forgotten that my ministry is in obedience to the one who loved his enemies so fully that he died for them? What then can I say to the "Vietcong" or to Castro or to Mao as a faithful minister of this one? Can I threaten them with death or must I not share with them my life?

Finally, as I try to delineate for you and for myself the road that leads from Montgomery to this place I would have offered all that was most valid if I simply said that I must be true to my conviction that I share with all men the calling to be a son of the living God. Beyond the calling of race or nation or creed is this vocation of sonship and brotherhood, and because I believe that the Father is deeply concerned especially for his suffering and helpless and outcast children, I come tonight to speak for them.

This I believe to be the privilege and the burden of all of us who deem ourselves bound by allegiances and loyalties which are broader and deeper than nationalism and which go beyond our nation's self-defined goals and positions. We are called to speak for the weak, for the voiceless, for victims of our nation and for those it calls enemy, for no document from human hands can make these humans any less our brothers.

Strange Liberators

And as I ponder the madness of Vietnam and search within myself for ways to understand and respond with compassion my mind goes constantly to the people of that peninsula. I speak now not of the soldiers of each side, not of the junta in Saigon, but simply of the people who have been living under the curse of war for almost three continuous decades now. I think of them too because it is clear to me that there will be no meaningful solution there until some attempt is made to know them and hear their broken cries.

They must see Americans as strange liberators. The Vietnamese people proclaimed their own independence in 1945 after a combined French and Japanese occupation, and before the communist revolution in China. They were led by Ho Chi Minh. Even though they quoted the American Declaration of Independence in their own document of freedom, we refused to recognize them. Instead, we decided to support France in its reconquest of her former colony.

Our government felt then that the Vietnamese people were not "ready" for independence, and we again fell victim to the deadly Western arrogance that has poisoned the international atmosphere for so long. With that tragic decision we rejected a revolutionary government seeking self-determination, and a government that had been established not by China (for whom the Vietnamese have no great love) but by clearly indigenous forces that included some communists. For the peasants this new government meant real land reform, one of the most important needs in their lives.

For nine years following 1945 we denied the people of Vietnam the right of independence. For nine years we vigorously supported the French in their abortive effort to recolonize Vietnam.

Before the end of the war we were meeting 80 percent of the French war costs. Even before the French were defeated at Dien Bien Phu, they began to despair of the reckless action, but we did not. We encouraged them with our huge financial and military supplies to continue the war even after they had lost the will. Soon we would be paying almost the full costs of this tragic attempt at recolonization.

After the French were defeated it looked as if independence and land reform would come again through the Geneva agreements. But instead there came the United States, determined that Ho should not unify the temporarily divided nation, and the peasants watched again as we supported one of the most vicious modern dictators—our chosen man, Premier Diem. The peasants watched and cringed as Diem ruthlessly routed out all opposition, supported their extortionist landlords, and refused even to discuss reunification with the north. The peasants watched as all this was presided over by U.S. influence and then by increasing numbers of U.S. troops who came to help quell the insurgency that Diem's methods had aroused. When Diem was overthrown they may have been happy, but the long line of military dictatorships seemed to offer no real change—especially in terms of their need for land and peace.

The only change came from America as we increased our troop commitments in support of governments which were singularly corrupt, inept, and without popular support. All the while the people read our leaflets and received regular promises of peace and democracy—and land reform. Now they languish under our bombs and consider us—not their fellow Vietnamese—the real enemy. They move sadly and apathetically as we herd them off the land of their fathers into concentration camps where minimal social needs are rarely met. They know they must move or be destroyed by our bombs. So they go—primarily women and children and the aged.

They watch as we poison their water, as we kill a million acres of their crops. They must weep as the bulldozers roar through their areas preparing to destroy the precious trees. They wander into the hospitals, with at least twenty casualties from American firepower for one "Vietcong"-inflicted injury. So far we may have killed a million of them—mostly children. They wander into the towns and see thousands of the children, homeless, without clothes, running in packs on the streets like animals. They see the children degraded by our soldiers as they beg for food. They see the children selling their sisters to our soldiers, soliciting for their mothers.

What do the peasants think as we ally ourselves with the landlords and as we refuse to put any action into our many words concerning land reform? What do they think as we test out our latest weapons on them, just as the Germans tested out new medicine and new tortures in the concentration camps of Europe? Where are the roots of the independent Vietnam we claim to be building? Is it among these voiceless ones?

We have destroyed their two most cherished institutions: the family and the village. We have destroyed their land and their crops. We have cooperated in the crushing of the nation's only noncommunist revolutionary political force—the unified Buddhist church. We have supported the enemies of the peasants of Saigon. We have corrupted their women and children and killed their men. What liberators!

Now there is little left to build on—save bitterness. Soon the only solid physical foundations remaining will be found at our military bases and in the concrete of the concentration camps we call fortified hamlets. The peasants may well wonder if we plan to build our new Vietnam on such grounds as these. Could we blame them for such thoughts? We must speak for them and raise the questions they cannot raise. These too are our brothers.

Perhaps the more difficult but no less necessary task is to speak for those who have been designated as our enemies. What of the National

Liberation Front—that strangely anonymous group we call VC or communists? What must they think of us in America when they realize that we permitted the repression and cruelty of Diem which helped to bring them into being as a resistance group in the south? What do they think of our condoning the violence that led to their own taking up of arms? How can they believe in our integrity when now we speak of "aggression from the north" as if there were nothing more essential to the war? How can they trust us when now we charge them with violence after the murderous reign of Diem and charge them with violence while we pour every new weapon of death into their land? Surely we must understand their feelings even if we do not condone their actions. Surely we must see that the men we supported pressed them to their violence. Surely we must see that our own computerized plans of destruction simply dwarf their greatest acts.

How do they judge us when our officials know that their membership is less than 25 percent communist and yet insist on giving them the blanket name? What must they be thinking when they know that we are aware of their control of major sections of Vietnam and yet we appear ready to allow national elections in which this highly organized political parallel government will have no part? They ask how we can speak of free elections when the Saigon press is censored and controlled by the military junta. And they are surely right to wonder what kind of new government we plan to help form without them—the only part in real touch with the peasants. They question our political goals and they deny the reality of a peace settlement from which they will be excluded. Their questions are frighteningly relevant. Is our nation planning to build on political myth again and then shore it up with the power of new violence?

Here is the true meaning and value of compassion and nonviolence when it helps us to see the enemy's point of view, to hear his questions, to know his assessment of ourselves. For from his view we may indeed see the basic weaknesses of our own condition, and if we are mature, we may learn and grow and profit from the wisdom of the brothers who are called the opposition.

So, too, with Hanoi. In the north, where our bombs now pummel the land, and our mines endanger the waterways, we are met by a deep but understandable mistrust. To speak for them is to explain this lack of confidence in Western words, and especially their distrust of American intentions now. In Hanoi are the men who led the nation to independence against the Japanese and the French, the men who sought membership in the French commonwealth and were betrayed by the weakness of Paris and the willfulness of the colonial armies. It was they who led a second struggle against French domination at tremendous costs, and then were persuaded to give up the land they controlled between the thirteenth and seventeenth parallel as a temporary measure at Geneva. After 1954 they watched us conspire with Diem to prevent elections which would have surely brought Ho Chi Minh to power over a united Vietnam, and they realized they had been betrayed again.

When we ask why they do not leap to negotiate, these things must be remembered. Also it must be clear that the leaders of Hanoi considered the presence of American troops in support of the Diem regime to have been the initial military breach of the Geneva agreements concerning foreign troops, and they remind us that they did not begin to send in any large number of supplies or men until American forces had moved into the tens of thousands.

Hanoi remembers how our leaders refused to tell us the truth about the earlier North Vietnamese overtures for peace, how the president claimed that none existed when they had clearly been made. Ho Chi Minh has watched as America has spoken of peace and built up its forces, and now he has surely heard of the increasing international rumors of American plans for an invasion of the north. He knows the bombing and shelling and mining we are doing are part of traditional preinvasion strategy. Perhaps only his sense of humor and of irony can save him when he hears the most powerful nation of the world speaking of aggression as it drops thousands of bombs on a poor weak nation more than eight thousand miles away from its shores.

At this point I should make it clear that while I have tried in these last few minutes to give a voice to the voiceless on Vietnam and to understand the arguments of those who are called enemy, I am as deeply concerned about our troops there as anything else. For it occurs to me that what we are submitting them to in Vietnam is not simply the brutalizing process that goes on in any war where armies face each other and seek to destroy. We are adding cynicism to the process of death, for they must know after a short period there that none of the things we claim to be fighting for are really involved. Before long they must know that their government has sent them into a struggle among Vietnamese, and the more sophisticated surely realize that we are on the side of the wealthy while we create a hell for the poor.

Somehow this madness must cease. We must stop now. I speak as a child of God and brother to the suffering poor of Vietnam. I speak for those whose land is being laid waste, whose homes are being destroyed, whose culture is being subverted. I speak for the poor of America who are paying the double price of smashed hopes at home and death and corruption in Vietnam. I speak as a citizen of the world, for the world as it stands aghast at the path we have taken. I speak as an American to the leaders of my own nation. The great initiative in the war is ours. The initiative to stop it must be ours.

This is the message of the great Buddhist leaders of Vietnam. Recently one of them wrote these words: *Each day the war goes on the hatred increases in the heart of the Vietnamese and in the hearts of those of humanitarian instinct. The Americans are forcing even their friends into becoming their enemies. It is curious that the Americans, who calculate so carefully on the possibilities of military victory, do not realize that in the process they are incurring deep psychological and political defeat. The image of America will never again be the image of*

434

revolution, freedom and democracy, but the image of violence and militarism.

If we continue there will be no doubt in my mind and in the mind of the world that we have no honorable intentions in Vietnam. It will become clear that our minimal expectation is to occupy it as an American colony and men will not refrain from thinking that our maximum hope is to goad China into a war so that we may bomb her nuclear installations. If we do not stop our war against the people of Vietnam immediately the world will be left with no other alternative than to see this as some horribly clumsy and deadly game we have decided to play.

The world now demands a maturity of America that we may not be able to achieve. It demands that we admit that we have been wrong from the beginning of our adventure in Vietnam, that we have been detrimental to the life of the Vietnamese people. The situation is one in which we must be ready to turn sharply from our present ways.

In order to atone for our sins and errors in Vietnam, we should take the initiative in bringing a halt to this tragic war. I would like to suggest five concrete things that our government should do immediately to begin the long and difficult process of extricating ourselves from this nightmarish conflict:

1. End all bombing in North and South Vietnam.
2. Declare a unilateral cease-fire in the hope that such action will create the atmosphere for negotiation.
3. Take immediate steps to prevent other battlegrounds in Southeast Asia by curtailing our military buildup in Thailand and our interference in Laos.
4. Realistically accept the fact that the National Liberation Front has substantial support in South Vietnam and must thereby play a role in any meaningful negotiations and in any future Vietnam government.
5. Set a date that we will remove all foreign troops from Vietnam in accordance with the 1954 Geneva agreement.

Part of our ongoing commitment might well express itself in an offer to grant asylum to any Vietnamese who fears for his life under a new regime which included the Liberation Front. Then we must make what reparations we can for the damage we have done. We must provide the medical aid that is badly needed, making it available in this country if necessary.

Protesting the War

Meanwhile we in the churches and synagogues have a continuing task while we urge our government to disengage itself from a disgraceful commitment. We must continue to raise our voices if our nation persists in its perverse ways in Vietnam. We must be prepared to match actions with words by seeking out every creative means of protest possible.

As we counsel young men concerning military service we must clarify for them our nation's role in Vietnam and challenge them with the alternative of conscientious objection. I am pleased to say that this is the path now being chosen by more than seventy students at my own alma mater, Morehouse College, and I recommend it to all who find the American course in Vietnam a dishonorable and unjust one. Moreover I would encourage all ministers of draft age to give up their ministerial exemptions and seek status as conscientious objectors. These are the times for real choices and not false ones. We are at the moment when our lives must be placed on the line if our nation is to survive its own folly. Every man of humane convictions must decide on the protest that best suits his convictions, but we must all protest.

There is something seductively tempting about stopping there and sending us all off on what in some circles has become a popular crusade against the war in Vietnam. I say we must enter the struggle, but I wish to go on now to say something even more disturbing. The war in Vietnam is but a symptom of a far deeper malady within the American spirit, and if we ignore this sobering reality we will find ourselves organizing clergyman and laymen-concerned committees for the next generation. They will be concerned about Guatemala and Peru. They will be concerned about Thailand and Cambodia. They will be concerned about Mozambique and South Africa. We will be marching for these and a dozen other names and attending rallies without end unless there is a significant and profound change in American life and policy. Such thoughts take us beyond Vietnam, but not beyond our calling as sons of the living God.

In 1957 a sensitive American official overseas said that it seemed to him that our nation was on the wrong side of a world revolution. During the past ten years we have seen emerge a pattern of suppression which now has justified the presence of U.S. military "advisors" in Venezuela. This need to maintain social stability for our investments accounts for the counterrevolutionary action of American forces in Guatemala. It tells why American helicopters are being used against guerrillas in Colombia and why American napalm and Green Beret forces have already been active against rebels in Peru. It is with such activity in mind that the words of the late John F. Kennedy come back to haunt us. Five years ago he said, "Those who make peaceful revolution impossible will make violent revolution inevitable."

Increasingly, by choice or by accident, this is the role our nation has taken—the role of those who make peaceful revolution impossible by refusing to give up the privileges and the pleasures that come from the immense profits of overseas investment.

I am convinced that if we are to get on the right side of the world revolution, we as a nation must undergo a radical revolution of values. We must rapidly begin the shift from a "thing-oriented" society to a "person-oriented" society. When machines and computers, profit motives and property rights are considered more important than people, the giant triplets of racism, materialism, and militarism are incapable of being conquered.

A true revolution of values will soon cause us to question the fairness and justice of many of our past and present policies. On the one hand we are called to play the good Samaritan on life's roadside; but that will be only an initial act. One day we must come to see that the whole Jericho road must be transformed so that men and women will not be constantly beaten and robbed as they make their journey on life's highway. True compassion is more than flinging a coin to a beggar; it is not haphazard and superficial. It comes to see that an edifice which produces beggars needs restructuring. A true revolution of values will soon look uneasily on the glaring contrast of poverty and wealth. With righteous indignation, it will look across the seas and see individual capitalists of the West investing huge sums of money in Asia, Africa, and South America, only to take the profits out with no concern for the social betterment of the countries, and say: "This is not just." It will look at our alliance with the landed gentry of Latin America and say: "This is not just." The Western arrogance of feeling that it has everything to teach others and nothing to learn from them is not just. A true revolution of values will lay hands on the world order and say of war: "This way of settling differences is not just." This business of burning human beings with napalm, of filling our nation's homes with orphans and widows, of injecting poisonous drugs of hate into veins of peoples normally humane, of sending men home from dark and bloody battlefields physically handicapped and psychologically deranged, cannot be reconciled with wisdom, justice, and love. A nation that continues year after year to spend more money on military defense than on programs of social uplift is approaching spiritual death.

America, the richest and most powerful nation in the world, can well lead the way in this revolution of values. There is nothing, except a tragic death wish, to prevent us from reordering our priorities, so that the pursuit of peace will take precedence over the pursuit of war. There is nothing to keep us from molding a recalcitrant status quo with bruised hands until we have fashioned it into a brotherhood.

This kind of positive revolution of values is our best defense against communism. War is not the answer. Communism will never be defeated by the use of atomic bombs or nuclear weapons. Let us not join those who shout war and through their misguided passions urge the United States to relinquish its participation in the United Nations. These are days which demand wise restraint and calm reasonableness. We must not call everyone a communist or an appeaser who advocates the seating of Red China in the United Nations and who recognizes that hate and hysteria are not the final answers to the problem of these turbulent days. We must not engage in a negative anticommunism, but rather in a positive thrust for democracy, realizing that our greatest defense against communism is to take offensive action in behalf of justice. We must with positive action seek to remove those conditions of poverty, insecurity, and injustice which are the fertile soil in which the seed of communism grows and develops.

These are revolutionary times. All over the globe men are revolting against old systems of exploitation and oppression and out of the wombs of a frail world new systems of justice and equality are being born. The shirtless and barefoot people of the land are rising up as never before. "The people who sat in darkness have seen a great light." We in the West must support these revolutions. It is a sad fact that, because of comfort, complacency, a morbid fear of communism, and our proneness to adjust to injustice, the Western nations that initiated so much of the revolutionary spirit of the modern world have now become the arch anti-revolutionaries. This has driven many to feel that only Marxism has the revolutionary spirit. Therefore, communism is a judgment against our failure to make democracy real and follow through on the revolutions that we initiated. Our only hope today lies in our ability to recapture the revolutionary spirit and go out into a sometimes hostile world declaring eternal hostility to poverty, racism, and militarism. With this powerful commitment we shall boldly challenge the status quo and unjust mores and thereby speed the day when "every valley shall be exalted, and every mountain and hill shall be made low, and the crooked shall be made straight and the rough places plain."

A genuine revolution of values means in the final analysis that our loyalties must become ecumenical rather than sectional. Every nation must now develop an overriding loyalty to mankind as a whole in order to preserve the best in their individual societies.

This call for a worldwide fellowship that lifts neighborly concern beyond one's tribe, race, class, and nation is in reality a call for an all-embracing and unconditional love for all men. This oft misunderstood and misinterpreted concept—so readily dismissed by the Nietzsches of the world as a weak and cowardly force—has now become an absolute necessity for the survival of man. When I speak of love I am not speaking of some sentimental and weak response. I am speaking of that force which all of the great religions have seen as the supreme unifying principle of life. Love is somehow the key that unlocks the door which leads to ultimate reality. This Hindu-Moslem-Christian-Jewish-Buddhist belief about ultimate reality is beautifully summed up in the first epistle of Saint John:

> Let us love one another; for love is God and everyone that loveth is born of God and knoweth God. He that loveth not knoweth not God; for God is love. If we love one another God dwelleth in us, and his love is perfected in us.

Let us hope that this spirit will become the order of the day. We can no longer afford to worship the god of hate or bow before the altar of retaliation. The oceans of history are made turbulent by the ever-rising tides of hate. History is cluttered with the wreckage of nations and individuals that pursued this self-defeating path of hate. As Arnold Toynbee says:

"Love is the ultimate force that makes for the saving choice of life and good against the damning choice of death and evil. Therefore the first hope in our inventory must be the hope that love is going to have the last word."

We are now faced with the fact that tomorrow is today. We are confronted with the fierce urgency of now. In this unfolding conundrum of life and history there is such a thing as being too late. Procrastination is still the thief of time. Life often leaves us standing bare, naked, and dejected with a lost opportunity. The "tide in the affairs of men" does not remain at the flood; it ebbs. We may cry out desperately for time to pause in her passage, but time is deaf to every plea and rushes on. Over the bleached bones and jumbled residue of numerous civilizations are written the pathetic words: "Too late." There is an invisible book of life that faithfully records our vigilance or our neglect. "The moving finger writes, and having writ moves on. . . ." We still have a choice today: nonviolent coexistence or violent co-annihilation.

We must move past indecision to action; We must find new ways to speak for peace in Vietnam and justice throughout the developing world—a world that borders on our doors. If we do not act we shall surely be dragged down the long dark and shameful corridors of time reserved for those who possess power without compassion, might without morality, and strength without sight.

Now let us begin. Now let us rededicate ourselves to the long and bitter—but beautiful—struggle for a new world. This is the calling of the sons of God, and our brothers wait eagerly for our response. Shall we say the odds are too great? Shall we tell them the struggle is too hard? Will our message be that the forces of American life militate against their arrival as full men, and we send our deepest regrets? Or will there be another message, of longing, of hope, of solidarity with their yearnings, of commitment to their cause, whatever the cost? The choice is ours, and though we might prefer it otherwise we *must* choose in this crucial moment of human history.

As that noble bard of yesterday, James Russell Lowell, eloquently stated:

> Once to every man and nation,
> Comes the moment to decide
> In the strife of truth and falsehood
> For the good or evil side;
> Some great cause God's new Messiah
> Offering each the gloom or blight
> And the choice goes by forever
> Twixt that darkness and that light.
>
> Though the cause of evil prosper
> Yet 'tis truth alone is strong
> Though her portion be the scaffold

And upon the throne be wrong
Yet that scaffold sways the future
And behind the dim unknown
Standeth God within the shadow
Keeping watch above his own.

Acknowledgments

This anthology is part of a larger program of public events entitled *War and Memory: The Aftermath of the Vietnam War* sponsored by Washington Project for the Arts. WPA has engaged contemporary artists across disciplines to present their work alongside the work of poets, writers, historians, and teachers. All of the individuals invited to participate in these events, many of them Vietnam veterans, continue to shape thoughtful personal and national responses to the Vietnam War. WPA offers this program not as a summation, but as an invitation to all, to expand the dialogue dedicated to a greater understanding of this critical period in our national history.

Washington Project for the Arts gratefully acknowledges the support of The William Joiner Center for the Study of War and Social Consequences at the University of Massachusetts in Boston, under the leadership of Kevin Bowen; The Robert A. Glassman Fund of the Boston Foundation (Mr. Glassman served as a platoon leader in Vietnam in 1966); The Best Products Foundation; and the National Endowment for the Arts.

As with every large book project, many people have generously contributed their work and support. The first person to be thanked is Jock Reynolds, the director of Washington Project for the Arts. Without his vision and intense work this book as well as the other events in the *War and Memory* program would not exist. I offer him my gratitude and respect most warmly. Also to Jane Creighton and Richard Posner who have worked as planners and organizers on the *War and Memory* program from the beginning, my thanks for their primary work on the book; and to Susan Ades, Susan Albright, Terry Allen, Paul Arkava, Marjorie Cohen,

Dorit Cypis, Sovann Doung, Brian Emond, Gloria Emerson, George Ewalt, Cathy Hillenbrand, Lucy Lippard, Don Luce, Phil Mariani,Lucy Nguyen, Meang Seak Tang, May Stevens, Richard Turner, and Ros Weiner for their contributions and advice.

And, in closing, a special thanks to each of the authors for their writing and also for their recommendations and guidance.   —RW

*

Notes on the Contributors

CRAIG ADCOCK is an art historian who teaches at the University of Notre Dame specializing in twentieth-century art. In addition to his work on Terry Allen, he has published essays about Dadaism and its influence and several studies of Marcel Duchamp, including a book in the avant-garde series of the UMI Research Press. He is currently preparing a monograph on James Turrell.

MICHAEL JAMES ASENTE is an artist who lives and works in the Williamsburg section of Brooklyn. The Hispanic people on his block call him "El Grasso." Soon he will marry his girlfriend, whom they call "La Flaca," the skinny one.

JOHN BALABAN graduated from Penn State University and Harvard, and went to Vietnam in 1967 as a conscientious objector, first with the International Voluntary Services and then as the field representative for the Committee of Responsibility to Save War-Injured Children. He is the author of two books of poetry, *After Our War*, which won the Lamont Prize and a nomination for the National Book Award, and *Blue Mountain*. In 1971-72, he returned to Vietnam to collect the oral folk poetry known as *ca dao*, which he later translated in *Ca Dao Vietnam: A Bilingual Anthology of Vietnamese Folk Poetry*. In 1985, Harcourt Brace Jovanovich published his first novel, *Coming Down Again*, set in Southeast Asia. In 1988, Harcourt will publish his children's story, "The Hawk's Tale." He teaches at Penn State University and is currently translating the works of the nineteenth-century poetess, Ho Xuan Huong.

JAN BARRY is a poet and the editor of three literary anthologies, including *Winning Hearts and Minds: War Poems by Vietnam Veterans* and *Peace is Our Profession: Poems of War Protest*. One of the founders of Vietnam Veterans Against the War, he is currently director of the Essex County Office on Peace (in New Jersey), an independent agency supported by the county government.

JEANNE BLAKE is vice-president of Courseware Development Associates Inc., a Minneapolis-based corporate training company. In 1981, she began a "barefoot" school, in which for two years she taught older adult Hmong the basics needed to enter formal ESL programs. She has lived with the Hmong in Thailand, both in refugee camps and in free mountain villages. During this time she was formally adopted into a Hmong clan and became fluent in the Hmong language. Currently she is teaching a course on Hmong culture at Hamline University.

ROBERT BLY is the author of *Silence on the Snowy Fields, The Light Around the Body* (winner of the 1968 National Book Award), *The Morning Glory, This Tree Will Be Here for a Thousand Years, The Teeth Mother Naked at Last,* and *Sleepers Joining Hands,* among others. Bly was a co-founder in 1966 of American Writers Against the Vietnam War and edited *A Poetry Reading Against the Vietnam War*. His poetry journals, *The Fifties, The Sixties,* and *The Seventies,* published many European and South American poets for the first time in the United States. A graduate of Harvard, Bly resides in his native state of Minnesota.

D. F. BROWN was born in 1948 in the Missouri Ozarks. He served as a combat medic with B Company, First of the Fourteenth Infantry, Vietnam 1969-70. He is the author of *Returning Fire,* the 1984 San Francisco State University Poetry Chapbook. His poems have appeared in *Transfer, Walking Point, Intervention,* and *Practising Angels*. He lives in Oakland, California.

CLARE CARTER, a native of Boston, Massachusetts, was ordained a nun in the Buddhist order, Nipponzan Myohoji, in 1981 and currently serves at the Peace Pagoda in Leverett, Massachusetts. She is working in whatever way she can to assist in the building of the Peace Pagoda in Vietnam.

NOAM CHOMSKY is Institute Professor in the Department of Linguistics and Philosophy at Massachusetts Institute of Technology, where he has been on the faculty since 1955. He has written and lectured widely on international affairs and U.S. foreign policy, and has been active for many years in the peace movement. His most recent books are *Pirates and Emperors* (1986) and *On Power and Ideology* (1987).

JANE CREIGHTON is the author of *Ceres in an Open Field,* a collection of poems from Out & Out Books. She edited and published the poetry magazine *Sailing the Road Clear* from 1973-78. Her articles and reviews on literature, film, and video have appeared in various publications, among them the *Texas Observer, Afterimage, American Book Review, Feminist Review,* and *The Independent.* She has been active in anti-intervention and solidarity work since 1982, most recently with the Center for Constitutional Rights on the Margaret Randall deportation case.

TRAN VAN DINH, a former senior diplomat, was born into a Confucian-Buddhist-Taoist family in Hue, the former imperial capital of Vietnam. He is the author of numerous articles and several books, including a novel, *Blue Dragon White Tiger: A Tet Story* (1983), *Independence, Liberation, Revolution: An Approach to the Understanding of the Third World,* and *Communication and Diplomacy in a Changing World* (both in 1987 by Ablex). Currently he is a professor at Temple University and an editorial advisor and contributor to the *International Encyclopedia of Communications,* a four-volume project of the University of Pennsylvania and Oxford University Press to be published in 1989.

W. D. EHRHART, an ex-marine and Vietnam veteran, is the author of three nonfiction books, *Vietnam-Perkasie, Marking Time,* and *Going Back,* and numerous collections of poetry, most recently *To Those Who Have Gone Home Tired* and *The Outer Banks.* In 1985 he edited *Carrying the Darkness,* an anthology of poetry of the Vietnam War (Avon Books). He lives in Philadelphia with his wife Anne and daughter Leela and teaches at Germantown Friends School.

MARK GERZON began his career as a nonfiction writer with his bestseller *The Whole World is Watching,* followed by *A Choice of Heroes: The Changing Face of American Manhood.* In 1983 he founded Mediators Productions Inc., a company specializing in feature film and television programing that deals with critical issues of our time. His current projects include a Movie-of-the-Week about apartheid in South Africa, co-produced with Lorimar for CBS, and an After School Special at ABC on children's fear of nuclear war.

ELIZABETH HESS has written on art for the *Village Voice, Art in America,* and the *Washington Post* among other publications.

KIM JONES: "I like to think about being a tree."

JOHN KETWIG is a middle-level manager with a major automotive manufacturer. His book, *. . . and a hard rain fell,* was originally a letter to his wife, Carolynn, attempting to explain his experiences in Vietnam. Ketwig is "mainly a daddy" but remains active in the peace movement. He and his family live in Severn, Maryland.

MARTIN LUTHER KING, JR. is remembered primarily as a great civil rights leader, but he also spoke powerfully against the war in Vietnam. A recent collection of his writings is *A Testament of Hope: The Essential Writings of Martin Luther King, Jr.,* edited by James Melvin Washington (Harper & Row: San Francisco, 1986).

CHARLES LITEKY was ordained as a priest in the Roman Catholic church in 1960. In 1966, he voluntarily entered the U.S. Army as a chaplain and served for two and a half years in Vietnam. In 1968, Liteky was awarded the Congressional Medal of Honor for heroism by President Johnson. He left the priesthood in 1974 and worked as a carpenter, painter, and a veterans counselor. In 1985, he made his first trip to Central America. ". . . incredible stories of cruelty started me on a search for truth that has led me through book after book and report after report on the conditions of poverty and oppression in Central America and my government's response to these conditions." On July 29, 1986, he renounced his Medal of Honor in protest of U.S. policy, and during September and October 1986 he took part in the Veterans Fast for Life in Washington, D.C.

BOBBIE ANN MASON is the author of *Shiloh and Other Stories* (which won the Pen/Hemingway Award) and the highly acclaimed novel, *In Country*. A native of Kentucky, she lives in rural Pennsylvania.

SARA MILES is a writer and researcher; she works with the Low-Intensity Conflict Clearinghouse project of the Resource Center in Albuquerque, New Mexico.

JAMES MOORE lives in Minneapolis where he teaches writing at the Minneapolis College of Art and Design. "For You" forms part of a book of personal essays, *Interruptions of Plot*, that he has been working on the past two years and recently completed. A third book of his poetry will appear in the spring of 1988 from Milkweed Press.

ADRIENNE RICH is widely acknowledged as a major American poet. She is the author of *Diving into the Wreck* (which received the National Book Award in 1974), *The Dream of a Common Language, On Lies, Secrets, and Silence*, and *Of Woman Born*, among many other books. She has been involved since the 1960s in the civil rights and antiwar movements.

DANIEL SWAIN, a native of Tucson, Arizona, served in the U.S. Navy aboard the USS Clarion River from July 1966 to September 1967. He has a master's degree in literature from Northeastern University and one in creative writing from the University of Illinois at Chicago. Currently he teaches writing at the Art Institute in Chicago.

VETERANS FAST FOR LIFE was a water-only fast on the steps of the capital by four U.S. war veterans, Charles Liteky, George Mizo, Duncan Murphy, and Brian Willson during September and October of 1986 to protest U.S. policy in Central America. The fast touched many people. Each day the office of the support group received hundreds of phone calls and letters in support of the veterans. All around the country individuals and organizations created support actions and events.

BRUCE WEIGL served with the First Air Cav. in Vietnam from December 1967 to December 1968. He has published four collections of poetry including, most recently, *The Monkey Wars* (University of Georgia Press). His poems have appeared in a number of magazines and journals including the *New England Review, Western Humanities Review, Black Warrior Review, Field, Mother Jones, Ohio Review, Triquarterly Review,* and the *American Poetry Review* among others. His essays have appeared in *The Nation, Ironwood, Rocky Mountain Review, Choice,* and others. Currently he is associate professor in the English department of Penn State University.

REESE WILLIAMS was the publisher of Tanam Press in New York from 1979-86. He is the recipient of two National Endowment for the Arts fellowships and an "Editors Award" from the New York State Council on the Arts Literature Program. Currently he is back in school studying Polarity Therapy.

HARRY WILMER was the founder, director, and president of the Institute for the Humanities at Salado and professor of psychiatry at the University of Texas Health Science Center in San Antonio. Awarded a Guggenheim Fellowship in 1969, Wilmer has written five books and over a hundred and fifty medical articles. While on active duty in the United States Navy in the 1950s he worked with Korean War veterans. And his work with the nightmares and post-trauma stress of Vietnam veterans at the Audie Murphy Hospital in San Antonio is reported in his book, *Dreams of Vietnam.*

SUSAN WOLF is the co-founder and co-editor of the journal *Feminist Issues.* She lives and works in New York City.

MARILYN YOUNG began her teaching life at the Residential College, University of Michigan in 1969, shortly after the college was founded. In 1980 she left Michigan for New York City where she now teaches history at New York University. She is the author, with William Rosenberg, of *Transforming Russia and China: Revolutionary Struggles in the 20th Century* (New York: Oxford University Press, 1982).

ABOUT THE COVER ILLUSTRATIONS

The Veterans Lobby is a 900 square foot glass hearth commissioned by the Veterans Administration Art-In-Architecture Program as the main entry to the new Seattle Veterans Administration Medical Center. As visitors enter the lobby, they walk past a pair of illuminated reverse-mirror 3-D murals set into the northern glass block wall. Inside the fireplace a glass fire glows while above the mantle a sword-bearing soldier becomes a farmer behind a plow. The images reverse as people exit the hospital. They are also visible day and night from outside the building. *The Veterans Lobby* was designed by Richard Posner, who served as a conscientious objector during the Vietnam War, in collaboration with the NBBJ Group, architects and completed in 1985 with the assistance of Robert Strini, Kevin Ryder and Meredith MacLeod. The photographs are by Steven Young.